State Capitalism

State Capitalism

Why SOEs Matter and the Challenges They Face

LALITA SOM

OXFORD
UNIVERSITY PRESS

OXFORD
UNIVERSITY PRESS

Great Clarendon Street, Oxford, ox2 6dp,
United Kingdom

Oxford University Press is a department of the University of Oxford.
It furthers the University's objective of excellence in research, scholarship,
and education by publishing worldwide. Oxford is a registered trade mark of
Oxford University Press in the UK and in certain other countries

First Edition published in 2022

Impression: 1

Published in the United States of America by Oxford University Press
198 Madison Avenue, New York, NY 10016, United States of America

British Library Cataloguing in Publication Data

Data available

Library of Congress Control Number: 2022931624

ISBN 978–0–19–284959–5

DOI: 10.1093/oso/9780192849595.001.0001

Printed in India by Rakmo Press Pvt. Ltd.

To my late grandparents.

Foreword

Much of the influence that governments have on their societies and economies occurs, in one form or other, through the medium of regulation. Nevertheless, devising regulations that promote economic and social advancement is rarely straightforward. There are technical complexities and uncertainties to grapple with, and often there are political constraints and pressures to surmount. The result can be regulatory initiatives that are deficient in various ways. They may have unintended consequences, including 'collateral damage' to those not directly targeted. They may achieve their goals at excessive cost. Moreover, in some cases they may not even serve their goals at all.

As ably demonstrated by the *OECD Regulatory Policy Outlooks* series, regulating in 'normal times' already represented a significant challenge for governments. The global financial crisis, the half-life of which is still affecting many countries, was a dramatic illustration of the consequences of regulatory failures—involving a combination of problems in financial market and consumer credit regulation, housing policy, and systemic risk management. Yet the consequences of these failures pale almost into insignificance compared with the seemingly insurmountable challenges societies currently face and will likely face in the coming years. Against a backdrop of a once in a century global health and economic crisis—coupled with climate change, inequalities from globalisation, ageing population, and seemingly insatiable spread of misinformation on social media platforms—sound even visionary public policy coupled with well-functioning regulatory frameworks have never been more needed.

The necessary rebuilding of economies and society will challenge the very foundations of the social compact—something that has become increasingly strained in recent times. It will require change to the regulatory frameworks that underpin the market economy, to better balance economic efficiency with inclusiveness, resilience, and sustainability goals. To combat the existential challenges of this era, the state will inevitably need to intervene in markets and society to a much greater degree than in the past.

Lalita Som's very timely and thoughtful book asks whether State capitalism is fit for purpose to rise to the challenges of the day. Based on a number of case studies around the world, she paints a not all too reassuring picture. An important lesson from the book is that State capitalism and ensuing poor regulatory outcomes should not be regarded as aberrations. On the contrary, poor regulation is better thought of as the natural order of things, being much easier to achieve than good regulation. It requires less effort and generally faces less political resistance, especially where certain groups can benefit from it in opaque ways at the cost of the wider community. State economic action, even when ill conceived, is often rewarded with public acclaim, as tangible evidence that government is 'doing something'. These uneven political pressures have often manifested themselves in a 'regulate first, ask questions later' approach—the antithesis of good policy process.

The case studies confirm that there are no simple prescriptions for achieving State capitalism 'nirvana'. Good regulation can only be secured through systems within government that actually foster it—systems that make it harder to regulate poorly than to regulate well. Dr Som points to what is really needed is cultural change. The culture within the State influences decisions at both the political and bureaucratic levels, about whether, what, and how to regulate, as well as how to administer regulation in place. In short, it exerts influence throughout the whole policy cycle. That said, while political and bureaucratic cultures are not immutable, they are not easily changed and do so only slowly.

The book focuses much attention on SOEs, an important yet often insidious instrument of State capitalism. In many countries around the world, SOEs remain an important presence and account for approximately one-fifth of the world's total stock market capitalization. As *State Capitalism* shows, SOEs remain a strong pillar of the economy in both large and small economies—even after successive waves of privatization starting in the 1980s. It also recognises that SOEs often play a vital role in delivering basic services, such as water and energy, and their performance is critical for citizens and the broader development agenda.

State Capitalism also documents very well, and no doubt disturbingly, the dark side of SOEs. The book shows that regulatory preference for, and regulatory protection of, SOEs continues to be high in most emerging market countries. Moreover, government backing and favour often times gives SOEs unfair competitive advantage in their domestic market, where they have crowded out private investment in new markets, products, and technologies and have usurped entrepreneurial activity. The book also shows that many large SOEs have provided services at below cost to preferred political constituencies for electoral gains and have consequently failed other consumers by maintaining unjustifiably high costs for goods and services. A disturbing trend is that in many instances SOEs have colluded to form the core of a public enterprise sphere of influence and have been proactively and successfully determining the terms under which the government allows them to operate.

State Capitalism rightly points to regulatory agencies as the public bodies that are best suited to ensure consumer's access to and the quality of key public services provided by SOEs. Regulators also need to play a critical role in the stewardship of SOE resource management including new investments. They also need to oversee markets, enhancing efficiency, and providing confidence, when SOEs compete in sectors that also include private sector interest. This is no easy task. Regulators operate in a complex environment at the interface among public authorities, SOEs, the private sector and end-users. As 'referees', they must often balance competing wants and needs from different actors through the application of good governance. This means that they must behave and act objectively, impartially, and consistently, without conflict of interest, bias, or undue influence.

The case studies in *State Capitalism* illustrate the challenges that regulators face in managing the interface between state and the market. Regulatory agencies have often operated with varying and sometimes ambiguous degrees of independence from the executive (and inherently more political) branch of government. Weak independence risks that a different set of norms is applied to SOEs or norms are partially applied by the regulator due to political pressures on how it discharges its powers. As such, the absence of strong and independent regulatory bodies in creating the necessary checks and balances against discretionary governmental action has sometimes, threatened the performance of SOEs. Likewise, the legislative framework that empowers regulators to provide an independent review of the economics of large-scale projects has failed to provide the important check-and-balance on decisions related to large SOE projects. For many new projects, by the time the SOE approaches the regulator with the license application, the decision has often been a fait accompli. These large projects then become a source of SOE underperformance.

The need for immediate regulatory reform in emerging markets has never been more critical. The international experiences, including those of OECD members, point to several general principles for effective regulation. Effective regulation depends on the existence of regulatory bodies with clear mandates, authority, and accountability. Regulators need to be independent, not simply (or even most importantly) in a formal sense, but free from interference from regulated businesses and other government agencies. Effective regulation focuses on making markets work, by fostering efficiency and innovation, promoting sustainable development, and maximising benefits to end-users, and is best separated from the pursuit of industrial policy or other government mandates. Regulation is a dynamic process in which transparency in rule formulation, effective dissemination to stakeholders, and mechanisms for consultation and appeal are essential. It is also an intensely empirical process requiring detailed knowledge of market conditions and trends and tools for assessing the impact of particular regulations and their costs and benefits. Successful regulatory reform embeds these principles and practices in the decision-making of each regulatory agency and its components.

Dr Nick Malyshev
Head, Regulatory Policy Division
Public Governance Directorate
Organisation for Economic Co-operation and Development (OECD)
Paris

Preface

This book is the result of ideas that emerged out of observing how the Washington Consensus, which held sway until 2007, was challenged and submerged by the Global Financial Crisis, the spectacular success of China, and other emerging economies which deviated from the free-market paradigm and embraced the active role of the State, and the role of State capitalism as a source of cross-border finance. The focus of the book is on the state of play and research on State capitalism and State-owned enterprises (SOEs). It also includes factors that affected SOEs and their performance in different countries through a country case study approach. The country case studies used the same analytical categories to arrive at principal common characteristics of, and practices followed by, successful SOEs independently of country context. While I was finishing writing the manuscript in 2020, the COVID-19 pandemic struck and reinforced the idea that only the State can intervene in offering holistic solutions in crisis situations while attempting to balance a wide variety of interests.

Despite the Washington Consensus and the many economic shocks and traumas of the 1970s through the 1990s, the State-owned sector has remained indispensable and popular in many countries. Experience with privatization has been mixed; in some countries it replaced state monopolies with private ones, with worse economic consequences. While a significant part of the State sector and individual SOEs have worked as well as the private sector in countries as diverse as Singapore, India, and Saudi Arabia. Well-performing SOEs have resulted in increased acceptability of state interventions and SOEs. These SOEs have markedly different operations, ownership, and governance systems from their previous archetypes. The contemporary views on SOEs have underscored how both the private and the State sectors could work together optimally in mixed economies that have characterized the countries chosen as case studies, to produce the best results in different political economy circumstances.

However, evidence suggests that a majority of SOEs misallocate capital, mismanage resources, and are less productive than private firms by one-third, on average. The performance of SOEs is symptomatic of the importance accorded to SOEs and the enormity and complexity of the challenges they face. SOEs have been expected to act in the long-term and holistic interests of the state and its citizens. They reallocate resources from one component of their operations to fund others. SOEs have enjoyed significant advantages compared to their private sector counterparts, but have been expected to be involved in implementing and financing critical public policies. They have been powerful tools able to restructure sectors and guide diversity in economies and development. Private interests with deep pockets in concert with politicians take advantage of these opportunities to extort from SOEs. The enormity and complexity of the demands made on SOEs have left them yearning for clarity that the profit maximization motive provides their private sector counterparts.

The separation between the State's roles as shareholder, policy-maker, and regulator has been laid down in an inconsistent and incoherent fashion in many countries. The uneven regulatory policy framework without an overarching guiding principle to state regulation is responsible for distortions in the market. The operational functioning of regulatory bodies has also been a constraint in creating a level playing field in terms of ensuring a competitive and fair business environment. The resultant regulatory capture by private near-monopolies has led to rising market concentration with existing competitors faced with extreme financial distress and overwhelmed to provide any meaningful competition.

What is incongruous to grasp is that while the State is accorded a very important role in the economy, it chooses to exercise its power to the detriment of State capitalism. The global public health crisis has yet again highlighted the need for more state productive capacity, government procurement capabilities, symbiotic public–private collaborations, and therefore, the continued relevance and use of SOEs. It is, then, imperative that there is a new paradigm to account for SOEs and reconceive the role of the State as viable policy tools. It is equally important to acknowledge that there are few other alternative policy means with the same puissance of SOEs in certain circumstances. These circumstances include state's intervention role that are indispensable *in extremis*, and the role that the State plays in fostering innovation, along with the private sector.

This book provides a comparative mapping of the role of SOEs, their performance, and the challenges they face in eight economies. It has explored across diverse national circumstances the factors that influence the performance of SOEs and has drawn some conclusions on the necessary conditions for SOEs to play a meaningful role. These have already formed a key input in many national reform processes and I hope that they continue to inspire reform-minded policy makers and officials in other countries.

Although implementing the demands of the State will remain the main rationale of all the SOEs, inefficient and ineffective SOEs are no longer publicly acceptable. SOEs no longer exist to provide jobs and to locate factories in underdeveloped areas of a country. SOEs need to revitalize their role as strategic, long-term, and mission-oriented investors (especially in healthcare, research, and education) in order to shape and grow economies and to bring about long-term benefits to their citizens.

Acknowledgements

Many thanks to all whose work, research, data, and support helped me write this book. I would like to especially thank Mr Percy Mistry who took time out to, discuss the analytical framework, provide constructive feedback on each chapter, push me to find more data and read my manuscript twice.

I take this opportunity to thank my friends at the OECD for their support and encouraging words and to Mr Nick Malyshev for writing the foreword.

Lastly, the confinement of 2020 played the most effective role in stopping me from getting distracted and allowing me to focus on the manuscript!

Contents

Illustrations

Figures

Tables

Abbreviations

ACSA	Airports Company South Africa
ANATEL	Agência Nacional de Telecomunicações
ANC	African national congress
ANEEL	Agência Nacional de Energia Elétrica
ANP	Agência Nacional do Petróleo, Gás Natural e Biocombustíveis
ANTT	Agencia Nacional de Transportes Terrestres
ASEAN	Association of south east Asian nations
B-BBEE	Broad-Based Black Economic Empowerment
BdB	Banco do Brasil
BEE	Black economic empowerment
BIFR	Board of industrial financing and reconstruction
BNDES	Brazilian National Development Bank
BPK	Badan Pemeriksa Keuangan
CBR	Central Bank of Russia
CBRC	China Banking Regulatory Commission
CCI	Competition commission of India
CEF	Central Energy Fund
CIL	Coal India Limited
CIRC	China Insurance Regulatory Commission
CNPC	China National Petroleum
CNOOC	China National Offshore Oil Corporation
CPSEs	Central public sector enterprises
CRC	China Railway Construction
CRG	China Railway Group
CRS	Contract responsibility system
CSCEC	China State Construction Engineering Company
CSR	Corporate social responsibility
CSRC	China Securities Regulatory Commission
CVM	Comissão de Valores Mobiliários
DBSA	Development Bank of South Africa
DoC	Department of Communications
DPE	Department of public enterprise
DPR	Dewan Perwakilan Rakyat
EBRD	European Bank for Reconstruction and Development

EDB	Economic development board
EPC	Exempt private company
FAT	Fundo de Amparo ao Trabalhador
FCGI	Forum for Corporate Governance in Indonesia
FGTS	Fundo de Garantia do Tempo e Servio
FIIs	Foreign Institutional Investors
FSB	Fundo Soberno do Brasil
GCC	Gulf Cooperation Council
GFC	Global Financial Crisis
GFCF	Gross fixed capital formation
GIC	Government Investment Corporation Private Limited
GLCs	Government linked companies
GoI	Government of India
IBC	Insovency and Bankruptcy Code
IICG	Indonesian Institute for Corporate Governance
IPO	Initial Public Offering
IPPs	Independent power producers
JSE	Johannesberg Stock Exchange
KPIs	Key performance indicators
KPK	Komisi Pemberantasan Korupsi
LAC	Latin America and Caribbean region
MoSE	Ministry of State-owned enterprises
MoUs	Memoranda of understanding
NBFIs	Non-bank financial intermediaries
NCCG	National Committee on Corporate Governance
NERSA	National Energy Regulator of South Africa
NIRC	Net Investment Return Contribution
NPAs	Non-performing assets
NPLs	Non-performing loans
NSA	Net sales to assets
OECD	Organisation of Economic Cooperation and Development
OI	Open innovation
PAP	People's Action Party
PASEP	Programa de Formacao do Patrimônio do Servidor Público
PFMA	Public Finance Management Act
PIF	Public Investment Fund
PIS	Programa de Integracao Social
PLF	Plant load factor
PLN	Perusahaan Listrik Negara
PPSA	Pre-Sal Petroleo S.A.
PRASA	Passenger Rail Agency of South Africa
PRC	Presidential Reform Commission on SOEs
PSCs	Profit sharing contracts

QE	Quantitative easing
RET	Radical economic transformation
RoA	Return on assets
RoC	Return on capital
RoE	Return on equity
SAA	South African Airways
SABC	South Africa Broadcasting Corporation
SABIC	Saudi Arabian Basic Industries Corporation
SAFCOL	South African Forestries Company
SAMA	Saudi Arabia Monetary Authority
SAPO	South Africa Post Office
SASAC	State-owned Assets Supervision and Administration Commission
SBs	Public Sector Banks
SCII	State-controlled institutional investors
SHCs	Sector holding companies
SOBFIs	State-owned banks and financial institutions
SOCBs	State-owned Commercial Banks
SOEs	State-owned enterprises
SPAs	Special Purchasing Agreements
STC	Saudi Telecom Company
SWFs	Sovereign Wealth Funds
TFP	Total factor productivity
TSR	Total shareholder return
VAA	Value added per assets
VAC	Value added per capital
VAE	Value added per employee
WTO	World Trade Organisation

1
Introduction

Controversy about the role of the State in owning, financing, and operating commercial enterprises has been rife for much longer than generally imagined by modern economic historians. Theoretical scrutiny of this issue began when private enterprises from the fountainheads of former empires forayed abroad to make remarkable fortunes through colonial trade and exploitation. But they overreached, eventually requiring the State/crown to intervene in their commercial affairs when they triggered political problems in a number of colonies that required statecraft to resolve.

Since then, convention, theory, practice—and the arguments they have generated about the legitimacy of the State being involved as an owner, financier, or risk taker of/in commercial enterprises—have evolved, especially in the post-colonial era since the 1950s.

Seventy years later, they are leading to a variety of conflicting assertions and arguments about the merits and demerits of State-owned enterprises (SOEs). The debate over 'State capitalism', and 'market or private capitalism', has been in sharp focus since 2000. China's growth experience over the last four decades has had much to do with shaping and assessing the merits of arguments about that emergent phenomenon.

The influence of the 1980s Washington Consensus, the 2008–10 Global Financial Crisis, and the COVID-19 pandemic on State ownership

Following the oil and debt crises of the late 1970s and through the 1980s, a consensus in global economic policy making formed around the view that large-scale privatization, economic liberalization, deregulation, non-interference in the economy except through macro-policy, and macro-stability were at the core of economic success (the Washington

Consensus). The idea of rejecting public ownership model, and relying more on market capitalism for economic revival, was advanced mainly by the Reagan and Thatcher administrations in the USA and UK, respectively. It was then bolstered and legitimized throughout the world by the World Bank and International Monetary Fund (IMF) when it became an essential feature in the large structural and sectoral adjustment programmes that they financed in debt-ridden countries.

Free market capitalism was advocated as the main resource allocation mechanism capable of generating sustained, efficient economic growth. This seemed to be borne out in practice as the socialist systems of Central and Eastern Europe collapsed under the weight of internal contradictions in 1989. Since then, the appropriate role of the State was perceived as being limited to pursuing conventional fiscal, monetary, exchange rate, trade, and 'big price' (for energy, labour, etc.) policies with a minimal role for intervening directly in the economy.

Three decades of economic reorientation, based on the 'Washington Consensus', had by 2005 relegated to irrelevance most other models for economic growth and development. The principal maxim applied throughout most of the world (excluding China and Middle Eastern autocracies) between 1980 and 2005 was that, regardless of the specifics of any economic challenges that a country confronted, reliance on the private sector and the market was its best hope of resolving such issues effectively and efficiently. The Washington Consensus, which held sway until 2007, was challenged and submerged by the crisis that followed.

With the 2007–10 Global Financial Crisis (GFC), a short-lived consensus emerged, almost everywhere that the State had a duty of care to intervene financially—by bailing out systemically important banks, other financial enterprises, and some systemically important industries (for example, the auto industry in the US, France, Italy)—in order to prevent global economic implosion and resuscitate growth. Often that required the State to own financial firms in an exigent emergency, thus, legitimizing the State ownership issue *in extremis*.

Concomitantly, the State was expected to pursue deep financial system reforms, while pumping vast amounts of liquidity (over US$10 trillion in total for the US, EU, Japan, and China or 12% of world GDP) through unprecedented monetary measures (i.e. quantitative easing—QE). With a revival of investment in finance and industry, those measures did resuscitate asset prices and confidence that prevented a prolonged global recession like the Great Depression of 1929–35. To an extent, they restored industrial and trade competitiveness through growth in productivity and the use of technology.

A decade after the crisis, looking at the world as a whole, profits bounced back in most sectors in most countries, and equity prices rose dramatically, especially for industrial and banking firms, while interest rates remained unprecedentedly low. New firms in the technology space made hyper-profits. Yet, apart from the technology space, overall levels of private and public investment have remained weak, due to a combination of heightened uncertainty, cash hoarding, and increased 'financialization'.

Many governments which took emergency action to rescue banks and other financial institutions in response to the GFC partially nationalized these in the process. Outside the US, these governments have been slow to unwind these ownership stakes, which has halted the long-term trend towards lower state ownership of business in many countries.

In the latter context, the GFC appears to have enhanced (at least for a while) the public appeal of State capitalism as an ideology, in contrast to reliance on creating competitive well-regulated markets, dominated by competing private firms, in driving output and growth.

A decade after the GFC, the need to address enduring economic weaknesses remains in developed and developing economies. There is an emerging realization that reviving an economy requires the State to revitalize its role as a strategic, long-term, and mission-oriented investor. It cannot simply be a facilitator of wealth creation, a redistributor of wealth, and a leveller of the playing field to ensure fair competition in the market. Economic policy must include actively shaping and co-creating markets as well as fixing them when they go wrong (Mazzucato, 2018).

Can State capitalism play this significant role? Or are its internal contradictions too many to play a meaningful role as a long-term and strategic investor in commercial enterprises? Can State capitalism manage markets effectively for specific policy ends and help build national economies and future leading sectors? Can SOEs play an effective role during emergency situations and economic crises, if overwhelming evidence shows mis-management and mis-allocation of resources at SOEs? These are the questions that this book seeks to address.

The GFC and the COVID- 19 pandemic have underscored the emergency role of the State and its smooth, seamless reactivation when necessary, for situations when private activity and markets are disrupted.

According to the IMF, the COVID-19 pandemic of 2020 will result in the worst recession since the Great Depression, far worse than the GFC. All its consequences for macro-prudential economic management, financial stability, and the global economy are as yet unknown. But there can be no doubt that there will be sharp declines in the level of output, household spending, employment levels, corporate investment, and international trade. The crisis has exposed a global lack of resilience, exacerbated by under-resourced healthcare systems in most countries which have been overstretched in coping with the pandemic while undertaking their normal functions at the same time.

Austerity policies pursued in so many countries over the last decade to restore fiscal discipline appear to have eroded the very public sector institutions that the world needed to manage the coronavirus pandemic. The pandemic has underscored yet again that faced with existential crises markets require support from the State.

They require support from the State when faced with the possibility of their short-term extinction as preserving them is necessary for long-term economic revival and survival. They need to be protected and maintained to resume operations and be resilient in the recovery stage.

Only the State can intervene in offering holistic solutions in such desperate situations while attempting to balance a wide variety of interests. In the face of the global pandemic in 2020, the State was expected to do much more than just save companies and markets when capital assets (like planes, ships, hotels, malls, manufacturing plants, etc.) are forcibly rendered inoperative or mothballed. To compensate for the loss of income and employment, resulting from state-mandated isolation and distancing policies, the State was expected, as a corollary, to protect minimal levels of individuals' incomes, save future livelihoods, and prevent implosion by propping up consumption and aggregate demand.

In the developed world, the State stepped up its role through extended welfare and massive stimulus by extending credit and making direct payments to businesses and individuals. Its actions were funded effectively by almost unlimited money creation and not by budgetary public financing which was already severely constrained.

It is almost inevitable post this crisis that, with dramatically expanded immediate lending to a vast number of firms that find themselves in liquidity (and possibly future solvency) distress, the State will eventually have to increase its ownership share of many private companies. They include, for example, airlines, cruise shipping firms, other firms in the travel/hospitality industries, as well as major manufacturing units, public utilities that provide essential services, and banks that lend to large and small businesses.

The massive loans that the State has extended immediately to such firms to avoid their closure, will need, inevitably, to be converted into equity with the passage of time. That will be essential to rejig debt-equity structures in ways that enable such firms to avoid filing for bankruptcy, and instead, ensuring their long-term financial survival on a sustainable footing. Thus, the State will automatically (if reluctantly in many countries) increase its portfolio of SOEs, as a consequence of the role, it has been obliged to play in saving lives and livelihoods in a dire public emergency.

Beyond this, the need for an entrepreneurial state investing (or co-investing with the private sector) in innovation to aid public health has never been more intense or acute.

Is State capitalism fit for purpose to rise to this challenge? It is perhaps too early to speculate on how the role of the State, and its relationship with the private sector, will evolve as the world economy builds in contingencies for emergency situations.

While SOEs are increasingly sought to play a role during emergency situations, evidence suggests that they misallocate capital and mismanage resources. In that case, will SOEs be effective in emergency situations and play the role expected of them in economic crises?

According to The Economist, most of the SOEs that raised equity or debt financing through international capital markets between 2000 and 2010, had a dismal record around the world. Their share of global market capitalization shrank from a peak of 22% in 2007 to 13% in 2014. SOEs accounted for just 4% of the market capitalization in developed economies but 35% of that of emerging economies in 2016 (FT, 2016). The root cause of that underperformance was the egregious mis-allocation of capital by SOEs. Given too much free licence by politicians and with little need to satisfy government investors, their capital investment surged, accounting for more than 30% of the total by large listed firms.

More than $2.5 trillion was invested in telecoms networks, hydro-carbons exploration, exploitation, and marketing, and other large but unproductive projects by SOEs since 2007. But much of that investment has not proven to be as successful as expected. State-owned banks, on the other hand, went on a lending binge in China, India, Russia, Brazil, and Vietnam. The resulting bad debts have now been recognized, even as the usual criticisms of the State as being slow and bureaucratic have not disappeared entirely.

Too many governments believe that profitable SOEs make the State stronger, with entitled cash-flow rights in key industries, without necessarily having to worry about running the companies efficiently themselves. They prefer lower dependence on tax revenues to finance public expenditures that positive net cash flow from SOEs permits.

But they disregard the fiscal impact of negative cash flows that loss-making SOEs necessitate, and the huge opportunity costs, thus, entailed in not being able to meet other social needs, like public welfare, health, education, and social safety nets because scarce resources are being diverted to cover SOE losses.

Moreover, in too many countries, the State's ownership of enterprises and financial institutions enables *the private agenda* (wealth accumulating through corruption and access to special privileges) *of public officials* (managers of SOEs, bureaucrats overseeing them, or politicians) to be accommodated opaquely, in ways that evade the necessary checks and balances of transparency, accountability, and responsibility which public trust demands.

As a result, policymakers in many countries (mainly developing) continue to extol the supposed virtues of State ownership—that is, its long-term steadiness, commitment to stakeholders, ability to make long-term strategic investments, and ability to provide a sturdy trellis on which to grow an economy.

The 'China Effect' on State capitalism and the developmental State

The rapid rise of China and other emerging markets with mixed economy models—none of which conformed to the traditional view of a free market economy—have resurrected reconsideration of the Washington Consensus and the idea that there is only one systemic path to good economic performance. Perhaps the most important way in which China and other successful emerging economies have deviated from the free market paradigm concerns the active role of the State in economic development (Musacchio and Lazzarini, 2014). The role of State capitalism is equally important as a source of cross-border finance and, particularly, a source of patient capital. For instance, the longer-term horizons of Chinese state-to-state lending provides more fiscal space to Latin-American debtors than when they borrow from financial markets, thereby, affecting their policy choices (Kaplan, 2016). Not just countries in Latin America, State and private actors in Germany and France have also actively sought to attract investment from Sovereign Wealth Funds (SWFs) (Thatcher and Vlandas, 2016).

State capitalism has expanded dramatically among some of the most important developing countries in the world over the past two decades. Many, such as China, Brazil, Russia, Indonesia, Saudi Arabia, South Africa, and India, are among the world's 30 largest economies. Others, like Singapore and Malaysia, though not as large, are significant exemplar economies within their regions that have a profound influence on economic thinking. State ownership is back in countries, especially where nationalist or authoritarian political leaders see the merits of control or push back against foreign ownership, such as in Poland and Hungary.

At the start of this millennium, the economic rise of a China dominated by SOEs and the seemingly inexorable rise in global oil prices fuelled by national oil companies (Russia, Saudi Arabia, Venezuela) pointed to a world more inclined towards State capitalism. On the face of it, that seemed paradoxical, given the disrepute that state ownership had fallen into immediately after the collapse of the Soviet Union in 1989, bringing into question the viability and durability of its economic model.

Retrospective analysis of the advantages of a 'developmental State'—as an activist in shaping, guiding, and socializing nascent markets, was exemplified by the success of Asia. It originated in post-war Japan but was more powerfully demonstrated by the unprecedented success of China, as well as that of Korea, Hong Kong, Singapore, and Taiwan. Although the 'developmental State' is not synonymous with 'State capitalism', the two phenomena intersect and overlap, thus, explaining part of the paradox.

Many economies (particularly developing ones like the BRICS, as well as many oil-surplus countries) with large levels of state participation in corporate ownership, grew strongly between 1990 and 2007, outperforming counterparts in the developed world significantly. Such economies (with China accounting for most of their collective weight) have also integrated more closely and more rapidly with the international economic system through two-way cross-border investment and trade.

In particular, China, India, and Brazil appeared to be more resilient economies through the 2008–10 GFC and immediately thereafter (2011–15) than the developed economies of the US, Europe, and Japan, which the crisis imperilled. Superficially, it suggested the superiority of a relatively greater capacity on the part of BRICS' governments to deploy resources for economic stimulus through State-owned banks and SOE holding companies.

It was felt by many observers that state ownership of banks in these emerging economies resulted in such firms being more tightly regulated and supervised by their central banks. That approach supposedly obliged State-owned Banks and Financial Institutions (SOBFIs) to be more conservative and prudent in risk taking than privately owned global financial firms in developed economies.

Post-2012 rethink about State capitalism

More careful analysis and scrutiny suggest a better nuanced, more accurate judgement about whether State capitalism with a predominance of SOEs and SOBFIs in the economy does actually work better than properly regulated markets dominated by private players. Was State capitalism the key variable in determining the earlier, stellar growth performance of China, India, South Africa, or the Gulf States? Despite holding up well through the GFC, growth in the BRICS economies has slowed considerably since 2012, raising questions about whether other variables and initial conditions might have played a more important part in explaining earlier growth than 'State capitalism' on its own.[1]

[1] Between 2005–08 SOEs performed well, because of State-owned natural resources enterprises. By 2016, SOEs generated lower return on equity compared to other listed companies: 8.1%

The slowing of growth in BRICS' economies after 2012 has occurred with the simultaneous explosion of non-performing loan assets. Their economies have financial systems dominated by SOBFIs and other State-owned financial firms (for example, insurance companies, asset managers, pension funds, and other intermediaries). They have brought to the fore the question of whether SOBFIs and their lending to financial as well as non-financial SOEs are now more the problem than the solution. Are they impeding the transformation and restructuring of these economies by prolonging the existence of zombie banks and firms as they attempt to escape the 'middle-income trap' and become 'developed'?

To reinforce that point, for example, many Brazilian, Chinese, Indian, and Russian SOBFIs—that saw themselves as impregnable and invincible compared to their developed country counterparts in the midst of the financial crisis in 2010—are now plagued with much higher levels of non-performing assets (NPAs) on their balance sheets. They have attempted to downplay and obscure that reality through ever-greening and implicit or explicit government support in bolstering their capital base.

The same is true of many agriculture or mineral commodity producing and export-manufacturing SOEs in BRICS and other developing countries as well. With the post-2012 collapse in commodity prices, the structural and operating weaknesses of all too many mining, hydro-carbon, and commodity producing SOEs have been laid bare.

Several influences have combined to convince many political leaders in Asia, Russia, and the Middle East that they needed to blend state intervention with private enterprise in a 'mixed social market economy' model rather than shift or resort to a purer 'market economy' model. They included Russia's post-1991 experience; the State's strategic role in post-war Japan and its imitators across East Asia; and China's phenomenal success post-1990 in building up powerful State-owned domestic industries and finding overseas markets for them.

In contrast to many governments now favouring recidivism and resort to some form of state capitalism in key sectors, most private enterprises see the rise of State ownership in the economy as a serious threat that is counterproductive and inimical to the functioning of a sound economy.

compared to a market average of 9.7% in developed markets, 9.6% compared to 11.2% in emerging markets. These results are from an analysis of 6600 businesses in 61 countries (FT, 2016).

That is because governments tend to use SOEs as privileged competitors to influence corporate behaviour in national and global markets.

For example, SOEs are often provided with privileged access to (cheaper) capital and guarantees that their private counterparts cannot avail of. SOEs are often given transparent or hidden subsidies, tax preferences, regulatory privileges, advantages in monetizing their international investments (for example, accessing resources to finance their investments in a more favourable way). Such advantages and many other immunities that SOEs enjoy, lower their cost of capital, often of labour and other inputs as well, are unavailable to private enterprises in the same industries/sectors. Such preferences result in distinctly un-level playing fields.

This has created a potential conflict between the developmental goals and the more widely shared common interest in maintaining a healthy international competitive environment. While countries have the means to ensure that their national SOEs can compete with private companies on an equal footing at home, it becomes more difficult when global SOEs operate in a jurisdiction other than their home country.

But there are many countries which have welcomed investment from foreign owned SOEs as a source of funding for capital formation. This is true for long-term investment in infrastructure—for example, the recent Belt and Road Initiative that China is pursuing aggressively in Central and South Asia, as well as in Eastern and Southern Europe, or investments in the hydro-carbon sector (for example, in Brazil, the Middle East, Central Asia, and Venezuela) by State-owned oil/gas companies from Russia, France, and Italy.

SOEs operating abroad benefit from advantages which distort competition in both their home and host countries. Governments and regulators have been more concerned with the cross-border activities of SOEs when it affects their strategic interests and national security considerations[2] (especially in sectors where SOEs are concentrated like network

[2] National security is, in most jurisdictions, defined broadly to include, in addition to national defence, issues such as initial infrastructure and national resource security. Applying domestic law to foreign sovereign investors may also be problematic. Governments already have tools at their disposal to deal with these issues, including investment review mechanisms and competition rules. However, these tools have drawbacks too as they can be used as a cover for protectionism or cannot fully shield the market place from any potential distortions of competition that may arise due to the favourable treatment of SOEs in the home jurisdiction.

industries, minerals, finance) rather than adhering to the objective of using SOEs to maintain competitive markets. Governments have, therefore, become more active in their efforts to formulate policies for dealing with international investment by SOEs. Provisions related to SOEs have increasingly been part of the newly concluded international investment agreements (OECD, 2015a).

Compared to the international investment environment, the trade environment has more developed rules to curb the support of governments to their SOEs, including the World Trade Organization's (WTO's) rules bearing on subsidies and countervailing measures and the protection of intellectual property rights (OECD, 2015a).

More complex regulatory challenges have emerged with the increasing clout of SWFs as they buy stakes in ailing Western banks, and as natural resources fall under the control of the State, sometimes a foreign one. That is particularly galling when home governments have spent years reducing their ownership in strategic SOEs, only to see them bought and controlled by foreign governments instead (even if indirectly by SWFs).

The domestic and international regulation and accountability of SWFs highlight some challenging contemporary governance themes. These include, inter-alia, issues, such as transparency, principal-agent connections, and conflicts, the relationship between states and markets, and cross-border financial governance, sometimes involving multiple governments involved indirectly in SOEs through their respective SWFs. As SOEs become increasingly active abroad, ensuring that they do not benefit from undue (or perceived) advantages at home is important for avoiding unwarranted protectionism and maintaining an open international investment and trade environment.

State capitalism and its different instruments

The State's participation in the economy as an owner or as pro-active interventionist—either by owning majority or minority stakes (with golden shares that retain the State's majority voting rights) in companies, or through the provision of subsidized credit, guarantees, and/or other privileges to private companies—is commonly referred to as '***State Capitalism***'.

Most forms of State capitalism rely on state guidance to manage and develop economies. This includes the use of domestic financial systems and industrial policy tools to foster national innovation systems and national champions, the creation of SWFs, and other state-guided measures. However, the defining characteristic of modern state capitalism in comparison to market capitalism is, in the end, a measure of scepticism about the extent of market efficiency. Yet, market capitalism remains an entrenched feature of the global economy and its trading system. It provides the basis for most established multinational corporations and attempts to optimize global production and knowledge networks through pricing mechanisms.

In order to improve its acceptability, State capitalism has emulated market capitalism in selected ways. More and more, SOEs operate like private firms, increasingly active internationally, and accounting for a greater market share. They employ performance incentives for top managers of state firms. They undertake mergers and acquisitions, relying on advisory services by international investment banks. They cater to the needs of fund managers, employ international accounting standards, stock market listings, recruit independent board members, and other efforts at corporate restructuring.

Profitability has become a key goal for many listed SOEs with large institutional investors (usually foreign) exercising influence over their boards and monitoring their activities. State ownership has increasingly taken the form of portfolio equity investment by governments and State-owned investment funds, rather than direct ownership/operation of SOEs.

Another transformation in State ownership is the emergence of firms in which the government is a minority shareholder. In such firms, the government outsources management to the private sector, keeping cash-flow rights and veto power over key strategic decisions (Musacchio et al., 2015). Modern state capitalists, drawing on the tools of powerful governments and the strategies of multinational businesses, have been able to adapt and innovate, to compete with established private, global multinationals, and enhance the growth and expansion of State-capitalist companies.

Modern state capitalism is, therefore, a hybrid that encourages the pragmatic use of markets and prices. Reliance on market forces, and on participation in state-owned joint ventures by foreign firms, is seen by State-capitalist policymakers as instrumental, providing state control and direction of key strategic and economic aspects remain unchallenged.

State capitalism usually involves a majority state-shareholding and direct management control of SOEs or SOBFIs, increasingly though it also involves (a) minority investments in SOEs by State-owned development or commercial banks, pension funds, insurance companies, and specially constructed SWFs; (b) the government continuing to own minor stakes in SOEs that have been partially privatized; or (c) minority stakes being held in such SOEs/SOBs by arms-length other State-owned holding companies.

In the majority-equity model, the government exercises control over SOEs directly, by appointing managers and boards of directors. In the other three cases, control and influence are exercised circumspectly and indirectly. A large number of SOEs are now listed on national and global stock exchanges. Their shares are publicly traded, even when the government remains the majority shareholder and exercises policy influence to achieve non-commercial objectives that are not in the best commercial or profitability interests of the firm.

Governments also exercise control as investors using large conglomerate structures that control a number of subsidiary/affiliate firms, or indirectly exercise influence through State-owned holding companies. Large developed and developing country SOEs and SOBFIs compete internationally and try to apply international standards of corporate governance. Many have professional managements, though they are rarely as independent as typically portrayed and are often subject to bureaucratic and/or political interference/intrusion.

As *minority shareholders* in partially privatized SOEs, governments continue to provide capital support, as well as extend privileges in the form of producer subsidies, subsidized loans or capital guarantees, and other entitlements like tariff protection to former SOEs that have become private enterprises, while relinquishing control and thereby avoiding the most common agency problems associated with state ownership. The influence by the government, if any in such instances, is indirect but palpable nonetheless.

State capitalism deploys industrial policy to foster innovation through national champions. These are created and developed through the strategic use of SOE joint ventures involving significant foreign investment by 'best-in-class' global multinationals, willing to transfer technological, organizational, and management know–how. Specific tools to achieve this objective include measures to foster technology transfers, specific trade-enhancing tools, government-guided mergers and acquisitions, competition policy, preferential access to credit, and the setting up of designated industrial zones in which preferential policies are applied to encourage innovation and develop new industries and technologies.

National champions are most common in industries that compete over scarce resources and that have the potential to capture a significant share of the global market in emerging new leading sectors such as artificial intelligence for example (Modelski and Thompson, 1996). There are, however, substantial variations in the types and amounts of state support available, as well as in terms of ownership structures and corporate forms.

All successful practitioners of state capitalism have, in one way or other, harnessed the resource mobilization capacity of domestic (state-owned) financial systems to support industrial policy goals and the nurturing of national champions. This has been done directly—via credit extended by state-controlled banks, insurance companies, and financial holding companies—or through indirect credit provision, not involving state-owned banks, by facilitating access of market sources of funding. In any event, the state tends to exert some control over the allocation of credit and investment to such enterprises (McNally, 2013).

Besides using industrial policy and fostering of national champions, SWFs have recently become another major plank of contemporary state capitalism, although they have existed since 1953. SWFs are state owned and managed investment funds that are invested in a variety of financial assets, including foreign currency, stocks, bonds, real estate, precious metals, and other financial instruments.

Between 2001 and 2012, governments *acquired* more assets through public stock purchases ($1.52 trillion) than they sold through share issue privatizations and direct sales ($1.48 trillion). Most of this was done through SWFs—which grew from less than $1 trillion in assets under management (AUM) in 2000 to over $7.5 trillion AUM in 2017. The number of SWFs increased from 50 to 92 between 2005 and 2017

(Prequin, 2018). The bulk of these stock purchases by SWFs has been cross-border transactions (Megginson, 2017).

SWFs were originally created—separately from central bank reserve management departments—to invest surplus national foreign exchange reserves in higher yielding assets other than traditional US, European, or Japanese government securities of various maturities. Some SWFs take strategic direct stakes in corporations; others are interested only in having a large number of minority shareholdings (bought openly in global markets) for long-term capital appreciation. Typically, most SWFs invest outside their home countries to keep a pool of savings in high-yielding foreign currency assets (quasi-reserves). However, some SWFs also invest in their home countries in both established as well as cutting-edge companies.

SWFs are funded not with budgetary resources (i.e. fiscal surpluses) but with accumulated surplus foreign exchange reserves, usually generated by income from resource exports (especially minerals and hydrocarbons). Their strategic long-term objective is to maximize returns on investment. Yet, there is a fear (on the part of recipient countries and companies in which they invest) that political goals could (and do) influence SWF investment decisions.

In 2007, prompted by concerns about political factors influencing investments by SWFs, the IMF spearheaded the promulgation of the Santiago Principles. Adherence to them is based on the presumption that SWFs invest primarily for commercial purposes. Given their increasing structural importance in global finance and feature significantly in cross-border investment flows, regulations for SWFs provide useful insights into cross-border financial governance.

Size, nature, and sectoral distribution of the State-owned sector

After over two decades of extensive reform and privatization, the State's *ownership* role in the economies of developed and developing countries remains significant. In some respects, it is more dominant than ever. SOEs as well as state-owned banks and other financial institutions—such as pension funds, insurance companies, SWFs, and other vehicles of governmental

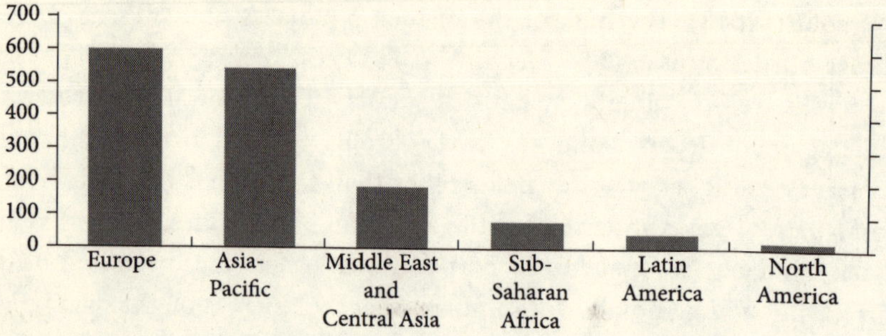

Figure 1.1 Number of SOEs across the world
Source: Gaspar et al., 2020.

capital—are now influential players as investors and traders in the global economy. Figure 1.1 shows the number of SOEs across the world.

For example, SOEs undertake 55% of total infrastructure investment in emerging and developing economies. The share of SOEs among the world's 2000 largest firms doubled to 20% over the last two decades, driven by SOEs in emerging markets—their assets are worth $45 trillion, equivalent to half of global GDP (Gaspar et al., 2020). An OECD (2017) study of 39 countries (excluding China) found that SOEs employ more than 9.2 million people and are valued at $2.4 trillion, with the largest portfolios residing in emerging market and post-transition countries. For typical emerging economies, the output from SOEs represents around 30% of GDP (Nem Singh and Chen, 2018). Figure 1.2 shows the share of SOE assets among the world's 2000 largest firms, and Figure 1.3 shows the share of SOE assets by sector.

Of the 10 largest listed companies globally, half include the State as a major shareholder. SOEs account for 22% of the world's largest companies and are often concentrated in sectors with strategic importance for the State and society, including for development. In OECD countries, for example, SOEs account for 15% of GDP; while in transition economies, SOEs can account for 20–30% of GDP. The World Bank (2018) estimates that SOEs account globally for 20% of investment and 5% of employment and SOE global revenues at $8 trillion, almost equivalent to the combined GDPs of Germany, France, and the UK. Another study found significant and growing state ownership among the top 500 global companies (PricewaterhouseCoopers 2015) as shown in Table 1.1.

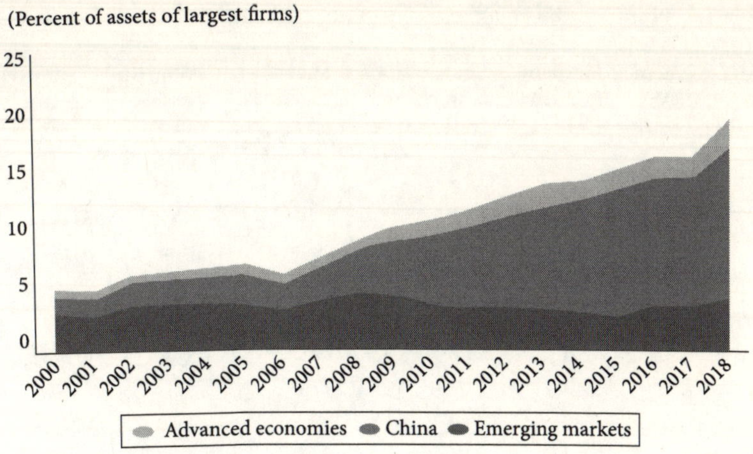

Figure 1.2 The share of SOE assets among the world's 2000 largest firms
Source: Gaspar et al., 2020.

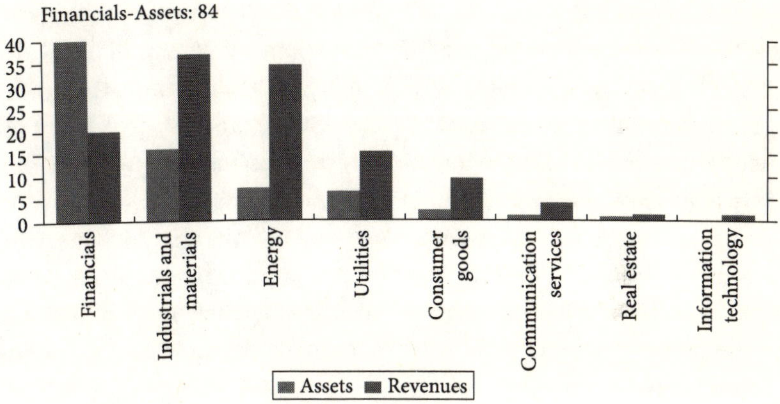

Figure 1.3 The share of SOE assets by sector
Source: Gaspar et al., 2020.

In addition, the State owns minority shareholdings in 134 listed companies valued at USD 912.3 billion and employing 2.8 million people. In absolute terms, the number of SOEs in individual countries ranges from ten or below (in Australia, Austria, Japan, and Switzerland) to over 100 (in Brazil, Czech Republic, Hungary, India, Lithuania, Poland, and the Slovak Republic). On the other hand, China alone has over 51, 000 SOEs, valued

Table 1.1 Number and share of SOEs in the Fortune Global 500 list

	No. of SOEs	Share by quantity (%)	Share by employment (%)	Share by revenues (%)	Share by assets (%)	Share by profits (%)
2005	49	9.8	18.4	8.0	8.9	8.2
2006	54	10.8	19.9	8.8	9.2	9.9
2007	55	11.0	19.7	9.2	8.8	10.4
2008	57	11.4	19.9	10.3	9.1	12.0
2009	69	13.8	23.6	14.5	15.7	11.9
2010	75	15.0	24.8	15.3	18.8	9.35
2011	86	17.2	27.7	17.8	22.2	16.95
2012	95	19.0	29.8	19.6	19.3	22.25
2013	107	21.4	30.4	22.0	19.7	23.15
2014	114	22.8	n.a.	24.1	23.0	19.9

Source: Kwiatkowski and Augustynowicz (2015).

at USD 29.2 trillion and employing approximately 20.2 million people. China alone, thus, accounts for 65% of total SOE assets around the world.

In those countries with relatively fewer SOEs, the average value of individual companies tends to be much higher than in countries with relatively higher numbers of SOEs. For example, Japan's eight SOEs have an average value of USD 10.3 billion, compared to Poland's 126 SOEs, with an average value of USD 125 million. Among OECD countries, SOEs have the largest economic weight as measured by their share of national employment in Norway, where they account for almost 10% of non-agricultural employment (OECD, 2017).

SOEs account for between 5% and 40% of the total economy (measured by output, value added, and employment) of developed and emerging economies. Table 1.2 shows data of the share of SOEs from developed and emerging economies in the Fortune Global 500 list. The largest concentration of SOEs is in public utilities, telecommunications, the financial sector (banking, insurance, pensions, and asset management), hydrocarbons, manufacturing, construction, retail services provision (shopping, hospitality), and to a much lesser extent, healthcare, and education services, which are sometimes provided by SOEs but more often than not directly by government ministries.

Table 1.2 SOEs from developed and emerging economies in the Fortune Global 500 list

	2005	2006	2007	2008	2009	2010	2011	2012	2013	2014
Developed economies										
SOEs	23	19	19	17	21	21	17	16	16	16
Private sector	444	436	432	427	410	404	389	376	360	352
Total	467	455	451	444	431	425	406	392	376	368
Share of SOEs %	4.9	4.2	4.2	3.8	4.9	4.9	4.2	4.1	4.3	4.3
Emerging economies										
SOEs	26	35	36	40	48	54	69	79	91	98
Private sector	7	10	13	16	21	21	25	29	32	34
Total	33	45	49	56	69	75	94	108	123	132
Share of SOEs %	78.8	77.8	73.5	71.4	69.6	72.0	73.4	73.1	74	74.2
Emerging economies share in total %	6.6	9.0	9.8	11.2	13.8	15.0	18.8	21.6	24.6	26.4

Source: Kwiatkowski and Augustynowicz (2015).

According to the same OECD study, telecoms, electricity, gas, transportation, and other utilities (including postal services) account for about half of all SOEs by value and 70% of all SOEs by employment. Among those sectors, electricity and gas is the largest, accounting for 21% of all SOEs by value and almost 10% of SOE employment.

The financial sector is the second largest sector, accounting for 26% of all SOEs by value and 8% of all SOEs by employment. The five largest national contributors to the state-owned financial sector (excluding China) are the UK, India, the Netherlands, Brazil, and Greece, accounting for over 60% of all financial sector SOEs by value.

The primary sector, which includes the production and refining of hydro-carbons, accounts for 11% of all SOEs by value and 6% by employment. Listed SOEs account for 45% of all SOEs by value and 25% of all SOEs by employment (OECD, 2017). In a few countries, the State has reduced its holdings in SOEs and SOBFIs for fiscal compunctions, though it still prefers to have controlling stakes in most.

SOEs in *developed* countries tend to be involved most often in strategic industrial sectors, such as energy (i.e. hydro-electric and nuclear power, renewable energy, oil, gas, and coal), postal and telecommunications services, transportation services, healthcare and education services, highly capital-intensive manufacturing (for example, automobiles, trucks, and aircraft), and to a lesser extent, financial services.

In *developing* countries, SOEs are more heterogeneous. As the objectives range from promoting growth in promising sectors or lagging regions, delivering services to the urban or rural poor or general population, addressing market failures such as natural monopoly, filling perceived market gaps, financing investments whose size or risk make private investment unlikely, to address issues of heightened national priority or security (World Bank, 2018a). In many such countries, the State may be as entrepreneurially diversified as any private global conglomerate.

Table 1.3 shows data on the area of activity of SOEs in the Fortune Global 500 list.

The State as a 'capitalist' in its own right plays a significant role not only in large emerging economies such as China, India, and Russia but also across the Middle East and North Africa (MENA), Southeast Asia, and Latin America despite wide differences in national incomes, sectoral

Table 1.3 Area of activity of SOEs in the Fortune Global 500 list

	2005	2006	2007	2008	2009	2010	2011	2012	2013	2014
Number of SOEs										
Financial institutions	10	11	10	11	15	18	15	16	14	17
Hydro-carbons	14	16	19	19	23	24	31	33	41	43
Utilities	21	19	18	17	18	18	20	22	23	25
Industry	1	5	5	7	10	11	16	18	20	22
Other	3	3	3	3	3	4	4	6	9	7
Total number of enterprises										
Financial institutions	112	115	116	123	103	116	109	105	109	110
Hydro-carbons	60	66	76	76	93	78	91	92	98	96
Utilities	80	75	73	69	70	67	67	71	68	69
Industry	79	82	79	80	83	82	82	82	78	84
Other	169	162	156	152	151	157	151	150	146	141
Share of SOEs (%)										
Financial institutions	8.9	9.6	8.6	8.9	14.6	15.5	13.8	15.2	12.8	15.5
Hydro-carbons	23.3	24.2	25.0	25.0	24.7	30.8	34.1	35.9	41.8	44.8
Utilities	26.3	25.3	24.7	24.6	25.7	26.9	29.9	31.0	33.8	36.2
Industry	1.3	6.1	6.3	8.8	12.0	13.4	19.5	22.0	25.6	26.2
Other	1.8	1.9	1.9	2.0	2.0	2.5	2.6	4.0	6.2	5.0

Source: Kwiatkowski and Augustynowicz (2015).

distribution, and the nature of strategic assets. Table 1.4 shows the predominance of Chinese SOEs in the Fortune Global 500 list.

Why do States own enterprises at all?

Governments around the world justify active state ownership as a way to resolve (or avoid) market failures; fill voids in domestic private capacity/capability; enhance economic competitiveness (especially in resource-based industries and public utilities); protect inherited institutional conditions and processes; and ensure stability through macroeconomic crises and financial shocks. But the current worldwide health crisis has pushed the role of the state in strengthening and supporting the public health system, to the forefront.

The unprecedented health crisis brought about by the COVID-19 pandemic has seen governments on a war footing and fighting the spread of the virus. While governments have been assigned to contain the disease, protect the vulnerable, and help create new therapies and vaccines, they have been caught ill-prepared and ill-equipped to deal with the crisis.

Critical institutions providing public services and goods have been weakened in many countries because of budget cuts and austerity measures over many years. The state now needs to invest in and rebuild institutions to help prevent such crises and to handle crises when they arise. It needs to coordinate and steer research and development activities towards public health goals including fair prices and safeguarding medicine and medical supplies.

In theory, through public ownership, the State can sustain sectors of long-term strategic or even national security interest, public goods[3] and goods with positive or negative externalities,[4] in financial and healthcare sectors[5] that are uneconomical for private investment. It is often argued

[3] The concept of public goods justified state provision because it implied that without such intervention, the market would undersupply such goods. The private sector would not have an incentive to produce public goods due to the difficulty of excluding from their consumption individuals who would not contribute to the cost of their production.

[4] The recognition that the consumption or the production of some goods may generate positive or negative externalities not reflected in the price of these goods created a further case of market failure requiring state intervention.

[5] In the financial sector and the healthcare sector, markets are incomplete or information is imperfect.

Table 1.4 Predominance of Chinese SOEs in the Fortune Global 500 list (in parentheses %)

	2005	2006	2007	2008	2009	2010	2011	2012	2013	2014
China	14 (88)	19 (95)	22 (92)	25 (86)	32 (86)	39 (85)	52 (85)	61 (84)	72 (82)	76 (80)
India	4 (80)	5 (83)	5 (83)	5 (71)	5 (71)	5 (63)	5 (63)	5 (63)	5 (63)	5 (63)
Germany	6 (16)	5 (14)	4 (11)	4 (11)	5 (13)	5 (14)	3 (9)	3 (9)	2 (7)	2 (7)
France	6 (15)	5 (13)	4 (11)	4 (10)	4 (10)	4 (10)	3 (9)	3 (9)	3 (10)	3 (9)
Russia	1 (33)	3 (60)	2 (50)	3 (60)	3 (38)	3 (50)	3 (43)	3 (43)	3 (43)	5 (63)
Japan	2 (2)	2 (3)	2 (3)	1 (2)	2 (3)	2 (3)	2 (3)	2 (3)	2 (3)	3 (5)
Brazil	2 (100)	2 (50)	2 (40)	2 (40)	2 (33)	2 (29)	2 (29)	2 (25)	2 (25)	2 (29)
Mexico	2 (100)	2 (40)	2 (40)	2 (40)	2 (50)	1 (50)	2 (67)	2 (67)	2 (67)	2 (67)
US	1 (1)	1 (1)	1 (1)	1 (1)	3 (2)	4 (3)	3 (2)	1 (1)	1 (1)	1 (1)
South Korea	1 (9)	1 (8)	1 (7)	1 (7)	1 (7)	1 (10)	1 (7)	2 (15)	2 (14)	2 (13)

Source: Kwiatkowski and Augustynowicz (2015).

that SOEs are important for the local economy (even in nonstrategic sectors), such as employing workers who cannot be easily employed elsewhere or providing livelihoods for households in economically depressed regions. Other examples include meeting public service obligations and protecting against foreign competition (Gylfason, Herbertsson, and Zoega, 2001). Governments argue that these non-financial objectives outweigh the fact that SOEs are less profitable, efficient, or productive than private firms (IMF, 2019).

Innovation and technological progress are fundamental engines of economic growth, but private sector underfunds innovative activities due to high levels of risk and information asymmetries. The development of technological capacity is a key element in any strategy to maintain global competitiveness and penetrate advanced markets. Because technological knowledge and capacity are to some extent public goods, states can play a role in expanding these. In addition, innovation of product and processes is equally important to achieve and maintain competitiveness. State action fosters, supports, and rewards innovation (OECD, 2015a).

The State sometimes serves as an enabler of innovation, subsidizing if not directing the deployment of transformational technologies (Janeway, 2018). In other cases, the State acts as a force for innovation and change, not only by 'de-risking' risk-averse private actors, but also leading the way with a clear vision. In innovation, the State not only 'crowds in' business investment but also 'dynamizes it in'—creating the vision, the mission, and the plan (Mazzucato, 2013).

The SOE structure also enables the State to launch firms in industries where start-up costs are significant, but returns, local demand, global market participation, and property rights are initially too uncertain for private entrepreneurs to risk their capital. State capital can help firms to develop *latent* capabilities by funding the acquisition of new knowledge that would otherwise remain unfunded. Constraints for financing latent capabilities are more binding in countries in the early stages of industrial development or with shallow financial markets (Yeyati et al., 2004).

For example, the launch of China's new technology-focused stock market in 2019 has underlined the importance of state funding to the country's fast-growing tech sector. Of the first 25 companies listed on Shanghai's Star board, 14 report State-owned investors among their top-three shareholders. These State-run venture capital funds, also known as 'guidance funds', which have proliferated since 2015 are intended to support the country's goal of gaining prowess in key technology sectors by 2025.

In 2011, the Russian government set ambitious goals in science, technology, and innovation and used its large SOEs as channels to achieve these targets. These initiatives focused on the collaboration among innovation actors and introduce open innovation (OI) principles. Russian SOEs have driven the demand for technology and have mainly absorbed incoming OI activities. SOEs have extended their OI activities to the country's knowledge producers, such as research and technology organizations, and leading universities. They work on incorporating scientific knowledge that could hold the key to globally competitive technological innovations (Gershman et al., 2018).

The *industrial policy* view hypothesizes that, under certain conditions in a nascent stage of development, state involvement might have a positive effect in the incubation of firms and industries. In this view, State capital and SOEs could be useful tools to remedy important sources of market failure and promote industrial upgrading (OECD, 2013c). Private sector can sometimes take a long time to effectively develop a critical sector of an economy. Economies develop SOEs to build vital economic sectors quickly. For example, Saudi Arabia established the Saudi Arabian Military Industries in 2017 to help develop world-class military products and services for the Kingdom and its allies.

The *strategic trade theory* approach suggests that comparative advantages in the modern economy are made and not found. Nations can actively pursue certain niches in the world economy through planning and targeted investment. With the proliferation of global supply chains, it is important for developing country producers to be in secure positions in global networks. States can assist in this process (OECD, 2015a).

State capitalism, through SOEs in particular, can also help utilize/coordinate the local deployment of complementary resources and support activities with high externalities and industrial linkages (Amsden, 2001; Rodrik, 2007). Hirschman (1958) famously proposed that backward and forward linkages in the production chain need to be created to spur local development. In other words, a 'big push' by the government may be necessary to promote coordinated, complementary investments (Murphy, Shleifer, and Vishny, 1989).

For sunset industries too, a SOE structure can be deployed to mitigate and control the negative consequences of potentially disruptive declines in obsolete industries/activities, such as outmoded shipbuilding, steel-making, or coal-mining plants, where direct subsidies are not possible and private ownership may no longer be viable.

The *social* view of SOEs suggests that governments use them to pursue social and development objectives such as generating employment to achieve greater equality and social stability. SOEs may serve as a conduit for subsidies that can sell certain kinds of goods. On other occasions, governments create SOEs to build the economy of an underdeveloped region.

SOEs are also often used as an insurer of last resort (through wide public pooling of risk) against catastrophic risks, such as natural disasters in the agricultural sector. Protecting citizens from various other risks[6] such as unemployment, loss of income due to old age, sickness, and risks inherent to some economic activities (for example, mining dangerous minerals, like uranium, or dealing with toxic chemicals or nuclear waste) have often been used to justify state intervention through enterprise ownership.

Governments step in to rectify environment externalities by imposing a tax to ensure firms take into account the damage to the environment. Emerging countries depend on SOEs to mitigate environmental externalities if there are inadequate institutions in the country or incentives for the private sector to do so. Recent research has suggested that the State can use its more visible hand, through stakes in SOEs, to implement its environmental policies.

The *environment* view of SOEs suggests that they have an important role to play in the low-carbon transition as they remain prominent actors in global energy markets, despite on-going liberalization and privatization in many jurisdictions. State ownership itself has a positive effect on investment in the renewable electricity generation sector in OECD and

[6] Market failure in dealing with risk is often due to two reasons: adverse selection and moral hazard. Adverse selection results from asymmetric information between those who buy insurance and those sell insurance. Normally those who buy it have more information than those who sell it; thus, it is difficult to establish the ideal price for each individual. As a consequence, markets do not develop fully and the government is expected to intervene. Moral hazard is a consequence of uninsured individuals tending to be less careful than those who are insured, or insured persons even precipitating the event for which they are insured, as with financial insurance.

G20 countries. This points to an opportunity for governments to use their ownership of SOEs to accelerate the low-carbon transition (Prag et al., 2018).

The role of the State in protecting individuals from risk manifests itself in three forms: public spending, regulatory protection, and guarantees. In deploying these instruments, the state guides the dynamics of a capitalist economy to accommodate specific social goals that are not directly the aims of private capital. Whether the State can play each of these roles effectively depends, *inter-alia,* on its ability to insulate its functioning from the influence of sectional vested interests within the sphere of private capital as well as of politics.

In countries where public accountability and institutions are weak and enforcement mechanisms do not operate well, governments prefer to opt for direct control of state assets (and, unfortunately, liabilities) rather than rely more on the oversight, regulation, and taxation of privately owned enterprises, ironically though, the same institutional weaknesses that impel governments to rely on direct control through state ownership, also undermine the State's ability to manage State-owned companies well. In weak institutional environments, the creation of large State-owned companies is likely to be associated with high levels of opacity, mis-management, corruption, and rent seeking by connected insiders and politicians.

Structure of the book

When organized effectively, the State's hand is firm in providing the vision and the dynamic push to make things happen that otherwise would not have. Such actions are meant to increase the courage of private business. It is a key partner of the private sector, willing to take the risks that business will not (Mazzucato, 2013). This ideal state of affairs is rare in many of the emerging economies covered in this book. The only exception is the case of Singapore.

The next chapter outlines a conceptual framework that is used in this book for understanding and evaluating the nature, structure, influences, and incentives that affect the operations of SOEs and their performance. This chapter looks at how State-owned banks and financial institutions contribute to the growth of State capitalism and at the contradictions in

State-led capitalism in the face of the rise of the regulatory state and the inherent conflicts of interest. More often than not, the State bows down to interest groups and it is 'captured' by private interests. Chapter 2 shows the link between State capitalism and crony capitalism, when interest groups approach the State to seek handouts, rents, and other privileges. When the State is not organized well, political authorities find it easy to grant favours with economic value to those who are closest to them and expect compensation of some kind in return.

Chapter 2 also looks at the private agenda of public officials running and managing SOEs. An entrepreneurial State does not only 'de-risk' the private sector but envisions the risk space and operates boldly and effectively within it to make things happen (Mazzucato, 2013). This role of the State is fulfilled only when SOEs allocate resources to their most efficient use and work towards increasing productivity at SOEs. The chapter looks at how SOEs allocate resources and their impact on total factor productivity. When not playing a leading role, the State becomes an imitator of private sector behaviour, rather than as an alternative. The State is slow and bureaucratic when it is sidelined to play a purely 'administrative' role (Mazzucato, 2013).

The chapter outlines the challenges of internal management in SOEs, the effects of adopting of private sector practices for better SOE management. Countries that do not have an entrepreneurial vision for the State, it takes a backseat and is blamed as soon as it makes a mistake (Mazzucato, 2013). Finally, the chapter looks at how states fare in fulfilling their primary roles when they are responsible for running and managing large and many SOEs.

The following chapters look at eight country case studies looking at these features of State capitalism and how they have evolved in each of those countries. The eight countries covered in the book include Brazil, China, Indonesia, India, Russia, Saudi Arabia, Singapore, and South Africa.

The country study of **Brazil** highlights the important role that the State-owned financial institution has played in supporting the minority State capitalism, the Petrobras corruption scandal, the abuses of minority shareholder rights, and the discretionary nature of the fiscal relationship between the SOEs and the government, and the State's responsibility to protect the environment (see Figure 1.4 and Tables 1.5 and 1.6).

The country study of **China** presents the importance of a coherent and efficient regulatory regime in developing the market economy and how SOEs maintain their status through marketplace distortions, such as soft budget constraints and opportunities and incentives to confer preferential treatment.

The country study of **Indonesia** brings out how nationalist sentiments have pushed SOEs to take on a more active role in the country's economic development and to provide special privileges to SOEs. And how the legacy of Suharto's patronage system has lingered and evolved into a

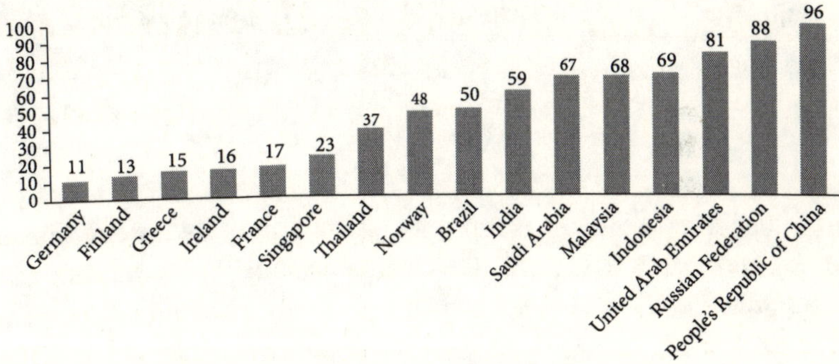

Figure 1.4 Share of SOEs among countries' top 10 firms (%)
Source: Buge et al., 2013.

Table 1.5 SOEs in country case studies

	No. of SOEs	No. of employees	Value of SOEs (USDbn)
Brazil (end of 2015)	134	597,505	145
China (end of 2015)	51,341	20,248,999	29,201.1
India (end of 2015)	270	3,284,845	338.5
Indonesia (2017)	143	—	549
Russia (2018)	32,000	—	—
Saudi Arabia (PIF portfolio) (end of 2015)	24	25,906	139.4
Singapore (2016)	30	—	229
South Africa (2014)	300	—	—

Sources: OECD (2017), OECD (2018), Fourie (2014), IMF (2019), FT (2016), Kim (2018).

Table 1.6 Performance of SOEs in country case studies

	Return on equity (%)	Return on assets (%)
Brazil (2016)	—	5.14
China (2016)	4.8	2.7
India (2016)	11.0	4.5
Indonesia (2006)	7.31	2.46
Russia	—	—
Saudi Arabia	—	—
Singapore (2019) Total Shareholder Value (TSR)	1.49	
South Africa	−0.2 (2018)	0.7% (avg 2006–10)

Note: TSR and RoE are not the same, but TSR has been used as an indicative proxy.
Sources: Kikeri (2018), IMF (2020), Fitriningrum (2006), The Economist (2018), Sheng and Carrera Junios (2018a), Jinrong Lin et al. (2020), Temasek Review (2019).

contest between dominant groups over the allocation of state resources and resulting crony capitalism. The chapter also highlights the collusion among power holders in SOEs, which has endured despite comprehensive reforms towards democracy and good governance.

The country study of **India** presents SOEs' complex relationship with the government and the multiple roles that the State plays with conflicting objectives. It highlights the large overall gains made by some large SOEs when their operational processes were allowed to function autonomously, and yet their absence from any coherent strategy to achieve higher rates of economic growth.

Russia's country study underlines the strengthened role of the State in resource allocation, including through stronger influence of SOEs and state development institutions, pseudo-privatization, and how the Soviet legacy still lingers on in monotowns. It presents the actual government strategy which is focused on consolidating, maintaining, and expanding political and economic power for the ruling elite through the control of select industries and enterprises whether publicly or privately owned.

The country study of **Saudi Arabia** highlights the top-down nature of decision making which has a politically demobilized society, allowing efficient SOEs to emerge. It also outlines how these efficient SOEs are used for mandates related to developing firms in their value chain and a range of other tasks in new sectors and how the prominent national role of the successful SOEs has resulted in their evolving into surrogate sub-national governments.

Singapore provides for a model country case of effective governance and efficient State capitalism. Its development experience has attracted long-standing fascination and interest from China and its leaders. The success of Singapore challenges the claim that private enterprise rather than the State is necessarily more efficient at allocating capital to its most productive use.

The country study of **South Africa** reveals how SOEs that were intended to be used as the principal means to engender radical economic transformation, have instead become the fountainheads in deepening a corrosive culture of corruption within the State and grafting a shadow state onto the existing constitutional state.

The concluding chapter brings out the myriad complexities, key points, and examples from each country to illustrate and illuminate the understanding of the SOE experience and the lessons that can be learnt from it. It seeks to answer questions related to government ownership of SOEs and quality of governance; explore whether conflicts of interest that SOEs create can be successfully resolved; ask if SOEs, instead of being instruments for accelerated development, reverse that role and become drivers of the direction and nature of politics in their countries; and whether they become engines that create wrong, self-serving incentives for politicians and bureaucrats that misguide policies and damage economies through their network effects.

2

A framework for understanding and evaluating SOE performance

This chapter outlines a conceptual framework that is used in this book for understanding and evaluating the nature, structure, influences, and incentives that impinge upon the operations of SOEs of different kinds in all countries and the impact that they have on influencing outcomes and performance. It provides the basic template for analysis in each of the eight country case studies that follow.

The framework used has seven distinct concepts that deal, *seriatim*, with: (a) State-owned banks and financial institutions (SOBFIs) as the central pillars of state capitalism; (b) the State ownership of enterprises and the rise of the regulatory state; (c) the emergence of crony capitalism and how that affects SOEs under State capitalism; (d) the private agenda of public officials involved with SOEs which invariably affects the latter's operations and finances; (e) the impact of state ownership on productivity and the allocation of resources; (f) challenges confronting the internal management of SOEs; and, finally (g) various conflicts (of interest) that arise in fulfilling the State's primary role of good, impartial, public governance vs its stewardship of the financial and commercial interests that arise from the government's ownership of enterprises. Each of these is discussed in detail below.

State-owned banks and financial institutions (SOBFIs) as the central pillars of State capitalism

Under State capitalism, the State's control over finance through SOBFIs plays a central, pivotal role. In State capitalist countries, SOBs dominate the banking sector. For instance, the market share of SOBs in banking assets is close to 60% in Russia and China. In India, which is characterized as a 'mixed' economy, it is close to 70%, while in Brazil it is more than 45% (see Figure 2.1).

SOBs grew in stature during the GFC in a 'flight to safety' away from private banks which were seen to have taken excessive risks in lending to uncreditworthy borrowers. SOBFIs were seen as potentially less volatile and more reliable vehicles for maintaining liquidity and providing credit in turbulent markets, as well as for medium term financial intermediation objectives and pursuit of policy goals, such as financial inclusion or sectoral growth.

'After the global financial crisis, SOFIs expanded more rapidly than the overall banking sector, independently of whether their mandate included a countercyclical role' (Ferrari et al., 2018). But this trend remained brief, with a substantial slowdown of asset growth after 2011. Government rationale for State ownership in the financial sector has echoed those found for SOEs (including the supply of specific public goods and services; supporting national economic and strategic interests).

In many countries, all deposits of whatever amounts at SOBs are guaranteed (implicitly or explicitly) by the State as owner, against limited deposit insurance in the case of private banks. State-owned banks account for 25% of the total assets of the global banking system. In the EU, the share rises to 30%, and it is much higher in the BRIC countries at 50–80% (OECD, 2012). In turn, financial firms account for 24% of the assets of all State-owned enterprises (SOEs). They represent the second largest industry, after the network industries, in which government holdings are concentrated (OECD, 2014b).

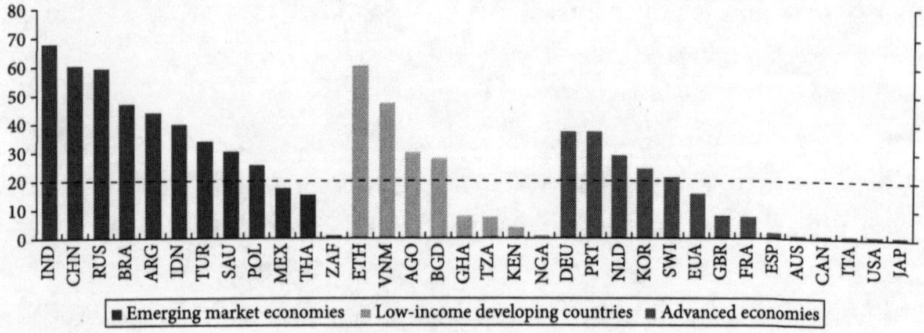

Figure 2.1 SOBFI's share of banking system assets (%)

Source: Gaspar et al. (2020).

By owning and controlling the banking sector and other parts of the financial system (like insurance, asset management, and pension funds), the State exerts considerable influence over the economy's investment pattern. Governments decide how much money is lent to, or invested in, which particular entities and on what terms. The State's dominance of the banking sector and financial system thus constitutes the central pillar of State capitalism (Yang and Lee, 2018).

Such control allows the State to allocate financial resources to strategic sectors to support specific industrial policies. These, in turn, influence the State's competitiveness in the world market (Musacchio and Lazzarini, 2014) and facilitate state control over the economy and society. SOFIs not only provide countercyclical lending but also direct that lending to new uncertain areas that private banks and venture capitalists fear. They operate in sectors and particular areas within those sectors that the private banks fear (Mazzucato, 2013). In addition, SOBs are invariably assigned other objectives, like providing access to banking services for groups of populations or regions not catered to by private institutions.

They are also tasked with mitigating market failures caused by asymmetric information and financing socially valuable (but possibly financially unprofitable) projects. Yet they compete aggressively with private institutions to try to lower the cost of financial intermediation.

This diversity of social, non-commercial objectives often leads to reduced profitability because SOBs are required to provide loans on non-commercial terms. Such practices increase credit risks that result in non-performing assets. Such risks demonstrate misallocation of capital in the economy. Moreover, if governance in these institutions is weak, profitability is likely to be even lower, and the amount of non-performing loans is higher, as they tend to be more sensitive to political interests.

SOBs have different operational objectives, different ownership structures, or different levels of state control. In some cases, the State mandates some SOBs, e.g. development banks, or rural banks to pursue specific state policies aimed at fostering particular investments.

For instance, Canada established the Business Development Bank of Canada to support Canada's entrepreneurs, especially in small and medium enterprises which commercial banks would only lend to a small proportion of requiring excess collateral to mitigate risk.

In other cases, the State runs its banks, like private commercial banks, that pursue profitability and maximization of shareholders' interests. The Development Bank of Singapore (DBS), for instance, is remarkable for its business-oriented operations even though the Singaporean state is its largest shareholder controlling nearly 30% of its equity (Yang and Lee, 2018).

In fact, most SOBs fall in between; they accommodate other stakeholders, but remain influenced mostly by the State. They might pursue business interests in principle, but when the government steps in, they follow government's instruction. By catering to government instructions, SOBs loosen implicitly the constraints under which both public and private sector entities are able to access funding that might not be available if the government did not own the lender.

In other words, if only private sources of financing were available, they would monitor more closely the financial situation of borrowing companies. The latter might then face binding constraints, or harder financing conditions, if their financial viability deteriorated to a point where it concerned the lenders.

However, having a financial institution owned by government reduces the risk to the borrower of facing such an obstacle. The looser constraint might not always result in a direct transfer of resources to borrowers whose creditworthiness is diminished; but it suggests that the amount of credit they have might not otherwise be available to them, or might be obtained only at a higher cost.

But softer financing constraints often result in fostering a sense of impunity among borrowing SOEs, as well as private, politically well-connected businessmen and industrialists, in being undisciplined about timely debt repayments to SOBs. This has led to a large volume of NPAs at SOBs in almost all countries where the State controls the banking system as show in Table 2.1. In such systems, bankers, regulators, and government tend to 'evergreen' bad loans (rolling them over to avoid recognizing losses on their books), or dilute their terms, instead of acknowledging reality sooner and making provisions (which reduce profitability) to write down sour loans.

This happens because SOBs are vulnerable to political influence. Politicians regularly put pressure on banks to ensure that favoured clients

Table 2.1 Non-performing loan ratio (%)

	2012	2015	2019
Brazil	3.8	2.8	2.9
China	0.9	1.3	1.9
Indonesia	2.2	2.1	2.6
India	2.7	4.3	9.1
Russia	17.2	13.5	17.9
Saudi Arabia	1.67	1.23	1.95
Singapore	1.04	0.92	1.31
South Africa	4.7	3.2	3.75

Source: CEIC data

have an easy access to credit. Such borrowers treat SOBs as their private kitties, expecting indulgent treatment during difficult times.

SOBs invariably end up being a captive source of financing for troubled SOEs and politically connected private entities, when borrower fragility necessitates bailouts. The State-owned sources of financing have therefore weak balance sheets that need intervention by the government to prevent bankruptcy.

Consequently, in countries where SOBs have a large presence, more credit is provided to SOEs and politically connected private entities than might be justified by rational resource allocation criteria. That feeds back inevitably into weakening the financial structure of SOBs and results inevitably in larger fiscal deficits and higher levels of public debt when SOBs need capital support (Gonzalez-Garcia and Grigoli, 2013).

When there is a structural bias on the part of SOBs towards allocating capital mainly, if not almost exclusively, to SOEs, the private sector faces challenges in securing bank credit or raising money from capital markets, implying a degree of crowding out. Private businesses are then forced to rely on non-bank financial intermediaries (NBFIs), or a variety of informal financing mechanisms, usually with high rates of interest. Indeed, the scope of informal finance has now expanded into the broader universe of shadow banking. Arguably, the contemporary map of informal finance and shadow banking represents a parallel political economy that complements, and is therefore just as functionally entrenched, as vested interests in the State sector.

The world trade regime faces a daunting challenge of disciplining State capitalism in interpreting and applying current World Trade Organization (WTO) rules consistently. As State capitalism has flourished, its compatibility with the WTO's trade regime has triggered heated debates. Among other issues, the funding of State capitalism, especially SOBs, has become increasingly controversial in recent years under the WTO's subsidy regime.

Contrary to the established discourse on the merits of having State-owned banks, the GFC has, ironically, revived interest on the part of governments (even relatively liberal ones) in owning banks. There is a weary acceptance that SOBs can undertake important countercyclical lending in times of crises. Moreover, attempts to re-regulate private banks following the GFC appear to have failed. This has led to even larger, more systemically important, global banks emerging after the GFC. For that reason, many countries now consider SOBs—owned and not just regulated by the State—to be one answer to the continuing conundrum of how to bring large private banks to heel (Tett, 2013).

The new approaches have introduced the concepts of 'credibility' and 'persistence over time' as a measure of the developmental superiority of SOBs vs private banks (Marois and Güngen, 2016). SOBs are seen as part of a more complex institutional landscape, in which the actual role they play needs to be seen in the context of a broader set of political economy issues. The empirical evidence from this strand of literature, that analyses the relationship between government ownership and bank performance, is more nuanced than before and has shown mixed findings.

Contemporary SOBs are quite different from their equivalents in the previous century. After the GFC, the ownership of many SOBs in a number of countries has been opened up to private shareholders. SOBs (especially from China and Singapore) now compete globally with large, systemically important private banks (mainly American, European, and Japanese) and face similar issues and challenges (Pargendler, Musacchio, and Lazzarini, 2013).

Overall, many contemporary SOBs have been reformed to a significant extent. There have been changes in corporate governance rules to accommodate the rules of stock exchange markets in which their shares are listed. This has led to more stringent regulatory frameworks being applied, greater transparency and accountability, and better compliance with ethical and deontological requirements (OECD, 2011). This process has been particularly important for 287 development banks in 117 countries (Musacchio and Lazzarini, 2014).

Some government-owned financial institutions have recently been acquirers of companies in a significant number of cross-border M&A deals. Since 2007, more than 10% of M&A deals have involved State-owned banks as acquirers in several sectors, such as electricity and gas, water supply and waste management, construction, transportation, information and communication, and financial insurance (Bacchiocchi et al., 2019).

A study analysing the relationship between bank ownership and performance for a large sample of banks (5,465 in 1995 to 6,677 in 2002) from 179 countries across the world found that SOBs located in developing countries have much lower returns on assets than their private counterparts. However, those located in developed countries are not significantly different from their private counterparts (Micco, Panizza, and Yañez, 2007).

What is perhaps more revealing in this context is that the traditional underperformance of SOBs is reversed for one particular type of bank, i.e. development banks as a specific sub-set of State-owned banks are no less efficient than private banks. There are clear differences between development and commercial SOBs, with the former performing much better than the latter (Bacchiocchi et al., 2019). There is a realistic appreciation in these studies that direct government ownership may be a necessary, if not sufficient, condition for a viable 'finance-for-development' alternative.

State ownership of enterprises and the regulatory state

In the 1970s, State-owned monopolies began to be deregulated and State-owned assets were divested through privatization. The outcomes have been ubiquitous, resulting in an expanded role for markets, greater private sector participation in all facets of society, and withdrawal of the State from being a direct provider of services and employer of last resort.

Privatization brought with it the imperative of establishing independent regulatory institutions. The underlying philosophy was that, without this coupling, a State-owned monopoly would be substituted with a privately held one in which the new owners might not prioritize public interest.

The 'regulatory State' is more circumspect than the 'ownership State', with a focus on setting in place the parameters for market expansion through private sector capital formation and efficient market operation.[1] In a regulatory state, the State is sometimes required to take up the role of a 'disciplinarian' -- because market economies requiring private capital need to be disciplined to induce good behaviour on the part of competing firms in ways that market competition alone cannot. This is the case, for example, with enforcing compliance with tax laws, environment regulations, labour regulations, etc.

In addition, the State often has to intervene to ensure that basic requisites—e.g. property rights—are respected and enforced, especially since competing private firms always have an incentive to encroach on each other's property rights. Therefore, the regulatory function of the State involves setting rules that define the allocative and settlement mechanisms of markets along with requirements for proper market participation. This involves defining rules, standards, procedures and practices, and enunciating codes that bring order into social, economic, and political engagement.

Across the OECD, the liberalization of domestic markets and international trade, coupled with the introduction of regulatory management tools, has led to a profound reformulation of the State's role in the economy. Scholars have labelled this trend the 'rise of the regulatory state' (Majone, 1994; Moran, 2003).

As a tool of government and a modality of governance, regulation now constitutes a new order, a set of governance standards and procedures that are both prescribed as preferred instruments to secure development, and a set of measures by which governments and governance are assessed for their quality and capacities. OECD member countries that previously relied on industrial strategies as the basis for influencing major sectors of

[1] By creating optimal investment conditions, attracting investment capital, securing the blessings of ratings agencies, and making markets work by sustaining private sector interest.

the economy have increasingly adopted arm's length regulation to oversee the development and performance of markets.

A vital factor behind this change has been the creation of a host of new institutions—oversight bodies, regulatory agencies, administrative courts, and ombudsman commissions—to manage newly liberalized markets (Thatcher, 2005). While these reforms were pioneered in OECD countries, they have become equally or if not more important for emerging markets in developing and transition countries. Poor regulation and implementation are still formidable barriers to entrepreneurship and investment in emerging markets.

But the institutional fabric necessary for the formation and functioning of a regulatory state is complex, costly to maintain, and rests on the availability of a variety of soft institutional capacities.[2] In developing countries, such capabilities are often absent, dysfunctional, too difficult, or too time consuming to construct in a way that would allow them to deliver the outcomes necessary to sustain regulatory efficiency. In such cases, the adoption of a regulatory state model may pose regulatory risks: unintended outcomes such as regulatory capture, reduced probity, or expose governments to possible regulatory failure.

Such risks notwithstanding, countries in the midst of economic and social transition (with a significant presence of SOEs) which have adopted the regulatory state model, their functioning is fraught with conflicts of interest in following clearly the multifarious roles of the modern State. When it owns SOEs, the State is obliged, to a greater or lesser degree, to play a dual role, i.e. that of market regulator and owner/shareholder, particularly in newly deregulated, often partially privatized industries.

Whenever this happens, the State is inevitably conflicted in its opposing interests as follows: *first*, a major market player/firm owner in its own right, and *second*, as an arbitrator in the neutral, impartial role of regulator. The conflict of interest involves a conflict between its public duty and the private commercial and financial interest of the State. Under such circumstances, the State's pecuniary interest may (and often does) improperly influence and compromise the basic functions of good governance.

[2] Capacities help structure the complex reflexive relationships between agential actors, formal institutions, procedural authority, and norms.

As a corollary to this, the growing role of SOEs as international investors raises questions whether their actions undermine a 'level playing field' in third party countries. Over the past 20 years there has been a growing trend in international investment by SOEs, sometimes a reflection of their government investment policies abroad motivated by commercial and/or geopolitical considerations. Part of the concern related to the internationalization of SOEs, for regulators and private competition, is that their decisions may not be driven by business objectives. When SOEs internationalize, concerns related to the spill-over effects emanating from their privileged position in the home market spreading to their international operations are significant. These include concerns related to national security, public interest, ad hoc political intervention, competition enforcement, insufficient information, 'renationalization' of private firms, and corruption risks.

The conflict of interest is difficult to resolve or reconcile, especially when it comes to (a) the State dictating the content of general corporate laws in its own favour as shareholder to the detriment of competitors in industries where private firms are competing with SOEs; (b) enforcing those laws and associated rules and regulations; (c) outside investor protection; and (d) ensuring competitive market efficiency.

Conflicts of interest also arise when the State has ownership interests in SOEs that improperly influence the performance of its *primary* legitimate statutory duties and responsibilities to discharge its fundamental constitutional responsibilities. Among others, these duties involve protecting

(a) its territorial integrity and borders;
(b) the integrity of its legal and judicial systems which ensure that basic human, physical, and intellectual property rights of citizens and foreign residents are respected with proper recourse to adjudication and dispute settlement;
(c) institutional machinery for maintaining law and order;
(d) individual and collective political and economic freedoms;
(e) the safety and well-being of citizens and foreign residents;
(f) investments in infrastructure, e.g. for transport, communications, water, power, and air quality;

(g) the environment for future generations; and, finally
(h) its economy, which the State must manage in a fashion that allows commerce to take place without excessive uncertainty and risk caused by poor, unsustainable policies.

In addition, there are the conflicting objectives of *optimality* (maximizing public revenues) and *efficiency* (maximizing social welfare via consumer and producer surpluses), which inherently cause friction in designing and implementing regulatory policies. On one hand, the theoretical approach to modern welfarism advocates that, under perfect market conditions, government could or should appropriate as large a share of rents as possible in the public interest. The pragmatic approach is on the other hand, which recognises that economic and political circumstances surrounding this issue are far from perfect so that the optimal sharing of rents must consider the economic risks undertaken by businesses (Guj, 2012).

Governments in most countries license private sector activities (and exempt SOEs from the licensing, yet allowing to compete with the private sector, effectively creating an un-level playing field) whether for regulatory purposes or to generate revenue, or both. Many states have not found a definite solution to managing such conflicts of interest appropriately in their multiple roles as shareholder and policy-maker. Nor have they reconciled this with their decisions to allocate regulatory functions to an independent regulator. This role confusion potentially limits the effectiveness of the governance system (Van Basten, 2007).

The presence of the State as a shareholder in enterprises and financial firms imposes negative externalities on the legal regime available to the private sector and to investors. The separation of administrative responsibilities for ownership and market regulation is therefore a fundamental prerequisite for creating a level playing field for SOEs and private companies, and thus avoiding the risk of unfair competition. However, regulatory institutions face broad challenges in overcoming these obstacles to achieve effective regulation.

Such challenges include the following:

(a) a lack of political support from ministries that formerly managed SOEs in a particular industry and may still have oversight over the newly formed regulatory institution;

(b) non-compliance with regulatory authority either *de jure or de facto*;
(c) regulatory inability to discipline SOEs (that were once effective monopolies in an industry being privatized) resulting in an inability to protect competing private players from monopoly abuse by the SOE incumbent;
(d) the inapplicability of some regulatory tools designed in anticipation of privatization, when the incumbent entity is a SOE;[3] and
(e) lack of knowledge and experience in applying the right tools in the process of regulation.

Legislative frameworks often empower regulators to undertake independent reviews of the economics of new projects, new entrants, and the fairness of competition in their regulatory domains. This provides important check-and-balance on decisions about large SOE capital projects and about new entrants distorting extant rules of play to gain market share. However, in practice, by the time a SOE or politically well-connected private firm approaches the regulator with a license application, the decision often becomes a *fait accompli*.

This happens because regulators are simply not equipped, nor adequately resourced, nor interested, in taking on the large, vested interests (with powerful political connections) that are behind such projects (Steyn, 2011).

Markets are subject to regulation for many reasons, e.g. to reassure consumers and investors, encourage healthy competition for a sustainable industry, ensure health and safety, encourage innovative start-ups, and protect the environment. To achieve these objectives, regulations must *first* encourage competition in product/service markets and *second* discourage anticompetitive behaviour.

But regulation always comes at a cost. Business may face excessive compliance burdens; entrepreneurs may be discouraged; monopolies may be rewarded; and result in the preferential treatment of SOEs, with

[3] Regulatory agencies establish incentives for performance, but they often have limited tools to deal with powerful (incumbent) SOEs. Information issues associated with SOE governance also apply to regulatory strategies. Information asymmetries characterize regulation, but when the firm reports to a powerful Ministry as well as to a new regulatory commission, the difficulties can increase. That is, in the case of a privately owned infrastructure firm, the licence conditions may require that the firm provide information to the regulator. Unless such information requirements are made clear (for either ownership type), the regulator is at a significant disadvantage.

domestic private companies and foreign companies being subordinated in that order. In companies in which the State has or retains a minority shareholding, regulations are often designed to protect the government while denying meaningful legal rights to other minority investors. Rules that favour the interests of the State as a shareholder over those of outside investors are often politically popular and governments often abuse such populism in their favour.

The regulatory preferences that SOEs enjoy exclusively include the following: exemption from disclosure requirements, exemptions from antitrust enforcement, rights-to-information rules, preferences in public procurement, monopoly rights, captive equity, exemption from bankruptcy rules, and insider information advantages. SOEs take advantage of preferential regulatory treatment and engage in economically irrational behaviour, such as excessive capital investments, excess employment of labour for political reasons, or anticompetitive business practices, thereby disrupting the order of fair competition. These privileges and immunities distort competition in the market between SOEs and private enterprises.

When regulatory preferences are extended to SOEs, such as being allowed to operate as monopolies and given exemptions from antitrust enforcement, the result is that SOEs entrench their monopoly/oligopoly status, which enables them to exercise a strong (often undesirable) influence in home markets. These privileges favour SOEs competing with foreign private firms in the domestic market, as well as in export markets and/or investment destinations in third markets, creating anticompetitive effects in the global market place and resulting in the suboptimal allocation of global resources. Creating a level playing field between SOEs and private firms (especially foreign private firms) or establishing competitive neutrality is a pressing issue for contemporary competition, trade, and investment.

Crony capitalism under State capitalism

Accumulated evidence has suggested that developing (and some high-income, but as yet not fully developed) economies, especially those that are in transition, run a real risk of the emergence and entrenchment of '*crony capitalism*'. This phenomenon occurs because of the natural tendency of businessmen to gain advantage over rivals through fair means or foul, the underdeveloped nature of key institutions (regulators, parliaments, legal systems, judiciaries, and ombudsmen), the power of political connections which cater to private interests, and, of course, the inevitable private agenda of public officials.

The term 'cronyism' refers to political authorities granting favours with economic value to those who are closest to them and expect compensation of some kind in return. These favours allow politically connected economic agents to earn returns above those that would prevail in an economy in which the factors of production were priced by the market.

Cronies may be rewarded with the ability to charge higher prices for their output than would prevail in a competitive market. They may also be rewarded with an official or quasi-official monopoly, thus allowing that group to earn monopoly rents (Krueger, 2002). Cronyism tends to thrive in an environment of discretionary decision-making, when governments are not richly endowed with sound, capable and experienced regulators yet play too large a role in making economic policy while also regulating economic activity at firm, industry, and economy levels.

State regulation creates enormous opportunities for granting favours to selected business groups willing to provide bribes and kickbacks in a variety of non-transparent ways for the privileges they secure. They, in turn, develop vested interests in ensuring that regulation is biased in their favour and devote significant resources to achieve that. This is known as 'regulatory capture', i.e. the subservience of the legal, regulatory, and policy environment to the interests of vested-interest groups. Reciprocally, it also leads to a predatory state when business is divided into competing groups, with the State apparatus ensuring business capture.

Democratization has increased the influence of capital over the State bureaucracy, making politicians more dependent on capital in the electoral process. Democracy has become money driven in many countries and running for office has become extremely costly. Most politicians therefore enter the legislature with a 'constant pressure to raise money' (Mietzner, 2015). Aspirants for political office typically bargain with various political parties. Political parties have been 'well-suited for the purposes and aims of the predatory interests that preside over them' (Hadiz, 2010). The rule of law and the role of mediating institutions are still too weak in many countries to control the dominating economic interests of big business conglomerates. Economies are therefore trapped in a vicious circle because of the collusion between dominant business and state representatives (Hellman and Kaufmann, 2001). Consequently, the role of oligarchs in democratic politics has now become a challenging issue in the governance of emerging economies.

Members of the government (politicians and bureaucrats) share in the rents generated by the selected business groups. This may take the form of cash compensation, the funding of elections, jobs, co-investments, or even direct transfers of stock. It is usually difficult to break the implicit contract between government and favoured business groups. This arrangement requires corruption to go hand in hand with cronyism and entrenches it. Public corruption is the sale by government officials, with authority and discretion, of government discretionary powers and rights (and property) and betrayal of the interests of principle for personal gain[4] (Shleifer and Vishny, 1998). Corruption encompasses bribery, nepotism, patronage, and clientelism.

Corruption has a deeper impact on how SOEs operate and on their performance given the close relationship between the State and the company. The risk of corruption is 'exacerbated when SOEs are not equipped with autonomous, professional and independent boards responsible for ensuring an arm's length relationship between the SOE and the government' (OECD, 2016).

While fair market competition reduces the scope for crony capitalism, corruption protects cronies from losing out to fair competition while benefitting from the inefficiency of State-run economic institutions, such as SOBs. This raises fundamental questions about institutional impartiality in ensuring market competition as well as the role of corruption. For example, how do crony capitalism and the political parties shape the boundaries of corruption? What is the State's trade-off between tolerating and cracking down on corruption?

[4] The other side of the coin is firms wanting to shape and influence the underlying rules of the game through private payments to public officials (Hellman et al., 2000) to enjoy a monopoly position in the market from where to extract rents. Towards this end, they resort to corruption which could mean bribes or illicit financial contributions to public officials who design state policies, legislation, and so on.

Collusion between public officials (in ministries and regulatory agencies) and businessmen usually results in regulations either being circumvented or being designed to favour chosen crony capitalists, and/or disfavour their rivals. For that to happen, and be sustained, forms of corruption are induced and encouraged by government. Close interaction between privileged businesses and public officials also means that public authority is used at strengthening the competitive position of the former and protecting them from the discipline of competition. However, some empirical studies show that in many developing economies, a higher tolerance of corruption can lead to higher output and therefore higher rents for officials (Li, Roland and Xie, 2019).

The absence of arm's-length principles in the governance and management of SOEs and SOBs is due to the related problems of inadequate institutional development and of state intervention in the economy. Large investors (mainly domestic, but occasionally foreign) bribe political leaders, whose families often go into business themselves. They exert influence over State-owned banks to lend to crony industrialists, while the latter are often nominated to Parliament, thus entrenching the insider crony-political nexus through a self-reinforcing circularity that is difficult to break.

This leads to the kind of cronyism on which too many countries (in transition and emerging) have relied in developing their economies and connecting them to the larger global economy. Many governments now believe that crony connections make it easier for them to attract new investment, acquire hard and soft know-how from foreign firms, and foster innovation in cutting edge industries, to capture a larger share of global trade and investment flows.

Cronyism has several major costs. It has a financial cost due to undertaxation of companies and dubious debts on the SOB balance sheets. It has a social cost when workers are underpaid and funding for public education or health has to be reduced for lack of fiscal resources, because crony capitalists are favoured with lower tax burdens. It has an environmental cost as crony capitalists often disregard the most basic standards for ensuring air quality, reducing carbon emissions, treating effluent discharge, and avoiding the use of toxic chemicals in industrial processes while minimizing toxic waste. Collusion, rent-seeking, and corruption among political and business elites as well as top officials in the government hinder governance reforms in SOEs.

Cronyism undermines the processes through which market mechanisms serve as efficient allocators of resources. It discourages long-term investing, undermines the functioning of any public authority and the disciplining of private capital by the State. Its arrangements are not transparent and its costs are hidden often showing up as profits. SOEs have almost the same effects as cronyism—in both instances, the enterprises owe their existence not to their performance in a competitive market but to non-market criteria by which they were established and are run.

Although SOEs are normally funded from the public budget, and allow for some transparency, the real costs of state ownership and cronyism are hidden; in that the full extent of profits is not necessarily publicly recorded. A large portion are siphoned off in a variety of ways. The true value of privileged positions (monopolies, protective tariffs against imports of competing goods, favoured access to subsidized credit, etc.) is difficult to gauge.

Under cronyism domestic credit expansion leads to an increase in the contingent liabilities of SOBs, which indirectly enlarges fiscal deficits. There is the risk of diversion of either credit extended to them or siphoning off profits to private uses.

Companies receive credit to expand from SOBs because their size becomes a political asset (too big to fail). They may locate their headquarters in the country's capital to be close to those they wish to influence regardless of cost. Since cronies receive subsidized credit from SOBs regardless of their prospective real returns, cronies can remain in business even when their activities are no longer viable. Since they receive subsidized credit, they in effect have a soft budget constraint (Krueger, 2002).

Paradoxically, on average, crony capitalists employ more competent professional managers—who are incentivized through structured performance-based compensatory mechanisms to achieve profits and reduce costs—than are employed by their non-crony competitors. This supports the case, for example, for the State retaining a minority stake in SOEs that are privatized and run by crony capitalist oligarchs.

Yet, power over SOEs provides a more direct mechanism of control, and so the temptation for politicians with predatory tendencies to exert influence over large SOEs has not disappeared. SOEs in strategic sectors, such as energy, still represent formidable tools for politicians to seek personal and political gains.

Whether the issue is crony capitalism or SOEs, it is clear that good economic performance can only be achieved and sustained over the long term when resources are allocated to optimal uses through arm's length transactions. Modern economic growth, even under inclusive institutions, can create tilted playing fields. The modern regulatory state can, within certain bounds, help redress these problems.

The private agenda of public officials

Three important direct links exist between the State and SOEs. The first is the extent of state intervention in the operational decisions of SOEs, including the setting of prices, investment, employment, and wages. The second is the extent to which the State provides direct benefits to SOEs, such as subsidies or favoured tax treatment. The third direct link between SOEs and the State is the extent to which different agencies of the State provide public officials the network by which they can entrench rent seeking behaviour and maximize personal gains.

The 'interventionist' State, along with its extensive bureaucracy and command-control governance mechanisms, has been dismantled progressively over time throughout the world. In a single generation, the world has witnessed one of the great transformations of the modern era, i.e. the death of the 'interventionist' State and the rise of the 'regulatory state' (Majone, 1999) which now derives its power through three functions: stabilization, redistribution, and regulation. The last two—i.e. redistribution and regulation—however, are not always reconcilable. They pose a paradox, i.e. an obvious 'decline of state power' has coincided with the increasing 'intrusion of governments into our daily lives' in a quantum that is palpably greater than at any time before in history (Strange, 1996).

This paradox lies at the heart of the rise of the regulatory state and the decline of the interventionist State. It produces both a reduction in the size of government while expanding its powers of governance. The regulatory state is thus a reconfigured state that uses alternative modalities of governance to wield its power (Majone, 1999). The profusion of statutory bodies and regulatory agencies has witnessed public officials in ministerial departments transfer into statutory and delegated agencies charged with regulatory oversight (Dowding, 1995).

In countries undergoing a social and economic transition from an interventionist state to a regulatory state, where perverse incentives, inefficient bureaucracies, and lack of accountability are still the norm, the privilege of having a position in state institutions could not be higher. The blend of both part-direct and indirect state influence has meant that the power of public officials in interpreting the new rules of evolving market engagement has never been greater.

With the muddled responsibility of the State in ownership and regulation, the discretionary power of public officials has increased. In many sectors, there is confusion with blurred lines of authority between ownership and regulation. The lack of formal administrative '*proceduralisation*' has led to enduring problems.

SOEs have been instruments of 'benevolent'[5] governments and of politicians and bureaucrats who use their control over SOEs to extract rents. Under the benevolent government concept, SOEs are deemed to suffer from weak managerial incentives to run firms efficiently; imperfect monitoring of managers; and the insulation of SOEs from market discipline.

Public administrators, elected (political leaders) and non-elected (i.e. bureaucrats, public managers), are unlike the ideal type envisioned and described in Weber (Hall, 1963). The latter are portrayed, in theory, as impartial, competent professionals with a strong ethic of working in public administration for the public good. In practice, however, SOE managers are self-interested individuals who use their control of SOEs to further their own private interests. They do not aim solely at enhancing the SOE's efficiency for the public good (Buchanan, Tollison, and Tullock, 1980). Thus their behaviour is often illegal and corrupt, resulting in the political capture of business objectives and activity. These individuals see state positions as a privilege. They achieve a higher rank in the civil service by abusing their office and position.

Rules, regulations, and sluggish bureaucracy are the means through which government officials maximize the opportunity of bribe-taking (Alam, 2000). A government official seeks to maximize his/her income

[5] A benevolent government is one which operates on behalf of its constituency consistently with the preferences expressed by voters and without making strategic use of undisclosed information in order to satisfy a private agenda.

from his/her public position weighing the benefits from the bribes he/she receives against the costs of being caught and punished. With strong competition for advancement within the bureaucracy and the pervasiveness of strong inter-unit rivalries and conflicts,[6] 'public bureaucrats want their own units and agencies to grow so that their status and freedom to act are increased' to give them more authority and discretion to seek higher rents (Box, 2005).

Opportunistic behaviour leading to corruption may be derived from a 'too public to fail' mentality in which SOEs are protected by their state ownership, their dominant position in the market or their involvement in the delivery of public services, and their insulation from the threat of bankruptcy and hostile take-over that private companies face. Opportunistic behaviour may also arise out of SOEs' operations in sectors with high value and frequent transactions or within complex regulatory frameworks that, unless well-designed, can provide a smokescreen for non-compliant behaviour.

Internal or external pressures, such as undue influence by the State in SOE operations, may further put employees and managers under pressure to break rules and/or provide opportunities to exploit their position. On one hand, SOEs with public policy objectives may be more able to justify illicit activity to compensate for financial losses or reduced profit margins that can be associated with delivering on policy objectives. On the other hand, SOEs (and other firms) with entirely commercial objectives may try to justify corruption because of the pressure to remain competitive or to perform (OECD, 2018a).

Corruption, or rent-seeking behaviour, is embedded in the hierarchical structure of public administration. Subordinates in administrative units are treated as 'family'. Gains obtained by their superiors through rent-seeking are shared with staff members, who are lower in the hierarchy (Rose-Akerman, 1999) and, sometimes, vice-versa. Similar is the case with politicians who are elected to office with the help of lower level politicians who have small power bases which they bring together during elections. Many such minor politicians, each representing a group of voters, coalesce to form a wider base under a top-level politician. In

[6] von Mises (1944), Parkinson (1957), Niskanen (1971), Warwick (1975), Tullock (1976), and Tinbergen (1985).

turn, top-level politicians need to feed this pyramid the fruits of power. The top-level politicians need important ministries, which control key resources. They share the gains down the pyramid through committee memberships, directorships of government departments and SOEs, contracts. This is the way political power is sustained and reproduced.

Corruption in public administration has adverse consequences on economic activity. When bureaucrats fuel rent-seeking behaviour, they hamper efficient decision-making, lower security of property rights and ultimately reduce incentives and opportunities to invest (Shleifer and Vishny, 1993; Mauro, 1995).

Empirical evidence suggests that higher tolerance of corruption leads to higher economic growth in ordinary times, but it undermines the State's ability to respond to exceptional exigencies—i.e. in crises—which, of course, is a fundamental attribute of state power. The State's crisis management capacity depends crucially on its ability to mobilize resources and to lead a coordinated response. This ability is jeopardized by tolerance of corruption, because the more rents created by crony capitalism that eventually flow to officials, the more the latter have an incentive to resist resource mobilization during crises (Li, Roland, and Xie, 2019).

Illegal behaviour emerges from conflicts of interest of public managers. A conflict of interest involves a conflict between the public responsibility and private interests of a public manager, in which the manager has private stakes that improperly influence the performance of his official duties. Common examples include the negotiation of future employment by a public manager prior to leaving an SOE and improper use of inside information (gathered in the course of official duties) aimed at realizing private gains. Therefore, public officials are often self-interested maximizers of their position in a bureaucratic world, who pursue future career advancement, financial security, and use the State's resources to serve their personal interests.

Public officials are considered therefore to be self-interested individuals who use their control of SOEs to further their own interests, rather than the SOE's efficiency resulting in corruption, political capture of business objectives. There is strong competition for advancement within the bureaucracy for civil servants (aided by politicians) to increase their status and freedom to act. Consequently, they are interested in not only growing their agencies but also government's indirect control over private agencies.

The impact of State ownership on productivity and the allocation of resources

Economics literature amplifies the importance of total factor productivity (TFP) as a source of sustained economic growth. TFP differs greatly across countries. One possible explanation is that frontier technologies and best practice methods are slow to diffuse in some countries. However, recent literature argues that misallocation of resources explains part of these productivity differences. This literature focuses on the benefits of reallocation of inputs from less productive to more productive firms as an important component of aggregate productivity growth. Policies associated with allocative efficiencies emphasize correcting or reducing market distortions.

The overall TFP of an industry depends not only on the TFP of individual firms but also on how resources are allocated to different firms. Theory suggests that in economies with low market distortions, productive firms will have access to more labour and capital inputs compared to less productive ones. This leads to an increase in the overall productivity of the sector (Hsieh and Klenow, 2009).

If an SOE and private firm in the same industry have the same marginal product of capital as the prevailing interest rate, the marginal product of capital of the SOE with access to subsidized credit will be lower than the marginal product of capital of the private firm that can only borrow at the prevailing interest rates. Capital will be misallocated in such a situation. Aggregate output would be higher if capital was reallocated from the SOE with a low marginal product of capital to the private firm with a high marginal product of capital. The misallocation of capital also results in low aggregate output per worker and low TFP.

Many studies show that market rigidities or direct government involvement distorts the allocation of resources from their most efficient use. Such rigidities are often induced by inappropriate regulation and other policies that shape the business environment. In particular, the argument that State ownership of firms distorts the allocation of resources (especially labour and credit) in the economy, and thereby gives rise to aggregate inefficiencies, is frequently made on theoretical grounds, and is supported by a number of stylized facts about the public sector.

First, the public sector has historically accounted for a substantial percentage of employment in a number of economies. *Second*, the public sector is significantly less efficient than the private sector. For example, the marginal factor productivity of SOEs in China is at least 40% lower than that of private enterprises (Hsieh and Klenow, 2009). *Third*, the public sector has tended to compensate workers at a rate that is not aligned with their productivity (Rama 1999), a factor that tends to 'lock-in' the inefficient allocation of labour.

Overall, labour misallocation is the larger problem for SOEs, as political considerations influence hiring decisions and lead to overstaffing, particularly by unskilled workers—whereas greater job security results in less motivated employees and contributes to lower labour productivity (IMF, 2019). Sectors with a larger share of workers employed by SOEs tend to have lower allocative efficiency.

State control affects competition in the product market. The key domains of state control as defined by the OECD Product Market Regulations (PMR) include the significance of SOEs in the economy, command and control regulation, price controls, governance of SOEs, direct control over enterprises, and government involvement in network sectors.

In practice, SOEs are likely to have unfair competitive advantages over their private sector counterparts. Such advantages are not necessarily due to better performance, superior efficiency, better technology, or superior management skills. Instead, they are due to direct subsidies, concessionary financing and guarantees, and other preferential treatment, including exemptions from antitrust enforcement, preference in public procurement, access to below cost energy inputs, and preferential tax treatment. This distorts competition in the market and affects competitive neutrality, where less productive firms command larger shares of output and overall productivity is hampered by inefficient allocation of resources.

Reallocation of resources through the elimination of distortions in the market enhances productivity because this allows productive firms to grow and the less productive ones to either shrink in size or exit. Empirical studies have shown that the productivity and profitability of SOEs tend to be lower than that of private firms across sectors, especially in the manufacturing sector. But this performance gap shrank during the GFC.

Market-oriented reform has involved changing the relative role of the State and the market in the coordination of production, exchange, and distribution activities with the main objective of improving efficiency. These reforms encourage and stimulate entrepreneurship by expanding market opportunities. During economic transition, the interaction of the State and the market becomes particularly important. The State plays an indispensable role in the establishment of the market system and associated institutional change.

Although the role of government in directing economic activity in a healthy economy is limited, transition from an 'ownership state' to a regulatory state' does require astute guidance. The only source of such guidance for the economy is the State. There is no denying that appropriate policy and leadership could smooth transition (Arrow, 2001). Given the key role of the State in economic transition, the interaction between market liberalization and state control of resources affects entrepreneurial activity significantly. The entrepreneurial potential of any economy is determined by the 'rules of the game' as set by government.

State control of resource markets creates substantial rents. Traditionally, these are directed towards building infrastructure and providing public goods, thereby facilitating economic transformation and transition to higher-income status. At the same time, such rents have pernicious side effects, such as rent-seeking by both governments and enterprises, leading to distortions in resource allocation. In turn, resource misallocation is linked to structural imbalances, such as overcapacity in certain sectors, and the negative impact of stifling the emergence of private entrepreneurship.

Even in Singapore, where SOEs operate much like private enterprises, critics of these SOEs contend that they perform better than the private sector only because of their relationship with the government. This gives them advantages resulting in large areas of the economy being closed to the private sector, thus stifling the growth of private entrepreneurship.

In some mature economies, where significant corporate assets are still owned by the State, policy-makers invariably assert that a number of public administration benefits occur as a result. These include as follows: maintaining ownership of core infrastructure assets often considered national icons; security of supply (particularly for essential services); continuity of service provision in markets where the private sector may not have sufficient interest; and increased accountability to the extent that SOEs are directly accountable to government (Chang, 2007). But, these SOEs are required to operate as efficiently as private sector equivalents in providing cost-effective, high-quality services to the public.

SOEs are also required to be more innovative, generate new revenue sources, operate with a strong customer focus under competitive market forces, and adopt creative and risk-taking activity.

The issue, however, is that a significant number of mature economies restrict competition from foreign government-controlled investments through provisions in their domestic laws and regulations in selected sectors. These specific restrictions are either carved out by invocation of national security safeguards or reflected as reservations to liberalization obligations under these countries' international investment treaties.[7]

The growth of SOEs, either in size or in numbers, leads to concerns that they encroach into too many industries, effectively crowding out the private sector and hindering the emergence of a critical mass of thriving local enterprises. As far as small and medium sized private enterprises are concerned, SOEs are perceived to have unfair advantages in terms of access to funds, tenders, and opportunities.

Workers in SOEs have traditionally gained relatively high wages and generous social rights (despite their low productivity) as compared to those in their private counterparts. The unintended consequence of this has been a reduction in the competitiveness of regions where SOEs are situated. This happens because a dominant SOE presence intimidates new investments from coming into the region while inducing a shift of extant investment to other regions. Where SOEs predominate, local people are invariably discouraged from finding jobs and developing careers in the private sector, and from starting their own companies because

[7] One of the most frequently cited concerns has been the perception that investment by SOEs and similar entities may be driven by 'political' goals rather than commercial considerations. SOEs may be acting on behalf of their government owners to secure control over scarce resources in the broader national interest. Another concern has been that SOEs may be buying into foreign technologies and know-how with the purpose of diffusing them widely in the domestic economy.

of the well-remunerated (especially taking pension benefits into account) and more secure jobs available in the public sector.

Challenges confronting the internal management of SOEs

SOEs suffer more agency problems than other firms in that they have a 'double agency' problem. An agent, usually a politician with his/her own agenda, will typically represent the State's interests in the company as well as his/her own. They also suffer a 'common agency' problem, because they are overseen by several levels of government, or by both the State and minority shareholders with potentially conflicting interests, which may be inconsistent with profit maximization. They usually operate in non-competitive industries, and therefore, they do not benefit from the discipline of market pressure in case of underperformance.

SOEs tend to do worse than their private sector competitors because their managers are mainly career civil servants who lack business acumen and their investment may be politically rather than commercially motivated. SOE employees are chosen on the basis of their political connections instead of merit or technical background as SOEs are used as vehicles of patronage. SOEs have typically a mix of social, economic, environmental, and strategic objectives in line with national priorities set by government.

Since the 1990s, SOEs around the world have faced renewed challenges to their survival. These include diminishing trade protection and reductions in cost-mitigating subsidies. There are fewer new employment opportunities in the private sector for successful managers of SOEs when they face the threat of privatization. Greater market competition, financial sector liberalization, and the restructuring and privatization of State-owned banks only add to these challenges. Finally, major new technological changes, new international agreements, and budgetary reforms combine to exert pressures on SOEs that few can cope with successfully.

Greater public scrutiny and higher pressure to improve operational and financial performance have proved beneficial for many SOEs, especially when they have been made more publicly accountable. The emergence of a new public management (NPM) approach has resulted in the adoption of private sector practices by public officials for better SOE management. Many SOEs have accordingly changed their charters to improve internal governance. They have allowed outside directors on their boards, provided incentives to managers for good performance, professionalized management, and improved financial reporting. With more monitoring by independent private shareholders, the oversight of stock exchange regulators, and the hiring of international audit companies, it has become more difficult and complicated for managers of SOEs to siphon off profits or employ fraudulent accounting practices.

Research by the World Bank indicates that a combined programme of privatization and corporatisation (i.e. incorporating government departments with a commercial focus such that they become separate legal entities, such as SOEs) is the most effective approach to manage the public sector (Shirley, 1999). The principles of NPM have since remained at the fore of numerous countries' political agenda.

For SOEs, profitability is not always a sufficient indicator of efficiency, and not all enterprises operate without subsidies and other forms of income. According to the IMF's Global Financial Stability Report 2019, based on a sample of SOEs from emerging markets examined by the fund, the profitability of the median SOE has plunged, with return on invested capital declining from 12.6 in 2007 to 6% in 2018, even as leverage, defined as debt-to-assets, has risen from 51.3% to 54.7% (see figures 2.2 and 2.3).

One of the most important factors driving SOE performance is the quality of governance. Studies on SOE performance show that good governance translates into better results, while weak governance is often at

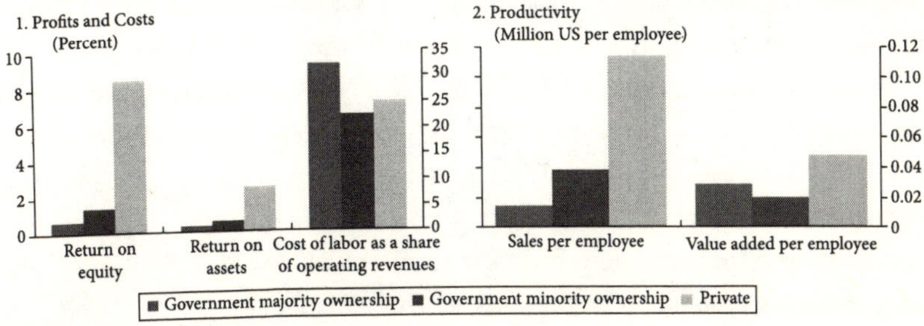

Figure 2.2 SOEs' performance relative to private firms
Source: Gaspar et al. (2020).

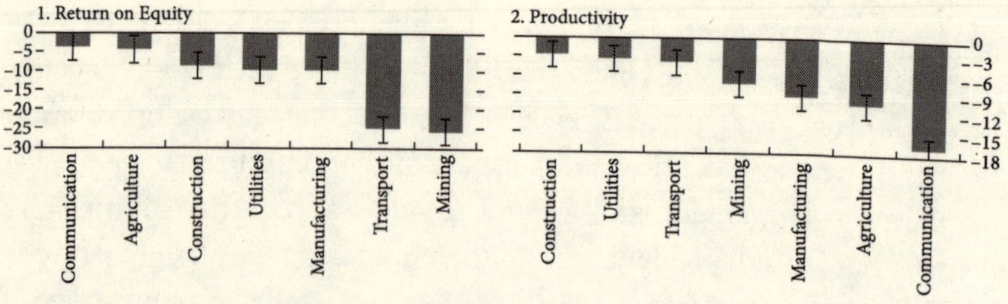

Figure 2.3 Relative performance of SOEs by sector
Source: Gaspar et al. (2020).

the root of many of the performance problems typically associated with State ownership.

A consistent theme in the analysis of SOEs is the extent to which they are, in practice, free of government or political involvement in operational and management matters. The choice and execution of large capital projects highlights the problem of political interference in SOE functioning. Capital projects are usually not decided upon by SOEs as a consequence of exercising their operational mandates. Often, projects are imposed on SOEs by politicians, or senior government officials, for political, 'strategic', or social reasons.

SOEs often accommodate the desire of those in political power to expand inefficient employment at any cost, despite the absence of productive opportunities. SOE plants are often put in sub-optimal locations for political reasons, regardless of significantly increased costs. To please (or avoid offending) political patrons, SOEs indulge in non-merit-based appointment of middle-level managers, senior executives, and board members, whose qualifications and competencies are questionable. SOEs usually find themselves unable to close down uneconomic plants. They are kept alive through the soft budget constraint.

Such projects are typically not financially viable. Politicians and senior officials often find it more convenient to pressure SOEs into undertaking these projects without providing a solution for the viability problem (see figure 2.4). The costs of such projects, referred to as 'unfunded mandates', result in an additional increase in tariffs to existing consumers, who are forced to effectively carry the cost of the subsidy the project requires. Even when SOEs are not pressurised into inappropriate capital projects, SOE managers face inappropriate incentives and are often biased towards

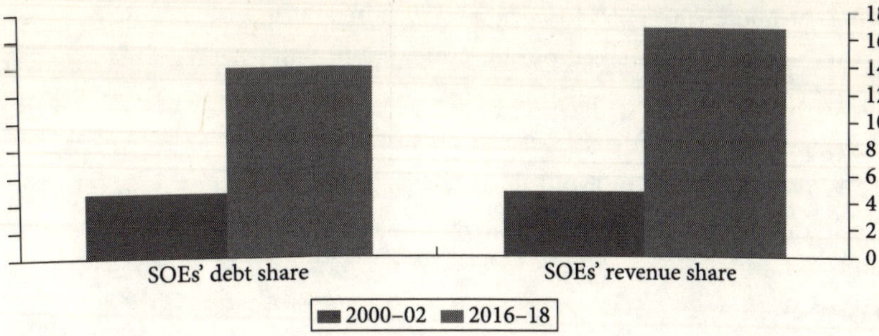

Figure 2.4 SOEs' debt and revenue of largest firms (%)
Source: Gaspar et al. (2020).

larger, and technologically more complex projects, rather than the more incremental or mundane solutions that would often be more appropriate and in the public interest (Steyn, 2011).

Once SOEs have committed to large capital projects, the next risk they (and ultimately their consumers) encounter is the likelihood of substantial cost overruns. The majority of large SOE projects end-up costing much more than the budgeted amount on which the decision to proceed was based. If such costs are disallowed from the rate base, they are inevitably passed on to the taxpayer. Lower SOE dividend payments to the fiscus create a greater need for tax revenues, often to fund SOE bailouts.

The relationship and communication between SOEs and their parent ministries, department, or statutory agencies, plays an important role in ensuring that appropriate corporate governance standards are adhered to. As shareholders, government ministries/departments have considerable ownership responsibilities and duties towards their commercial enterprises, including providing them with competent, effective boards and ensuring clear policy frameworks and operating guidelines in their respective sectors.

The board of directors of any SOE should be its principal governance and oversight forum. But, in a majority of SOEs boards, directors are appointed primarily by ministers, with or without consultation with senior bureaucrats and cabinet colleagues. This discretionary behaviour on the part of political leaders undermines usual governance mechanisms and ensures that the debate on the State's role of rowing vs steering continues unabated.

Policy-makers are also looking at new, alternative paradigms to public sector management, such as public value. Public value argues for a renewed emphasis on the important role public managers can play in maintaining an organization's legitimacy in the eyes of the public. Far from advocating a return to inefficient public services, public value embraces notions of valued public services and efficiency. It calls for more rounded accountability whereby organizations face their citizens as well as their political masters, rather than static, top-down models that focus public managers on meeting centrally driven targets and performance management.

Yet, with the inherent conflicts concerning the roles and private agendas of politicians and public servants, and their influence on governance mechanisms, the extent of administrative discretion and concepts of the public interest have been difficult to reconcile (Coats and Passmore, 2008).

Conflicts that arise in the State's primary role vs its ownership of enterprises

The visible hand of the State has helped build the national economy in many countries. It is equally true that many other countries have survived (if not thrived) in spite of their governments, rather than because of them. In addition to protecting the basic human rights of its citizenry, creating economic opportunity and equality of access to it, the traditional role of government has been associated with policy-making and administration—implementing appropriate legislation and regulations to establish a stable, progressive society.

As a reflection perhaps of increased competition and risks in the global economy, governments feel (rightly or wrongly) that they are being looked upon increasingly not only for macroeconomic policy-making and stability but also for the promotion of continued economic development by way of fostering growth, innovation, and entrepreneurial activity (Reynolds et al., 2004). The role of the State has changed over time, around the world. It has had ideologically driven cycles to it; especially post-decolonization.

Highly interventionist eras have been followed by episodic neoclassical liberal market eras, stressing minimal state intervention. The State is supposed to play a significant role focused on its core activities. These include public protection, providing justice, law and order, defence of the country from foreign aggression, and running a stable, sustainable macro-economy.

In addition, modern governments are expected to provide essential public works and functioning infrastructure. They have to correct or ameliorate the negative impact of externalities, and provide for social insurance and safety nets. They also have to guarantee the protection of individual, collective and corporate property rights, enforce contracts, and provide a full panoply of public goods. As societies and economies grow more complex, the greater the range of the protections that are sought.

Among the most pressing challenges now facing the global economy is ever-increasing wealth and income inequality and climate change and global warming. Excessive individual wealth has made political power expensive to acquire. It encourages potential supporters to focus on common enemies (inside and outside the country) and on cultural values. The more unequal are incomes and wealth and the more determined the 'haves' are to avoid being compelled to support the 'have-nots' through increased taxation, the more politics will take on such characteristics.

It is now widely felt that economic liberalism since the 1980s may have gone too far in posing their confidence in market arrangements and their indifference to the social and political consequences of inequality. The State's role has now become significant in reducing inequalities through the application of simultaneous policy tools at its disposal.

It is becoming increasingly evident that environmental problems, such as climate change and global warming, constitute existential threats to human societies, without effective policies enacted by the government; these problems will very likely persist and even intensify. Governments are increasingly being ascribed a pivotal role in protecting the environment, for instance, through the implementation of environmental policies that protect the environment directly or solve environmental collective action problems (Mansbridge 2014). One of the most obvious lessons of the Covid-19 crisis is that an effective government is necessary for managing large-scale emergencies.

The implicit focus of these core activities is to improve the efficiency of the market by opening it to fair competition; removing monopolies and monopolistic practices; and eliminating obstacles to entry into productive activities. States are supposed to do all this through better provision and diffusion of information and the establishment of efficient regulatory bodies that provide needed information to consumers and establish transparent rules of the game that are known to all and applied impartially to all market participants.

In countries, where SOEs will continue to play a significant role for the foreseeable future, they are relied upon as pioneers of national infrastructure projects and as actors with diverse developmental mandates, regardless of fiscal pressures. SOEs' prominent national role reflects their capabilities and gives them considerable political capital.

Past evidence suggests that rising state intervention in economies is accompanied inevitably by a dereliction of attention to the core activities of the State. Limited time, knowledge, and resources are available to technocratic policy-makers and political decision-makers. As they assume more secondary roles and functions in managing/directing SOEs/SOBFIs, they become distracted and overwhelmed (if not seduced) by these secondary responsibilities. Consequently, they are unable to dedicate to the core activities of government the resources, time, energy, and attention that these activities require for the State to deliver on its primary role.

The hyperactive state then does more but does it less well. This deterioration in quality and deflection of attention has negative implications for market functioning.

In the real world, the normative and the positive roles of the State tend to diverge, implying that many state interventions have not resulted in expectations based on those policies being met, nor the desired (public interest) outcomes being achieved. The countries that seem to have the greatest need for an expanded public sector role are often the ones where the public sector is least able to play that role efficiently. Therefore, when policy-makers in these countries attempt to play a larger, more intrusive role, they end up damaging economic activity and retarding progress toward national development.

Policy-makers who invariably seem too aware of the limitations of markets should be equally aware of the limitations and the difficulties governments have in addressing many public failures that disable the effective functioning of markets—i.e. unnecessary red tape, difficulties of dealing with bureaucracy, the problems of regulatory capture, and socialization of national enterprises.

No country in the 21st century has relied solely on market forces or on state intervention in enterprise ownership. There has been, accordingly, a continuing debate on the extent to which market forces should be relied on to drive the growth engine, when to intervene, and how to govern these forces. Making that assessment requires an understanding not only of the nature of information asymmetries, and market imperfections and failures, but also of government and public failures in policy-making, implementation, rule enforcement, and in managing commercial SOEs.

It requires an understanding not only of the limitations of government and political processes and the relative strengths and weaknesses of the public and private sectors but also about how and how easily/quickly these deficiencies can be improved. Therefore, the search of the ideal model of state intervention is still a work in progress. Redefining the scope of state intervention will be a continuous process that takes into account a country's own experience and that of other economies both mature and emerging and through trial and error during the course of market transition.

3

Country case study 1: Brazil

SOEs in Brazil

The universe of SOEs in Brazil in 2017 included 150 enterprises directly or indirectly owned by the federal government, 102 of which indirectly controlled, subsidiaries of SOEs. Of these SOEs, 48 were from the energy sector, 35 from oil and derivatives, 15 from commerce and services, and 14 from the financial sector. They employ around 516,000 people (0.7% of total employment); the aggregate budget for SOEs is approximately 30% of GDP; and total investment by SOEs amounts to roughly 2.3% of GDP (Filho and Alves, 2018).

Brazilian SOEs have assets of R$4,678.4 billion (approximately US$1.5 trillion) in 2017. The three largest federal SOEs, listed on the Stock Exchange, had a market value of R$262.2 billion (US$84 billion), with Petrobrás alone accounting for 63% of that value (Filho and Alves, 2018). SOEs pay dividends and contribute to government finances by paying taxes and fees that amount to almost 3% of the GDP or 9% of total government revenue. SOEs which finance their activities with their own resources or through the market are indirectly controlled by the State.

Despite the large-scale privatization that occurred in the 1980s and 1990s, the Brazilian government still maintains a large and influential number of SOEs under its control. Although the absolute number of SOEs declined sharply following the wave of privatizations in the 1990s, their economic clout remains significant. Brazil's SOEs are some of the largest companies (SOE and private) in the Latin America and Caribbean region (Musacchio and Pineda, 2019).

SOEs in Brazil operate in both competitive and non-competitive markets. Across sectors, 43% of Brazilian SOEs operate in the oil and natural gas sector, and 37% in the electricity, finance, and service sectors. A few large SOEs play a lead role in their respective sectors: Petrobrás is the largest company in oil and natural gas with a budget that represents almost 7% of Brazil's GDP. The Brazilian Energy Company (*Centrais Elétricas Brasileiras S.A.*—Electrobras) leads the electricity sector with a budget of 0.3% of GDP.

Banco do Brasil, *Caixa Econômica*, and *Banco Nacional de Desenvolvimento Econômico e Social* (Brazilian National Development Bank--BNDES) are the most important actors in the financial sector with an aggregate budget equal to approximately 4.3% of GDP. These government-owned financial institutions control over 40% of total banking assets. During the 2008–10 GFC, these three large federal government-owned banks played a major role in the compensation of private investors and lenders, while also sustaining the government's long-term plan of expanding access to finance and credit in support of development.

Eight SOEs are listed on the Brazilian stock exchange, accounting for approximately 25% of the total market capitalization; Petrobrás alone represents 17% of market capitalization. By 2009, around 5% and 30% of the SOEs with majority control by federal and state governments respectively were listed.

The unique features of Brazilian state capitalism include SOEs being minority shareholders in a number of supposedly private corporations in Brazil. For example, Petrobrás is one of the large shareholders in the chemical firm Braskem.

Through its lending activities BNDES plays a central guiding role in the economy. When President Fernando Collor (1990–92) started the National Privatization Program, BNDES was selected as an 'operational agent' and remained so in the subsequent wave of privatization under President Fernando Henrique Cardoso (1995–2002). BNDES is run by a technical elite with expertise in many industrial sectors (Schneider, 1991). For that reason, the Brazilian government insisted on its close involvement in the privatization process to guarantee credibility and smooth execution.

Between 2000 and 2013, the value of BNDES' lending operations relative to GDP more than doubled, from 4.8% to 11.1%. During that period, total credit extended by it to the private sector increased from 19% to 21%. BNDESPAR, a wholly owned subsidiary of BNDES that operates as its equity arm, holds stakes in 74 closely held firms and 71 publicly traded corporations (which account for nearly 60% of Brazil's total market capitalization). By the end of 2012, the market value of the equity held by BNDESPAR was US$44.8 billion (OECD, 2015b). BNDESPAR plays a central role in supporting Brazil's national champions (Pargendler, 2014).

The history of SOEs in Brazil

SOEs were first established during the 19th century when the Crown of Portugal migrated temporarily to Brazil. The Banco do Brasil (BdB) was set up in 1808 and the Caixa Econômica Federal (Caixa) in 1861. These early antecedents notwithstanding state ownership of enterprises in Brazil became more prominent after World War I when the government had to bail out a number of railway companies to avert their bankruptcy.

During and after World War II, the Brazilian state began to invest heavily in large, capital-intensive industries in which private capital had either no interest or lacked the financial capacity to risk making the large-scale investments that were needed. SOE formation gathered momentum in the 1940s, when the government created more SOEs in '*commanding heights*' industries to establish a solid foundation for sustained future economic development, such as in mining, steel, chemicals, and electricity.

This was when Brazil ceded its agrarian commodity orientation with emphasis on modernization through industrialization and urbanization. But it was not until later that State capitalism became the main pillar of the Brazilian economy, flourishing in the 1970s over two decades of military rule (1964–85).

For the first fourteen years of the junta rule (1965–79) Brazil grew at an average of 9–10% annually. Part of that rapid growth came from labour moving from agriculture to manufacturing. The remainder came from the accumulation of capital. Value added in manufacturing grew at 10% per year between 1967 and 1980. By 1976–77, the public sector accounted for 43% of total gross fixed capital formation (GFCF) with about 25% being attributable to SOEs (Trebat, 1983).

Although state investments in finance can be traced to the 19th century, government intervention in Brazilian enterprise through the 20th century evolved in three phases. In the *first phase* (1910–40), the government acted as a risk-taker and insurer against enterprise failure through direct ownership. In that phase, the government ended up owning and operating SOEs more by accident than by prior design.

There was no national plan designed for the State to promote industrialization until 1940. It was under President Getúlio Vargas (1930–45) that large, dominant SOEs, such as National Steel Company in 1941 and the Vale do Rio Doce Company (Vale) in 1942, were created. The government stepped in partly because it wanted to promote industrialization aimed mainly at import substitution.

The *second phase* occurred in the 1950 and 1960s, when President Vargas was re-elected. He adopted a policy of 'development nationalism'. SOEs were created to build the country's infrastructure, supply important inputs to domestic industry (e.g. electricity, oil, and steel), and prevent market failure in capital markets. The State monopolized large, long-term investments in infrastructure and strategic industries. Foreign companies were involved in industries that were technology and capital intensive.

BNDES was set up in 1952, while Petrobrás, the flagship State-owned national oil company, was created in 1953. Industrialization in the early 20th century was financed through large stock and bond markets. But, by the 1950s, there were only a few initial public offerings (IPOs) and the long-term bond market had virtually disappeared because of high levels of inflation. Under those circumstances, BNDES was created to provide long-term financing for the renewal of large infrastructure projects. In the late 1950s, the bank's focus extended to supporting the development of the still infant steel industry. Under the military government (1964–85), and with the encouragement and substantial financial support of the World Bank, BNDES changed its focus from lending solely to public projects to financing private companies as well (Schneider, 2015).

The *third phase* of SOE proliferation in Brazil occurred in the 1970s and early 1980s when SOEs, such as EMBRAER (aircraft manufacturer), INFRAERO (airspace regulator), EMBRATEL (telephone), Correios (mail), and RADIOBRÁS (radio, TV, and other telecommunications), among others were created during the military dictatorship (1964–85). This wave grew stronger during the administration of President Ernesto Geisel (1974–79), a former army general who had served as the CEO of Petrobrás between 1969 and 1974. He was a strong believer in state planning and saw a clear need for the government to guide and support economic development (Gaspari, 2003).

Geisel believed that foreign participation was only warranted in cases where domestic technology and financial capacity were lacking. State ownership was justified by the industrial policy argument that State-led intervention was necessary to promote risky, coordinated investments. The government ventured more heavily into petrochemicals, created firms to control the distribution and storage of food, and invested in research and development at the National Agricultural Research Company (known as Embrapa). It also supported or bailed out private firms in petrochemicals, metals, and technology.

By 1981 there were 530 federal public entities and many others owned by provincial sub-sovereign governments. The rapid growth in SOEs, however, did not lead to an overwhelming dominance of SOEs in the Brazilian economy. The Brazilian government allowed private sector to remain the dominant player in other sectors where state intervention through ownership was not perceived as necessary.

In the third phase, the Brazilian government ventured into industries beyond utilities, mining, steel, and petroleum, not necessarily by design, but motivated by the actions and ambitions of SOE managers. Thus, the industrialization process in Brazil was largely state induced, and large public investments were made in energy production, mining, and petroleum extraction and, later, in infrastructure and telecommunications.

However, Brazil's State capitalism model collapsed in the 1980s due to the failure of many SOEs to adjust to the first and second oil shocks (in 1973 and 1979) followed by the debt crisis of 1982. Brazilian SOEs had expanded investment fuelled by foreign borrowings and increased employment, whereas comparable private firms had downsized. Faced with losses and large liabilities in foreign currency, a limited privatization scheme was launched at the urging of the IMF and World Bank in the mid- and late 1980s, with 38 SOEs being privatized.

Obliged to adjust its structure under Washington Consensus terms, the Brazilian economy was transformed during the 1990s. There was a historical move towards privatization and deregulation that ended a long period of uninterrupted state intervention in the economy. State ownership of enterprises was reduced significantly through huge transfers of public investments into the private sector and the emergence of huge private conglomerates that were often controlled or owned by foreign investors. Privatization programmes in the 1990s and 2000s reduced the size of the SOE sector relative to the population to one of the lowest levels in the Latin America and Caribbean (LAC) region (Musacchio and Pineda, 2019).

This change was embodied in the National Plan for Privatization (Programa Nacional de Desestatização, PND), launched in 1990 and sustained through the decade. Between 1990 and 1992, 15 more SOEs were privatized, yielding about US$3.5 billion in total proceeds. By 1994, 25 SOEs had been sold, mostly in exchange for debt certificates and little hard cash. Post-1994, SOEs in the energy, transportation, and communications sectors were privatized. However, Brazil's largest SOE, Petrobrás, remained outside the privatization programme because of constitutional restrictions.

An interesting feature of the privatization process in Brazil is that around 50% of privatization auctions involved 'mixed consortia' controlled by domestic private groups and foreign investors, often with funding from state-related actors, such as BNDES and pension funds of SOEs (Lazzarini, 2011). The privatization process thus led to the expansion of a 'state-minority model' in Brazil.

A substantial source of domestic participation in the privatization auctions was constituted by the public sector using the resources of the public sector pension funds. For instance, in the case of the steel industry—among the earliest privatizations—the Banco do Brasil pension fund, Previ, was a key player. By the end of 2002, the fund had acquired major stakes across a range of key privatized companies. Since 2003, there has been a clear move towards strengthening of private national companies or groups, with the active involvement of the state and private entrepreneurs to create 'national champions' or 'leading global' corporations.

The particular type of State capitalism prevailing in Brazil today reflects a combination of governmental control of traditional SOEs with the noticeable exercise of shareholder activism by State-controlled institutional investors (SCIIs) both in private and public companies.

Brazil is currently coping with the consequences of various corruption scandals, which has included the gross misuse of SOEs resources. The Federation of Industries in the State of Sao Paulo has estimated that corruption amounts to as much as 2.3% of Brazil's GDP.

Politicians are reluctant to pursue further privatization because, in most Latin American countries, there is little public support for this approach (Shirley, 2005). In 2017, a survey of 500 to 600 residents across Argentina, Brazil, Chile, Colombia, Ecuador, Mexico, Peru, and Venezuela found that 35% of those interviewed believed that SOEs were inefficient and 42% thought they were a major source of corruption. Yet almost 30% of them also believed that SOEs were important for the economy, and 14% thought that SOEs defended the country's natural resources. Only 7% of those interviewed believed that SOEs should be privatized (Musacchio and Pineda, 2019).

Regulation vs public ownership of SOEs

Currently, the major influence of the Brazilian State on economic activity is through its regulatory agencies and through the development bank BNDES. Through regulation it influences the country's electric power supply, its telecommunications system, its rail and road transportation network, and its oil exploration and production sector (both through the still publicly owned Petrobrás and the regulation of the activities of foreign oil prospectors).

While BNDES is the major source of investment funds. Through these instruments—both as a regulator and as financier—the State has continued to exercise a major influence over the development of above-mentioned sectors.

One notable feature of Brazil's privatization has been that it was implemented through the granting of concessions rather than a permanent transfer of assets. The winner of the concession contract operated the facility for a limited period of time (usually 20–25 years), at the end of which the assets reverted to the State unless a new concession was granted either to the old operator or a newcomer after an auction.

The concession contract included provisions for rate or tariff readjustment, investment for maintenance, and upgrading of the relevant facilities. For instance, in the telecommunications sector, strict targets were set to increase provision of fixed and cellular lines, while service quality was monitored and enforced (Amann and Baer, 2005). The administration of the concession contract was the responsibility of either regulatory institutions−–e.g. ANATEL (*Agência Nacional de Telecomunicações*); ANEEL (*Agência Nacional de Energia Elétrica*)−–or ministries.

The setting of tariffs is one of the State's significant regulatory responsibilities. In this regard, the State has had to balance the influence of competing constituencies. In the period of rapid privatization, the State in an effort to attract bidders prioritized the interests of investors and raised tariffs sharply. As a result, profits of public utilities increased dramatically. This policy led to a rapid upsurge of private sector investment in utilities and infrastructure.

However, the high level of tariffs led to popular opposition. For example, the protests of associations of truck drivers in various states forced the government to reduce tolls. In the case of the telecommunications sector, the Lula administration heralded a similar downward pressure on tariffs. These reductions were contested by a number of concessionaires for violation of the concession contracts. This raised the possibility of concessionaires abandoning their concession contracts, resulting in a process of re-nationalization.

The regulatory model was changed in the early 2000s, selecting bidders on the basis of those able to offer low tariffs rather than on the basis of their capacity to deliver. Correspondingly, the pace of private sector-driven upgrading of the relevant facilities has lagged, while high disparities in tariff levels still exist. For example, tolls on highways constructed during Cardoso and Lula/Rousseff presidencies vary between R$1.99 and R$18.56 per 100 km (Amann et al., 2014).

The absence of strong regulatory bodies in the power sector failed to create the necessary checks-and-balances against discretionary governmental action threatening the performance of SOEs. Similarly, political pressure on ANEEL to rein in tariffs underpins at least in part, the failure of much needed additional power generation and distribution capacity to be put in place in the urbanized South and South East. Consequently, Brazil has remained vulnerable to electricity shortfalls (Mourougane and Piso, 2011). In 2021, President Jair Bolsonaro replaced Petrobrás' chief executive after publicly criticizing him following steep increases in the prices of petrol and diesel, which sparked unrest among truckers and threats of strikes.

Another key regulatory issue faced by the concessionaires was uncertainty over future tariff adjustments and the transparency around their setting and enforcement. In the case of the energy sector, the regulator, ANEEL, has come under consistent criticism for the opacity, complexity, and inconsistency of its management in tariff setting (Amann and Baer, 2005).

An additional aspect of privatization through concessions was that the BNDES helped finance both domestic and foreign bidders in the auction process. The concessionaires were required to upgrade the facilities they administered under the concession contract. This was often made easier by the government through generous loans from BNDES. Above and beyond the State's regulatory and financing role, it has not entirely relinquished its position as the channel through which savings are accumulated (through pension funds) and then directed towards favoured sectors, like utilities.

Many Brazilian utilities experienced liquidity problems as the State's inclination, to allow essential upward tariff adjustments, diminished. The financial precariousness of utilities affected BNDES adversely, as a large proportion of the financing of public utilities in Brazil was provided by it. Given these constraints, sustaining investment meant active participation by the state, either by providing subsidies to consumers or through direct government control. A populist bearing on regulating public utilities and the resultant precariousness of the debtors has put the security of public savings in jeopardy, implying that the Brazilian economy has continued to be strongly affected by the actions of the State.

Another reason for the persistence of high regulatory risk in Brazil emanates from the weak autonomy of the regulators. This is due to political interference and the influence of the service providers. A survey of 21 of Brazil's 27 infrastructure regulators found that 13 reported that the executive had made 'highly' or 'very highly' effective attempts to intervene while 8 reported direct interventions (Correa, 2007).

The energy regulator, National Agency of Petroleum, Natural Gas and Biofuels (ANP—*Agência Nacional do Petróleo, Gás Natural e Biocombustíveis*), comes under the direct control of the government. The power regulator (ANEEL) possesses fewer institutional guarantees of independence (Prado, 2013). There is a strong political party influence at *Agencia Nacional de Transportes Terrestres* (ANTT), the road transport regulator (De Paula and Avellar, 2008).

The contrast between the experience of the independent ANATEL (telecoms regulator) one hand and the more politically influenced ANEEL/ANTT on the other can be discerned from the rapid expansion in the telecommunications sector following its liberalization in 1998, while slow progress has been observed in expanding electricity generation and distribution and accelerating highways construction (Amann et al. 2016).

In the oil sector, Brazil has extended regulatory preferences to SOEs, entrenching Petrobrás' monopoly status. In 2010, the Brazilian government made significant legal changes in its oil sector, reversing previously undertaken market reforms, and intensifying state interference in the sector. The main goal was to increase state control over a strategic resource to guarantee that future Brazilian generations benefitted from the proceeds of the oil reserves. It created Pre-Sal Petroleo S.A. (PPSA), a wholly SOE responsible for monitoring the production-sharing contracts in pre-salt layers and areas deemed strategic.

The overlapping responsibility of PPSA and ANP has, inevitably, added elements of uncertainty to the institutional governance structure in the sector. All consortia operating in pre-salt layers and areas deemed strategic are required to form operational committees and 50% of the committee's votes belong to PPSA. Petrobrás has at least a 30% voting share, since this is the minimum required percentage for its participation in pre-salt and strategic domains (Florencio, 2016).

Together with PPSA, the current regulatory regime has provided Petrobrás with undue influence which can be exploited by it to gain an unfair advantage to the detriment of the consortia. PPSA is also responsible for managing the production-sharing agreements on behalf of the government and has a significant role in the consortium's decisions. However, it is not legally liable for any potential major breach of contract affecting operational activities.

The State's dual role as an active investor and referee has meant that the government is uniquely positioned to shape the applicable legal regime with its interests as shareholder in mind. Corporate law has provided only weak and feeble constraints to the behaviour of SOEs.

The example of Petroquisa's privatization has demonstrated that the original corporate law regime is made particularly amenable to the interests of the State as shareholder. The State sponsors legal reforms to change the applicable rules when they prove to be inconvenient. However, courts and regulatory agencies have been reluctant to enforce legal obligations on state actors. This has contributed in increasing the degree of discretion enjoyed by the State as the controlling shareholder (Pargendler, 2014).

The federal government has relied on Petrobrás' investment capacity in order to advance its macroeconomic programmes and needs—such as inflation control by banning fuel price readjustments. It is clear that, ideally, whenever Petrobrás has been called upon to promote public policies, all company expenses and/or waivers should be duly accounted for and refunded by the National Treasury. The accountability of these policy expenses and their refund are important instruments in the maintenance of the separate roles played by the government—namely, as the major shareholder of Petrobrás and as the regulator.

SOEs have experienced a clear conflict between the social and political objectives of the government as a controlling shareholder, on one hand, and the interests of outside investors, on the other. In recent years, Brazilian SOEs have engaged in actions that have been widely perceived as detrimental to the interests of the company and its private minority shareholders. The use of price controls by Petrobrás and the renegotiation of concession contracts by power company Electrobras have illustrated the tendency to pursue objectives that are not in the financial interest of the firm.

Finally, the very definition (and legal treatment) of government control raises challenging questions. Brazil has increasingly relied on minority, rather than majority, shareholdings by the State. The prevalence of SCIIs in the Brazilian stock market, as well as the widespread use of shareholder agreements by state actors, has raised the spectre of government intervention even in firms where the government does not directly hold a majority of the voting capital.

SOEs and the emergence/impact of crony capitalism

During Cardoso's government a greater emphasis was placed on private sector competition with regulatory oversight detached from direct political intervention. But during the governments of Lula and Rousseff, there was a preference for a State-led concession approach that guaranteed a majority stakeholding for the Brazilian State. During both these periods government bank credit was a major source of finance for firms in Brazil and was allocated through BNDES.

Government control over banks has led to significant political influence over operational and investment decisions of firms, with non-financial companies allocating capital to accommodate political pressure, instead of economic efficiency. This provides politicians with the control to choose projects being implemented in the economy (Carvalho, 2014).

A study of 13,000 of Brazilian manufacturing firms between 1995 and 2005 with at least 50 employees has concluded that government bank lending is believed to have helped in re-electing local governments of political allies. Politicians use control over bank lending decisions to influence firms to expand employment in regions with allied incumbents.

This suggests that government control over banks has led to a significant influence of political considerations over firms' decisions. These considerations seem to have systematically influenced the way in which financial firms allocate resources. Corruption consequently has been a considerable risk for the efficient operation of the development bank (Carvalho, 2014). The absence of arms' length principles has led to the same kind of crony capitalism on which many emerging economies have commonly relied, to develop their economies.

Brazil's Congress has more than two dozen political parties; it is nearly impossible for a single party to ever win a majority. Brazil's presidents must therefore form coalitions in order to govern effectively. Individual political parties have little influence over who wins a seat for their party. Instead, to win a seat in the lower house, candidates often must vie for support from big companies that are happy to help candidates win.

In exchange for investing in candidates' campaigns, companies expect to receive help in winning government contracts. In addition to inducing corruption, this candidate-centred electoral process creates both intra- and inter-party competition that leads to party polarization. Brazil's electoral rules have allowed candidates to switch parties at low cost, undermining any chance of ideological coherence within coalitions. Since party whips cannot control their own congressmen, presidents must bargain with legislators on an individual basis in order to pass legislation.

Progress is impossible unless individuals are paid off to vote a certain way (Galbreath, 2017). The need to win over so many individual allies—with their own interests and constituencies to please—has led Brazilian presidents to pump vast amounts of patronage and protection into the system.

Presidents often allow legislators to appoint their allies to jobs in Brazil's SOEs and regulatory agencies. Once in these posts, the new officials gain a say over which companies will receive lucrative government contracts. And many of them have proven all too happy to make those decisions based on bribes, which they then share with their patrons in Congress.

The emergence of the Petrobrás contractors' scandal in 2014 is a prime example of crony capitalism based on corruption. Operation Car Wash, as the investigation, has come to be known, uncovered massive corruption involving government officials, business leaders, and Petrobrás. Prosecutors have claimed that the illegal proceeds were used to finance electoral victories in 2010 and 2014.

This scandal has involved contractors for Petrobrás bribing executives of the company in exchange for lucrative contracts. Executives at Petrobrás and a cartel of contractors then collided to siphon large sums from inflated construction and service contracts. Public prosecutors have alleged that some of the illicit cash paid to Petrobrás made its way to the country's political parties. Over US$2 billion is estimated to have been sucked away in corruption involving the federal government, governors, and members of Congress, many of whom received payments in return for allowing Brazil's biggest construction firms to overcharge Petrobrás for building contracts (Galbreath, 2017).

Most of the contractors identified have been among Brazil's largest builders of infrastructure, including construction giant Odebrecht and multinational conglomerate Andrade Gutierrez. Estimates have suggested that since 1997 these companies secured subsidized credit of $20 billion from BNDES. To ensure continued access, the companies in question have lavished gifts and other favours on politicians and have contributed large sums, both on and off the books, to their reelection campaigns.

As a result of the Operation Car wash investigation, Odebrecht entered into a plea-bargain agreement with authorities in Brazil, the US, and Switzerland in December 2016, agreeing to a record USD 3.5 billion in criminal penalties shared between all three countries. These cases have contributed to reinforce the perception shared by many Latin American citizens that governments have not acted in public interest but have been captured by powerful private crony interests (OECD, 2019).

Aside from its broader political ramifications, the Car Wash affair has threatened future infrastructure projects given the indictment of senior executives from Brazil's largest construction and capital goods firms (Amann et al., 2016). A study by the São Paulo State Industrial Association (FIESP) has estimated that the money lost to corruption in the first stage of the PAC (Growth Acceleration Program), between 2007 and 2010, could have built 124% more roads and 525% more railways (Amann et al., 2016).

At a more fundamental level, the Car Wash scandal illustrates the dangers of having large powerful SOEs dominant in the economy and ineffective regulators. Despite the enormous scale of bribery in the system, the energy regulator, ANP, failed to step in to prevent it.

The unveiling of massive corruption surrounding the relationship between Petrobrás and its contractors has significantly raised regulatory risk. Unfortunately, the problem is not just restricted to the energy sector but pervades throughout the system in which SOEs predominate.

The private agenda of public officials

The President appoints (supposedly) exceptional, qualified people to high positions in the administrative structures of the State, because they are considered, legally, to be offices of public trust. The Constitution has established that SOEs are subject to the standard principles of public administration. This implies that both the board of directors and top administrative officials must act within strict legal boundaries and not serve their personal pecuniary or other interests. They must observe administrative ethics and morality, be transparent about the company's performance and their own work, and act in pursuit of public and collective interests.

SOE board members and appointed high officials are subject to civil, penal, and administrative law regarding ethics. Any misconduct could lead to judicial consequences, although the administrative and penal laws are difficult to enforce. They require proof of malign intent to harm the company; mere poor performance is not enough.

In addition, exceptions in law absolve public personnel acting within their professional capacity for the damages or losses caused by SOEs to third parties. For SOEs that offer public services, there is no underlying government responsibility assumed, for damage and losses caused to third parties. Given the significant protections provided to public officials by law, and other exceptions in laws related to fiscal responsibility, public officials have pursued their private agenda in their official capacity with impunity.

Exceptions in law related to fiscal responsibility have allowed the government to generate primary budget surpluses, while keeping massive resources flowing to both SOEs and private companies through public banks during economic crises. But these exceptions have made SOEs more vulnerable to political influences that affect market behaviour.

In Brazil, public debt is divided into consolidated (or capital, long-term) debt (*dîvida consolidada ou fundada*)--composed of total financial obligations undertaken by the State through laws, contracts, agreements, treaties, and credit obligations that exceed 12 months in duration—and fluctuating (or short-term) debt. Fluctuating debt comprises 'unpaid bills' (*restos a pagar*), amortizations and interest on consolidated debt, third-party guarantees and collateral, and National Treasury debt (Tautz et al., 2014).

In contrast with consolidated debt, fluctuating debt does not need previous legal authorization to be incurred. The fluctuating debt is thus harder to identify and control; it serves as a massive and fertile field for manipulation of balances by public officials. Brazil has no procedure that allows the identification, transparency, and control of such expenditure, thus creating a non-transparent 'parallel budget' that competes for resources and funds with the Enacted Budget. There has been a constant increase in this 'hidden debt' and has been clearly accompanied by a sustained or increasing flow of public resources from the National Treasury to public banks, destined to stimulate private and public enterprises.

In addition to regulatory agencies and BNDES, the role of public pension funds[1] is equally significant. Political interference in directing

[1] Public pension funds are not legally owned by the government but are organized as separate legal entities managed for the benefit of SOE retirees. Pension funds of SOEs play a particularly dominant role in Brazil's equity markets. Previ, the pension fund of Banco do Brasil's employees, is the largest such fund in Brazil and holds equity stakes in 43 publicly traded companies, which together account for over one-half of Bovespa's market capitalization. In 2006, Previ alone held

pension fund investment has been commonplace in Brazil and has provided another avenue through which public officials extend their private agenda. The governance structure of SOE pension funds is particularly conducive to political interference. By law, the SOEs appoint half of board members, as well as the board chairpersons at SOE pension funds, with the remaining directors being elected by the fund's beneficiaries. Typically, the CEOs of SOE pension funds are appointed by the CEOs of the respective SOEs, who, in turn, are directly or indirectly appointed by the country's president (Pargendler, 2016).

Pension funds of SOEs have played a dominant role in Brazil's equity markets. Previ, the pension fund of Banco do Brasil's employees, is the largest such fund. Private pension funds in Brazil have typically allocated less than 30% of their investment portfolio in corporate stocks, given the historically high interest rates paid on sovereign debt. Previ, by contrast, apportions over 60% of its portfolio to equity investments in large Brazilian corporate groups. Its equity investments consist of large stakes—an average of 15.87% of the equity capital in strategic sectors, like energy, banking, tourism, and telecom.

These sizable stakes have translated into significant governance influence. Every year, Previ elects over 100 members of boards of directors and supervisory board (*Conselho Fiscal*).

The well-publicized role of Previ (and BNDES) in ousting the chief executive of mining giant Vale do Rio Doce, a private firm, illustrates the use of pension funds to further the government's economic agenda. Despite Vale's robust financial performance, its CEO Roger Agnelli attracted the ire of President Lula for what he viewed as unnecessary employee firings and underinvestment in the country. Through the use of 'minority' holdings by state actors (and especially Previ's holding of nearly 15% of Vale's equity), Agnelli was replaced by an executive presumably more sympathetic to the government's policy priorities (Pargendler, 2014).

Brazil has established two SCIIs that have reinforced the government's influence in private firms. The FI-FGTS, an investment fund of FGTS (a fund designated for workers—Fundo de Garantia do Tempo e Serviço) *Brazilian* Indemnity Funds, was created in 2007 to

the equivalent of 5% of Brazil's market capitalization. Taken together, public pension funds in Brazil accounted for 64.6% of the country's pension fund industry as of 2013 (Pargendler, 2014).

finance investments in energy and infrastructure. In 2008, Brazil created its SWF (Fundo Soberno do Brasil—FSB). The fund has since invested in Brazilian government debt and in SOEs, such as Petrobrás and Banco do Brasil. These state actors have held minority positions.

The State's minority investments in SOEs might at first appear puzzling. It would seem that the government has little to gain in terms of additional influence by accumulating stakes through SCIIs in firms that are already under state control. By sharing control with private actors, the exercise of state power can pretend to be distant. But Brazilian corporate law confers significant rights on minority shareholders and allows holders of at least 15% of the company's voting stock or 10% of the company's nonvoting preferred stock to appoint one board member each. SCIIs had a decisive voice in electing the representatives of minority shareholders to the board, thereby ensuring an even greater degree of dominance by the State in Petrobrás' governance. SCII have also made ample use of shareholder agreements to influence corporate strategy and governance (Pargendler, 2016).

The creeping influence of the State and public officials over large swathes of the economy has been responsible for the main public corruption scandals of the last decade. These include the Congressional vote-buying scandal orchestrated by government officials, which implicated *Banco do Brasil* (Milhaupt and Pargendler, 2017), and the bribery scheme involving several Brazilian construction conglomerates and Petrobrás.

State influence over corporate governance in Brazil extends far beyond SOEs and firms in which SCIIs hold significant equity stakes. The State and public officials can make an influential appearance in unexpected contexts (Pargendler, 2014). Minority stakes have allowed state actors to entrench their influence and required them to broker deals with private actors.

SOEs and the misallocation of resources

The public sector presence in Brazil's financial system is significant. Government-owned financial institutions control over 40% of total banking system assets (IMF, 2012). During the financial crisis, three large federal government-owned banks—BdB, Caixa, and BNDES—played a major role.

Altogether the fiscal stimulus, including the quasi-fiscal operations of BNDES, amounted to 3% of GDP (IMF, 2017). According to the IMF, the BNDES performs a number of quasi-fiscal activities, such as loaning funds below market rates to privileged sectors, and participating as a central instrument in the masking of debts in the government's budget. In addition, the bank works within the government's policy of strengthening 'national champions' to compete in international markets, including both SOEs, such as Petrobrás and Eletrobrás, and private companies, such as Vale. Table 3.1 shows Brazilian SOEs' and SOBFIs' finances.

The Brazilian government, besides relying on majority-owned SOEs until the late 1980s, has been very active in the financing of private companies through BNDES. Between 1952 and 1964 almost 84% of the lending activity of BNDES went to Brazilian SOEs (Leff, 1968). Over time, the bank has expanded its operations, with new lines of credit and lending to many large private corporations. By the late 1970s, 87% of all BNDES's loans went to the private sector (Najberg, 1989). In the last decade this has changed, SOEs accounted for 20–40% of all of BNDES' loans (Musacchio and Lazzarini, 2014).

An analysis of the sources of funds of BNDES shows the extent of misallocation of public resources. Since 1974, BNDES has used tax revenue from two payroll taxes, the Programa de Integração Social (PIS) and the Programa de Formação do Patrimônio do Servidor Público (PASEP). Since 1990, worker unemployment insurance funds which

Table 3.1 Brazil—Public corporations and finances, 2014 (in % of GDP)

	Number of entities	Revenue	Expenditure	Balance
Nonfinancial public corporations (including Petrobrás and Eletrobrás, another 59 federal corporations, 394 state corporations, and 664 municipal corporations)	1.119	11.2	12.5	−1.3
Other financial public corporations	12	7.0	6.2	0.8

Source: IMF, 2017.

were consolidated under the Fundo de Amparo ao Trabalhador (FAT) have also been transferred to BNDES in the form of subordinated debt.

Essentially, the bank has relied on involuntary savings to channel resources to foster new investment. FAT funds are transferred to BNDES and are paid long-term interest rate (TJLP), which has been below the benchmark market interest rate (SELIC), set by the Central Bank of Brazil (Prochnik and Machado, 2008). Over the years, BNDES has seen its retained earnings grow—including the returns from investments by BNDESPAR—and has begun using them as its main source of funds.

Yet, after 2009, the government has pursued an aggressive expansion of the bank's operations and has transferred funds from the National Treasury to the BNDES. This has allowed the government to simultaneously sustain large-scale investments and obtain a primary surplus during adverse international economic scenarios. An exception in the law of fiscal responsibility has allowed transfers from the Treasury to the BNDES, and from the BNDES to public or private corporations, need not observe the criteria of confirmation with key budget documents (Tautz et al., 2014).

In 2009 and 2010, such direct transfers reached R$180 billion (around US$100 billion) (Pereira and Simões, 2010). BNDES' portfolio of soft loans with subsidized interest rates expanded fivefold over by 10 years to R$876 billion in 2016.

The constant increase in 'hidden' debt has been clearly accompanied by a sustained or increasing flow of public resources from the National Treasury to public banks, and correspondingly, a steady and robust rate of disbursement destined to stimulate private and public enterprises. The transfers to BNDES, done through the issuing of public bonds in the market, are loaned to the bank at a lower interest rate, are then loaned again by BNDES at low interest rates to beneficiaries of its programmes and credit lines. Not only does this generate a revenue loss in many cases but also most of the government's expenditure, from transfers to the BNDES, have ended up in growing 'unpaid commitments,[2] (Tautz et al., 2014). These 'unpaid commitments' grew from around 5% of the central government budgetary expenditures to 13.4% at end of 2014 (close to 4%

[2] In 2003, some US$3 billion 'Unpaid commitments' in 2003 amounted to US$3 billion, which increased to US$21 billion in 2010 and to US$50 billion in 2011.

of GDP). In 2015, despite an effort to reduce those, they still remained high (12.3% of budgetary expenditures). The large size and some of the 'unpaid commitments' include liabilities accrued more than a decade ago (IMF, 2017). Figures 3.1 and 3.2 show the balance sheets of SOEs and SOBFIs in Brazil and the comparison of the SOE liabilities with other countries.

Taking into account the opportunity cost of BNDES funding, the money used to capitalize the bank could be, in principle, used to reduce public debt or support activities with a higher social rate of return. Between 2005 and 2009, the difference between the net interest margin

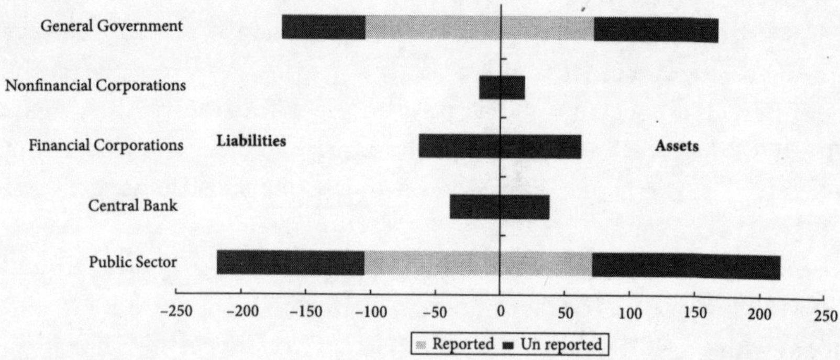

Figure 3.1 Brazilian SOEs' and SOBFIs' balance sheets, 2014 (as % of GDP)
Source: IMF, 2017.

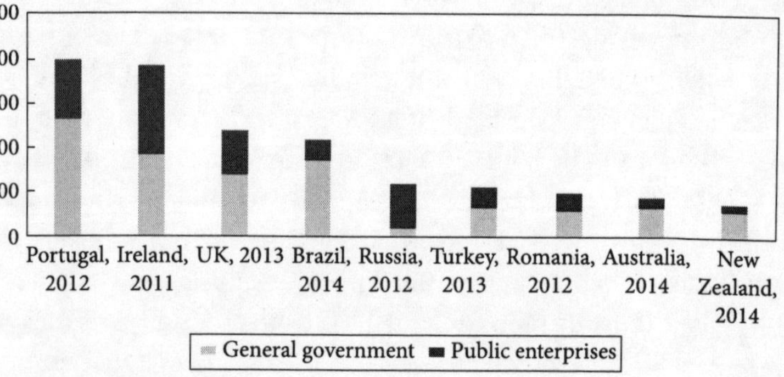

Figure 3.2 Brazilian SOEs' gross liabilities as compared to select countries (as % of GDP)
Source: IMF, 2017.

of loans and the SELIC rate was, on average, –7.6%, which is close to the difference between the TJLP and the SELIC in the same period (–6.7%). Given the subsidies embodied in its loan operations, BNDES actually incurred losses, paying around 7.6 cents per each dollar loaned (Musacchio and Lazzarini, 2014).

In providing credit, BNDES has targeted large, established firms that would be able to borrow elsewhere using private and foreign sources of capital. Although there are growing credit lines to small firms, large corporations still represent a large portion of BNDES' borrowers. Therefore, misallocation entails from its focus on extending credit to firms that are not necessarily financially constrained (Cull, Li, Sun, and Xu, 2015).

A related potential problem is the effect BNDES has had on the private credit market. As BNDES has been, by far, the most important source of credit with long maturity and its key borrowers have been large, established firms. Consequently, private banks have been reluctant to provide long-term credit as they are left with higher-risk borrowers. In other words, BNDES as a lender to large firms has 'crowded out' the development of a private market for long-term credit.

Since 2007, BNDES has aided in industrial consolidation through debt and equity to acquire competitors and to compete in international markets. However, the criteria used to select these firms are not clear (Musacchio and Lazzarini, 2014).

The recent case of JBS, one of the Brazil's biggest multinationals, has demonstrated the system of political patronage, endemic corruption, and corporate favouritism, with BNDES at the heart of that problem. JBS has been one of the principal beneficiaries of subsidized public loans. JBS, founded as a small butcher in the 1950s, boomed during the 13-year rule of the Workers' party, or PT. Starting in 2007, BNDES invested R$8 billion in JBS equity, accumulating a 21.3% stake. It also lent directly and indirectly nearly R$4 billion in subsidized loans to the group. Revenue at JBS grew from R$4 billion in 2007 to R$170 billion in 2016. The company diversified into unrelated businesses, like pulp and paper and plastic flip flops. Investigations into JBS have implicated many of the political elite, dismantling the corrupt nexus between government and big business (Leahy and Schipani, 2017).

In light of the corruption cases, Brazil introduced the SOEs' Governance Law in 2016. Among other governance rules, it has established requirements of transparency in how SOEs conduct their business. These requirements are similar to those that the Brazilian Securities and Exchange Commission (Comissão de Valores Mobiliários, or CVM) applies to publicly-held companies. It also seeks to disengage the management of SOEs from party politics by constraining campaign expenditure (during election years) of federal government offices to which any given SOE is linked (CFA Society Brazil, 2016).

As the Brazilian economy grows, BNDES' capacity to remain the single financier of long-term investments will be constrained. BNDES should therefore focus on supporting market-based financing by crowding in private sector intermediation. BNDES should also move away from direct financing of large corporations with market access towards developing the long-term corporate debt market (IMF, 2012).

Performance of SOEs and their corporate governance

The State minority model which is prevalent in Brazil arose during privatization when equity purchases by BNDESPAR facilitated an indirect state ownership of corporations. BNDESPAR acquired minority equity positions in a variety of public and private firms such that, by 2004, the market value of BNDES' equity participations totalled US$13.5 billion. By 2013, BNDESPAR's holdings were valued at US$53.4 billion (Inoue, Lazzarini, and Musacchio, 2013).

In 2018, the government held more than 5% of the voting shares in 4 out of the top 5 and in 11 out of the top 20 Brazilian MNEs (ranked according to the value of foreign assets), both directly and indirectly through BNDES and pension funds of SOEs (Sheng and Carrera Junior, 2018b). The State minority model has allowed partial mitigation of the negative effects present in majority SOEs and has allowed financially constrained firms to undertake long-term strategic projects by benefitting from government resources and political assistance (Inoue, Lazzarini, and Musacchio, 2013).

A study of 367 non-financial Brazilian listed companies between 1995 and 2009 found a positive effect of minority ownership, through BNDES, on firms' financial performance (measured by RoA) and on capital expenditures of financially constrained firms with investment opportunities (Inoue, Lazzarini, and Musacchio, 2013). There was a positive relation between both direct and indirect state ownership and financial performance (measured by RoA and RoE) in publicly listed MNEs during 2000–2015 as well (de Alcântara et al., 2017).

However, the positive effect on performance is balanced out, when firms in which BNDES holds equity are associated with business groups, especially State-owned and private–domestic groups. The negative correlation is particularly strong in the case of State-owned groups, in which internal allocations may be driven by reasons other than efficiency.

These results thus suggest that a development bank's minority stakes can positively affect performance to the extent that they are able to promote long-term investments and are shielded from governmental interference and potential minority shareholder expropriation (Inoue, Lazzarini, and Musacchio, 2013).

During the global financial crisis, majority held SOEs underperformed the most (Carrera Jr, 2018). These results are consistent with the view that majority and fully owned SOEs underperform when they need to respond quickly to pressures from their external environment, since the problems of 'liabilities of stateness' disturb corporate reorganization initiatives (Lazzarini and Musacchio, 2015). In the case of firms with minority state ownership, their performance compared to large private companies and majority held SOEs was better due to the existence of profit-oriented shareholders (Carrera Jr, 2018).

Given the importance of large SOEs, the problem of 'too-big-to-fail' has persisted. It has not allowed SOEs to be insulated from political intervention. Petrobrás was burdened with excessive exploration commitments off the coasts of Sao Paulo and Rio de Janeiro. This increased the amount of investment that the company required to fulfil these commitments, overstretched the finances of this oil giant, and opened up more opportunities for corruption and political intervention. In 2010, Petrobrás needed a capital injection of nearly US$50 billion to pursue the exploration projects that the Brazilian government had requested.

The company issued a mix of debt and equity (to keep debt/equity ratios from increasing further). However, the government negotiated directly with Petrobrás without including minority shareholders. They exchanged exploration rights for new equity. The price at which exploration rights were negotiated was convenient for the government and the voting power of minority shareholders was diluted with the deal. Thus, having access to the government as an investor of last resort has created an implicit contract in which governments take for granted their ability to extract resources from SOEs at their discretion (i.e. governments can force SOEs to undertake quasi-fiscal operations) (Musacchio and Pineda, 2019).

According to the 'SOE Act' of 2016, the members of the Board of Directors of SOEs and the nominees for executive positions, including directors and the president, must be chosen by citizens of unimpeachable reputation and of relevant expertise and experience.

However, in a survey conducted by the Ministry of Planning, out of the 147 SOEs controlled by the central government, 84 did not adapt their statutes to comply with the new legislation until January 2018 (Tomazelli, 2018). The composition of the boards of SOEs has varied significantly, and it is common for the supervising ministry to have the most representatives, other line ministries also have their share of representatives, as does the employee's organization and company executives. Brazil's President appoints the representatives of the public to the SOE board.

In terms of other corporate governance structures, Brazilian law provides for all types of SOEs to be created under private company law rather than having their own statutes. Generally speaking, SOEs that have adopted legal forms of private law are governed by commercial law. This governs their creation procedures, the structure and powers of the board of directors, shareholders' rights, disclosure of financial and non-financial information, and liquidation procedures. Companies listed on national and international stock exchanges are also governed by regulations issued by the relevant securities commissions (World Bank, 2014b).

The Federal Public Administration Act provides that SOEs are subject to the same operating conditions as private sector companies. In Latin America several State-owned oil enterprises, including Petrobrás, have voluntarily changed their organic statutes to promote good corporate governance, establishing standards that exceed the minimum requirements set forth in legislation. Petrobrás has also established an 'Integrated Evaluation System and Internal Oversight Methods', which has created a risk management committee with participation from employees and executives (World Bank, 2014b).

Yet through extensive use of requirements such as sourcing raw materials and equipment from relatively costlier national suppliers, especially in the energy sector, has led to substantial delays and cost overruns in the implementation of large projects like the exploration of the pre-salt oil fields (Musacchio and Pineda, 2019). The enhanced governance measures also failed to prevent the largest corruption scandal involving Petrobrás.

Conflicts that arise in the State's primary role vs its ownership of enterprises

The Brazilian government has increasingly used key SOEs—such as BNDES and Petrobrás—as effective branches for executing national development programmes and policies. Since 2008, these SOEs have been part of several large-scale government programmes, such as the Program for Accelerated Growth (PAC), in which the emphasis has been on infrastructure and civil construction, the Program for Sustained Investment (PSI), in which production, acquisition, and export of capital assets and technological innovation were stimulated.

Cartão BNDES has financed the purchase of and investment in specific products by accredited suppliers by micro, small, and medium enterprises. BNDES has been involved with the financing of sporting events, such as the World Cup in 2014, and the *BNDES ProCopa Turismo* has helped construct a national hotel network.

The quasi-fiscal activities of Petrobrás have included curbing inflation which has resulted in a growing gap between the prices of domestic oil and gas by-products refined by Petrobrás and the prices charged by international oil companies in international markets. The government's policy creates a self-defeating contradiction: sustaining subsidized prices for domestically sold oil and gas by-products results in financial losses to Petrobrás, thus reducing potential revenues that could have been used to fund future investments and promote other public policies.

The OECD has described these subsidies as 'implicit price support for fossil fuel' and has recommended that they be removed in order to promote the use of ethanol (OECD, 2015b). This policy has created further contradictions in the domestic fuel market and for Petrobrás itself, when it came to the production and commercialization of ethanol, whose competitiveness has been undermined by the government control over the price of gasoline.

According to the Sugar Cane Industry Reunion (UNICA), the federal government has promoted 'dumping' in the fuel market as it granted fiscal incentives for gasoline production and set its prices below the production cost, thereby imposing unfair competition on national ethanol production.

The quasi-fiscal activities of Petrobrás have saved the company from any discernible pressure from the federal government to set up basic public services and infrastructure in the communities affected by its activities. There has been growing political pressure on SOEs to take into account their social and environmental obligations. It is understood that there is no underlying government responsibility for covering the cost of environmental and social damage or loss caused by national oil companies in undertaking oil/gas exploration activities.

The quasi-fiscal activities of Petrobrás have also had various pernicious side effects, including imposing significant costs on Petrobrás for suppressing demand for ethanol and reducing incentives for energy efficiency. This has created several economic and political dilemmas characteristic of national oil companies that must deal with environmental and economic issues and, at the same time, serve political interests. In contrast with many of its global peers, Petrobrás has not made any intensive effort to diversify into green energy. In the face of the emerging climate crisis, it has increased its investment in fossil fuels, with plans for a 30% increase in daily oil production by 2024.

Petrobrás is expected to end its effective monopoly over refining in Brazil in 2020 when it sells 50% of its operations in the sector. However, the programme of asset sales has been criticized by environmental activists, who think it is the wrong time for Petrobrás to divest from thermoelectric generation and renewable fuels, such as vegetable oils and ethanol. This divestment strategy does not pay adequate attention to what lies in store for the environment.

Pressure, on the other hand, for more transparency and accountability regarding BNDES' disbursement and investment has been growing in proportion to the bank's portfolio. In light of the negative social and environmental impact of BNDES financed projects demands for clearer objectives and civic responsibility have strengthened. Despite the legal and institutional framework regarding social and environmental protections, BNDES has continued to finance projects that involve high social and environmental risks and costs.

Although recent research has suggested that the State can use its more visible hand, through stakes in SOEs, to implement its environmental policies and to deal with environmental externalities, the example of Petrobrás shows that the role of SOEs has been ambiguous in practice.

Conclusions

The unique features of Brazilian State capitalism include (a) a combination of governmental control over SOEs, with these SOEs being minority shareholders in a large number of supposedly private corporations, and (b) the noticeable exercise of shareholder activism by SCIIs both in private and public companies. There has been a positive relation between both direct and indirect State ownership and financial performance (measured by RoA and RoE) in publicly listed MNEs between 1995 and 2015.

But SOEs have experienced a clear conflict between the social and political objectives of the government as a controlling shareholder, on one hand, and the interests of minority investors, on the other. The prevalence of SCIIs in the Brazilian stock market, as well as the widespread use of shareholder agreements by state actors, has raised the spectre of government intervention even in firms where the government does not directly hold a majority of the voting capital.

Government control over banks has also led to a significant influence of political considerations over firms' decisions. These considerations seem to have systematically influenced the way financial markets allocate resources. Corruption consequently has been a considerable risk for the efficient operation of the banks. The creeping influence of the State and public officials has been responsible for the main public corruption scandals of the last decade.

The government has continued to use key SOEs for executing development programmes and policies. The quasi-fiscal activities of these SOEs have had various side effects, including imposing significant costs on the

SOEs themselves, suppressing demand for alternative competing products, reducing incentives for improving efficiency, and increasing environmental costs. State-owned financial institutions' latest priority has been to encourage Brazilian firms, to adopt a 'global' strategy in order to improve Brazil's balance of payments.

4

Country case study 2: China

Contours of SOEs in China

China's remarkable, unique experience with rapid economic development, sustained at an unprecedented growth rate (averaging 10% annually) over three decades (1978–2007), has resurrected global economic and political debate about the role that SOEs can play in fostering economic and social development with strong public welfare characteristics.

China's SOEs have been crucial to the success of its economic reform and transformation process which started more than three decades ago. That process catapulted China from the status of a low-income economy in 1978 to becoming the world's second largest economy (the largest when measured at PPP exchange rates) by 2018.

China's transformation reveals important links between SOEs, the financial system, and social welfare. SOEs in China are the most capital rich with total net fixed capital of RMB 734 million per firm, which is almost twice as large as the average for foreign-owned firms (RMB 403 million). SOEs are also the second largest contributor to economic activity in China. SOEs record the highest valued added per firm on average (RMB 30.5 million) just ahead of foreign firms (RMB 28.7 million). SOEs employ considerably more workers on average (544 for SOEs compared with 238 and 381 for domestic and foreign firms, respectively). SOEs and entities directly controlled by SOEs accounted for more than 40% of China's non-agricultural GDP by 2011 (Elliott and Zhou, 2013).

At their peak in 1978, when China was still a low-income country, its SOEs produced 78% of total industrial output and employed 60% of the non-farm workforce. Collectively owned enterprises accounted for the rest, with no other type of business enterprise permitted at the time. After the approval of private firms in 1979, the share of output produced by non-state and non-collective enterprises increased rapidly. Although

SOEs continued to expand until 1990, their share in total employment declined gradually over this period as the private sector grew more quickly.

During the 1990s and early 2000s, the rationalization of SOEs and liberalization of the private sector were two key policy priorities underlying China's industrial development. The ownership of small- and mid-sized SOEs was diversified and privatized and loss-making SOEs were encouraged to merge or to go bankrupt.

As a result, the State-owned sector of the economy shrank dramatically. After peaking at over 112 million workers in the mid-1990s, SOE employment began to fall in absolute terms. After twenty-six years of rapid reform, the privatization process slowed down in 2004. Since 2012, however President Xi's strategy has been to place SOEs at the heart of the economy once again. One indication of that choice has been an increase in bank lending to SOEs from 36% in 2010 to 83% in 2016 (Lardy, 2016).

The State sector in China consists of three main components. *First*, there are enterprises fully owned by the State through the State-owned Assets Supervision and Administration Commission (SASAC) of the State Council and by SASACs of provincial, municipal, and county governments. *Second*, there are SOEs that are majority owners of enterprises that are not officially considered SOEs but are effectively controlled by their SOE owners. *Third*, there is a group of entities, owned and controlled indirectly through SOE subsidiaries, based inside and outside of China (Table 4.1) (Szamosszegi and Kyle, 2011).

Centrally owned SOEs include entities managed by the SASAC; State-owned financial institutions supervised by the China Banking Regulatory Commission (CBRC), China Insurance Regulatory Commission (CIRC), and China Securities Regulatory Commission (CSRC); and entities managed by other central government ministries, such as the Ministry of Commerce, Ministry of Education, Ministry of Science and Technology, and others (Szamosszegi and Kyle, 2011).

SASACs are analogous to holding companies. They hold shares of SOEs which were previously held directly by the State. In all, there are approximately 300 SASACs—about 30 provincial SASACs overseeing provincially controlled SOEs, and scores of municipal SASACs supervising local SOEs (Szamosszegi and Kyle, 2011). Figure 4.1 shows the participation of central and provincial SOEs in the Chinese economy.

Table 4.1 Classification of SOEs in China

SOEs	Examples
Central SOEs	Aluminum Corporation of China Limited, China Minmetals Corporation, China nonferrous Metal Mining (Group) Co., Ltd., etc.
Local SOEs	Bailian Group, Jinjiang International Holdings Co., Ltd., etc.
Entities supervised by MoF	China Publishing Group Corp, China Arts and Entertainment group Ltd., China Railway, etc.
Financial institutions controlled by Central Huijin Investment Co. Ltd, an investment company owned by the Chinese government	Industrial and Commercial Bank of China (ICBC), Agricultural Bank of China (ABC), China Construction Bank (CCB), Bank of China (BOC), etc.

Source: Zhang (2019).

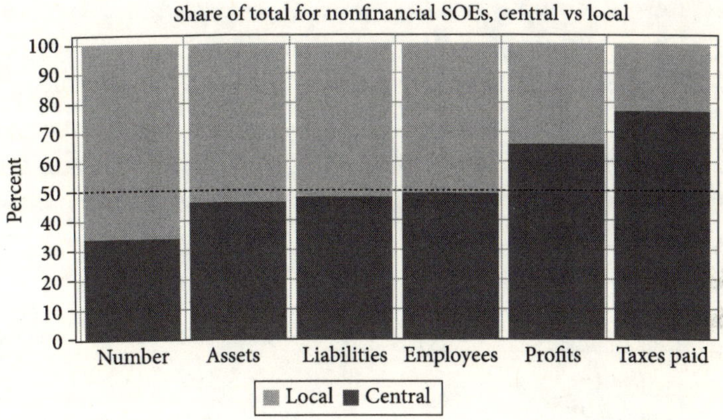

Figure 4.1 Central vs provincial SOEs in Chinese economy (%)
Source: Batson, 2017.

Most SOEs are controlled by local governments, though it is those in the care of the central government that receive the most attention (Cary, 2013). In 2016, the central SASAC controlled 173 SOEs, with $154,914 billion in total assets (Jingrong Lin et al., 2020). Central SOEs control 53% of overall SOE assets. 66% of these 102 companies are now listed on stock exchanges domestically and/or internationally (University of Alberta, China Institute, 2016).

Central SOEs are all large conglomerates which own many second-tier and third-tier SOEs. They have subsidiaries listed on the Shanghai Stock Exchange, the Shenzhen Exchange, or in Hong Kong. Within these central SOEs there are 53 SOEs located at an even higher political position denoted as 'top central SOEs'. The chief executives of top central SOEs are often directly appointed by the Central Organization Department of the Chinese Communist Party and have the political rank of vice minister.

The Central SOEs have been critical to the success of China. All central SOEs have mainly been outcomes of specific government mandates and planning; they determine the business goals of these SOEs. The objective of central SOEs is to contribute to the aggregate growth of China, to the development of the domestic economy, and to enhance peoples' lives. Figure 4.2 shows the contribution made by central SOEs to the Chinese economy.

The top 10 centrally controlled non-financial SOEs are Sinopec Group, China National Petroleum Company (CNPC), State Grid, China Mobile, China State Construction Engineering Company (CSCEC), China National Offshore Oil Corporation (CNOOC), China Railway Construction (CRC), China Railway Group (CRG), Sinochem Group, and China Minmetals. Based on their core business activities, these top 10 SOEs can be classified into six sectors: oil and gas (Sinopec, CNPC,

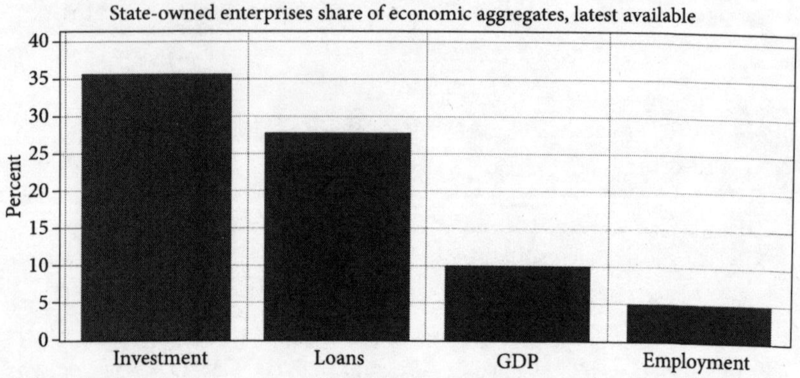

Figure 4.2 Contribution of central SOEs to the Chinese economy (%)
Source: Batson, 2017.

and CNOOC), electricity distribution (State Grid), mobile network operations (China Mobile), construction (CSCEC, CRC, and CRG), chemicals (Sinochem), and resource trade (China Minmetals) (Chen, 2013).

Most of the top 10 SOEs are relatively young in terms of their current corporate structures. SOEs are now increasing their presence in the fast-growing technology and services sectors. Their share in less-strategic sectors is gradually declining, and at a much slower pace than in the pre-2008 period (Batson, 2017). Figure 4.3 shows sector-wise investment of SOEs.

Since the late 1970s a series of economic reforms have been put in place to introduce market principles. The five main stages of reform included management reform (1978–84), the contract responsibility system (CRS) (1984–92), ownership reform (1993–2002), and governance and oversight (2003–12), extensive SOE reform (2012–present).

- In the *first* phase, SOEs' were allowed relative independence in decision-making over their operations. A small number of select SOEs were allowed to keep a proportion of their profits to reinvest and innovate. By 1980 this incentive mechanism was rolled out to include over 6,000 medium and large SOEs.
- In the *second* phase CRS was implemented. CRS was a system in which managers were assigned the operating rights of SOEs by the government through employment contracts. In turn, they paid a predetermined amount of profits to the government and retained excess profits. SOEs were allowed to sell products outside of the State

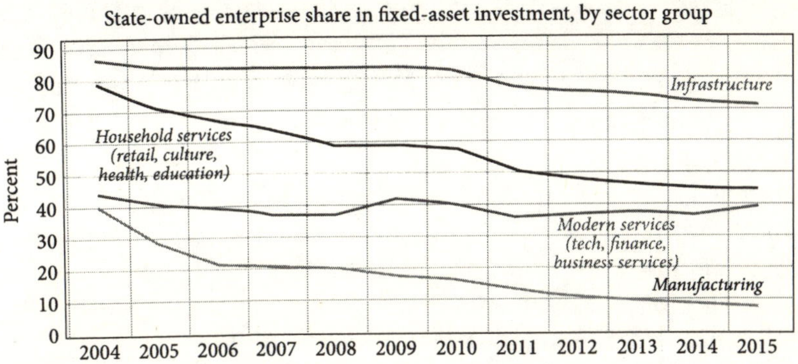

Figure 4.3 Sector-wise SOE investment in China (%)

Source: Batson, 2017.

plan with a premium over the State price of around 20% (known as the Dual Track system). Some hiring responsibilities were accorded directly to the managements of firms. At the end of the second phase formal contractual arrangements between the State and SOEs were introduced.

- In the *third* phase, SOEs were allowed to be sold either to the public or employees and many SOEs were corporatized. The corporatization of SOEs focused on the reform of ownership rights. The establishment of the Shanghai and Shenzhen Stock Exchanges provided platforms for listing and financing SOEs in the capital market. There are more than 1000 SOEs which are listed on both stock markets. The second achievement was the codification of Company Law which came into effect in 1994.
- The *fourth* phase began after 2003, when China's SOE reform entered a stage focusing on the reform of large and important SOEs. In 2003, SASAC was established which aimed to centralize the administration of national-level SOEs and promote mergers and acquisitions among large SOEs.
- The fifth phase began in 2013 after the launch of an increasingly comprehensive and thorough reform of SOEs. The core document guiding the reform, entitled 'Guiding Opinions on Deepening the Reform of State-owned Enterprises', was published in 2015. The idea that SOE reform should be guided by one core policy document (the 'one'), supplemented by supporting policies (the 'N') is called the 'one plus N' (1 + N) policy system. The '1 + N' policy system promotes the reform of SOEs based on their classification as commercial SOEs and public service SOEs and seeks to reorganize central SOEs. SASAC facilitated the merger of 20 central SOEs during the 2012–2018 period (Jingrong Lin et al., 2020).

The importance of Chinese SOEs in the domestic economy has generally diminished, despite the relative dominance of SOEs in several key sectors. According to the 2016 China Statistical Yearbook, the total number of SOEs decreased from 10% to 5% of the total industrial sector from 2005 to 2015. Meanwhile, the proportion of SOEs to total industrial assets decreased from 48.1% to 38.8%, and the contribution of SOEs to total employment fell from 27.2% to 18.2% (University of Alberta, China Institute, 2016).

This coincides with a decline in SOE share of revenue from principal business lines, which dropped from 34.4% to 21.8% in the same ten-year period. Consequently, the share of SOEs in GDP has declined to less than 30%. The 'China 2030' study of the World Bank and the Development Research Center of the State Council envisages a continuation of this trend with the share of SOEs in industrial output dropping further—to around 10% by 2030 (University of Alberta, China Institute, 2016).

The number of SOEs that SASAC now controls reflects the rapid state withdrawal since the 1990s. This was due to a rise in competition that ensued as China implemented market reforms and a fiscal system that put growing budgetary pressures on local governments. Lower margins and smaller market shares meant that less-efficient State enterprises faced increasing financial difficulties, and local governments were forced to subsidize the loss-makers (OECD, 2000).

Hard budget constraints in the context of deteriorating financial performance led to restructuring and privatization but were held back by excess employment, outstanding debt, and ideological pressures (Guo and Yao, 2004). Till the mid-2000s, it was the better performing firms which were restructured because they could compensate their workers that were laid off. The space that was vacated by SOEs was more than filled by private firms which have thrived in the gradual economic transition, despite the many market imperfections and lack of property rights enforcement. China has been a striking example of this paradox.

Since 2010s it has been taken for granted that SOEs should be instruments of government policy. Their mandate to act as growth stabilizers, however, requires them to make investments that deliver low public sector returns while funding themselves at a higher cost of capital (Batson, 2017). The State sector in China will continue to play an important role, even if the State's share of GDP shrinks further.

SASACs have listed a number of industries that are important to China's economic and national security and indicated that these strategic industries (defence, power and grid, petroleum and petrochemicals, telecommunications, coal, civil aviation, and shipping) will remain wholly or largely under the government's control. In the other important so-called pillar industries (autos, information technology, construction, iron and steel, non-ferrous metals, chemicals), the State will remain a major player, with significant, though not majority, ownership (Szamosszegi and Kyle, 2011).

China's latest five-year plan indicates it is pursuing a 'national champion' strategy for certain industries that the government views as important. SOEs appear to be a key enabler in the government's plans to encourage indigenous innovation in China. The current model of State capitalism is likely to remain in place for some time. As such, the Third Plenum confirmed that the public ownership system should remain the 'dominant' characteristic of the economy (Szamosszegi and Kyle, 2011).

The latest development in the Chinese government's 'Go Global' strategy, which began in the mid-1990s, is the proposed 'Belt and Road Initiative' (BRI) announced in 2013. Through enhanced global infrastructure, capacity building, and selected trade and investment arrangements, BRI will link China to Europe, the Middle East, Eurasia, and Africa. Under BRI, China's SOEs were encouraged to 'go abroad' to acquire strategic assets overseas mainly to access key minerals and commodities. Overall, the initiative has been met with interest from both domestic investors looking to expand their businesses abroad and target countries that hope to attract Chinese investment, as well as those that look at Chinese investment sceptically with suspicion (University of Alberta, China Institute, 2016).

Regulation and ownership issues in SOEs

The State is both the controlling shareholder and the regulator of SOEs in China. It is both the judge, jury, and the most powerful player in corporate China. China's system of business regulation has been emerging from the heritage of central planning, under which it was characterized by a very large number of rules formulated and enforced by a wide range of agencies with sometimes overlapping responsibilities; differential treatment of businesses according to their role in the plan; heavy reliance on administrative discretion and limited transparency; and extensive decentralization of regulatory responsibility, leading to wide differences in practices and standards among industries and regions (Wang, 2014).

The regulatory system became further fragmented during much of the reform era as new rules enforced by new or expanded agencies were added. As a result, by the late 1990s, the large costs and uncertainty imposed by the regulatory regime had become a major concern for China's foreign partners—and probably an even greater burden on domestic private businesses.

Competition and market exchange are now well-established features of China's economy. A coherent and efficient regulatory regime that can promote development of the market economy is a priority. China's new competition policy system has adopted many familiar elements of modern competition laws and institutions. But the State has restricted entry (no non-State entry, domestic sector only, or foreign investment through joint ventures) into strategic sectors, thereby enhancing their monopoly status (OECD, 2009).

It has counterbalanced limited competition in strategic sectors by initiatives, such as separation of enterprises from government bureaucracy, corporatization, business restructuring or creation of SOE groups, public listing, and the emergence of competition between SOEs and (sometimes) the non-State sector.

Regional governments have continued protecting local business interests, while some ministries promote national champions. Anti-competitive measures, taken by sub-national governments and enterprises connected with them, have included banning or discouraging foreign products—that is, products from other parts of China—from entering the local market or by preventing local products from being shipped elsewhere. Other measures have ranged from imposing discriminatory fees to fining offending sellers or refusing them licences, in some cases even setting up checkpoints to enforce compliance and to intercept and confiscate shipments and rules requiring use of locally produced inputs (OECD, 2009). Some local governments have conferred competitive advantages on enterprises affiliated with local bureaus or ministries, or have set up entities that combine administrative functions with market operation.

Local governments have sometimes blocked mergers that would dilute the separate identity of local firms or prevented firms from exiting unproductive businesses. By interfering with restructuring to protect local business interests, local governments have undermined the efficiency-promoting goals of reducing excess capacity and realizing economies of scale. These measures, including discrimination in tax treatment, standards, inspections, and licensing, have created significant barriers to competition.

Given the importance of SOEs in the Chinese economy, marketplace distortions that typically accompany State ownership, such as soft budget constraints and opportunities and incentives to confer preferential treatment have been common. SASAC is not only responsible for ownership exercise but also has several regulatory responsibilities. Although the best assurance of competitive neutrality in the treatment of SOEs is to keep antimonopoly enforcement independent of the missions of industrial policy and promotion, complete independence and transparency are difficult to design in China's system of government.

Although regulatory bodies responsible for enforcing competition law are structurally independent from the government, interference by government agencies and government and Party officials in business decisions has been widely prevalent. Regulators in China owe their positions to the political bureaucratic elite. Prospects for the exercise of independent judgements and action are, therefore, limited (Minogue, 2006). Thus, the core ideal of regulation in China rests on the view that economic governance cannot be completely insulated from overriding political considerations (Minogue and Carino, 2006).

China's system of economic governance has faced problems of powerful competing claimants to the authority of regulatory institutions and institutional fragmentation. These have led to inadequate information sharing, incongruities among regulations and standards adopted by the different agencies, widespread shirking, and buck-passing. Regulatory cartelization and capture are rife and manifest themselves in tolerance of counterfeiting by local government officials, lax enforcement of safety regulations, and regulatory forbearance (Mushkat and Mushkat, 2012). The governance regime cannot therefore be considered as strategically focused, tightly managed, and vigorously shielded from undue influences.

All this suggests that, although there has been a normative preference for fostering a more competitive economy, deploying state assets to support state goals is still important. This manifests itself repeatedly in market restructuring designed to avoid 'harmful competition' for SOEs.

China's SOEs in strategic sectors are at the heart of the deregulation-liberalization-reregulation seesaw movement. They are corporatized, distanced from the ministries overseeing them, and undergo a degree of diversification in their ownership (Mushkat and Mushkat, 2012). At the same time, parallel steps are taken to bolster central authority and tighten supervision of such firms and sectors. China's regulatory system exhibits such interventionist neo-mercantilism because it considers this to be the 'best' course of action for the country to follow in prevailing politico-economic circumstances. Therefore, the regulatory system has been more a transitional arrangement rather than a deeply entrenched system.

Avoiding competition for strategic SOEs involves several entry barriers for foreign service providers, for example, restrictions on their ownership form; ceilings on the maximum share they may own in a domestic firm; restrictions on their geographic scope of operations and lines of business; and other requirements, such as minimum capital requirements. These restrictions, however, have been substantially relaxed since China's entry into the WTO. But competition remains curtailed between State-owned and non-State parts of certain sectors, especially in 'strategic' industries and utilities (OECD, 2009).

Large SOEs dominate certain activities not because they are competitive enough to retain dominance but because market competition is restricted and they are granted oligopolistic status by the State (Lin 2010). SOEs have been favoured for government procurement as well. Given that many government-funded projects are large in nature, in many cases only SOEs are large enough to participate. Lack of transparency, technical barriers, in particular technical regulations (indigenous innovation legislation), and domestic content requirements restrain competition in the procurement market.

SOEs that raise capital in international capital markets continue to benefit from a number of subsidies and other forms of preferential treatment. The Chinese government has long used lower tax rates to reward firms for undertaking investments. Another form of benefit conferred upon SOE subsidiaries is the direct transfer of funds through grants or capital injections. Government grants, typically treated as 'other revenue' in the income statements, are not always large. The government has also provided certain SOEs with preferential access to inputs. State-owned banks and the SOE parents provide access to low-cost capital. SOE subsidiaries frequently make significant purchases from and sales to related entities (Szamosszegi and Kyle, 2011).

The government has used cheap credit, selective rule enforcement, and forced consolidation to support SOEs in strategic sectors (Hsueh 2011). Thus, administrative barriers and state's direct and indirect support have precluded significant efficiency-enhancing competition in China and have helped SOEs in maintaining their dominance in sectors shielded by the State.

SOEs were partially divested to non-state interests through minority shareholding, but lack of proper institutional framework of checks and balances has compounded insider control problems. Reorientation of China's SOEs towards becoming more market oriented would have entailed reducing the State's involvement to passive minority ownership. As that has failed to happen, China's SOEs continue to operate in a corporate governance vacuum, with managers and other insiders exercising *de facto* control over the enterprises, at the detriment of outside investors (Yu, 2013).

Communist Party officials, government bureaucrats, and crony capitalism

The institutional foundations of China's extraordinary growth from 1990 to 2010 lie in what is now referred to as 'Crony Capitalism with Chinese Characteristics'. Crony capitalism is pervasive in many countries with weak formal institutions. Yet, it is relatively new in China. The communist party's nationwide campaign in the 1950s against capitalism and corruption exhibited the party's zero tolerance for rent-seeking.

Anti-business sentiment continued to grow during the 'Cultural Revolution' from 1966 to 1976. But the Party has subsequently moved away from that intensely ideological agenda, with change being driven primarily by party cadres at the grass-roots, aiming to increase the wealth of local cohorts (and themselves). The top leadership's focus on rapid economic development provided the justification for party cadres to drive economic activity, from which they benefited personally. Many party cadres reaped substantial economic benefits from the rise of private business in rural China in the 1980s and the first wave of privatization in the mid-1990s (Bai et al., 2014).

Gains from promoting their local economy ranged from direct economic returns from legal or grey channels to materializing political ambitions (Jia, Kudamatsu, and Seim, 2014). The emergence of regional competition was a key factor in fostering new institutional arrangements by local officials to promote economic growth. Since then the relationship between the government and firms has evolved considerably. In the past local governments often directly intervened in firms' internal affairs, especially in SOEs. When SOEs were privatized, government–firm relationships were extended into the private sector.

The long-term symbiotic relationship has evolved into informal, implicit collusion between governments and firms (Zhou et al., 2014). In exchange for political protection and support, firms provide resources for and invest in public projects developed by their local governments.

The Chinese central government controls strategic economic resources as well as the high-level administrative capacity. While this power is often used by the central government to develop its own SOEs, the actions taken by local governments over the last two decades focus on their empowered role in regulating entrepreneurship both to increase their fiscal revenue and personal gain.

The Chinese central government oversees a vast patronage system that secures the loyalty of supporters and allocates privileges to favoured groups. Corporate reforms since the late 1990s—designed to turn wholly State-owned firms into shareholding companies—have not made a dent in patronage. The domination of the Party and the State's economic control[1] has bred a virulent form of crony capitalism, as the ruling elites convert their political power into economic wealth and privilege at the

1 Chinese SOE's are controlled by powerful political families. Most senior executives are screened for loyalty by the Central Organization Department of the Party. The Economist reported that in early 2012, 17 prominent Chinese political leaders were at one time senior executives in large SOEs, and 27 prominent business leaders were serving on the Party's Central Committee. The party appoints 81 % of the chief executives of SOEs and 56 % of all senior corporate executives. In large- and medium-sized SOEs (ostensibly converted into shareholding companies, some of which are even traded on overseas stock markets), the Communist Party secretaries and the chairmen of the board were the same person about half the time. In 70 % of the 6,275 large- and medium-sized SOEs classified as 'corporatized' by 2001, the members of the party committee were members of the board of directors, while 5.3 million party officials—about 8 % of its total membership and 16 % of its urban members—held executive positions in SOEs in 2003.

expense of equity and efficiency. The State's economic dominance preserves systemic inefficiency as scarce resources are funnelled to local elites (Pei, 2009).

Market reforms led to substantial regulatory power being delegated from the central government to local governments but without a robust legal framework. Private entrepreneurs face constant risks of expropriation and discrimination and legal recourse to protect their property is limited. Local governments have been empowered to make discretionary decisions on a wide range of issues, like freedom from formal regulatory frameworks, informal levies, intellectual property rights protection, and the use of local resources.

The variety of taxes and fees extorted by various levels of the local governments from private enterprises is high (Li, Zhang and Meng, 2006). For instance, fees can be charged in the name of administering businesses, to support associations set up by the government of which membership is mandatory, and so forth.

A survey done by the Chinese Academy of Social Sciences in 2003 found that 70% of the profits of private enterprises went towards paying fees imposed on them by local authorities and the high transaction costs arising from 'red tape'. It has therefore become imperative that entrepreneurs continue to maintain intricate networks of mutual obligations with local power holders for survival and growth.

Political connections have served as a substitute for missing or weak property rights. Entrepreneurs typically depend on connections inherited from their family's political capital, past, and current connections with government, party, and SOEs (when government/Party officials or senior managers in SOEs set up his/her business)[2] (Chi et al., 2019).

Over 80% of the private entrepreneurs have reported that they have at least one 'friend' who is a government and/or Party official (Kung and Ma, 2016). They embed themselves within various government institutions, such as the Party, national or local people's congresses and political consultative committees, and state-sponsored NGOs, like business associations, to maintain and strengthen their links with public officials.

[2] Significant numbers of Chinese private entrepreneurs are former government officials (19%) and a majority of them previously managed or worked for SOEs (51%).

The special relationship with political leadership has allowed them to either break formal rules or obtain exclusive access to resources (Taplin, 2019). The support that entrepreneurs have obtained ranges from exercising political power to lobbying the central government for the right to break the rules, to utilizing economic resources to strike special deals, obtaining cheap credit, improving infrastructure, blocking competitive entry by new firms that may threaten the profits of cronies, and offering land below market prices.

Party leaders at central and local levels also have the power and the incentive to reduce day-to-day frictions with officialdom for their cronies. Local officials have influenced the growth of private entrepreneurship not only as a referee but also as active players in market activities. A large number of local officials in positions of authority have their own private companies registered under the name of family members.

Politically connected enterprises have been successful in obtaining bank loans and enjoy a higher profitability, which suggests that political connections contribute to enterprise growth by helping these enterprises overcome the property rights obstacles and/or obtain business favours. Therefore, politically connected enterprises are both larger and have grown faster than their non-connected counterparts (Kung and Ma, 2016). The private economy has therefore benefitted from social networks that have converted power to wealth.

The economy has expanded dramatically and hence the set of cronies. Tens of thousands of firms, supported by empowered leaders, enter, survive, and many of them excel without major institutional improvement. Local leaders have derived higher private benefits associated with the success of their cronies as compared to their counterparts in the central government (Bai et al., 2014).

This explains why local governments, rather than the central government, have played a central role in China's growth. Supporting private firms have offered higher returns to political leadership as compared to SOEs, but leaders have had to make extra efforts to get around policies and regulations discriminating against private firms.

But there are checks on the power of crony capitalism in China from market competition, both global and inter-regional. Career incentives in the Party hierarchy that put considerable weight on aggregate economic performance, and on generating fiscal revenue for the local area, have put limits on rent extraction by entrenched local public officials (Bardhan).

Individual entrepreneurs may have a 'clientele' relationship with the State, but the State is now sufficiently enmeshed in a profit-oriented system that has been identified with legitimacy-enhancing, international economic prowess and nationalist glory (Denizer et al., 2011).

The Chinese economy is largely dualistic in a vertical economic structure, with the State deriving profits and political rent from its monopolistic control in the upstream sectors ('the commanding heights') that provide capital and inputs and services to the successful downstream largely private (including joint venture) or hybrid sectors (Li-Liu-Wang, 2012). So, the government is not inclined to kill the latter sectors that support the former.

Crony capitalism has undoubtedly brought huge benefits to entrepreneurs in China who could hardly exist otherwise. Crony capitalism with Chinese characteristics has also meant that although each of the local governments protect its cronies by mobilizing local resources, it cannot stop other local governments from supporting their own firms that may produce better products.

Competition between local governments have played a central role in allowing new firms to emerge and challenge incumbent firms (Bai et al., 2014). This has ameliorated to some extent the negative dynamic consequences of crony capitalism. But this support comes at the cost of other unattached firms.

The private agenda of public officials

Economic theory and practice have both propagated the belief that the inherent tendency of a typical developing state or government is to resist, or proceed very slowly with, market-based reform and economic liberalization. But market reform in China has produced a contrary phenomenon. Mid- and lower-level officials within the Chinese bureaucracy have embraced markets enthusiastically by facilitating business in a manner that was unanticipated in earlier dominant thinking on market reform.

The transition orthodoxy in the late 1980s and early 1990s had ridiculed the possibility that a 'gerontocratic', 'hard line' communist bureaucracy might possess the skills to successfully lead a transition from a command control economy to a market economy. China's experience shows that, when personal incentives are conducive, mid- and lower-level officials do not always aim at maintaining the status quo. Instead, for personal reasons, they develop strong career interests in accepting, facilitating and promoting change (Nolan and Wang, 1999).

China on its long, slow path of institutional and technical reconstruction has bequeathed a large and significant role to local public officials. Its bureaucrats may not have had individual ownership stakes in China's large SOEs. But it was the bureaucracy (local and national), which restructured state industry, by withdrawing the State from downstream sectors, including light and processing industries.

The bureaucracy consequently concentrated SOE focus on upstream sectors, including natural monopolies and capital-intensive industries. They expanded the operating and financial autonomy of large SOEs' through careful, persistent, institutional experimentation, by mobilizing resources that the market would have been unable to organize. A principal reason as to why China's large SOEs have grown so powerful is that bureaucrats have been proactive in sectors where China's emerging big businesses needed help. This ensured that different levels of government secured revenue streams and resources that they could use for patronage and reinforce their control.

Bureaucratic norms changed during the reform period. While legal boundaries and civil service rules on bureaucratic behaviour have remained ambiguous and unclear, the earlier sole emphasis on political loyalty has been replaced by demand for younger, better educated, able officials, who demonstrate adaptability, flexibility, and dynamism in the new market environment. The process of changing bureaucratic behaviour has also been influenced by generational change in the bureaucracy, with younger officials being encouraged to adopt more readily a dynamic pro-market style of work.

These normative and generational changes have transformed bureaucratic behaviour and led officials to adopt entrepreneurial strategies. Local bureaucrats also had strong incentives to employ, dynamic, profit-seeking managers who could make money for the whole community. The reform drive persuaded officials at every level that continued 'marketization' of the economy was inevitable; so their adaptation became necessary.

Given their access to state resources and business contacts, the lack of clarity on bureaucratic activities, their discretionary power given weak property rights,[3] officials saw revenues from successful businesses as a means of relieving their own financial constraints. Tax income from businesses was used to raise salaries and refurbish offices in local departments. By improving overall working conditions for the bureaucracy as a whole in this way, a measure of legitimacy and protection from charges of malpractice was acquired (Duckett, 2001).

Public officials also realized that in the absence of effective factor markets, the government will naturally play an influential role in allocating scarce resources. State officials understood the key role they played by determining who gets what and thus created opportunities for themselves to create and extract rent. In addition, the Chinese bureaucracy has been fragmented by conflicting goals and functions between departments, interlocking directorate, and complex vertical vs horizontal responsibilities (Lieberthal 1992; Mertha 2009).

These institutional characteristics and exclusive access to basic factors obliged firms to build broad coalitions. The symbiotic relationship has offered mutual benefits to both bureaucrats and entrepreneurs. But private firms have had to maintain a delicate balance between distance and closeness in their relationships with the government. The two most significant political events in China in the past decades—the removal of Shanghai Party boss Chen Liangyu in September 2006 and that of Chongqing Party boss Bo Xilai in March 2012—point that these relationships have been fraught with perilous consequences.

The Communist Party has exhibited a high degree of tolerance towards private benefits that party cadres as individuals, and the bureaucracy as a whole, obtained from their interactions with businesses. Such benefits were broadly defined and took a variety of forms. Economic benefits

[3] Weak property rights faced by Chinese private enterprises are primarily manifested in policies that systematically discriminate the private enterprises vis-à-vis the SOEs and the 'grabbing hand' of the government in extorting a variety of unregulated taxes and fees from the private enterprises.

ranged from legal income as bonuses to illegal income as bribes, from private consumption (including tuition payment at overseas schools for their children) funded by firms to explicit equity stakes in private business held by family members.

Another popular means by which many private entrepreneurs in China have obtained tax concessions from officials is to provide them and their families with a variety of free entertainment, such as sumptuous banquets, gifts, karaoke, and hosting sports club membership and financing overseas travel (Cai, Fang, and Xu, 2011). The party cadres who were successful in achieving economic development targets were promoted in the political system's hierarchy.

But as marketization has proceeded, the opportunities for high-ranking government officials to use public office for private gain have increased sharply. In particular, 'gradual reform' accommodating the temporal coexistence of planned and market sub-economies has created an environment evolving from petty to high corruption involving not only SOE executives but also Party and state executives and law enforcement agencies.

In the 1980s, the main form of corruption involved rent-seeking exploitation of reforms to open up the command economy. Since the 1990s, bureaucratic control over the sales of state assets, bank loans, tax benefits, awarding of infrastructure projects, regulatory fees, sale of land, appraisal of state assets, arbitration/resolution of business disputes have all created opportunities for illegal profits.

Government officials have been rewarded for delivering or appearing to deliver growth. This incentive structure has fuelled large-scale misallocation of capital to 'image projects' (for example, new factories, shopping malls, and unnecessary infrastructure) that burnish local officials' records and strengthened their chances of promotion within the Party hierarchy (Finn, 2006 and Pei, 2009).

Investigations by various Chinese authorities reveal that 90% of recent Chinese millionaires are family members of high-ranking Communist Party or government officials. They also reveal that, in highly regulated businesses, such as finance, trade, land development, and infrastructure, most key corporate positions are occupied by such family members. This class of 'bureaucratic entrepreneurs' with links to the powers that be has converted their positions of unaccountable authority into unprecedented wealth and power.

SOEs and the misallocation of resources

The output share of SOEs in the Chinese economy has been declining but the State has increased its control over a number of 'strategic' and some 'not so strategic' sectors. Total government investment is about 25% of GDP, roughly half in the public sector and infrastructure, and half in the private sector. State control of capital, land, and resource markets have created substantial rents that have been directed to important infrastructure projects and provision of public goods, thereby facilitating economic transformation and contributing to rapid growth (Chu and Song, 2014).

Data on government and private investment from 1980 to 2011 suggest that government investment in public goods 'crowds in' private investment significantly, while government investment in non-strategic sectors 'crowds out' private investment.

Private investors have faced a complex regulatory system in China, which involves comprehensive licensing of firms' entry, expansion, and diversification plans; forbidding private enterprise to enter certain sectors; and mandatory credit allocation schemes imposed on the banking system. Government competes with private firms for access to factor, product, and capital markets. Therefore, public capital in those sectors crowds out the private capital.

On the other hand, government investment in fields traditionally reserved for the State, such as public goods and infrastructure, has resulted in raising the profitability of private production and thus has had a crowding-in effect on private investment (Xu and Yan, 2014). This suggests that for future growth, the Chinese State should increase public investment and withdraw from sectors in which there is direct competition with the private sector.

The State control of factor markets has created some pernicious side effects which include rent-seeking by both governments and enterprises, thus distorting resource allocation. Distortions in factor markets have often resulted from government intervention to address market failures during the transition from a centrally planned to a market-based economy and have acted as subsidies, helping in raising corporate profits and export competitiveness.

The prices of capital, land, and energy do not reflect the true environmental cost of production, making for a widespread misallocation of resources which has been exacerbated by local authorities' growth-seeking behaviour, as they have competed to offer low-cost or free land, cheap credit, tax concessions, and other subsidies to attract investment (OECD, 2015c).

Since SOEs monopolize a few strategically relevant sectors, the prices of energy, water, and resources are kept artificially low, not just for them, but across the board. This, of course, serves the interests of both Chinese consumers and private enterprises as well, but at the cost of an unnecessary subsidy that compounds overall resource misallocation throughout the economy.

The misallocation of resources has been found to be linked with structural imbalances, such as overcapacity in certain sectors, and significant negative impact on private entrepreneurship, which holds the key to increasing future productivity and China's growth potential (Chu and Song, 2014).

Despite SOEs enjoying substantial product/market protections, SOE productivity has been lower than in foreign and private firms. At the time when SOEs were facing less political pressure to serve as 'iron rice bowls', SOEs benefited from their connections to the State in obtaining cheap capital. During 1978–1998 growth in China's non-agricultural state sector was achieved by mobilizing labour, and not through productivity gains.

Total factor productivity (TFP) in Chinese industrial companies over the period 1998 to 2003 was markedly higher in private firms than SOEs. Overall, using a value-added measure of output, TFP in private firms was twice that in SOEs. SOEs in the industrial sector do not just compare poorly with private firms in terms of productivity; there remains a long tail of enterprises that continue to waste investment and drain financial resources from the economy (Pandey and Dong, 2009).

The gap in TFP between the private sector and the State sector suggests difference not only in productivity levels but also in productivity growth, suggesting that the State-controlled sector not only lags behind the private sector but is also falling increasingly behind as time progresses. Nevertheless, there have been improvements in some parts of the State sector. The absolute (not relative) degree of efficiency has steadily increased between 2004 and 2009 (OECD, 2009).

With larger declines in employment relative to value added, and significant increases in capital intensity, labour productivity growth in SOEs has been faster than in the private sector—5.6% vs 3.6% per year, respectively, from 1999 to 2007. These increases in SOEs' labour productivity corresponded to improvements in the return on assets (RoA) through better allocation and use of capital (OECD, 2010a).

Part of this better performance can be explained by SOEs that have moved to majority shareholding by legal person (LP) and other institutional shareholders. SOEs with this structure have performed significantly better than firms under direct State control (OECD, 2005).

The pattern of improving labour productivity alongside low TFP indicates that SOEs use capital much less efficiently than private firms. If capital were used more efficiently, total investment could fall by 5% of GDP without sacrificing economic growth (Dollar and Wei, 2007).

Increased competition and ongoing SOE governance reforms have led to better capital structures and greater returns. The State sector has moved strongly into profitability with the average RoA of industrial SOEs increasing almost ten-fold from 2.2% in 1998 to 21% in 2007 (OECD, 2010a). Figure 4.4 shows the performance of Chinese SOEs.

Currently, SOEs earn half the level of profits at comparable private firms. Much of the SOE profitability is explained by a relatively small

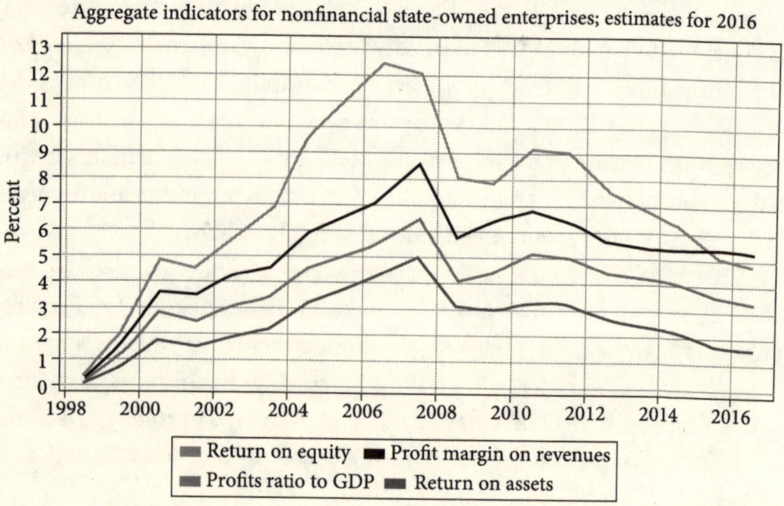

Figure 4.4 SOE performance in China
Source: Batson, 2017.

number of central SOEs operating in resource extraction and processing sectors. These have experienced a period of unprecedented demand that massively boosted commodity prices. With the onset of global recession in 2008, the profits of central SOEs fell by 30%. Since then, the productivity gap between State-owned and private firms has widened. Average RoA for State entities was about 4.6%, compared with 9.1% in private companies, according to estimates by GaveKal Dragonomics. Yet SOEs continue to thrive because of their preferential access to cheap loans from State banks for financing investment (Song, Storesletten and Zilibotti, 2011).

SOEs have handled the post-2008 slowdown poorly, hampered by less pressure to reform and more pressure to spend to support growth. Post-2008, the longstanding gap in profitability between state and private firms in the industrial sector, has widened. The RoA of the State sector has declined to 1.8% in 2015 from its peak of 5% in 2007 (Batson, 2017). Figure 4.5 shows the performance of SOEs in comparison to the private sector.

Before 2008, there was a debate about large SOE profits, which led to a new system for SOEs to pay dividends to the government. Figure 4.6 shows the profits of central SOEs and dividends paid to the government. The result has been that required dividend payments have been ramped

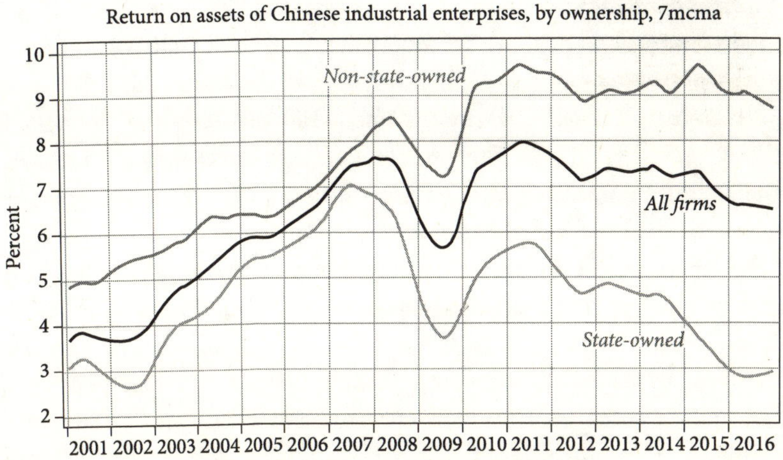

Figure 4.5 RoA of Chinese SOEs and the private sector

Source: Batson, 2017.

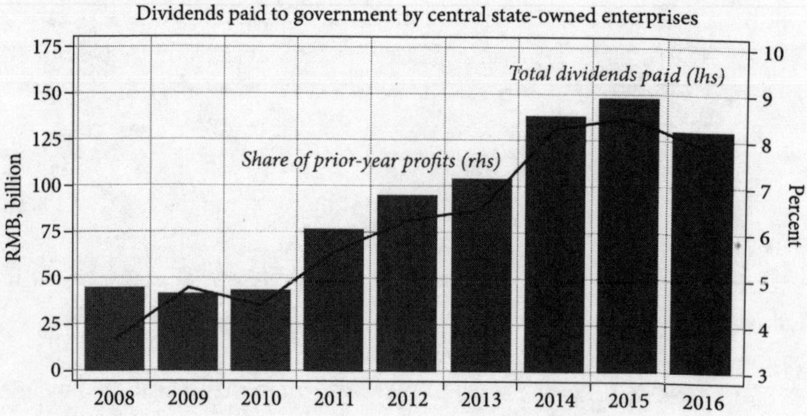

Figure 4.6 Dividends paid to the government by central SOEs
Source: Batson, 2017.

up just as SOE profits worsened. This has left SOEs with fewer retained earnings, increasing their reliance on debt. SOEs have increased the size of their assets, largely funded by debt rather than retained profits (Batson, 2017).

Higher leverage is maintaining the State sector's Return on equity (RoE) from falling further than it already has. Figure 4.7 shows the RoE of Chinese SOEs. Listed company data suggest that about 46% of SOE liabilities are financial debts. This ratio implies that SOEs had RMB 47 trillion in outstanding debt in 2016, equivalent to 63% of GDP. By mid-2018, SOE debt had increased to 82% of the GDP[4] (Molnar and Lu, 2019).

The returns on SOE investments are so low that they may not be able to pay back these debts. This puts pressure on the government to keep interest rates low. It also means many of these SOE debts will eventually have to be nationalized (Batson, 2017).

The high degree of State ownership of financial institutions has been accompanied by a dominant emphasis on bank lending to SOEs, while largely ignoring the non-state sector. With State ownership of financial institutions being dominant, government officials and politicians

[4] According to the latest data release by the State Council, as of end 2017, non-financial SOE debt reached CNY 118.5 trillion, for the first time exceeding 100 trillion in November of the same year. This is an increase of nearly four-fold compared to end-2007. During the same time, SOE assets grew 337%, revenues 159%, and profits 60% (OECD, 2019).

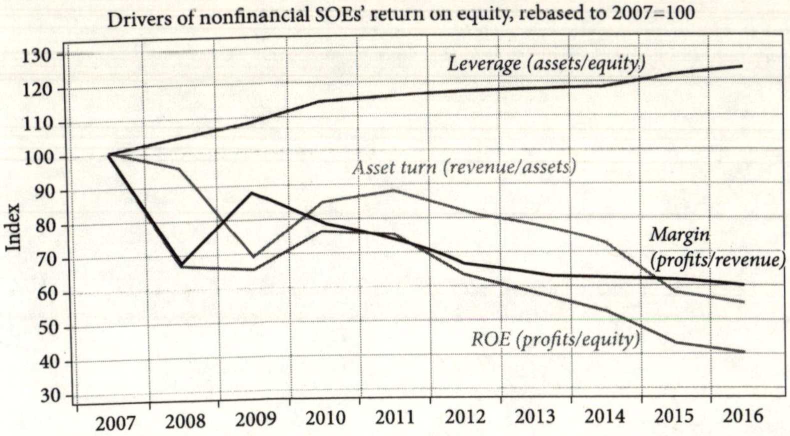

Figure 4.7 RoE of Chinese SOEs
Source: Batson, 2017.

in China have a substantial say in influencing the allocation of financial resources. The four large State-owned Commercial Banks (SOCBs) concentrate particularly heavily on lending to SOEs.

Traditionally, SOCBs have functioned as government agencies whose principal mandate has been to support government's economic and social objectives. Banks' bias in favour of SOEs stems from government policy priorities and implicit government guarantees on the loans made. Close ties between government and bank officials at local level have created a culture that has given local government officials inordinate influence over bank lending decisions.

Consequently, there is widespread and considerable inefficiency in the allocation of credit, as manifest in the high level of non-performing loans (NPLs) as shown in Figure 4.8. The Chinese government has also intervened in the credit market *ex-post* by bailing out troubled SOEs or State-owned banks. Government bailouts take various forms, such as the restructuring of ailing SOEs, the takeover of nonperforming loans, and deliberate delays in the long drawn-out closure of insolvent financial institutions (Lu et al., 2005).

This reflects a traditionally weak credit culture in China. State-owned lending institutions have few incentives and little ability to assess and enforce rigorous credit standards, while State-backed borrowers are often

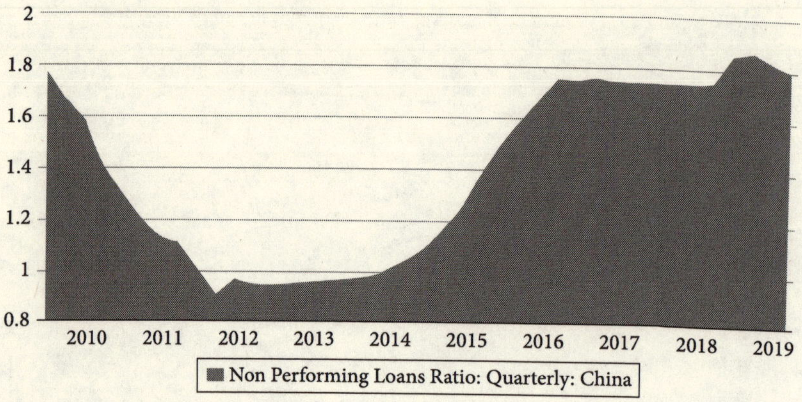

Figure 4.8 China NPL ratio
Source: CEIC Data.

able to avoid repaying their debts. The high level of NPLs has arisen partly because of circumstances beyond the control of the State-owned banks. They include notably the operating and cash-flow problems of many of their SOE customers arising from 'chain-debt' with SOE suppliers not being paid by other SOE customers for goods delivered; outside interference by local governments in bank lending decisions; and the limited legal or other means available to banks to enforce loan agreements.

Weaknesses in State-owned banks' internal loan appraisal and risk management systems, and poor corporate governance, have also been important contributors to the large level of NPLs. Financial discipline has been uneven, with much tougher lending standards being applied to smaller SOEs and non-State enterprises than to large, powerful SOEs (OECD, 2015c).

Official data from the Chinese bank regulator indicates that NPLs have declined over the past decade from over 15% to 1.9% at the end of 2019. These data hide facts, such as 'rollover ever-greening' and rapid credit expansion in China since 2008 with overall credit as a share of GDP rising by almost 80%. It is almost impossible (especially in emerging markets) to distribute so much credit at such a pace in an efficient manner. This is manifest in the percentage of liabilities of listed companies—represented by companies whose cash flow is less than interest expense—which has ranged between 8% and 16% over the past decade.

China's financial system has progressed considerably towards a market rather than fiat driven system since the 1990s. Competition in the banking sector has risen markedly as SOCBs have moved away from their traditional specialization and as joint-stock private banks have emerged. Credit quality has improved significantly. Accounting practices and internal risk management systems have been modernized. Regulatory authorities have taken a number of steps to reduce interference by local governments in the operations of SOCB branches. But, as rapidly as the financial system has evolved, the real economy has been changing even more rapidly (OECD, 2005). The low capital adequacy ratios of Chinese banks and limited loan provisions are inadequate to deal with the high level of NPLs.

In the 1990s, SOEs accounted for only one-third of GDP, but two-thirds of total domestic loans (China Academy of Social Sciences). The World Bank estimated that, between 1991 and 2000, almost a third of investment decisions in China were misguided. The Chinese central bank's research shows that politically directed lending was responsible for 60% of bad bank loans in 2001–02. Chinese economic planners revealed in 2006 that 11 major capital-intensive manufacturing industries were overproducing (Pei, 2006).

Excess capacity has plagued many industries, weighing on profitability and on capital spending in steel, cement, aluminium, flat glass, and electrical and railway equipment. Sectors with excess capacity account for about 10% of total SOE assets (Batson, 2017). The National Development and Reform Commission (NDRC) has long called for avoiding 'blind' investment and redundant construction of steel mills, copper smelters, and electrolytic aluminium producing plants (OECD, 2015c). The excess capacity sectors performed so poorly over 2012–15 that they had a huge impact on total SOE profits.

In 2008, when the central government began its economic stimulus programme, much of it was channelled through State-owned banks. They extended low-interest credit to local governments to support mega-infrastructure projects and to SOEs. Despite official figures showing that private small- and medium-sized enterprises (SMEs) employed 75% of China's workers and produced 68% of gross industrial product in 2008, these private firms have been virtually excluded from preferential access to low interest loans (Nee, 2011). Figure 4.9 shows the cost of capital and return on capital in China.

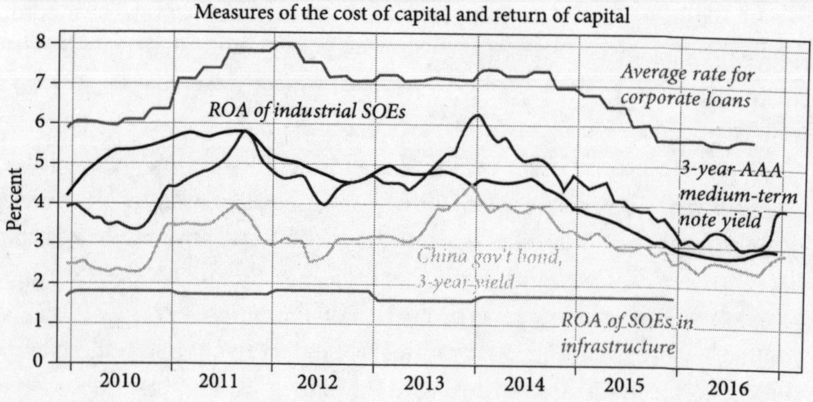

Figure 4.9 Cost of capital and return on capital in China
Source: Batson, 2017.

The financial vulnerability of SOCBs, in the form of bad loans, financial losses, and undercapitalization, endangers both the stability of the economy and the sustainability of growth. Misallocation of capital will become more conspicuous as savings and investment rates decline in the future.

Internal governance and management of SOEs

SOEs in China have come a long way from functioning as an extension of the government to resembling private businesses. But they continue to pursue the twin goals of maximizing profits and contributing to national welfare. The current organizational system of Chinese SOEs is best described as a 'networked hierarchy' that centres on a core holding company, often 100% owned by SASAC (China Economic Review, 2012).

The core company owns stakes and coordinates resources and information for a group of subsidiaries, including any listed entities, as well as a financing arm and related research institutes. SOEs are then linked into the broader 'China Inc' network through a web of joint ventures, strategic alliances, and equity holdings (Lin and Milhaupt, 2013 and China Economic Review, 2012).

Against this backdrop, the four stages of reform (as outlined earlier in the chapter) since the 1970s have allowed SOEs to retain profits and the government gave SOEs responsibility for dealing with their own gains and losses in the market. Furthermore, the reforms introduced incentive contract schemes for managers and workers.

Under the contract responsibility system from the late 1970s, enterprises were required to hand over agreed amounts of profits and taxes to the State, in return for which management was given extensive autonomy and large responsibility for raising investment funds from retained profits, bank loans, and eventually other sources (for example, joint ventures, stock market flotations, bonds) (Nolan and Wang, 1999).

The contract responsibility system played a positive role in guaranteeing the steady growth of government revenue, promoting the separation of enterprise ownership from management, and the separation of government from enterprises. It provided SOE employees with greater autonomy, better incentives, and made SOE development more sustainable. But experience over time has shown that the contract responsibility system also had embedded weaknesses. It failed to avoid short-term performance-oriented behaviour. The basis of these contracts was often arbitrarily decided. It was neither fair nor objective. Contractors shared the gains when enterprises were profitable but were not personally liable when they incurred losses. In other words, profits were privatized, while losses were socialized (OECD, 2011a).

The contract system ended in 1994. It was replaced with a system of joint-stock ownership companies with 'handovers' decided by a combination of dividends from share ownership and a new structure of corporation tax and value-added tax. Although the reform of traditional SOEs in this period significantly reduced the role of governmental intervention in the management of SOEs, the rights and responsibilities of SOE stakeholders and management were ill-defined.

From 1987 to 1992, professional managers were brought into the SOEs, and modern corporate governance was introduced from 1993 to 1998. Over the course of the reform years, the central authorities engineered a gradual decline in resource allocation through the material balance planning system. By the mid-1990s, even in the largest of upstream industries, managers decided all key issues. They needed to co-ordinate input supplies through the market. They were forced to evaluate the capability of different suppliers and had to learn to bargain about price and delivery. They had to decide the product mix and product price. They had to compete for markets. Accountancy, marketing, and legal compliance departments grew rapidly. In large SOEs producing complex engineering products, such as power equipment, product reliability and after-sales service became significant elements in inter-firm competition (Nolan, 2004).

In 1993, a system of Corporate Law was introduced and the internal governance of SOEs was restructured along the lines of a modern corporation. Under the 'modern enterprise system', the largest SOEs were restructured under company law (without their social service liabilities). SOEs had to have a board of directors, as well as a supervisory board if their shares could be bought by non-state shareholders. When the latter bought in, the State retained a one-third direct stake. The remainder was split between 'legal person' shares, indirectly controlled by the State, and individual shares that could be held by management, employees, or outside private investors (Green and Liu, 2005).

For other types of corporations, the law required that they form four governing bodies: (1) shareholders, acting as a body at the general meeting; (2) a board of directors; (3) a board of supervisors; and (4) a CEO (Aivazian, Ge, and Qiu 2005).

By the mid-1990s the joint-stock company in China had once more become a powerful weapon to transcend the limits of previous forms of ownership and operation, in this case the government as the sole owner and operator of SOEs. The introduction of this form of ownership was welcomed by SOEs, partly because of the flexibility provided by the corporate shareholding structure, but more importantly because it gave a separate identity to the secured corporation.

Large SOEs have maintained a leading role throughout the reform process. The central focus of reform of large SOEs has been aimed at enlarging managerial autonomy, in other words towards the 'separation of ownership from management control'. China's planners also supported emerging indigenous large private businesses by enabling them to attract capital and technology transfer from foreign multinational companies. The government was confident that it could control the conditions under which foreign investment occurred because the economy was so large that no individual foreign investor could exercise a large influence on the State.

By opening up to foreign investment, the joint venture signalled further ownership reform. Most joint ventures involving foreign investors were initially small value downstream firms. A smaller number were large investments undertaken jointly with large SOEs. The main purpose of these, from the Chinese side, was to secure technology transfer. From the side of the foreign joint venture partner, it was the lure of investing in China's huge potential market.

In the mid-1990s, the Chinese government allowed selected large SOEs to issue and list shares on foreign stock exchanges. The vast majority of these were in Hong Kong, and a small number in New York. Prior to flotation in foreign markets SOEs went through a process of institutional restructuring to meet listing requirements.

The emergence of the multi-plant firm formed another avenue for the development of independence of managers relative to State owners. The CSRC and the National Economic and Trade Commission jointly issued the *Code of Corporate Governance of Listed Companies* in early 2002. It propounds the basic principles of corporate governance, the means to achieve investor protection, and the basic code of conduct and professional ethics that need to be observed by directors, supervisors, managers, and other executives of listed companies (OECD, 2011b).

There was a process of mergers and acquisitions in China during the early years of 2000s with the State acting as the mediator. The State required large SOEs to absorb and reorganize loss-making enterprises, change their management methods, and upgrade their technology. Large SOEs used their bargaining power with local governments to increase the size of their business empires.

The establishment of SASAC of the State Council in March 2003 marked a milestone in SOE reform. SASAC's main responsibility was to represent the State Council to 'exercise the duties and responsibilities of the State investor'. The creation of SASAC at both the central and local levels was an effort by the Chinese government to consolidate the control rights over SOEs. Before SASAC came into being, the ownership of SOEs within the government was fragmented, with too many bureaucracies, from central ministries to departments of local governments, having control over tens of thousands of SOEs (Wang, 2014).

The *Company Law* and the *Securities Law*, both introduced in 2006, provide the foundation for drawing up and developing a corporate governance framework in China. The revised *Company Law* improved companies' governance structure and mechanisms to protect shareholders' rights and public interest. It highlighted the legal obligations and responsibilities of those in actual control of the company—the directors, senior management, and supervisors. SASAC carried out corporatization reforms of large SOEs and piloted the establishment of boards of directors according to the *Company Law* (OECD, 2011b).

In reality, SOEs in China have a system of corporate governance that features two parallel structures, one for legal governance and the other for political governance. Mechanisms and controls in the legal governance structures stem from the corporate form based on the *Company Law* and other relevant state laws. Political governance is the Party-dominated process that actually controls personnel appointments and decision-making in SOEs (Wang, 2014).

The two structures run separately, although the same group of players participate in the decision-making processes of both structures. In most cases, the informal, non-legal, rules of political governance prevail over legal rules under China's corporate laws.

Although Chinese SOEs are now legally organized in corporate form, featuring all or most of the attributes of the separation of ownership and management, real control has remained vested in the Communist Party. The Party controls SOEs through both general requirements on policy compliance and specific powers, such as appointing the senior executives of SOEs. Top leaders of SOEs (for example, the chairperson and deputy chairperson of the board of directors, and senior corporate executives) are appointed by the Party's organizational departments. Party cells within the SOEs convene meetings to make important decisions for the company and to ensure that the operation of the company is consistent with the Party line (Wang, 2014).

The board of directors and top managers are required to consult and respect the opinion of the Party before making any important decisions, and brief the Party on the implementation. The Party directly controls not only the personnel but also sometimes the operation of SOEs, bypassing the legal governance structure consisting of the board of directors and management (Wang, 2014).

China's SOEs have undergone large changes due to enhanced enterprise autonomy, the impact of market forces, rapid growth of domestic demand for upstream products, strategic integration with the world economy, and the State's policy of promoting large businesses (Nolan, 1999). But various studies have shown that corporatization has not improved efficiency.

Corporatization policy in China has induced SOE insiders to preserve their rents by choosing diffuse outside investors and selecting weak corporate boards (Qian, 1996). The Communist Party has used organizational and financial schemes to keep control over SOE corporate boards and Communist Party secretaries ignore or overrule boards and CEOs (Deng, Morck, Yu, and Yeung, 2011).

In 2014, SASAC implemented a pilot scheme designed to raise efficiency without privatization and to close the widening productivity gap between SOEs and private companies and the even wider disparities in RoA. The plan called for transferring control of state equity to State-owned holding companies that will 'focus more on capital management'. The goal was to reduce political interference in the management of SOEs by designing the holding companies to focus on maximizing shareholder value rather than advancing the government's policy goals (Wildau, 2014).

Some of the largest Chinese SOEs have transferred assets from their unlisted parents into their listed subsidiaries as part of their restructuring. But current restructuring proposals are unlikely by themselves to change the current pattern of State dominance in the economy. The reforms outlined so far suggest that there are no plans to fundamentally restructure SOEs or to curb their monopoly privileges. So far there has been no suggestion that the regulatory protection SOEs enjoy in their main operating sectors—whether aviation, defence, energy, or telecommunications—should be pared back (OECD, 2015c).

Instead, they appear to envisage that State-backed companies will be able to enjoy the benefits of private investment, but without ceding control or opening their markets to more competitors (OECD, 2015d).

The 2015 document guiding another round of comprehensive and thorough reform of SOEs, entitled 'Guiding Opinions on Deepening the Reform of State-owned Enterprises', supported the idea that SOE reform should be guided by one core policy document (the 'one') supplemented by supporting policies (the 'N') called the 'one plus N' (1 + N) policy system. The new policy system promotes the reform of SOEs based on their classification—as commercial SOEs and public service SOEs. The government is at its discretion to allocate resources between different types of SOEs. The new policy system aims at strengthening the leadership of the Party in SOEs and is mandated to incorporate the Party's role into their Articles of Association. The new policy system has reorganized central SOEs and merged 20 central SOEs during the 2012–2018 period. Through these mergers China promoted the competitiveness of SOEs to support the 'One Belt, One Road' initiative and advanced 'supply-side reform' at home (Jingrong Lin et al., 2020).

The reforms in Chinese SOEs have obliged them to adopt strategies conducive to fulfilling administrative tasks or empire building. The political control of SOEs is associated with treatment of the SOEs as favourites. Accordingly, in order to continue receiving government-allocated resources, SOEs have helped fulfil government goals and policies in return, rather than solely focusing on making profits.

Conflicts that arise in the State's primary role vs its ownership of enterprises

As outlined in the previous section, the multiple roles and objectives of Chinese SOEs are to implement and comply with the Party's policies and follow the Party's orders in order to improve macroeconomic management and to safeguard the country's 'economic security'.

This is broadly defined as controlling strategic sectors affecting state security; enhancing the basic well-being and prosperity of the Chinese people through transfer of profits; and undertaking 'significant special tasks' in China's economic and social development. This evolution in the role of SOEs has been a significant shift from the command economy and the ideological hostility to the market that prevailed in the pre-reform era.

Given the long history of SOEs and the enormous social responsibilities imposed on them, China took a gradual approach to reduce the scope of state intervention since the late 1970s. By the early 1980s, the view that the market was not incompatible with socialism had become widely accepted. To increase efficiency and economic output and to focus on macroeconomic stability, reformers found it imperative to enlarge the role of the market and weaken state intervention (Fan and Hope, 2014).

In 1987 the Party's Thirteenth Congress defined the Chinese economy as one in which 'the State regulates the market, and the market guides firms'. By the early 1990s the concept of market had become fully legitimized in China. The gradual legitimatization of the market profoundly changed the mode of resource allocation.

After a 'socialist market economy' was declared the ideal in 1992, the discourse changed in determining relations between the State and the market. The role of the market no longer needed to be justified, but the sanctity of government intervention was preserved in defining the appropriate role of the State in economic management.

In the mid- and late 1990s, the government realized that the presence of thousands of small SOEs disallowed an efficient state control. It embarked on a policy of 'grasping the large' which resulted in the emergence of State-preferred 'winners'. Since 1999, the government has been exiting industries of lesser national importance.

The remaining SOEs have been consolidating. The State directed and protected the largest SOEs to create ventures able to exploit economies of scale and form vertically integrated systems of production, while encouraging smaller firms to reorganize as component suppliers. The State highlighted the need to withdraw from controlling the less successful SOEs to reduce the fiscal strain (of subsidizing small SOEs) and focus on core activities in the commanding heights.

The State's withdrawal from less important industries has facilitated it to invest in new and fast-growing tech sector. For example, the launch of China's new technology-focused stock market in 2019 has underlined the importance of state funding. Of the first 25 companies listed on Shanghai's Star board, 14 report State-owned investors among their top-three shareholders (Hancock and Xueqiao, 2019).

It focused on building successful State firms in the commanding heights by providing significant support to SOEs in industries that it considered to be the 'backbone' of industrial manufacturing. SOEs in the commanding heights were prevented from going bankrupt. The State believed that ensuring growth in the State sector, especially the largest enterprises, was important for the entire Chinese economy.

It therefore redefined its mechanisms of economic control, by maintaining control of the banking industry to ensure that credit was directed towards supporting the prominent SOEs. The State negotiated contracts for the large with suppliers of high-quality materials, especially other core SOEs, to ensure high-quality and value-added production.

As the next logical step, China orientated the largest SOEs towards export markets. This was partly due to the pressure from overseas multinational corporations seeking market share in China. This competition encouraged the government to push key SOEs to 'Go Global' (Dickie, 2005). The large SOEs were restructured around this policy to turn them into global companies.

The Chinese State utilized joint ventures with foreign enterprises to achieve technological catch-up for its large SOEs. The exporting SOEs' TFP was higher than even foreign exporters[5] by 2013 (Elliott and Zhao, 2013). China's large SOEs have therefore thrived under the State's policy to promote large businesses as part of a wider policy of strategic integration with the world economy.

The gradual withdrawal of the State in China and the replacement of state bureaucratic allocation by market coordination was justified by pragmatic as well as ideological reasoning. It provided the space for dynamic and competitive private enterprises to emerge, survive, and grow. The State clearly understood the futility of doing more and more but doing it less and less well. The continued, exceptional growth of the large SOEs in the commanding heights has contributed remarkably to the growth of the private market and must be accounted for in any explanation of the Chinese experience (Sutherland, 2003). In addition to the important role played by Chinese SOEs in employment, the country has witnessed substantial growth in Corporate Social Responsibility (CSR)-related activities (Zhang et al., 2010), as the Chinese government has strongly promoted the concept of CSR and encouraged corporations to actively engage in socially responsible activities, including environmental protection and corporate philanthropic giving. Corporate philanthropic giving in China has grown rapidly. According to statistics, philanthropic

[5] Higher productivity of exporting SOEs could also be a result of increased competition from the exposure to international markets. If SOEs export to high income countries, whilst others export primarily to developing countries, then the higher levels of competition from exposure to high income country markets will force SOEs to improve their productivity levels (Elliot, 2013).

donations from China's listed companies in 2017 totalled about RMB7.2 billion (about US$1 billion), up 14.71% from the previous year, of which RMB3,776 billion came from SOEs. The total contributions of SOEs in 2017 represented 2.49% of their total assets (RMB151,711 billion in 2017) (Jingrong Lin et al., 2020).

Conclusions

The State has defended its proactive role by providing not only the capital-intensive investments needed by the private sector to grow but also in creating an entrepreneurial role for itself with a bold vision and targeted investment. It has successfully envisaged the risk space in the international markets and has operated effectively within it to facilitate the entry of Chinese private companies.

This has amplified the importance of key large SOEs in Chinese growth. In acting as a force for change in China during its transition, the State has done what Keynes in *The End of Laissez Faire* (1926) argued for 'the important thing for Government is not to do things which individuals are doing already, and to do them a little better or a little worse; but to do those things which at present are not done at all'.

Yet the large presence of firms which have survived through their political connections especially to local government interests now poses a threat to the State becoming beholden to local interests. It also runs the risk of becoming a poor imitator of private sector behaviours, because the State is unwilling to curb the monopoly privileges given to some SOEs, thus creating entrenched vested interests in continuing State ownership.

Today, deficiencies in China's market infrastructure continue to prevent the government from fully allowing free market forces to run the economy. The government will continue, therefore, to have an important role to play in resolving these transition problems in China's development.

In the coming years the biggest challenge for China will be in dealing with SOEs with high leverage. SOEs had an outstanding debt equivalent to 82% of GDP in 2018. However, the returns on SOE investments are low which will make it difficult for SOEs to repay these debts.

5

Country case study 3: India

The origins, emergence, and significance of SOEs in India

At independence in 1947, India had a weak bourgeoisie, limited domestic savings, a tiny capital market, a small banking sector, and limited private entrepreneurship that had been deliberately suppressed for nearly two centuries. It was emerging as a sovereign country in a global economy that had been disrupted since 1914 by two debilitating world wars. The law-and-rules-based, multilateral world order that prevailed for the next seventy plus years had only just begun to take shape.

In those circumstances, the early intellectual consensus in newly independent India (forged by Mahalanobis and Nehru, both of whom were bedazzled by the experience of the Soviet Union from 1920–47) was that the nascent nation state should induce economic development through rapid industrialization under a State-driven planning process (Chattopadhyay, 1987).

So, the Government of India (GoI) launched its first five-year plan (1951–55), modelled on the USSR, with emphasis on fiscal measures to raise resources for industrial investment through public planning. Consequently, the State sector became the driver of economic growth in the Indian economy. It was the Industrial Policy Resolution (of 1956) that reserved the commanding heights of the economy for SOEs. The private sector was allowed to play a limited role and private property was protected by the Constitution. But the areas open to private entrepreneurs for investment were limited. The key role assigned to SOEs in early industrialization strategy was to help India achieve economic self-reliance (Khanna, 2012).

Since 1947, enterprises in public utilities and infrastructure, including the railways, ports, airports, and telecommunication, and power units had largely been in the public sector. The Industrial Policy Resolution earmarked several basic and capital good sectors exclusively for the public sector. During the Second Five-Year Plan, which coincided with the announcement of the Industrial Policy of 1956, new SOEs were established in several core and basic industries. Enterprises producing steel, heavy engineering, fertilizer, electricity generation equipment, machine tools, etc., were set up (Khanna, 2012), several of them with technological and financial assistance from the Soviet Union and other Eastern European countries.

Subsequently, in the late 1960s and 1970s, the government nationalized the coal industry, large commercial banks, and all insurance companies. It also took over several firms in the private sector that were facing bankruptcy and had closed down or were on the verge of closure.

From the Second Five-Year Plan onwards, the State sector has accounted for about 45–50% of gross capital formation. From independence until the early 1980s, the private sector accounted for about 20% of total capital formation (less than 3% of GDP). Until a decade ago, the household sector (including medium and small enterprises, largely in the unorganized sector) accounted for 30–40% of total Indian capital formation.

After the epochal 1991 liberalization, the State sector's contribution to India's mixed economy has remained significant; indeed, it remains crucial in key sectors. Liberalization did not result in a large reduction in SOEs' contribution to GDP nor to State sector employment outside the central bureaucracy. Privatization has been slow and patchy. Between 1991 and 2008 the central government divested its majority ownership in only 14 SOEs, mostly hotels (Chatterjee, 2017).

Especially striking is the resilient longevity of SOEs that are majority owned and controlled by the central government—even after decades of criticism from domestic and foreign observers for being inefficient, and for benign neglect by several administrations. SOEs have continued to play a significant role in the Indian economy by transforming themselves despite the twin pressures of growing competition and criticism.

Central SOEs: Since independence, the number of CPSEs (Central public sector enterprises established by the federal government) in India has grown manifold. In 1951, India had only five SOEs with a total investment of just Rs. 290 million. These grew to 339 SOEs (out of which 257 were operational) with Rs. 13,734.12 billion in investments in 2018 (Dun

Table 5.1 Key indicators of CPSEs

	2017–18	Year to year growth %
Employment (excluding contract workers)	1,08 million	
Contribution to the Treasury	Rs. 3.5 trillion	−3.0
Foreign exchange earnings of CPSEs	Rs. 869.8 billion	−1.0
Total assets	Rs. 19.8 trillion	12.0
Financial Investment in CPSEs	Rs. 13.7 trillion	10.0
Dividends from CPSEs	Rs. 765.7 billion	−2.0
CSR expenditure by CPSEs	Rs. 34.4 billion	3.0

Source: Dun and Bradstreet India's Top PSU 2019.

and Bradstreet, 2019). Concomitantly, employment within CSOEs shot up from 0.7 million in 1971–72 to 1.94 million a decade later, peaking in 1990 at 2.24 million (Chandra and Chatterjee, 2019). In 2018, SOEs employed 1.08 million full-time employees (see Table 5.1).

CPSEs listed on India's bourses, contributed 41% of aggregate combined public and private Indian corporate profits in 2011 (measured by profits of the largest 100 listed firms). In 2015, six of India's ten largest firms (by sales or gross revenues) were CPSEs, down from eight in 1982. Energy and infrastructure SOEs have remained important (Chatterjee, 2017). The State has continued to intervene heavily in other sectors as well using its control of credit, land, and natural resources (Chandra and Chatterjee, 2019).

In 2017, there were seven Indian companies in the Global Fortune 500 list. Three were SOEs. Of the total CPSEs, the 8 largest SOEs are called Maharatnas, 16 are Navratnas, and 73 are Miniratnas. About half of them are in manufacturing and mining. The rest are in the main services sectors—transport, telecommunications, financial services, etc.

The federal government has invested in about 400 companies through Life Insurance Corporation[1] (LIC) mostly in minority stakes, which make up about 4% of India's total stock market capitalization. The median investment of LIC was 4% of a company and the mean was 7.4%. The government controls LIC and selects its board and management teams.

[1] Life Insurance Corporation plays the role of a large holding company for the government. It is the largest active stock market investor.

But LIC has remained a passive investor. LIC has been often directed by government to invest in the shares of SOEs, especially when demand for a firm's IPO is low. However, these investments have significantly underperformed the market (Musacchio and Lazzarini, 2014).

State (Provincial) SOEs: Although the most significant SOEs were established by the federal government, a large number of enterprises were established by state (provincial) governments as well (SSOEs), including many in the joint sector where private partners held up to 49% of the shares. A few enterprises were established by municipalities or jointly by provincial and federal governments.

There are now about 838 SSOEs with investment above Rs. 2.7 trillion (compared to only 249 CSOEs with investment of Rs. 9 trillion), their role in the growth story (with the exception of a few states) has been marginal (Khanna, 2012). Two-thirds of the investment of SSOEs is concentrated in electricity generation and distribution, with the rest spread unevenly across manufacturing, finance, transport, and infrastructure (Khanna, 2012). The political economy of electricity pricing, with subsidized or free electricity to farmers and other favoured sections, with no clear budgetary support for these, has undermined SSOEs and their viability.

In 1991, many key sectors of the economy were dominated by mature public enterprises that had successfully expanded production, opened up new areas of technology, and substituted imports in an array of capital goods sectors. Their technical competence enhanced India's ranking in terms of industrialization, with a large pool of trained workers, with technical skills, especially in chemical and manufacturing industries. The share of SOEs in GDP had gone up from 8% in 1959 to 26.1% in 1991 (Nagaraj, 2006).

By 1995, the private corporate sector had overtaken both the public sector as well as the household sector in terms of investment and capital formation. This expansion in the private corporate sector's share has been entirely at the expense of the public sector, where capital formation has fallen from 49% of total investment to 25% (Khanna, 2012). Nearly three decades after opening up of the economy, the 47 SOEs listed on the Stock Exchanges in 2018 accounted for about 10% of total market capitalization (Chandra and Chatterjee, 2019) with the rate of growth of the private corporate sector accelerating significantly. Figure 5.1 shows the accumulated investment made by CPSEs.

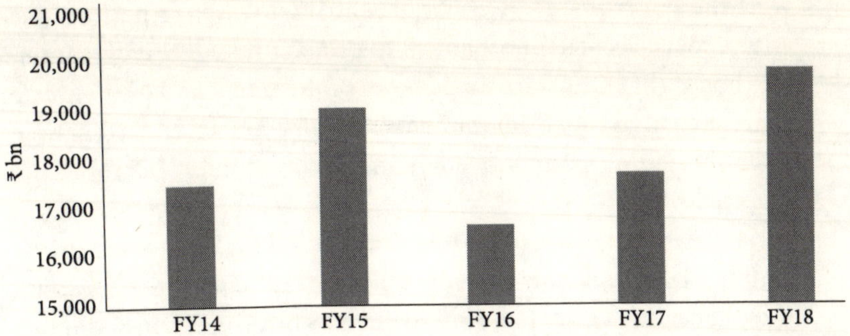

Figure 5.1 Accumulated investment of CPSEs
Source: Dun and Bradstreet, India's Top PSUs 2019.

A paradigmatic change in 1991

After pursuing State-led capitalism for over four decades after Independence, India introduced a new industrial policy in 1991 that emphasized delicensing and a reduced role for the public sector. The industrial policy opened up most sectors of the economy to private entry and investment. The new industrial policy restricted the role of the public sector to a few strategic sectors. Many SOEs, though incorporated as companies, were largely not listed on stock exchanges until 1990. The entire equity of most SOEs was held by federal or provincial governments.

The key feature of the new regime beginning in 1991 has been the expansion of the capital markets and listing of SOEs on the stock exchanges. With that, SOE reforms have gone through three distinct phases from 1991 to now:

- *First Phase* (1992–98): India embarked on a policy of divesting up to 20% of shares in SOEs to mutual funds (fractional equity sale), the general public, and workers. From 1993 to 1994, Foreign Institutional Investors (FIIs) were allowed to bid for shares. The Board of Industrial Financing and Restructuring (BIFR) was created to track the performance of SOEs and advise them, especially the loss-making ones, on investment and restructuring. Three categories of SOEs were formed: Maharatnas, Navratnas, and Miniratnas. Performance contracts (Memoranda of Understanding) were signed with the government to create incentives for better performance with a social security mechanism to protect the interest of workers. The boards of SOEs were made more professional and given greater powers to undertake investments, acquire assets and companies in India and abroad, and enjoy greater autonomy (Chibber and Gupta, 2017).

- *Second Phase* (1998–2004): India embarked on large-scale privatization or strategic sale of a controlling stake to private parties and introduced measures to improve the functioning of the better performing SOEs. In all, a dozen SOEs were privatized during this period and in two cases the government's controlling block was sold to other SOEs in the same sector. Further privatizations were met with considerable opposition from vested interests and labour unions.
- *Third Phase* (2004 onwards): India has made serious efforts to revive underperforming CPSEs. Between 2004 and 2008 it encouraged their restructuring by creating the Bureau for Restructuring of Public Firms with a mandate to undertake financial restructuring and revival of loss-making SOEs. During this period, 60 SOEs were restructured, two were closed, and two were privatized. The Arjun Sengupta committee was set up to look at ways of granting 'full managerial and commercial autonomy' to CPSEs, to enhance their ability to respond to competition from the private sector. The committee recommended significant changes in the relationship between the controlling ministry and the SOEs, in order to curtail the numerous and detailed interventions in routine operations of SOEs which seriously eroded SOEs' autonomy. It recommended that all major decisions, both strategic and operational, should be taken by the board of directors, where at least half of the members were independent. It also sought to insulate SOEs from 'parliamentary interference' that could require SOEs to reveal commercially sensitive information. A National Investment Fund was created to collect disinvestment receipts, with the idea that it would be strategically deployed rather than used as part of budget receipts. Following fiscal pressures after the 2009 crisis, this condition was relaxed until the Fund, for all practical purposes, became part of the fiscal budget (Khanna, 2012).

Since 2009, GoI has continued to sell small stakes in SOEs listed on the stock exchange, in order to raise resources to bridge its deficit. In recent years, it has required SOEs to increase dividends paid to it. The government has continued its policy of selling its stake in SOEs to mutual funds, and financial institutions, but these stake sales have not resulted in any change of control.

Governance reforms in the public sector led to the better-performing CPSEs enjoying greater autonomy, being listed on stock exchanges and having independent directors on their boards. CPSEs have played an important role in the economy, and despite opening up most sectors to private players, most industrial CPSEs have continued their growth and expansion.

Between 1997 and 2011 with reforms and empowered boards, manufacturing CPSEs with sales of above Rs. 1 billion (US$25 million) improved their performance substantially. Through market-driven pricing they were able to match the private sector's return on capital (RoC). They have also made significant contributions to government revenues: between 2004 and 2009, CSOEs' contributions to central revenue grew 27% annually (Xu, 2012).

SOEs kept pace with the accumulation and investment in the private sector, both in the manufacturing and the services sector up to 2007. Since then, however, assets controlled by the private sector have accelerated and have overtaken the total assets of SOEs.

But SOEs have continued to play a key role in the politics of rents that has defined India's pluralist competition between powerful interest groups (Bardhan, 1998). They fund a multiplicity of subsidies, which have also gone to privileged (well-connected) private firms and have continued to pacify rival groups.

Successful SOEs are expected to compensate for the financial weaknesses of other State-owned firms. SOEs have been traditionally seen as a 'captive tax base', which 'generate predictable source of taxes and compulsory payments to various fiscal agencies' (Waterbury, 1993). They have provided regular dividends but at times of financial hardship they are mined still harder for short-term fiscal convenience, and as a source of revenue to window-dress budgets. They have been forced to buy back the government's holdings or to buy equity in other SOEs, to bolster government finances. The State has used SOEs in more indirect ways to support the political agenda of the government of the day, i.e. SOEs have been used to expand investment and employment when private capital has proved slow to bend to government will or fiat.

From ownership to regulation

Economic reforms of the 1990s allowed for private entry but did not entail privatization of incumbent State-owned monopoly service providers in many sectors. The government has continued to be the policy-maker and auctioneer of operating licences, while it owns some of the largest companies in those sectors.

But the nation's governance structure has become increasingly regulatory in character. The admission of private actors into several domains has meant that the prior model of administration, where the State had a monopoly and the executive performed the managerial role through its ministries or departments, has been altered (Kapoor and Khosla, 2019).

A noticeable feature of many of the regulators is that they are responsible for the promotion and development, as well as regulation, of a certain industry. This can result in the regulator thinking more of the interests of the industry rather than that of other stakeholders. The inadequate institutional distance between regulators and SOEs, especially when there are no firewalls between them, has meant that the regulators have not promoted enough competition.

Regulatory bodies have operated with varying and sometimes ambiguous and controversial—degrees of independence from the political executive. This has led to a different set of norms being applied to SOEs or being partially applied by the regulator due to pressures on its functioning. Banking is a classic example of the former, while infrastructure and renewable energy exemplify the latter. Both jeopardize the level playing field for the country to make an effective transition from a licensed business regime to a regulatory state.

The infrastructure sector in general has exemplified government preference for SOEs, undermining regulatory independence, the dilution of rule-based decision-making, and disregard for contractual arrangements for political gains, such as providing free electricity and other welfare measures. The renewable energy sub sector has been targeted for differential and favourable regulatory treatment within the broader ambit of the Electricity Act 2003 (Kapoor and Khosla, 2019). The renewable sector suffers from the conflicting goals of procuring cheap solar equipment, while boosting a domestic manufacturing base through imposition of import duties, and simultaneously wanting to keep the lowest possible prices for power to help indebted and loss-making State-owned power distribution companies keep their costs down.

Sector regulatory bodies were created to meet India's international obligations to its multilateral creditors. Almost all the major sectors that were opened up for increased participation of the private sector—telecoms, power, mining, petroleum and gas, banking, insurance, airlines, etc.—have seen sector regulators constituted for each of these sectors. But ministerial departments, earlier responsible for operating in those specific sectors have had overriding powers over the regulatory bodies' decisions. As a result, over time, the regulatory bodies have been reduced to advisory bodies which lay down rules that do not conflict with ministerial departments. Regulatory bodies therefore have limited ultimate authority.

Many of the sector-specific regulators have been administratively located within and financially provided for by the concerned ministries, which also own and control the regulated SOEs. In addition, these regulators depend on relevant ministries for staffing, often contractually engaging personnel from the regulated SOEs themselves. Dependence on the executive is entrenched through budgetary allocations made by the ministry, with extensive reporting requirements placed on the regulator. In some sectors regulatory bodies have faced further regulatory turf battles with the Competition Commission of India (CCI) over predatory pricing (Kapoor and Khosla, 2019).

Further, the extent of reporting required from regulators to the concerned ministries has compromised their operational autonomy. Accordingly, the government has had a greater incentive to monitor and control the regulator in order to protect its SOEs, as well as a greater opportunity to do so because of the regulator's place within the government hierarchy.

It is evident to the regulated SOE as to where the real seat of authority lies—the ministry rather than the regulator. Therefore, when choosing between the regulator's verdict and conflicting policy directives from the ministry, SOEs ignore the former, diminishing market confidence in the regulator. The State's decision to leave the relationship between the formal executive and a specific regulatory body open ended has allowed the State to exercise control when it desires and to claim independence when matters go awry (Kapoor and Khosla, 2019).

Sanctions against SOEs have hardly deterred them from breaking regulatory directives or carrying out their operations as always because the government tends to make good the SOEs' losses. As a result, regulated SOEs do not appear to have much reason to abide by regulatory directives that are in conflict with populist measures and policy decisions taken by the executive. Regulators have had limited authority and freedom to enforce regulations against SOEs to the same degree as against their private counterparts.

Despite these regulatory hurdles, the telecom sector in the country grew explosively until it was severely compromised in 2019. The objectives that have guided telecom regulations so far have included coverage and penetration, revenue maximization, and national security. The result of this has been that mobile users in India have increased hundred-fold from about 10 million in 2002 to 1.2 billion in 2018 (Kapoor and Khosla, 2019). However, this framework of departmentally driven regulation and a near-sidelining of the 'independent regulator' has served its time. The already consolidated telecom sector is now faced with extreme financial distress resulting from regulatory capture by one private near-monopoly with existing competitors rolling over.

Crony capitalism

Oligarchic control is often prevalent in the corporate sector of countries whose bureaucracies are less efficient, whose governments are unable to perform their primary functions of providing basic public good governance and more interested in directing economic activities, whose political rent-seeking opportunities are lucrative, and whose financial markets are less functional. Most of these conditions of rent seeking by officials have existed in India throughout its long history. They have persisted since independence and continue to do so.

The concept of self-sufficiency was exploited by vested industrial interests to perpetuate and exploit a monopolistic, socialist economy.

Much of the formal Indian economy has been controlled by a handful of family-run conglomerates that have been quick to use their political and financial muscle to move into sectors that have showed promise (Bajaj and Yardley, 2012; The Economist, 2012). The core competence of many Indian businesses has remained the ability to buy and manipulate politicians and civil servants (Chawla, 2012; Shourie, 2009).

Economic liberalization of the early 1990s was supposed to eliminate the potential system of patronage in-built into the old system of industrial regulation—with its artificially created barriers to entry—that allowed business opportunities in them to be rationed between a privileged few business houses (or 'cronies'). With liberalization, entrepreneurial ability and not command over patronage or resources should have become the driving force that separated the successful businesses from the failures.

However, the ability to influence government decisions has remained an important facet of business success even after 1991 (Guha Thakurta, 2014), suggesting that some essential features of Indian capitalism have survived the transition to liberalization. Indian capitalism today has 'two faces', one entrepreneurial and innovative, the other more 'crony-istic' (Kar and Sen, 2016). Large businesses have been able to manipulate political and civil service officials for tweaking policies and decisions to secure an advantage for themselves and to ensure that rivals are kept down. This has created obstacles for independent companies trying to attract talent and capital.

Business success in India has relied much less on technology, innovation, and fair market competition and much more on securing means—financing, technology, and state support—from the outside, rather than on creating technological and managerial capabilities within firms that are proprietary in nature. Many businesses have been able to use precisely this feature to transform their enterprises and grow even as the industrial landscape changed and the industries in which they had originally established themselves declined in importance.

Relationships with politicians have continued to be the 'master key' in enabling large businesses gain access to natural resources (Bajaj and Yardley, 2012). Business survival and success have continued to depend on the degree of influence commanded by a business firm, highlighting the persistence of the mercantile element in Indian capitalism. In the world of the Indian 'promoter'—as controlling shareholders are known in the country—cronyism is not an aberration; it is, in fact, the norm.

Given India's opaque sources of political funding, with every political party and leader intent on maintaining the non-transparent, corrupt, *status quo*—cronyism, reinforced through political contributions made to secure reciprocal political patronage for unfair business advantage—remains one of the main organizing principles of economic activity. Businesses, in collusion with the State, have garnered surplus/monopoly-profits/rents for long. The lack of properly regulated competition has allowed all the surplus to be cornered by a few, favoured rentiers and disallowed to contribute either to the benefit of labour or to providers of genuine, retail shareholder capital.

The Indian State has struggled historically to discipline such large business houses. In order to secure favourable policy and regulatory decisions, prominent business tycoons have often exploited close personal links with politicians, who rely on under-the-table donations to fund increasingly expensive and fiercely competitive election campaigns—or, sometimes, even cut out the middlemen and become politicians themselves.

The State's continued influence over the financial system has distorted the shape of many of India's largest conglomerates. Until recently, through cross-holdings across subsidiaries, promoters were able to 'funnel' away cheap state financing from one arm of the conglomerate to the other, often leaving taxpayers, or small individual shareholders, on the hook for any losses (Bertrand et al., 2002). This system has facilitated asymmetric risk sharing between Public Sector Banks (PSBs) and private firms in large projects. Figure 5.2 shows the non-performing loan ratio of PSBs.

Due to a lack of interbank communication and regulatory oversight, private promoters have been able to borrow from multiple lenders and invest less equity than expected. Many promoters have managed such 'riskless capitalism' for long. Max Weber described this system as 'political capitalism': a system in which profit-making activity is oriented towards 'opportunities for predatory profit' through proximity to the State (Weber, 1978).

For politically well-connected industrial families, the very idea that State-owned lenders would appropriate the assets of loan defaulters and sell them to competitors or third parties has been unthinkable so far.

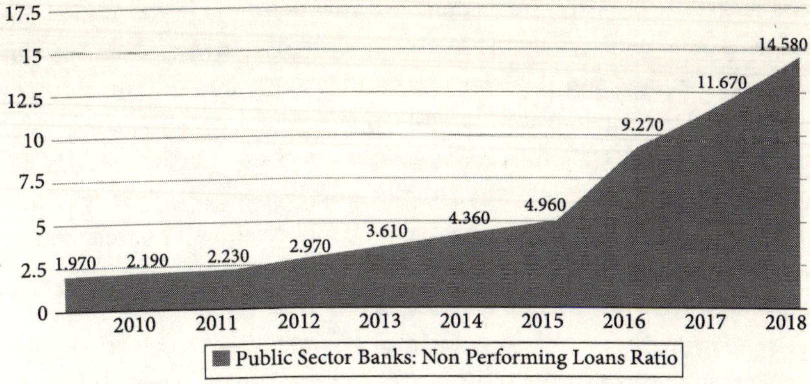

Figure 5.2 NPL ratio of Indian PSBs
Source: CEIC Data.

Undercapitalized State-owned lenders have preferred to (or been obliged by politicians to) keep kicking the can down the road.

The Insolvency and Bankruptcy Code (IBC) of 2016 has been a long-awaited reform with the potential to resolve India's overwhelming non-performing assets (NPAs) in a transparent and time bound manner through formal bankruptcy proceedings in open courts. Consequently, IBC has led to creating an M&A momentum with several domestic and international investors actively participating. Despite the introduction of this code, State-owned lenders have still been unable to change the balance of power with big businesses. The strong business-state nexus in India has made the exercising of public authority subservient to the interests of private profit, especially when such profit has political backing.

The State has remained an important actor in the economic management and decisions of state or quasi-state institutions have played an important role in determining the quantum and distribution of economic benefits. The State's role—in granting property rights to land; exploitation of natural resources; influencing the development of infrastructure and its pricing; influencing the value of property; extending tax benefits; public procurement, spectrum allocations; etc.—has created opportunities to grant favours of large economic value.

In the past few years, public power and resources have been actively involved in the process of private capital acquiring land on a vast scale for industrial projects, Special Economic Zones, mining and exploration, and real estate projects. India's rapid growth after the reforms of 1991 has been accompanied by a higher intensity of corruption, as the demand for natural resources and the associated rise in rents on natural resources rose and as the gap between domestic demand and supply had widened for urban land, electricity, and transport networks.

In India's federal set-up, the leverage of private capital over the State has also been enhanced by the competition for investment between states. A narrow group of large businesses have consequently acquired significant influence with different hierarchical levels of the State and have been able to secure major benefits through such influence.

There has been a strong resistance from big businesses against further change and reforms to create a level playing field, open doors to further competition, and to bring down entry barriers. Investors who benefit from reforms have been diffused and scattered, and the benefits of which accrue to them in the indefinite future. On the other hand, the dislocations that reforms are likely to cause are here and now, and those immediately affected by them are concentrated and organized (Shourie, 2009). Most of the entrenched businesses have preferred to cut private deals with the concerned minister or civil servant than work to change the system, inflicting significant harm on institutions by the deals they cut.

Private interests of public officials

If big businesses have resisted further changes, politicians and bureaucrats have equally resisted administrative reforms that separate policy-making from policy implementation. Separating policy-making from implementing takes away from them their ability to shower favours on their cronies. Politicians have traditionally run the elaborate system attached to India's command capitalism through extensive state controls and cumbersome licensing.

Bureaucrats have been the vanguard of resistance to attempts to change this status quo and have been largely successful because of the political leadership's undue dependence on them. Indian bureaucrats have become power centres in their own right at both the national and state levels, and have been extremely resistant to reform that affects them or the way they go about their duties (Saxena, 2010). Consequently, the civil service has been corrupted extensively and has served the interests of patrimonial politics (Das, 2001; Shourie, 2009).

According to a survey of bureaucracies in 12 Asian economies, India's bureaucracy was ranked as the least efficient, and working with the country's civil servants was described as a 'slow and painful' process (Rana, 2012). The 'system' of corruption has worked well in coordinating rents and getting them shared across both the official and political realms.

The existing system of rent collection has wide support among those in bureaucratic and political office. Day-to-day administration provides ample opportunities for corruption, such as transfers and postings of public officials, awarding of major contracts and concessions, and the provision of goods and services free or below market prices (Das, 2001). As the implementing body for all government policies, state laws, and regulations, the various civil services have been at the heart of seemingly intractable governance problems in India (Shourie, 2009).

The nature, extent, reach, and domain of corruption have been profoundly altered since liberalization in 1991. Under the 'license-control' regime, the number of places where rents could be extracted was extremely large because industrialists had to obtain a government licence not only to open a new business but also to expand an existing one. By eliminating most of these controls, liberalization reduced the number of points at which bribes could be collected.

Liberalization was also accompanied by the rapid expansion of services and other industries, many in new sectors, such as Information Technology (IT), where already established, routine mechanisms of rent extraction were not in place. This also reduced the *number* of 'pressure points' where government officials could extract rents.

Liberalization contributed to the reduction of corruption by narrowing the sources of rent extraction. But there still exist four significant areas each connected with a source of rent extraction by bureaucrats and politicians. The first revolves around the acquisition and sale of land, the second around the construction of infrastructure, the third around the sale of public assets, such as the mobile phone spectrum, and the fourth concerns welfare programmes.

The acquisition of land has been a very complex political task, one that has required a great deal of local knowledge and manipulation of the legal system. Large corporations and big builders leave that task to 'brokers', who are mostly low-level politicians, good at bribing people and threatening landowners. Political support at higher levels has been necessary to neutralize the ability of the victims to turn to law enforcement for help or restitution.

Successful land consolidation has placed tremendous informational demands about the complexities of 'local' life—power relations, kin ties, caste connections, and family dynamics. The asymmetry in social knowledge and information about community dynamics has provided the space for politicians to extract rents from land (Gupta, 2017).

Infrastructure development has often been associated with corruption in at least three different ways—there are significant kickbacks to be collected in the bidding process. Infrastructure development has often depended on acquiring and rezoning land, and political help is necessary before the project begins and during its construction. Finally, politicians and senior bureaucrats have benefitted from insider knowledge related to the location of new infrastructure projects. The location of an airport, or the route of a metro line, is altered in such a way as to lie adjacent to land that already belongs to powerful politicians, or has been recently acquired by politicians and senior bureaucrats (Gupta, 2017).

The largest corruption scandals in the recent past have involved the sale of public assets, like the mobile phone spectrum, and the sale of mining rights. In these cases, assets over which the State has monopoly power which are supposed to be auctioned to the highest bidder were sold at a much lower price in exchange for a kickback. This was done by giving some companies insider information, or by rigging the auction process to exclude competitors, or by granting rights to an illegitimate company in which the politician or his family have a significant share.

Politicians and bureaucrats have been paid to rig the rules favouring one bidder over another. In the process, however, the treasury was deprived of large sums of revenue that could have potentially funded redistributive social programmes or infrastructure. The large outlays for many of the welfare programmes have been accompanied by complaints of 'leakage' (Gupta, 2017).

The anti-corruption movement in India has focused largely on demand for institutions (Jan Lokpal) with the power to investigate corruption and prosecute at all levels of officialdom. This would have been certainly better than the existing Prevention of Corruption Act of 1988, under which 'permission to prosecute' has to be given by the Government.

An important administrative reform needed in India is to change the current system of bureaucratic 'transfers and postings', which has been a major source of illicit income of politicians in state secretariats. In general career promotion for officials in India depends more on seniority than on performance, so an official has the incentive to maximize bribe taking in the short period of local posting before transfer (Gupta, 2017). It is typically the case in India that senior officials in various services actually bid and pay large sums to their superiors or selection boards, for transfers to lucrative postings where they can derive large rents for personal income and share them with key connections in the administrative bureaucracy.

While bureaucrats and politicians have often been seen as naturally hostile to administrative reforms, senior CPSE staff have comprised an unlikely pro-reform constituency. The reinvention of CPSEs has therefore been carried forth within the organizations themselves. Many of India's largest CPSEs, like NTPC, have thus not survived into the liberalization age unchanged. The ideas of efficiency have positively affected their modes of operation and management (Chatterjee, 2017).

Misallocation of resources and SOE productivity

Despite playing a significant role in the Indian economy till the reforms of 1991, their mounting losses, low productivity, and under-utilization of capacity over time have made SOEs a net drain on the treasury and have heightened the case for reform. CPSEs accounted for nearly 85% of the public sector's total capital assets in 1991. Post-1991, the concern with public sector reform was subordinated to the drive for increasing private investment. Rewarding SOE efficiency was less a concern than simple resource mobilization and fiscal containment. With short-term finance becoming the government's main concern, successful SOEs were neglected, in favour of attention towards loss-making enterprises. SOEs have been partially or wholly privatized since 1991 to bring market pressure to release labour to more productive sectors of the economy (Chatterjee, 2017).

Over the years several studies have mapped the performance of SOEs and compared it to their peers in the private sector. Studies before 1991 (Dholakia, 1978, Gupta, 1982, and Bhaya, 1990) found that the performance of SOEs had improved marginally over time. In terms of partial labour and capital productivities, State or private ownership did not appear to have had any significant impact on performance. However, in terms of returns on investment, the private sector performed better than SOEs.

Post-reforms, research has shown (Ahluwalia, 1995, Ahuja and Majumdar, 1998, Ramaswamy, 2001, Mohan and Ray, 2003, and Gupta, 2005) that ownership did not affect the gross RoC employed, but without the SOEs in the petroleum and refinery industry in the sample, there was a significant decline in the returns of the public sector. Studies from the late 1990s and early 2000s showed that SOEs were not performing as well as their private counterparts. The magnitude of the difference increased with increasing competitive intensity and partial privatization had a positive effect on profitability, productivity, and investment.

When performance was measured and compared in terms of productivity and technical efficiency, the mean technical efficiency score of SOEs ranged between 0.35 and 0.39 and the private sector performed better in terms of productivity. Studies offered contradictory conclusions whether privatization could help in improving the efficiency of SOEs. This was mainly because the performance was measured across highly heterogeneous samples of firms belonging to diverse industrial sectors with widely differing technologies.

More recent studies on ownership and performance (Kaur and Kumar, 2010, Gupta, Jain and Yadav 2011, Jain 2017, Chibber and Gupta 2017, Singh 2019 and Baird et al., 2019) found that foreign-owned firms performed most efficiently, followed by domestic private firms and then the SOEs. The difference in performance was related to the technology used. There was a strong and positive relationship between privatization and efficiency of SOEs.

SOEs have been a source of distortion in the labour market and the associated efficiency losses. Privatization has resulted in rationalization within the State sector that has effectively released surplus workers, more efficient use of labour through restructuring, and also possibly due to investment in new equipment from the retained proceeds of privatization.

This has been the mechanism underlying the observed increase in economy-wide output and productivity.

Value added per employee (VAE) as a measure of labour productivity increased rapidly from Rs. 400 per employee per hour in 1989–90 prices to Rs. 1600 in 2003–04. But it fell sharply after that before recovering back to Rs. 1600 per employee by 2014–15. Overall, VAE increased by fourfold between 1990 and 2015. This translated to a 2.0% annual increase in VAE against the average labour productivity growth of around 5.2% for the economy as a whole (Chibber and Gupta, 2017).

In terms of efficient use of assets and capital and operational efficiency in SOEs measured by value added per assets (VAAs), value added per capital (VAC), and net sales to assets (NSA), there has been no significant change between 1990 and 2015. VAA has remained around 0.2, while value added per unit of capital has remained around 0.5. However, net sales per asset has increased from 0.5 to 0.8 between 1990 and 2015 (Chibber and Gupta, 2017).

State-owned manufacturing firms have shown higher returns on capital employed than private firms from 1995 (Khanna, 2015). The return-on-assets and return-on-capital in the largest 7 SOEs—i.e. the Maharatnas, have been better than foreign companies of similar size. But in the case of the next category of SOEs—Navratnas, the performance of the private firms of similar size is better. The return on assets and on capital have declined quite sharply since the GFC of 2008–10. The Maharatnas have lower VAA, the efficiency variable, although they have higher financial profitability measured by RoC or Return on assets (Chibber and Gupta, 2017).

The Maharatnas also have higher labour productivity as measured by VAE but that is due to greater capital intensity in the large SOEs. In manufacturing, SOEs provided better RoC than either private sector as a whole, including Business Group-controlled firms, independent private Indian firms, or foreign-owned private firms.

The performance of SOEs in terms of technical parameters, like plant load factor (PLF) in electricity generation or yields in the steel and petroleum industry, is not inferior to their private counterparts. SOEs in the service sectors have performed poorly relative to those in mining and manufacturing. They have made losses primarily because the State demands that they underprice their services for political reasons. Not only is the performance of SOEs in service sectors poor but also their presence has adversely affected the performance of private sector firms in those sectors especially in the airline sector (Mukherjee, 2015).

The profitability of SOEs has been affected by subsidies, discouraging further investment especially in the petroleum sector (exploration and production) and the power sector. In the power sector, SOEs have been known for their efficient operations and technical parameters, with their power plants operating at 90–95 PLF, but have been starved of liquidity because of subsidized prices of power (Khanna, 2015).

The unintended consequence of dismantling the price control mechanism over the last two decades and the new regulatory regime has seen the resurgence of the State sector. In sectors where they have always been efficient, dismantling of price controls and market-driven pricing have allowed SOEs to improve their profitability. But the power to influence policy and regulations has moved to the private sector, thus preventing SOEs from adding capacity and allowing the private sector to capture the expanding market (Bhargava, 2013).

In short, the reinvention of state intervention since the 1980s has allowed the best of the CSOEs to be retrofitted for the market era, with greater autonomy, with exposure to competition and endowed with the trappings of corporate governance (Chatterjee, 2017). Given the profitable and more efficient performance of the large CSOEs, it has been difficult for successive governments to decide between allowing these successful SOEs to become world class companies or to privatize them to extract better value for their assets.

In terms of the allocation of state resources, the most important challenge has been India's State-owned banks and financial institutions and the State's inability or reluctance to discipline well-connected firms. Many of the large private firms that had benefited from the State's generous incentives to make heavily leveraged infrastructure investments have resulted in overcapacity and project delays undermining their profits. The resulting industrial stagnation has left many PSBs overexposed to non-performing assets.

This misallocation of public resources has seen a decade-long dual crisis of overinvestment, known as the 'twin balance-sheet problem': private firms have become increasingly unwilling to invest either because of their debt burdens or pessimism about the future, while bad-loan-stricken PSBs have been unable to expand corporate credit (Chandra and Chatterjee, 2019).

Internal Management and post-reform performance of SOEs

Till 1991, SOEs were wholly owned by the government and were merely an extended arm of the State. The governance structures of the SOEs allowed administrative departments in the concerned ministry to exercise complete control over SOE functioning (Varma, 1997). While full privatization was considered politically unpalatable, a policy of malign neglect and partial equity sales remained the key solution for state sector reform through much of the 1990s.

Indian policy-makers have generally favoured the introduction of private enterprises and competition in parallel with the continuation of large SOEs in certain sectors (Chatterjee, 2017). SOEs have persisted and even flourished when entrepreneurial bureaucrats have been able to leverage their firms' political influence to gain access to lucrative resources.

They have fared less well when they lacked the resources to resist political interference in their everyday operations. Nonetheless, while many surviving CPSEs are profitable, several SOEs barely break even. Just ten SOEs—most of them in the energy sector—account for two-thirds of the entire State sector's profits (Chandra and Chatterjee, 2019).

On paper, CPSEs have enjoyed a more arms' length relationship with the government and the imposition of greater market discipline, albeit on an ad hoc and asymmetric basis. Nonetheless, the State has generally been careful not to relinquish control entirely: it retains stakes above a controlling 51% in virtually all CPSEs.

A partial attempt made by the government between 1999 and 2004 to dismantle the public sector legacy with strategic disinvestment (privatization) met with considerable opposition from vested interests and labour unions. In practice, the actual proceeds from disinvestment were modest and dwarfed by the finances flowing to CPSEs. Between 1991 and 2008 (partial and complete) privatizations raised $12.9 billion at 2011 exchange rates, compared with a cumulative investment in the 242 surviving CPSEs of $91 billion during that period (Pratap, 2011).

Subsequent governments have tried to further improve the performance of these companies through better performance contracts (MoUs) and bringing more SOEs into the 'Ratna' classification. The number of MoUs increased rapidly in the early 1990s from four in 1988–89 to over a hundred by 1994–95. The second phase of increase saw the number of MoUs jump to 215 in 2015–16 from 197 in 2009–10.

Almost 50% of the SOEs were making losses in the 1990s, but from 2002–03 onwards with private equity and when Memoranda of Understanding (MoU) or performance contracts were applied, the number of loss-making SOEs declined to about a quarter of the total. Since then, however, and especially after 2012, the share of loss-making SOEs has increased again to almost one-third of the total. Profitability of the SOEs—measured by profits over total sales—has increased from 2% in 1990–91 to around 3% by 2000–01, then peaked at almost 9% between 2003–04 and 2006–07 and has since fallen to between 5 and 6% (Chhibber and Gupta, 2017). Table 5.2 shows data on the performance of CPSEs.

Much of the financial performance improvement of SOEs—earlier attributed to privatization—has been due to the performance effect of MoUs (Gunasekar and Sarkar, 2014). MoUs have had a positive impact on SOE performance by increasing their return on capital. This result has been true mainly in the non-service sector (manufacturing, mining) (Chhibber and Gupta, 2017).

Post-1996, the programme ('Ratna' classification) that conferred autonomy on some SOEs led to higher profits, value added, and sales

Table 5.2 Performance of CPSEs

Year	Gross revenue (y-o-y %)	Net revenue (y-o-y %)
2013–14	6.2	6.5
2014–15	−3.4	−4.4
2015–16	−8.0	−10.3
2016–17	6.6	3.3
2017–18	10.2	11.6

Source: Dun and Bradstreet India's Top PSUs 2019.

(Figures 5.3 and 5.4). The Navratnas were given greater everyday financial and managerial autonomy from ministerial oversight, delegated substantial powers to incur capital expenditure and enter into joint ventures for technology transfer. Their boards, which had traditionally taken only unanimous decisions (Singh, 2009), were partially revived with greater emphasis on independent directors. SOEs that were eligible for autonomy had a higher value added to begin with and witnessed a 41% increase over mean value added and a 58% increase relative to mean profits after the programme was implemented. Figures 5.6 and 5.7 show total income of all CPSEs and profits after tax of all CPSEs.

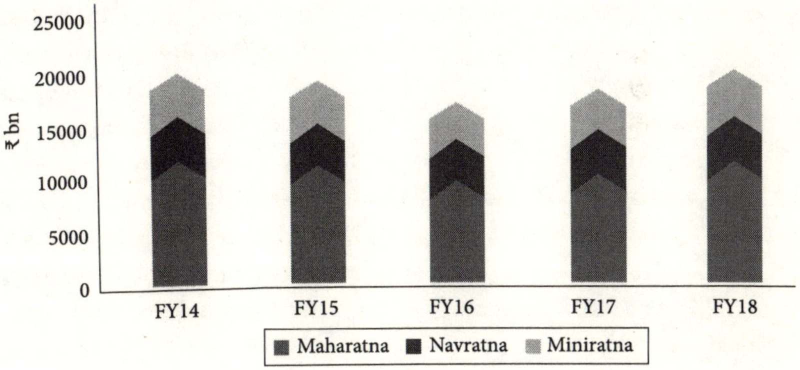

Figure 5.3 Total income of Ratna category CPSEs
Source: Dun and Bradstreet, India's Top PSUs 2019.

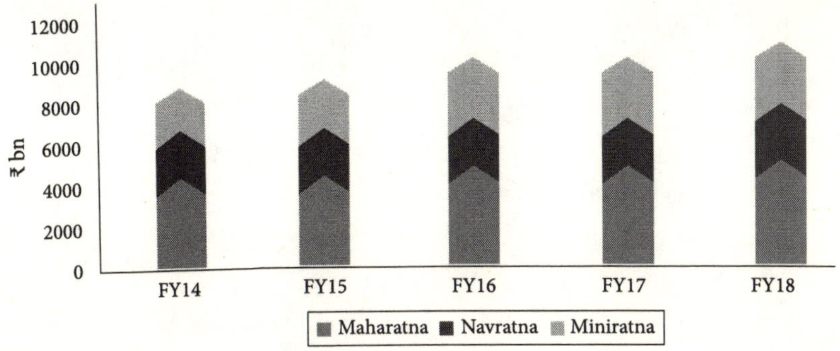

Figure 5.4 Net worth of Ratna category CPSEs
Source: Dun and Bradstreet, India's Top PSUs 2019.

On measures of labour productivity—sales per employee and VAE—greater autonomy increased profit, sales, and productivity significantly. These outcomes were driven partly by SOE managers' incentives to receive board seats in the private sector. In the long run, the volatility of SOE returns has increased, indicating that managers may be engaging in higher return and higher risk projects. Overall, large gains in SOEs' performance have proven to be possible without any changes to the ownership structure (Kala, 2019).

There were large increases in labour productivity after the programme—an increase in Rs. 4.5 million for sales per worker and an increase in Rs. 1.086 million for value added per worker. Autonomy provided a substantial effect on sales and profits (see Figure 5.5). There was an increase of about 3.5 times higher sales relative to the mean, and an increase in profits over twelve years of about 45% relative to the mean. These effects imply that not only did autonomy allow SOEs to increase profitability and expand output relative to other SOEs but also allowed them to perform effectively relative to the private sector. Dividends and retained earnings increased too—the increase in dividends has been about 54% relative to the mean, and the increase in retained earnings has been about 55% relative to the mean. The government, as the majority shareholder in these SOEs, got a substantial increase in the revenue it has received.

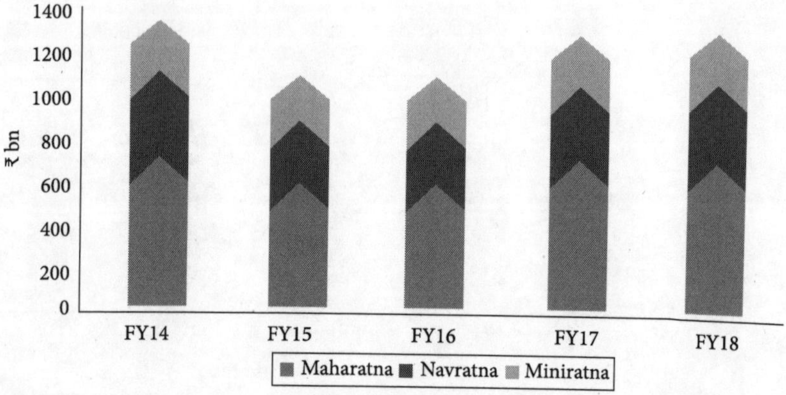

Figure 5.5 Growth in profit after tax (PAT) of Ratna category CPSEs
Source: Dun and Bradstreet, India's Top PSUs 2019.

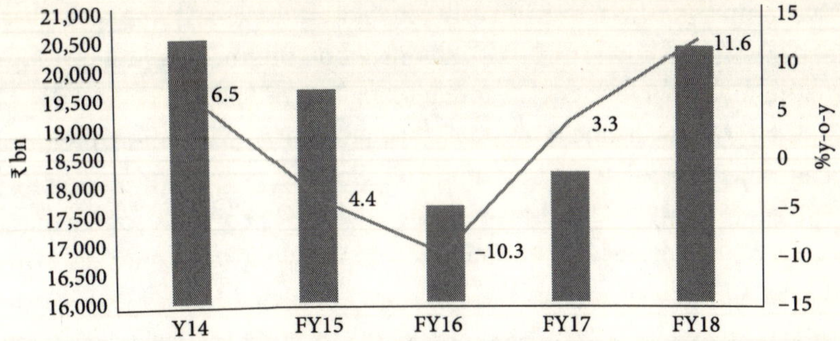

Figure 5.6 Total income of all CPSEs
Source: Dun and Bradstreet, India's Top PSUs 2019.

However, there has been no substantial change in the relative allocations between the government and SOEs which have borrowed less from the government and more from non-governmental sources. That is consistent with the conditions for capital expansion under the autonomy programme (that expansion be financed out of non-governmental sources). With their increasing profitability, a large part of the investment has been internally financed. Interest payments have not changed as a result of the autonomy programme, SOEs have not used autonomy to increase their high-interest borrowing (Kala, 2019).

During the same time, however, the ratio of SOE sales to GDP declined from 20% of GDP in 1990 to about 16% of GDP in 2015, a much smaller decline indicating that the sales to asset ratio increased from 0.5 in 1990 to around 0.8 in 2015. Value added by SOEs, as a share of GDP, and the ratio of SOE employment to total organized employment in the economy declined from around 8% of GDP in 1990 to below 5% of GDP in 2015 (Chhibber and Gupta, 2017).

The entry of minority shareholders nominally improved CSOE governance through board diversification. In practice, however, it was motivated in large part by the State's revenue raising through divestment, i.e. the State's equity holdings tend to become more valuable with increased autonomy. The revised governance structures of at least the largest CPSEs have ensured that the SOEs' erstwhile objectives—employment generation, social equity, and their use as a political resource—were nominally subordinated to the profit motive (Chatterjee, 2017).

Nevertheless, the CPSEs have occupied an awkward space between stock market favourites and old-fashioned tools of the State. SOE commitment to meeting older 'social' and 'political' considerations—like the enhancement of government revenues through dividends, employment, and social objectives—has not disappeared. Beyond corporate profitability, CPSEs have continued to advance state goals and provide a source of patronage. CPSEs have been bound in a complex political economy of subsidies and even well-managed CPSEs have struggled to escape the wider political ecosystem within which they are embedded (Chatterjee, 2017). Table 5.3 shows the number of loss-making and profit-making SOEs in India over a period of 10 years starting from 2008–09 (see Figure 5.7).

Persistent corporate governance problems in SOEs have therefore had a structural dimension. The government plays multiple roles with respect to SOEs, as a regulator, owner, adjudicator, and executive, but with conflicting objectives. The multiplicity and ambiguity of roles have helped the government in using the SOEs as agents of political interest rather than public policy. Subsidies to consumers or targeted (i.e. politically favoured) sections at the cost of the SOE, and special grants and bail-out packages, have provided the government reason, even if misplaced, for continued special controls and rights (Reddy, 2001).

Table 5.3 Number of loss-making and profit-making SOEs in India

Year	No. of loss-making SOEs	No. of profit-making SOEs
2008–09	55	158
2009–10	60	157
2010–11	62	158
2011–12	64	161
2012–13	78	151
2013–14	70	164
2014–15	76	159
2015–16	79	164
2016–17	81	175
2017–18	71	184

Source: Department of Public Enterprises.

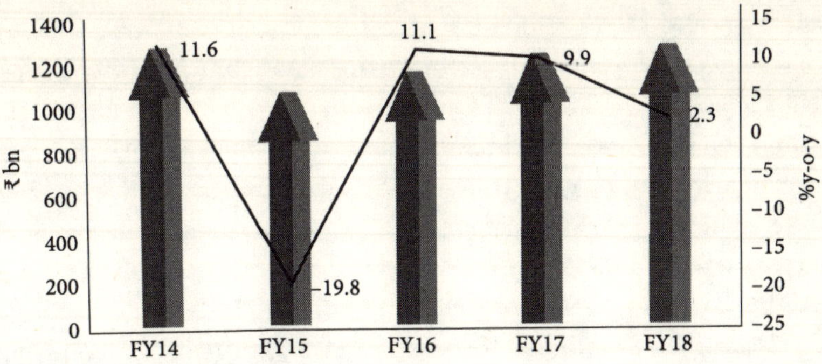

Figure 5.7 Net profit of all CPSEs
Source: Dun and Bradstreet, India's Top PSUs 2019.

As a result, relations with the parent ministries have remained unclear. While there has been considerable operational flexibility in CPSE's day-to-day operations, and even capital decisions, they continue to be remote controlled by parent ministries through quarterly performance reviews and ministry appointed board members. At times, the board is 'effectively paralyzed' through slow board appointments and approvals for capital investment above the delegated levels (which sometimes even require cabinet approval). SOE managing directors and finance directors are invariably appointed through politicized processes. The controlling line ministries have had little formal redefinition of role or responsibilities and continued political interference has undermined the veneer of good corporate governance installed since the 1990s (Xu, 2012).

CPSEs are strongly linked to the national interest, and are expected to behave in some respects as market players. But they clearly owe their dominance to their political connections. For example, NTPC benefits from upstream linkages with the centrally controlled coal sector; access to cheap land, railway freight, and finance via public sector banks; and from preferential treatment by international financial institutions. This preferential access to budgetary support tends to dilute its accountability to shareholders and the market.

CPSEs' weight and influence—the source of both their appeal and doubts for investors—thus lie in their complex relationship with the government. But it is not unusual for well-connected private firms in

India to have similar preferential access to natural resources, land, and finance and they have on occasions benefitted from minority government stakes.

The evolving version of India's State capitalism post-1991 has been far from a straightforward, coherent, or successful alternative to liberal market states or to first-generation state intervention. While the State's everyday control may have waned, successive administrations have continued to draw on CPSEs for social and political ends. For that reason, CPSEs continue to struggle to reclaim the full costs of the goods and services they supply to state-level customers. Nonetheless, CPSEs have continued to expand and added capacity and their surprisingly healthy profits have provided a regular stream of revenues to the government.

Yet CPSEs are not part to any coherent strategy to achieve higher rates of economic growth. The resilience of CPSEs against the odds has not only provided the welfare system in the country a degree of stability but has also facilitated businesses.

Conflicts that arise in the State's primary role vs its ownership of enterprises

The low returns from SOEs in the 1970s and 1980s (and in the first half of 1990s) were due to very low product prices fixed for their output. Often SOEs were expected to perform a promotional role—like supporting the growth of handicrafts, exports, exhibitions of Indian products, development of backward regions, supporting regional language films, etc. These 'promotional' activities added to the already low returns of SOEs.

Since the 1990s policy-makers have experimented with transferring State-owned assets with low returns to the private sector, hoping that would unlock profitability and generate more funds for building badly needed infrastructure—roads, power transmission lines, sewage systems, irrigation systems, railways, and urban infrastructure. But India's reform process has been characterized by a 'very special type of gradualism'. Incremental, partial reform has often been seen as strategic 'reform by stealth' (Jenkins, 1999) and as a pathway towards second-best 'reform without losers' (Joseph, 2010). There has been persistent inter-elite competition which has fostered a distinctive dynamic of institutional change, different from the conventional accounts of liberalization as a linear process of displacing the statist system.

India's state organizational structure has provided multiple points of entry for new rent-seeking strategies and multiple veto points by which liberalization policies could be resisted. Residential and agricultural elites have relied upon their influence on state governments through the ballot box and have typically sought to influence policy decisions, such as tariff rises.

Private firms have instead relied on high-level lobbying, seeking to influence earlier stages of the policy process—agenda setting and policy formulation—as well as ad hoc renegotiation attempts behind closed doors. The fragmented State system has enabled both sets of groups to exercise influence upon different levels of the State. In this way 'reform by stealth' has produced unreformed zones outside its heartlands.

Liberalization usually involves the explicit dismantling of older institutions through direct assault. In contrast, the mode of liberalization in India has been a form of 'dualization'. It 'does not necessarily imply any direct and comprehensive attack on organized interests, but only the enlargement of certain areas of the economy within which market forces are able to operate more freely than in others' (Thelen, 2012).

The institutional change that this type of liberalization brings has been marked by compromise and continuities, because it is shaped by persistent inter-elite competition. The practical result has been the creation of a layered and improvised State-market hybrid that institutionalizes the uneven involvement of the private sector alongside the continuation of older subsidies and statist instruments. Market institutions and producer subsidies have not displaced the statist system, but have been grafted onto it. Subsidies for politically important consumer groups on one side, and politically connected producers on the other, have been institutionalized in a segmented 'dual-track' economy. Just as interest-group competition has constrained the potential for sweeping institutional change, the politics of the reform era has been in turn informed by this segmented system (Joseph, 2010).

This hybrid system is neither stable nor coherent. Not only does it fail all categories of consumers but it is also financed through the short-term exploitation of natural resources and SOEs. The ad hoc compromises of the reform process have so far institutionalized a system which is technically, financially, and environmentally dysfunctional. This pattern of subsidies and rents has had limited and regionally uneven impact, reflected starkly in India's dismal performance on almost all dimensions of human development (Dreze and Sen, 2013). Low levels of human capital and inadequate access to basic infrastructure have highlighted the failure of governance in India in delivering public services.

The dual dynamic of institutional change that has emerged from dominant class competition has been a hallmark of Indian liberalization. It has disallowed the State from withdrawing itself from certain industrial sectors and has led to negative synergies between the State and the private sector, resulting in sub-optimal economic outcomes and output.

The regulatory regime has been symptomatic of the same dominant class competition and the negative synergies between the State and the private sector. A half-hearted reform process and a non-effective regulatory regime have enmeshed the State in economic activities from which it should have been displaced long time ago. The State sector has functioned sub-optimally and where it has showed resilience despite the constraints, there exists no coherent strategy to make it globally competitive. Disallowing profitable CPSEs from generating higher returns means inability to unlock funds for building badly needed social infrastructure—roads, power transmission lines, sewage systems, irrigation systems, railways, and urban infrastructure.

Consequently, the State sector has failed to provide a solid base of minimum social infrastructure (broad-based education and health) for workers; a fast pace of rural electrification that could facilitate the growth of agro-processing and rural industrialization; a system of regional economic decentralization and the foundation of a national system of basic scientific research and innovation; and in promoting industrial capabilities across sectors and regions.

Conclusions

CPSEs have played an important role in the economy, and despite opening up most sectors to private players, most industrial CPSEs have continued their growth and expansion. Successful SOEs are expected to compensate for the financial weakness of other State-owned firms.

SOEs have been a 'captive tax base' and have provided a regular stream of dividends to enhance public revenue. But, at times of financial hardship for GoI, they are squeezed even harder for short-term fiscal convenience, and as a source of revenue to window-dress budgets. They have been forced to buy back government's holdings or to buy equity in other SOEs, to bolster government finances. The State has used SOEs in many indirect ways to support its agenda.

CPSEs especially have continued to expand and add capacity and their surprisingly healthy profits have provided a regular stream of revenues to the government. Yet CPSEs are not part to any coherent strategy to achieve higher rates of economic growth through greater efficiency, innovation, and competition nor to make them globally competitive.

The resilience of CPSEs against the odds has provided the not-so-obvious welfare system in the country with a degree of stability. But the State sector has been allowed to function only sub-optimally and disallowed to play a potentially significant role in building the social infrastructure that the country so desperately needs.

On the whole, the suboptimal operating and financial performance of SOEs, and the opaqueness with which they fulfil implicit political demands and objectives, leads to the inevitable suspicion that they exist at a considerable cost to the economy—a cost that is difficult to estimate accurately and transparently.

6

Country case study 4: Indonesia

SOEs in Indonesia

SOEs have existed in Indonesia since Dutch colonial times in the early 19th century. They are more pervasive across the Indonesian economy than in any other country in the OECD's Product Market Regulation database, except China. Indonesia has 143 SOEs spread across almost all sectors of the economy, ranging from manufacturing, construction, and transportation to agriculture. Listed SOEs represent one-quarter of Indonesia's equity market capitalization (OECD, 2018b). The equally weighted average of Indonesian SOEs among the country's top ten firms' sales, assets, and market value is 69% (Apriliyanti and Kristiansen, 2019).

In 2016, total SOE assets amounted to 51% of GDP and total SOE liabilities to 33% of GDP (IMF, 2018). The largest SOEs are leading companies in their respective industries, for example, Pertamina's market share was 96.0% in the special fuel retail sector, and Perusahaan Listrik Negara accounted for 72.8% of the total installed electricity generation capacity in 2016.

In terms of assets, Indonesian SOEs include its largest telecommunications service provider, the two largest banks, and the four largest construction firms. Mining SOEs are major producers in their segments, such as tin, copper, gold, silver, nickel, and bauxite. SOEs also hold dominant positions in various transport modes, such as toll roads, railways, seaports, and airports, as well as in manufacturing industries, such as cement, steel, train, ship, airplane assembly, and defence (Kim, 2018), as shown in Figure 6.1. Indonesia's SOEs operate in 31 industries (Ministry of Finance of Republic Indonesia 2016).

The Indonesian government holds partial ownership in 40% of its SOEs. Many of these SOEs have been the product of partial privatization over the past two decades. Full privatization, and even privatization of majority stakes, has been rare in Indonesia, with the State continuing to

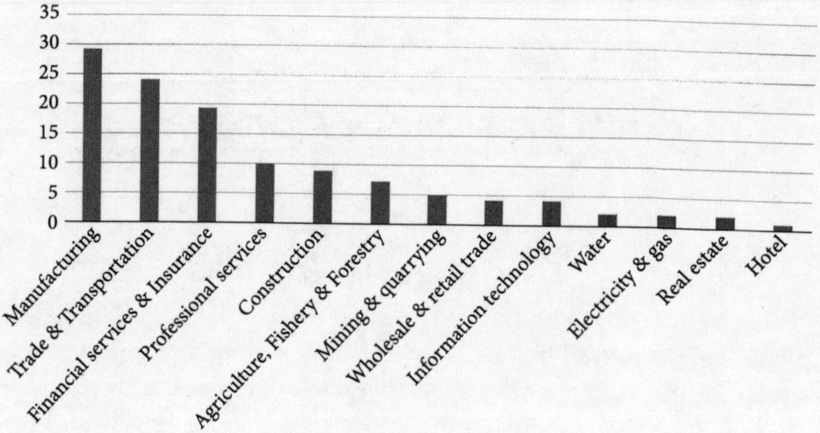

Figure 6.1 Classification of Indonesian SOEs by Industry
Source: IMF, 2018b.

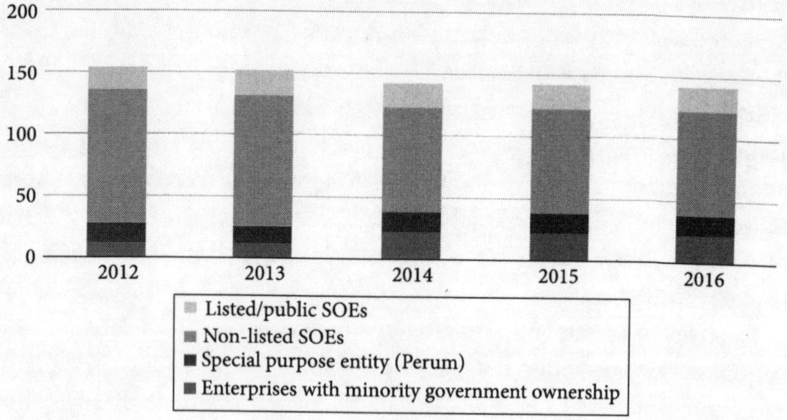

Figure 6.2 Ownership of Indonesian SOEs
Source: IMF, 2018b.

be the dominant owner of most privatized SOEs. Many large SOEs have been partially privatized through stock market listing, joint ventures, acquisition of strategic assets, and shifting ownership to other SOEs as shown in Figure 6.2 (Kim, 2018).

Indonesia's SOEs were first established by the Dutch colonial government to provide public utilities, such as rail transportation, electricity generation, and distribution. In the early years of independence in the 1950s, Indonesia's political leaders and policy-makers were quite averse to having a market economy and private enterprise. They were strongly influenced by a particularly aggressive form of economic nationalism as a reaction to the continuing dominance and control of Dutch[1] and, to a lesser extent Chinese, businesses in the Indonesian economy.

Following a political dispute over the status of Papua Island (West Irian), Dutch properties, including mining operations and large plantations, were seized by labour unions and administered by military boards (Pangestu and Habir, 1989). After the nationalization of Dutch enterprises, ethnic Chinese emerged as the community controlling various important economic activities, like trading, rice mills, and money lending, with significant effect on the livelihoods of the Indonesian population. Although the economic activities of the ethnic Chinese, particularly in rural areas, were intertwined with the economic activities of indigenous Indonesians (*pribumis*), resentment towards ethnic Chinese was higher because of their control over domestic trade (Thee, 2006).

Despite concern about the possible adverse economic effects of dealing too harshly with the Sino-Indonesian traders, successive Indonesian governments felt compelled to take measures to reduce the economic dominance of ethnic Chinese and foster the growth of indigenous Indonesian businesses and SOEs were viewed as the bulwark against further expansion of Sino-Indonesian wealth. The political imperative of having a sizable sector of the economy that was not under the control of Sino-Indonesian conglomerates required a commanding state sector (Thee, 2006).

Accordingly, under President Sukarno, the number of SOEs increased dramatically as the new constitution stipulated that 'sectors of production which are important and affect the life of the people shall be controlled by the State'. With the introduction of 'Guided Democracy' and 'Guided Economy' in the late 1950s, government focus shifted to building a national industrial economy facilitated by State-owned capital. State-owned

1 Under the terms of the Financial-Economic Agreement (Finec), reached at the Round Table Conference in The Hague in late 1949, the Netherlands' agreement to transfer sovereignty speedily to Indonesia was accompanied by a commitment by the Indonesian government that the legal rights and interests of Dutch enterprises operating in independent Indonesia would be protected (Thee, 2006).

trading firms were given a monopoly over the import of essential commodities and were provided with state credit. At the end of the 'old order' (of Sukarno in 1965), the government owned about 800 companies in agriculture (plantations), banking, trade, industry, and tourism. These SOEs were staffed with managers from the military or the civil service (Thee, 2006).

With President Suharto coming to power in 1966, private enterprise was favoured in the early years of his 'New Order' regime. He staked his political legitimacy on economic development[2] being the guiding principle for supervising, rather than controlling, economic activity. In the first decade of Suharto's New Order, the military sold many of the forestry and plantations concessions to private interests and transferred control of the remaining SOEs (mainly resources-based operations) to civilian public administration (Mcleod, 2000).

The total number of SOEs was reduced to 233 through reorganization and consolidation. In 1967, SOEs were given more autonomy and were restructured into three categories functionally divided along the axes of public service and level of fiscal support they could expect from the government—Departmental Enterprise (Perusahaan Jawatan or 'Perjan'), Public Enterprise (Perusahaan Umum or '*Perum*'), and Limited Liability Enterprise (Perseroan or '*Persero*') (Fitriningrum, 2015).

In addition, there were large stand-alone SOEs governed by their own specific legislation and local SOEs owned and managed by the various regional governments. Their activities—usually localized in nature and utility oriented—included such operations as water supply and banking. During the New Order, the 'State control' over SOEs was under the Directorate General of SOEs in the Ministry of Finance (ASOSAI).

The two oil booms of the 1970s, however, provided the government with much larger resource rents and tax revenue. They enabled the government to undertake ambitious State-led industrialization with SOEs coming under the supervision of line ministries. Another important influence on industrial policy in Indonesia emerged when in 1978 a new Minister of State for Research and Technology, Dr. B.J. Habibie, a

[2] In 1966, Indonesia was one of the poorest countries in the world, with per capita GDP (in 1985 US$, based on PPP) of $612—similar to that of India's $653. Three decades later in 1992, with an average GDP growth of almost 7% per capital GDP (in 1985 US$ based on PPP), was $2102, almost twice that of India's $1282.

German-trained aeronautical engineer, was appointed. Under him, Indonesia initiated the development of a range of State-owned, 'strategic industries', including a 'hi-tech' aircraft assembling company, a ship-building company, and eight other SOEs, deemed crucial for Indonesia in view of their strategic importance (Thee, 2006).

By 1980, 70% of total capital investment was undertaken by the public sector, with SOEs accounting for about 70% of overall economic activity. SOEs were, by now, operating in various strategic industries, with many assuming leading positions in them (Hill, 1987). With no sizable *pribumi* (indigenous Indonesian) presence in the economy, Indonesia maintained a large state sector to avoid further concentration of wealth in Sino-Indonesian conglomerates.

The SOE sector often faced financial constraints but survived difficult circumstances with repeated government support. Plans were announced to improve the performance of SOEs, but the actual implementation of the reform policies was slow (Pangestu and Habir, 1989; Robinson and Hadiz, 1993). Despite social pressures to solve the problems of SOEs, which had become a serious budgetary burden, the government maintained fiscal support for SOEs to ensure that they continued to play a pivotal role in the economy (Gonzalo, Pina, and Torres, 2003).

The end of the oil boom in 1982 resulted in considerably diminished fiscal capacity. So, the government once again attempted to promote the development of a more efficient private sector through a series of deregulation measures to improve the investment climate for private entrepreneurs. This policy was maintained up to the onset of the Asian economic crisis in 1997 (Thee, 2006). The crisis led to a sharp contraction of almost 14% in Indonesia's GDP in 1998. Although less leveraged and not so severely affected as private enterprises, SOEs suffered from growing operational and financial inefficiencies; many required financial restructuring.

In the process of negotiating a rescue deal, the Indonesian government and international organizations (such as the IMF, World Bank, and Asian Development Bank that had stepped in to enable recovery) recognized SOEs as a major source of corruption and economic inefficiency. As a result, the incoming government devised policies to shrink the SOE sector and privatize all but a few selected enterprises in the next decade (Government of Indonesia, 1998).

However, the implementation was slow, as the government faced strong social and political opposition, which was strengthened during the process of selling shares in Semen Gresikand Indosat to foreign companies. Responsibility for the management and restructuring of SOEs was shifted from line ministries to the Ministry of Finance, and a new Privatization Board was established. A 1998 presidential decree separated the State's shareholder and regulatory functions, establishing the Ministry of State-owned Enterprises (MoSE) as a single ownership entity for Indonesia's 141 SOEs and 18 companies in which the State held a minority share. In addition, Government Regulation 41 of 2003 was promulgated to strengthen the role of the Ministry of SOEs as the sole government representatives of SOEs (Republic of Indonesia, 2008).

After graduating from the IMF structural adjustment programme in 2003, the Indonesian government continued to seek opportunities to sell government stakes in SOEs till 2014 with the aim to strengthen its fiscal position amid weak tax revenues and rising fuel subsidies. However, the privatization plan was unambitious, involving divestment of only minority stakes in majority of cases. During this period of gradual ownership reorganization, the SOE sector as a whole experienced paradoxically, rapid expansion from the mid-2000s when Indonesia again recorded stable and healthy economic growth (Carney and Hamilton-Hart, 2015).

The country became less a hydrocarbon and mineral economy and became more a service-driven economy. Yet it enjoyed another (China-driven) commodity price boom between the mid-2000s and early 2010s (Hill, 2015), SOEs in the banking, telecommunication, energy, and mining sectors recorded impressive growth. Since 2014, President Joko Widodo has been trying to turn SOEs into efficient 'agents of development' by bringing competing SOEs under single holding company structures.

Since independence, the importance of SOEs was derived from their recognized contribution in the country's development, the large number of workers they employed, and the socially important role they played in avoiding public impression that the ethnic Chinese dominated economic activity. Their importance evolved during Suharto's regime as they constituted an important vehicle for achieving the economic emancipation of *pribumi* business (Johansson, 2014).

Along with rising importance of SOEs, post-colonial development in Indonesia saw the transfer of concentrated power and corrupt practices from old to new elites, without a subsequent mobilizing of people through political participation. A culture developed, based on the inherited logic of negotiations, gift giving and solidarity networks, which facilitated dubious and hidden economic transactions. From independence to 1998, strong forces worked to concentrate power in the hands of the executive bodies at the federal level in Jakarta (Apriliyanti and Kristiansen, 2019).

In the aftermath of the Asian financial crisis, the objective of the Ministry of SOEs has been to transform SOEs from being bloated, inefficient, resource-absorbing behemoths, into becoming more significant contributors to the economy. Since 2014, SOEs have played a key role in the government's $415 billion infrastructure development strategy (Salna and Dahrul, 2020). The 2016 Plan to accelerate 245 national strategic projects assumed that 30% would be financed by SOEs with the government focused on strengthening the institutional capacity[3] of SOEs to plan, select, and execute high-quality infrastructure projects.

Despite reforms of the last 20 plus years, corruption has remained endemic as little has changed in business–state relations by the substitution of authoritarian rule with democracy (Aspinall, 2013). Running for office is extremely costly in comparison with Indonesian income levels (Aspinall and Sukmajati, 2016). It has become the job of politicians to seek funding partners (Aspinall, 2013), and conglomerate business owners, or oligarchs, are the main sponsors of politicians and political parties (Carney and Hamilton-Hart, 2015). Indonesian SOEs are the main source of funding for the democratic political system (Apriliyanti and Kristiansen, 2019).

Regulation vs public ownership of SOEs

From the late 1980s up to the onset of the Asian economic crisis in 1997, Indonesia experienced a surge in domestic and foreign investment. Although fuelled by a recovery in oil prices in the mid-1990s, the surge

3 The government's strategy includes recapitalizing a number of SOEs in 2015 to increase their borrowing capacity (including external) to support infrastructure investment.

was attributable in large part to successive deregulation measures which the Indonesian government had introduced after the end of the oil boom in 1982 to improve the investment climate for private investors, both domestic and foreign. It was hoped that with a better investment climate, a more dynamic and efficient private sector would develop which would function as the new engine of growth and a major source of non-oil export revenues to offset the fall in oil export revenues (Thee, 2006).

The government attempted to open the economy further to private participation by divesting its holdings in some of the SOEs and encouraging foreign investment. But the energy, mining, and utilities sectors have remained firmly in the hands of government. Large SOEs in these sectors have colluded to form a public enterprise sphere of influence and have been successfully proactive in determining the terms of the government's support to SOEs. They thrived during the Suharto regime, thanks in part to the protection they received from the military in early years, and from the technical ministries that governed them in later years.

The historical legacy which established SOEs, and bestowed political privileges on them, created natural monopolies which established a firm state control over substantial resources. Understandably, it also resulted in the emergence of powerful constituencies (connected with the military) with vested interests aligned with the political structure of the Indonesian State. Despite putative efforts at opening up the economy on a number of occasions since the early 1980s, Indonesia's developmental ethos has continued to be dominated by highly nationalistic *pribumi* State-led development attitudes and priorities with a consequent reluctance to cede State ownership/control of key state assets and enterprises.

While democratization has been an important step in reforming systems of patrimonial politics, achieving effective regulatory governance over dominant patrimonial relations has proven to be exceedingly difficult.

The Indonesian government has continued to face major challenges in trying to build capable, effective, and responsive regulatory institutions for oversight of SOEs in an environment that still reeks of powerful vested interests and the vestiges of a patrimonial state. The State has, so far, been ineffectual in challenging well-established networks of entrenched vested interests. Nor has it been able to change significantly the pervasive influence of a long-established nexus of power relations that operates through deep-rooted civilian–military networks.

Recognizing that its various roles as owner, regulator, supervisor, and manager of SOEs have led to serious conflicts of interest, and posed constraints on potential growth, the government has made privatization a key strategy to increase economic efficiency, promote growth, and generate revenues for debt repayments and bank recapitalization. But transforming the developmental state model into a strong impartial state, capable of efficient and effective regulation at arms length, has remained an elusive goal.

Currently, exemptions from sound principles of commercial management have continued to be provided to SOE monopolies that produce or market goods or services concerning 'the needs of the people in general and production vital to the State'. The government amended existing laws in 2014 to terminate the monopoly status of most SOEs, especially in infrastructure and utilities. But since then, SOEs have been chosen to take on a more active role in the country's economic development agenda through infrastructure investment.

Sector-specific reforms in some cases have led to the establishment of sector-specific regulators in a process of opening SOE-dominated sectors to more private sector participation. Although the government has allowed the entry of new operators in most sub-sectors, the structure of the industry, together with the existing regulatory framework have allowed incumbents to deter entry of potential rivals (OECD, 2010b).

Not only do regulatory systems of governance seem antithetical to Indonesia's historical approach to development but also SOEs suffer from fuzzy, often confused, regulatory governance. More fundamentally, effective state and institutional capacities are necessary for effective regulatory systems of governance to emerge. Such systems require specific capacities and institutional endowments that presume efficient operation of administrative practices and procedures, many of which are only partially (or superficially) adhered to in Indonesia.

SOEs, with their public service obligations to fulfil, alongside processes of economically efficient and profitable commercialization, have made the entire SOE sector a contested space for a complex bureaucracy. Multiple institutional actors, agencies, and a plethora of bureaucracies compete within the SOE sector, blurring lines of authority, responsibility, thus contributing to rule confusion and inter-organization competition. The effect of such confusion and blurred lines of authority makes for a series of enduring problems in SOEs. They have served not only to empower SOEs especially in utilities and natural resources sectors but also in shaping their management culture and adversely affecting their operating procedures and finances (Jarvis, 2012).

Multiple and overlapping jurisdictions allow SOEs to make their operations and finances quite opaque, limiting the possibility of formal administrative 'proceduralization' to emerge. Thus, blocking transparency and accountability systems might enable them to operate efficiently. In the absence of effective institutions that are able to command legitimacy, and orchestrate effective co-ordination of sectors with significant SOE presence, SOEs are exposed to the unpredictable politics of governance by executive decree, but again in a porous institutional environment that shows little capacity to implement executive decrees. The prevalence of weak institutions in the sector has allowed SOEs to operate in a governance vacuum.

Diffused governance of SOEs has created a legacy of contested legitimacy. Some sectors with a strong SOE presence suffer from a legitimacy crisis, partly because they are overpopulated with agencies, sectional interests, and contested rule and authority ownership, where no single institution or agency has emerged with the legitimate authority to assume a leadership role. The lack of sound regulatory governance has meant that popular perceptions of endemic patrimonial politics have persisted, with vested interests and collusion being assumed to operate at the expense of the national interest (Wells, 2007).

In particular, collusion between government elites and the kickbacks secured in exchange for lucrative contracts, coupled with the involvement of SOEs (especially in natural resources and utilities) and the various arms of government, has led to feeding these unfortunate negative public perceptions. These historical legacies continue to affect SOEs, creating widespread perception that all SOE activities occur under such conditions and operate more for the private gain of their managers and officials and against the wider public interest.

Another legacy from Suharto's regime has also affected the emergence of regulatory governance in Indonesia. Under Suharto, people in Indonesia witnessed how the legal system was used to maintain his absolute power. There is little faith in the purpose of law and its enforcement system. This has affected the adoption of new laws, especially laws that have been adopted from foreign legal systems.

The example of BP Migas, the Upstream Oil and Gas Regulator in Indonesia, has shown that the principle of regulatory governance has not been fully embraced in policy-making. In 2012, the Indonesian constitutional court had held that BP Migas was unconstitutional. Islamic organizations and community interest groups expressing nationalist sentiment had applied for a judicial review of certain provisions of Indonesia's Oil and Gas Act 2001. They believed that BP Migas had awarded too many lucrative resources-based contracts to foreign investors to the detriment of the Indonesian population (Gibson Dunn and Crutcher LLP, 2012).

The 1945 Indonesian constitution provides that natural resources are to be controlled by the State and must be used in such a way as 'to provide maximum benefit to the people'. This provision tends to be restrictively interpreted in the Indonesian courts. In this case, the constitutional court effectively held that 'maximum benefit' could only be delivered if the State exercises 'full control' over natural resources extractive industries by being directly involved in their exploration and extraction through SOEs and making related policy decisions.

BP Migas was set up in 2002 as an independent, non-profit state entity to replace the regulation and licensing function of Pertamina. It managed and controlled the development of the Indonesian upstream oil and gas industry (exploration, production, exploitation, and marketing activities). The constitutional court's decision was based on the reasoning that the State should have sufficient control of its own natural resources and re-establish full control by granting exploitation rights to SOEs.

SOEs could then enter into Profit Sharing Contracts (PSCs) with the private sector. There was a conflict of interest in BP Migas entering into PSCs directly fettering the discretion and sovereignty of the State by restricting it from issuing new regulations or policies that conflicted with those PSCs. The creation of BP Migas was part of a proliferation of governmental bodies that created inefficiency and resulted in greater bureaucracy and potential for corruption (Gibson Dunn and Crutcher LLP, 2012). The constitutional court on its part has encouraged the government to reassert State control in the oil and gas sector through the new legislation.

SOEs and crony capitalism

The rapid growth of the Indonesian economy for nearly two decades prior to Suharto's downfall can be partly explained by crony capitalism along with Indonesia's general openness to trade and equity investments. Crony capitalism in Indonesia was the result of excessive government intervention in some targeted industries, which created close, symbiotic but not transparent relationships with certain business groups and cronies.

Crony capitalism in Indonesia resulted in blatant corruption among the government bureaucracy, particularly at the top levels, intimate State-business relationships with native Indonesian military officers, ethnic Chinese businessmen, and carefully selected indigenous Indonesian businessmen. Indonesia has had a long history of authoritarian governance and corrupt business practices. Dramatic democratization and decentralization reforms have been made over the last 20 years, but corruption remains endemic (Freedom House, 2017), and 'money politics have become the main political game' (Hadiz, 2010). There has been 'corruption in substantive amounts' in Indonesian SOEs (Sari and Tjoe, 2017). New cases of bribery and collusion among power holders, involving SOEs, are regularly revealed in Indonesian newspapers and magazines. The endurance of collusion in and around SOEs in Indonesia is a clear indication that it has become institutionalized (Apriliyanti and Kristiansen, 2019).

Since independence policies towards the private sector have often been influenced by the consideration to promote the development of *pribumi* Indonesian entrepreneurship. Under Suharto, major *pribumi* capitalists had emerged. Apart from the Suharto family, the *pribumi* capitalists included those that had been cultivated under the patronage of the State, through the tendering of government projects, serving as contractors for large SOEs.

Suharto's New Order, especially after the deregulation policies, became a quintessential example of crony capitalism and to a large extent, supported the expansion of his network. Liberalization in the 1980s withdrew monopoly licences that Suharto had passed out as patronage since the late 1970s. By the early 1990s, the only heavily protected industries were those directly linked to the President's immediate relatives and closest cronies.

New export-related opportunities opened up in many sectors, including agriculture (palm oil) and manufacturing (furniture, plywood, and garments). New foreign investment also sought the security of partnering with the president's family or closest associates driving corruption to new heights. During the deregulation period, Suharto's financial resources increased enormously and were put under his direct control, making his political authority highly personalized. The sudden expansion of Suharto's family's businesses combined with the increased dependence on Chinese conglomerates and a small number of dependent indigenous businesses made Suharto's patrimonial network complex, but still personal.

These policies distorted market incentives and rewarded unproductive rent-seeking activities. During Suharto's tenure, State power gradually evolved into an instrument of the newly ascendant family-based oligarchy. As reward for political support and kickbacks, loyal businessmen received privileges and protection from the government. Such privileges were manifold and included (a) licensing arrangements providing monopoly rents inter alia in importing, distribution, and exploitation of natural resources; (b) privileged access to inputs including finance and land; (c) tax breaks and subsidies; (d) privileged treatment in public procurement; (e) designation as mandatory partners in foreign joint ventures and with SOEs; and (v) price regulation resulting in supra-normal profits (McLeod, 2000).

By the late 1980s official corruption had reached extraordinary levels, whereby the idea of a competitive bid meant that each team needed one of the regime cronies just to qualify. This cronyism meant that virtually all new businesses—i.e. toll roads, mobile phones, video, and eco-tourism—had to come within the ambit of one or more of the family members and key cronies.

In spite of extensive corruption, Indonesia grew rapidly during the 1980s and 1990s, a phenomenon often referred to as the 'East Asian Paradox' (Vial and Hanoteau, 2010). If rent-creating corruption led to significant efficiency losses, in profit-sharing corruption, there was an incentive to enhance efficiency. This seems to have been the case with Indonesia where, along with rent-creating examples, there were profit-sharing examples. In many cases, the blurring of the difference between SOEs and family enterprises meant that Indonesian taxpayers had to pay for the inflated costs of crony capitalism. To moderate the burden on citizens, Suharto installed a national patronage network that covered the entire country. This network was financed from extra budgetary sources maintained through an intricate and widespread system of corruption.

SOEs channelled huge, unaccounted sums to Golkar, the government party. The party, in turn, distributed the patronage to the lowest and smallest units of the government bureaucracy, including village headmen. Patrimonialism thus became the cohesive factor in Suharto's regime, not only as the foundation of his legitimacy but also as a means for exchanging material rewards for favours, protection, and loyalties to Suharto's clients.

In addition, numerous private charitable foundations headed by Suharto had the authority to demand contributions from private individuals, corporations as well as State companies. Although run by officials of the State, family members, and Suharto's business associates, these foundations were involved in their own investment activities. Oligarchs not only controlled the State apparatus but also utilized State power to protect themselves.

Economic policies were often dictated by the political elite's interests, particularly the business interests of Suharto's family and their cronies. When efforts to reform SOEs were successful, and pain was felt by 'clients' of the system—military and civilian functionaries with positions in SOEs—Suharto's cabinet simply rescinded the measures whenever it felt some pushback.

Privatization was selective. For example, the privatization of electricity supply to industrial estates resulted in control by a group of businesses headed by a close Suharto relative. The concentration of economic power in Indonesia exacerbated the financial crisis and eventually transformed the crisis into a political one. Following the crisis, one of the IMF's requirements for *Reformasi* was to improve governance in the political economy. In complying with IMF requirements, the *Reformasi* governments have established regulatory frameworks to remove the practices of corruption, collusion, and nepotism in the economy.

However, several aspects of the New Order patronage system still persist. The *Reformasi* governments cannot be categorized entirely as being patrimonial. State power is much too fragmented and diffused now to constitute a single group presiding over the interests of a single, largely cohesive oligarchy fusing business, political, and bureaucratic interests as it did during Suharto's time. The complex system of intertwined social and personal hierarchies and patronage relationships still permeate the economy and society (Raffiudin, 2015).

The new economic–political system is dominated by forces that were established under the Suharto regime (Robinson and Hadiz, 2004). The collapse of authoritarianism has given rise to an 'untamed oligarchy' in Indonesia. The old oligarchy has been able to seize the new political and market institutions. Institutional reforms have also enabled oligarchs to access power by becoming members of parliament, or even being appointed as cabinet ministers in the *Reformasi* governments. These intertwining interests have made the use of money politics more than ever before. Oligarchs have utilized the 'power of their wealth to overwhelm the legal system' (Winters, 2011). The rule of law and the role of mediating institutions are still too weak to control the dominating economic interests of the big business conglomerates and generate transparency and accountability in the economic system (Winters, 2011). Even leading figures in auditing and law enforcement agencies, like Badan Pemeriksa Keuangan (BPK), Komisi Pemberantasan Korupsi (KPK), and the Attorney General, are 'clients of powerful people'.

The current President Jokowi, who does not belong to the old ruling elite and who had ambitions to change the system, has failed to break from the political traditions (Fukuoka and Djani, 2016). President Jokowi has had to 'strike deals with oligarchs and engage in patronage distribution', and he has avoided 'institutional changes that might confront or disrupt' strategic political alliances (Warburton, 2016).

What has occurred seems to be a repeat of the previous pattern, when the oligarchy hijacked deregulation policies back in the 1980s. In 2012, Indonesia's constitutional court dissolved energy regulator BP Migas and integrated its role into the energy ministry. Many political observers believed that the changes were driven by the lobbying of crony capitalists as they would benefit from the new law which gave greater power to SOEs with which they have had close ties.

Patron–client relations have now evolved from allocating state resources to SOE policy-making, for example, the distribution of governmental 'projects', appointment of top managers of SOEs, adoption of new technologies, and so on. In 2012, executives connected to political parties and the Presidency were on the board of about half of the top 25 State companies, according to data from the MSOE. Two presidential decrees issued in 2005 gave the authority to choose top managers of SOEs to a 'final assessment team' led by the president. Policies related to the implementation of new technologies have been based on the strength of lobbying activities surrounding the main policy-makers, in particular, the President.

The private agenda of public officials

Indonesian SOEs have operated in businesses with 'well-established opportunities for extracting personal benefits, through contracting, access to resource rents, or the provision of loans' (Carney and Hamilton-Hart, 2015). Collusion around SOEs in Indonesia has involved agents from various elite groups and different layers of hierarchies—from private businesses to the national parliament, and from state auditors to the President. Financial means illegally tapped from SOEs are used for both political and private ends (Apriliyanti and Kristiansen, 2019).

Suharto realized the effectiveness of private sector monopoly privileges for generating rents. These rents were then shared between the favoured recipients and Suharto, his family, and their supporters. Suharto's patrimonialism needed a sufficient number of people willing to play the game so that opportunities for harvesting rents could be exploited. Important to Suharto's patrimonialism were public officials employed in providing protection from imports, awarding contracts without bidding, providing access to cheap loans, granting rights to exploit natural resources, designating mandatory partners in foreign joint ventures, in obtaining land and purchase of inputs at artificially low prices and the tax office (Mcleod, 2000).

In Indonesia, where the State lacked a mechanism of regulatory control over policies made for the public or private sectors, the vested interests of key actors have been crucial in determining national policy. In Indonesia, this context was shaped by the personalized relationship of power and the nature of a soft state. The former encompassed various practices, for example, favouritism. Exchanges between patron and client focused on reciprocal support for the promotion of particular interests and the satisfaction of mutual needs. Public officials played an important role in this exchange. In addition, they played a significant role in the absence of properly functioning formal law. The vacuum was filled by informal arbitration, with Suharto and his civil service and franchises playing the role of arbitrators and enforcers (Simandjuntak, 2014).

Just as Suharto used his position as the head of the government to bestow privileges on selected firms, he effectively awarded franchises to government officials at lower levels to buy their loyalty. This included many of his ministers and senior bureaucrats, government administrators at all levels from provinces to villages (Mcleod, 2000). Suharto's new vision of a 'development state' required a massive expansion of the State bureaucracy. Between the mid-1970s and the mid-1980s, the core bureaucracy grew from fewer than 500,000 to at least three million. As the New Order's top managers became increasingly entrenched, the system became a well-oiled mechanism for extracting patronage rents. Some of these resources went to supplement income, and therefore to consolidate and cement the loyalty of the bureaucracy to the Presidency.

Suharto's patronage network was financed from off-budget transfers and asset pools involving military businesses (which were phased out in large part by the mid-1980s), large-scale infrastructure construction kickbacks, access to national resource concessions. The president's closely managed 'foundations' kept this system working. If systemizing patronage was the first prong in Suharto's strategy to maintain stability, the second prong was protection of that system. The network controlled life's opportunities for all participants in the governing system, and it required a tremendous flow of resources to keep it running effectively (Baker, 2012).

A significant portion of the actual income of all officials came through projects, either *legally* in the form of 'incentives' or *illegally* through theft of project resources or kickbacks from government contractors. Officials at all levels became adept at designing annual budgets for projects, used to expropriate resources. Budgetary procedures, as well as the bureaucratic culture that emerged during the next few years, guaranteed the pervasiveness of bureaucratic corruption, both petty and grand. Bureaucratic corruption under the New Order became systemic and routine, but it was organized and contained within limits that did not seriously threaten broader security and development goals.

The New Order's integrated system of *administrative* and *political* control obscured the boundary between the two. It was difficult to discern where the interests and actions of Suharto's top lieutenants ended and those of the professional managers began. Under the New Order, mandatory membership in the civil servant association—until 1998, in Suharto's political party, *Golkar*—ensured that the bureaucracy would not become independent from political leadership. At the highest levels, senior administrative officials were expected to provide protection and opportunity to the Suharto family and to crony enterprises.

The loyalty of public officials was clearly divided between the so-called technocrats (a group of US trained economists known as 'Berkeley mafia') and *pribumi* nationalists. The technocrats and nationalists sparred for influence at the top table. In the 1980s technocrats gained the upper hand and controlled the vital Ministry of Finance, the Bank of Indonesia, and the powerful coordinating Ministry of Economy. The nationalists controlled many of the secondary ministries—for example, technology, telecommunications, and transport. The technocrats guided government policies towards liberalization in many sectors of the economy. It was remarkably successful and the country's economy grew rapidly throughout the 1980s and early 1990s (Hertzmark, 2007).

Liberalization in the 1980s threatened the interests of many state officials because much of their power derived from the allocation of licences, monopolies, and concessions. SOEs in the upstream sector were also threatened by the retreat of the State. These changes withdrew monopoly licences to importers that Suharto had passed out as patronage. By the early 1990s, the only heavily protected industries were those directly linked to the president's immediate relatives and closest cronies.

Liberalization opened up new export-related opportunities in plantation agriculture and export manufacturing. Banking was deregulated, and most large Indonesian conglomerates entered the banking sector. Liberalization attracted foreign investment, but lack of an effective regulatory enforcement mechanism and of a sound commercial law system drove corruption to new heights. Uncertain foreign investors sought the security of partnering with the president's family or closest associates.

Till the end of the 1990s, these two closely inter-related systems of rent-seeking and patronage had co-existed. The Asian Financial crisis and political transition sparked a number of changes, including liberalization, decentralization, and democratization. The collapse of Suharto's regime decreased the value of connections to him (Hallward-Driemeier et al., 2020). Restructuring of politically connected companies, elimination of a number of production and trade monopolies, and elimination of investment restrictions were arguably all manifestations of reduced capture.

But corruption during the Suharto era was, and in the post–Suharto era has continued to be, ubiquitous in Indonesia—despite a formidable array of legislation prohibiting it, and notwithstanding several successful prosecutions of corrupt officials both during and after Suharto. Corruption has been exacerbated by competitive multiparty politics, such that political parties and other entities compete to establish their own separate patronage networks.

Decentralization reforms redistributed political, administrative, and economic power to provinces, districts, and cities, which encouraged competition (Hill, 2007). They have resulted in a renegotiation of state–business relationships. In fact, many businessmen have elected themselves as heads of administrative units. In many other cases, they have managed to win the support of local politicians by supporting them during election campaigns (Hadiz, 2004).

Thus, the 'gift-exchange' nature of state–business relationships appears to have changed very little. Competition for control over key state institutions by state officials representing different political parties and hence coalitions of interests, aspiring towards oligarchic status, is also seen in the case of the scramble to take charge of SOEs. Control over monopoly SOEs still offers a potential economic resource base. Newcomers are encouraged to identify and affiliate with other members in an organization by rewards and co-optation. The system of reciprocal loyalty and obligations, and the threats of sanctions have obliged new members to accept and engage in the ongoing practices (Apriliyanti and Kristiansen, 2019).

SOEs and the misallocation of resources

The economic policies pursued by successive Indonesian governments since the early years of independence were shaped by (a) the interplay of major economic challenges faced at the time; and (b) the economic ideas of key, influential policy-makers, and economic nationalism. Widespread social discontent was a major underlying political issue that has plagued every Indonesian government. It arises from a persistently widening gap between the privileged rich and the numerous poor—specifically between visibly rich business tycoons and the indigenous (*pribumi*) majority. The State has had to play an essential role in helping the country to face this fundamental politico-economic challenge. Policies to promote the development of *pribumi* Indonesian entrepreneurship put SOEs at the centre of the divide, as a proxy for representing the interests of the majority *pribumis* (Thee, 2006). This strategy was not too different from what was followed in other countries at the time.

The New Order government took several measures to help *pribumi* businessmen advance faster. New foreign investment projects required an Indonesian partner in joint ventures. State-owned banks were required to extend credit only to domestic companies. Government contracts of up to Rp. 20 million were reserved for businessmen from the 'economically weak groups in society'. While contracts up to Rp. 100 million were awarded by tendered bids, preferential treatment was extended to businessmen from the 'economically weak groups in society', if their tenders were up to 10% higher than the others (Daroesman, 1981).

This led to ethnic Chinese businessmen collaborating with *pribumi* businessmen, who held the required business licenses (Suryadinata, 2001) and fronted for them. State-owned banks favoured companies in which the majority share ownership was held by *pribumi* businessmen, while the ethnic Chinese managed and controlled actual operations. The State banks were resigned to these practices as otherwise too few companies were able to meet the minimum own capital requirements to qualify for these bank loans (Sadli, 1988) or to operate successfully enough to ensure that loans were repaid. Ethnic Chinese businessmen had long commercial experience, better access to capital, managerial, and technical skills, and networked with other Chinese businesses throughout Asia. Through collaboration with *pribumi* businessmen, they were able to move into various economic activities on a large scale. Although government-driven economic nationalism was aimed at reducing the economy's dependence on ethnic Chinese conglomerates, the government's affirmative action programme actually (and paradoxically) led to further economic concentration in Chinese hands.

Suharto's government introduced other policies, like the 'Foster Father scheme'. Under this scheme, large enterprises and SOEs (referred to as 'Foster Fathers') were urged to establish partnerships with cooperatives and small enterprises, largely owned by members of the economically weak groups in society (Thee, 2006).

The government often used SOEs to provide public goods and services. Frequent political interference in the pricing of such services and inadequate accountability of SOEs resulted in the inefficient delivery of goods and services, with profitable business units within SOEs cross-subsidizing public service delivery. The government usually provided no compensation or made only inadequate subsidy payments to meet the SOEs' cost of delivery, thus affecting adversely the commercial viability of several SOEs (IBP, 2007).

It was during Suharto's rule that giant business conglomerates owned and controlled by his children emerged and grew rapidly with State backing. These conglomerates enjoyed preferential treatment, including large subsidized credit from the State banks, protection, and monopoly positions, and assured government procurement. They were extended monopsony and monopoly rights to purchase from SOEs and sell at monopoly prices (Johansson, 2014).

The State has always been the major instrument through which the interests of oligarchs were consolidated, entrenched, and protected. As in many countries the oligarchy in Indonesia appropriated State power for itself and used it to further its interests. The State's resources were deployed to create an oligarchy insulated from any accountability.

SOEs became cash cows. They over-priced contracts with suppliers and under-priced contracts with customers. The most egregious example of how state resources were deployed to aid Suharto family's businesses was in the case of the 'national car' or Timor. Suharto's son's company was granted national car status under the terms of a State decree to encourage the production of a local car. When Timor failed to reach a target of 20% local content within the first year, the company gained a series of further concessions. In 1996 the government allowed the company to produce Indonesia's `national cars' entirely in Korea. But as sales flagged, in 1997 the government instructed State departments, enterprises, and other agencies to purchase the 'national car'. Projects, like these which did not take into account Indonesia's resource constraints, became 'devouring tapeworms' (Nasution, 1995) depleting resources of the State. These practices eventually eroded the legitimacy of the New Order regime.

State-owned banks and enterprises were not only instrumental in enriching a select group of conglomerates close to Suharto and ethnic Chinese businessmen, but they also provided jobs to members of the armed forces after their retirement, and to relatives and friends of Suharto's supporters, such as his ministers and senior bureaucrats. State power provided the catalyst for the emergence and consolidation of an oligarchy in Indonesia.

A culture of patronage has long existed in Indonesia, and state resources have been used to reward individuals for political support. Since the fall of Suharto there has been a contest between dominant groups over the control of the State apparatus and its authority in relation to the allocation of state resources and patronage. Power relations between politicians and the business elite may have changed since then, but influential positions are still offered to people who are willing to make economic decisions in favour of wealthy sponsors (Apriliyanti and Kristiansen, 2019).

The performance of Indonesian SOEs

At the end of Sukarno's rule in 1966, SOEs had become the dominant force in the domestic economy. Traditionally, SOEs provided public goods and services, but frequent political interference in the pricing of such services and inadequate accountability of SOEs resulted in inefficient delivery, with profitable business units within the SOEs cross-subsidizing public service obligations. The government provided no compensation or made only inadequate subsidy payments to meet the SOEs' costs of delivery.

The arrival of Suharto's New Order government was expected to improve the economic efficiency of SOEs through reform of the State sector. But the ability to perform efficiently was constrained, as SOEs were manipulated for political purposes—to pay off political cronies or to serve the personal ambitions and accumulate enormously the wealth of political leaders. With the increase in oil prices in the early 1970s, the urgency diminished for Indonesia to push through reforms of its SOEs. In fact, reform of SOEs went into reverse with the government increasing its proportion of ownership in the domestic economy (Sungkar, 2008).

During the 1980s, the government continued with its relatively modest reform of SOEs. These reforms included introduction of performance measures commonly used for private companies, such as profitability, liquidity, and solvency. Most of the SOEs evaluated on these measures were deemed as 'unsound' (Irianto, 2004). In the late 1980s, the government actively privatized SOEs to generate revenue to maintain the government's spending programmes. Some of the bigger SOEs went public successfully and, after privatization, some of these firms were successful in improving their performance quite significantly (Van der Eng, 2004).

At the start of the Asian financial crisis in 1997, SOEs, although less leveraged and not as severely affected as private enterprises, suffered from growing operational and financial constraints and most needed restructuring. They had very low rates of return on assets (RoA), new investments, and their total equity, often less than the cost of capital. At the end of 1997, with total assets of US$57.6 billion, the average return on investment and return on equity of SOEs was, respectively, 3.5% and 9.6%, which showed the low level of asset utilization and the high level of production costs (Sungkar, 2008).

Privatization continued after the Asian financial crisis, and new systems were established to separate the functions of shareholders and controllers and to centralize the supervision of SOEs (Aprilinyati and Kristiansen, 2019). Privatization was given considerable emphasis in the IMF's post-crisis recovery programme between 1997 and 2003. There have been several resultant sales of minority shareholdings to private investors. Consequentially, there are some entities that are fully owned by the State and others whose ownership has been partially moved to private investors. However, privatization has had limited success in Indonesia (Sungkar, 2008). The proportion of publicly listed companies with a dominant share of state ownership actually grew after the crisis, and the value of SOEs' total assets increased more than four-fold from 2004 to 2014 (Carney and Hamilton-Hart, 2015). There was no intention to decrease state ownership in the Indonesian economy at the time (Carney and Child, 2013).

In the aftermath of the crisis, a separate Ministry of State-owned Enterprises was formed to represent the government as the State shareholder in SOEs and to separate the functions between shareholders, regulators, and centralized supervision. According to the World Bank's categorization of 16 countries with a centralized ownership arrangement, Indonesia is the only country with a ministry-level ownership structure (World Bank, 2014a). In 2003, a new law was issued to specifically address the restructuring and privatization of SOEs. Indonesia has since promoted competition in several sectors and reduced the privileges accorded to SOEs.

To improve SOE governance and performance, the MSOE has, since 2003, appointed more-professional directors/commissioners, improved the design of annual performance contracts for managers and listing minority stakes in many companies. The MSOE appoints directors and commissioners in conjunction with other line ministries (ROSC Worldbank, 2010). But in reality, 45% of SOE board members are bureaucrats, recruited mostly from the MSOE or technical ministries, like the Ministry of Industry or the Ministry of Energy and Mineral Resources. High-ranked officers are placed in the largest and most powerful firms. The recruitment of persons to leading positions in the bureaucracy and agencies involved in managing or controlling SOEs has also been subject to selection procedures that do not mainly emphasize professional competence or merit (Aprilinyati and Kristiansen, 2019).

The government along with a number of stakeholders, such as the Capital Market Supervisory Agency (Badan Pengawas Pasar Modal—'*Bapepam*', currently known as Financial Service Authority—OJK), the Jakarta Stock Exchange (currently known as Indonesian Stock Exchange), and certain professional bodies launched a series of initiatives to improve corporate governance in SOEs. These included, for example, establishing the National Committee on Corporate Governance (NCCG), the Indonesian Institute for Corporate Governance (IICG), and the Forum for Corporate Governance in Indonesia (FCGI). The Audit Board of Indonesia, BPK, formally strengthened its independence from the government by coming under the supervision of a Board of nine members, who are elected by the Parliament. The Corruption Eradication Commission, KPK, started operating in 2003 with the mandate to prevent, fight, and prosecute corrupt practices. The KPK is accountable to the public and submits reports openly and periodically to the President, the Parliament, and the BPK. Other instruments to control SOEs and investigate and prosecute corruption cases include the National Police (POLRI), which was separated from the Armed Forces in 2000, and the Attorney

General of Indonesia (Kejaksaan Agung). Finally, the Commission 6 of the Indonesian Parliament, DPR (Dewan Perwakilan Rakyat), has a special responsibility of overseeing and controlling SOEs (Aprilinyati and Kristiansen, 2019).

Another significant change affected the final products sold by Pertamina (State-owned oil and natural gas company) and Perusahaan Listrik Negara (PLN, the State-owned electricity company), whose prices have been administered by the government. While energy subsidy reforms since 2014 have effectively discontinued gasoline subsidies for all, and electricity subsidies for medium and large users, there are other products which are still subsidized by the government. But for such subsidized products, the government budget compensates Pertamina and PLN with payments calculated on the basis of agreed formulae to reflect economic costs, including changes in the exchange rate.

The government established sectoral holding companies (SHCs) as part of the SOE reform plan after the crisis, though the focus was firmly on privatization (Ulfa, 2017). After Indonesia was relieved of the drawn-out effects of the crisis in the mid-2000s, the government began to pay greater attention to SHCs. In the longer term, the government has envisioned to create a super-holding company similar to Singapore's Temasek Holdings or Malaysia's Khazanah Nasional. Under the current government, the emphasis of SHCs has shifted from professionalization and streamlining to corporate expansion. But there is a risk that consolidating the SOEs into SHCs will probably make their financial situation more opaque.

Despite these changes, Indonesia's 124 SOEs with assets worth $350 billion (see Figure 6.3) and revenue of $155 billion (in 2012), their total profits were only $9 billion, and only about 20 SOEs paid a regular dividend. Revenues from SOEs represent less than 2% of Indonesian State incomes, and they continue to receive huge capital injections from the national budget (Ray and Ing, 2016).

Comparing efficiency indicators of SOEs with private sector counterparts in certain key industries, such as banking and plantations, showed SOEs lagging behind. In the banking sector, State-owned banks showed lower rates of RoA at 2.2%, compared to 2.6% for private banks, but with a much higher proportion of non-performing loans (NPLs) than private banks (Wicaksono, 2009).

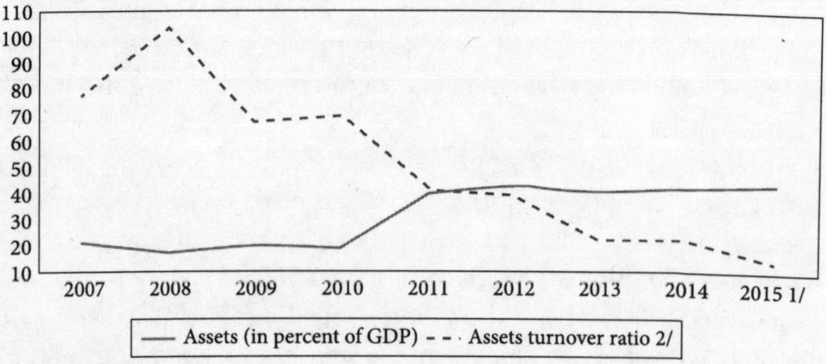

Figure 6.3 SOEs assets and turnover ratio
Source: IMF, 2018b.

More than 90% of total assets of the SOEs were accounted for by the 12 largest SOEs. These SOEs also accounted for more than 91% of debt, 79% of total revenues, and 84% of total net profits. The overall average SOE RoA is 2.92%, while the mean RoA of the 12 largest SOEs was 6.36%. Partially owned SOEs accounted for only 25% of total SOE revenues, but this group produced a far bigger portion of net profits—60% of the total net profits of all SOEs (Astami et al., 2010).

The significant challenge now facing key SOEs in Indonesia is their high level of total and external indebtedness, in the face of inadequate hedges against their foreign exchange exposure. Although still relatively low, the total debt of SOEs doubled as a share of GDP between 2009 and 2013. About two-thirds of this increase originated from debt issued to non-residents, with external debt reaching 2.8% of GDP at end 2013 (54% of total).

Similarly, the share of foreign currency-denominated debt rose to about 70% in 2013. Pertamina and PLN accounted for the majority of the increase in the aggregated debt level of non-financial SOEs, using the proceeds from new borrowing to finance investment in physical assets (for example, oil pipelines, power plants). Since 2014, SOEs have been encouraged to increase investment in infrastructure through direct and indirect financial incentives. As a result, financial vulnerabilities have been rising at some SOEs (IMF, 2015).

While their balance sheets have become more leveraged in recent years, low world oil prices have affected Pertamina's revenues from upstream production and lowered its profit margins. The profits of non-financial SOEs' have also fallen in the past few years, while facing higher interest payments. PLN recorded losses of about 0.3% of GDP in 2013, mainly due to exchange rate depreciation (IMF, 2015).

Improvements in the operational efficiency of Indonesian SOEs and maintenance of sound debt management remain important. The current government is recapitalizing a number of SOEs to increase their borrowing capacity (including external) to support infrastructure investment. This would require a strengthening of the institutional capacity of the SOEs to plan, select, and execute high-quality infrastructure projects.

Conflicts that arise in the State's primary role vs its ownership of enterprises

The State has an important role in negotiating rules that level the playing field for investment, rules that ensure that private and State-owned firms compete on the same terms. When state support enables some companies to crowd out others, it casts doubts on the fairness of the business environment. Where fairness is questioned, the sustainability of investment is at risk.

Since 2014, SOEs have been chosen to take on an even more active role than before in accelerating the country's economic development. The current government has been critical of past governments' use of SOEs as cash cows. With this policy direction, privatization has now largely been excluded from the government's agenda.

SOEs have been contributing to development mainly through infrastructure investment, loans to small businesses, and price restraint, including, 'one fuel price policy', '35,000 megawatt electricity project', and other projects in line with Indonesia's long-term re-industrialization goal. SOEs have been actively participating in projects that are expected to improve national connectivity, such as the 'Trans-Sumatra toll road', 'Greater Jakarta light rail transit', and 'Jakarta-Bandung high-speed rail'. SOEs have been increasingly taking over projects previously owned by the private sector with little progress, such as the 'Bocimi toll road' (Kim, 2018).

To encourage SOEs to increase investment in infrastructure, the government has taken a multipronged approach, including injecting capital, limiting dividend payments, and upgrading the financing framework. To expand their investment capacity and provide confidence, the government has injected new capital into SOEs, especially in the power, construction, and transportation sectors. This capital injection amounted to 0.6% of GDP in 2015–16 (Breuer et al., 2018).

To encourage capital spending, the government has allowed SOEs to lower dividend payments to the government since 2015–16, so long as the retained earnings were channelled into infrastructure investment. Direct borrowing by SOEs from international financial institutions has been allowed under a sovereign guarantee. The scope of the Indonesia Infrastructure Guarantee Fund has also been expanded to include state guarantees for borrowing by SOEs. SOEs' capital expenditures increased to 2.8% of GDP in 2015 and 3.1% of GDP in 2016, from 2.2% of GDP in 2013 (Breuer et al., 2018). Since 2015, SOEs have amassed a combined debt of $98 billion and that has grown by 15% in 2019–20 (Salna and Dahrul, 2020).

The government's direct project funding, and preferential lending by State-owned banks, project guarantees, and asset securitization, have also supported SOE participation in development programmes. Although the aim of these measures is to implement specific projects, the government is also enabling SOEs to finance future projects without relying mainly on funds provided directly by the government through the fiscal budget. The government, therefore, has been pursuing policies to strengthen SOEs' capital structures (Kim, 2018).

As a result, financial vulnerabilities have been rising at some SOEs. Rapid investment, higher leverage, institutional and coordination weaknesses, and continued weak execution capacity could expose SOEs involved with infrastructure projects to cash-flow difficulties, particularly if interest rates increased or projects are delayed. Measures to contain retail electricity and fuel prices have been slowly generating financial pressures in those firms.

For example, the price of low-octane fuel ('premium') has not been changed since 2016 despite the increase in the international oil price, although that has now crashed in the face of the COVID-19 crisis. Fourteen SOEs made losses in 2017, although that was a fewer number than in 2016. State-owned banks' exposures to SMEs and the construction sector have risen rapidly (OECD, 2018b).

On-balance-sheet loans and guarantees to SOEs are relatively small. Other potential adverse effects of increased public borrowing on interest rates include crowding out private investment and of higher contingent liabilities. But, recognized contingent liabilities were only 0.01% of GDP in 2017, as these are confined to government-guaranteed loans. Still, the potential need for future capital injections could represent an indirect fiscal risk (OECD, 2018b).

The government has been resorting to public–private partnerships (PPPs)—between SOEs and private firms—quite extensively in recent years. In 2017 there were 11 PPPs underway, totalling US$15.4 billion (World Bank, 2018b).

Greater private sector involvement in infrastructure projects would reduce the pressure on SOEs, but the private sector is being crowded out. Prospective investors have faced legal and regulatory uncertainty and a lack of viable projects due to deficiencies in the project cycle (World Bank, 2017). SOEs have sometimes acted as 'private' bidders which has also deterred private investors (OECD, 2012a). Indonesia's drive to increase infrastructure investment through SOEs risks polluting the business environment while increasing fiscal risks in the long run.

Conclusions

Since 2000 the objective of the Ministry of SOEs has been to transform SOEs from being bloated, inefficient, resource-absorbing behemoths that encourage unbridled corruption, into becoming significant contributors to the Indonesian economy. Since 2014, SOEs have been a key plank in the government's infrastructure and development strategy.

The historical legacy that governed the establishment of SOEs, and bestowed political privileges on them, resulted in the emergence of powerful constituencies with vested interests aligned with the political structure of the Indonesian State. Despite many efforts at opening up the economy since the early 1980s, Indonesia's developmental ethos has still continued to be dominated by highly nationalistic state-led development attitudes and priorities with a consequent reluctance to cede State ownership/control of key state assets and enterprises.

State power is much too fragmented and diffused now to allow a single group presiding over the interests of a single, largely cohesive oligarchy, that fused business, political, and bureaucratic interests as it did during Suharto's time. But the complex system of intertwined social and personal hierarchies, patronage relationships, and endemic corruption still permeate the economy and society.

The government has often used SOEs to provide public goods and services. Frequent political interference in the pricing of such services and inadequate accountability of SOEs has resulted in the inefficient delivery of goods and services, with profitable business units within SOEs cross-subsidizing public service delivery.

After the Asian financial crisis, a separate Ministry of State-owned Enterprises was formed to represent the government as the State shareholder in SOEs and to separate the functions between shareholders, regulators, and centralized supervision. The significant challenge now facing key SOEs in Indonesia is improving the operational efficiency of SOEs and maintaining sound debt management. The current government is recapitalizing a number of SOEs to increase their borrowing capacity to support infrastructure investment.

7
Country case study 5: Russia

SOEs in Russia

Russia has over 32,000 SOEs. Normalizing by population puts Russia at about 220 SOEs per one million inhabitants (IMF, 2019). The State accounted for about one-third of Russia's total value added in 2016, a share that remained largely unchanged for about a decade. The State sector's share of GDP has increased since the late 1990s, according to the European Bank for Reconstruction and Development (EBRD), from 30% in 1997 to 35% in 2010 and has remained at this level till recently.

The State, comprising general government and SOEs, represents two-fifths of formal sector activity and one-half of formal sector employment. SOEs are present in almost all strategic sectors but not that pervasive in the direct production of consumer goods. Over the past 5 years, the State's share has increased significantly in energy and banking, although this has been mostly offset by some reductions in other sectors. The prevalence of SOEs means that the State accounts for a higher share of employment compared to other middle-income and advanced economies, even though general government spending is relatively lower.

About 1.5% of SOEs represent more than 85% of revenues, suggesting room for consolidation of smaller enterprises, efficiency gains, and better management of state assets (IMF, 2019). The Russian State is a prominent controlling shareholder in listed companies, accounting for half of the market capitalization MICEX 50 Index in 2014. SOE share in formal employment was 25% in 2016–17 (IMF, 2018).

A study in 2018 by the Center for Strategic Research, a Russian think-tank, has claimed that the State's size stopped expanding in the last few years, but that the State's role in resource allocation has strengthened, including through stronger influence of SOEs and State Development Institutions, pseudo-privatization, and expansion of regulation. It has highlighted that the number of State entities declined in 2010–16, but that the State's direct and indirect participation in key sectors has remained considerable (Di Bella et al., 2019).

The State's share is large in sectors deemed strategic (oil/gas extraction and processing, and defence equipment production), in natural monopolies, public utility services (electricity, water and sanitation, heating, pipeline, and railway transportation), finance (banking and other financial services) and, naturally, in security, health, and education. There is, however, little State ownership in most other sectors of the Russian economy, including consumer goods, non-defence manufacturing, agriculture, insurance, and services. From a regional perspective, the presence of the State across Russian regions has been diverse. Regions with lower per capita income (which receive relatively larger federal transfers) generally have a larger state size, as shown in Table 7.1 (Di Bella et al., 2019).

Over two-thirds of Russia's banking system is dominated by State-owned banks (divided into development institutions, commercial banks, and hybrid banks). The large State-owned commercial banks (groups) include Sberbank, the VTB Bank group, and Gazprombank, which had over 50% of the banking system's assets at the end of 2017 (Di Bella et al., 2019). The State now controls four of the top five companies in Russia: Gazprom, Russian Railways, Rosneft, and UES. The State's shareholding in the ten largest Russian companies is very high; it is topped only by the UAE and China in their shareholding of the top ten companies in those countries.

Pervasive state control in the Russian economy reflects not just the communist legacy of the Soviet era but also the Russian government's policy of maintaining a controlling stake in strategic enterprises and promoting 'national champions'.

Accordingly, the number of majority stakes of the federal government has increased from 25% of total holdings in 2005 to 61% in 2008 (Sprenger, 2008).

Another related development is the emergence of large, State-controlled conglomerates. These have, in some cases, been established through the consolidation of existing SOEs (for example, Rosneft and Gazprom, United Aircraft Corporation), established in late 2006 to consolidate all SOEs engaged in the manufacture, design, and sale of military and non-military aircraft. Similarly, Rosatom was established in late

Table 7.1 Number of SOEs in Russia

	State	Subsidiaries	State + Subsidiaries
Market activities	28.125	445	28.57
Agriculture, Fishing, Logging	1.692	0	1.692
Mining	131	60	191
Manufacturing	2.015	43	2.058
Electricity, Gas, Hot Water	2.774	54	2.828
Water Supply and Sanitation	2.779	1	2.78
Construction	1.066	12	1.078
Trade and Repairs	2.119	72	2.191
Transportation and Storage	1.973	49	2.022
Hotels and Restaurants	697	6	703
Information and Communication	1.455	47	1.502
Financial and Insurance	490	13	503
Real Estate	5.206	16	5.402
Professional, Scientific and Technical Professions	5.095	67	5.162
Administrative and Related Services	813	5	818
Non-Market Activities	4.012	4	4.016
Total	32.137	449	32.586

Source: Di Bella et al., 2019.

2007 by amalgamating SOEs involved in the nuclear industry; United Shipbuilding Corporation amalgamated 40 shipbuilding yards; and Rostechnologii was established to consolidate ownership of pre-existing conglomerates.

After the collapse of the Soviet Union in 1989, the Yeltsin administration initiated an aggressive process of economic transformation, at the heart of which was the transfer of State assets to private ownership. This led to a dramatic transformation of Russia's economy. An economy previously based on State ownership, central planning, and a high degree of autarky gave way to one based on private ownership, market forces, and integration into the world economy. According to EBRD's estimates, the Russian State's share in value added dropped from 95% in 1991 to 30% in 1997. Before privatization began in the early 1990s, there were 349,300

SOEs owned by all levels of government (national, federal, and municipal) with total assets valued at RUB 35.6 billion and 80,100 non-business organizations with total assets of RUB 24.1 billion (Goskomstat 1992).

Data from the beginning of the privatization period suggest that 36,800 SOEs were privatized in 1991–92 and another 64,800 were privatized in 1993–94. By mid-1994, the State's average holding in industrial firms had fallen to 38%. According to official data 57.9% of the workforce, including 76% of the industrial workforce, was employed in privatized or in new private firms. Over 70% of small-scale enterprises had been transferred to private ownership. But between 1995 and 97, the pace of privatization slowed and, post-1997, privatization transactions ceased to be conducted on a large scale.

By the mid-2000s, the State had re-assembled substantial stakes in formerly privatized companies and strategic sectors (Grosman et al., 2016). Today the State has not only held on to old companies but has also established new SOEs, including, by some estimates, around 600 unitary enterprises[1] per year (Kovaleva et al., 2019).

Privatization in Russia

So far, there have been three distinct phases or waves in Russia's privatization process:

(1) mass 'voucher' privatization programme executed during 1992–94[2];

[1] In Russia, SOEs are defined as any public non-budgetary establishment with a positive direct government share. Russian SOEs can take four legal forms—1. *Commercial companies with state participation* include joint stock and limited liability companies; 2. *Unitary enterprises*, like mixed companies, are commercial establishments of different sizes. They differ from mixed in their use of state property for operations; 3. *State corporations* which are large non-commercial SOEs with 100% State ownership, created to carry out strategic research and social functions, using government properties and funding; 4. *Public interest entities* which are non-commercial establishments, often created through the organization of State corporations, that work in defence of specific public causes.

[2] In the first phase, the method of privatization was determined by the size of the enterprise. Small-scale privatization involved small enterprises largely active in trade or retail being sold through competitive tenders or through lease purchase agreements with managers. The federal government transferred ownership of such entities to municipal control with little involvement thereafter. Larger enterprises were corporatized as joint stock companies before being privatized. But these enterprises were still highly dependent on state policy. Privatizations began with

(2) 'loans-for-shares' privatizations undertaken in 1994–97[3]; and
(3) selective case-by-case privatizations post-1997 in the Putin era.

Although the methods used were different in the first and second waves of privatization, the outcome was the same with insiders (i.e. extant management and staff of the SOEs being privatized) predominating in post-privatization ownership. As a consequence, public proceeds from privatization were modest compared to the underlying intrinsic value of the assets sold. In 1997 (which was, until 2004, the peak year for privatization revenues) proceeds from the sale of state property totalled 0.9% of GDP.

Through most of the 1990s annual proceeds from privatization amounted to around 0.1% of GDP. The processes involved led to the transfer of assets to those who already managed (i.e. controlled) them. The first two phases of privatization therefore served to formalize and extend the pre-existing pattern of *de facto* asset control (OECD, 2006) achieved through under-payment, cutting corners, intimidation, or outright physical force.

The transition from state to private ownership in Russia occurred quite rapidly with State-owned firms being privatized (perhaps too hastily) without sufficient forethought and preparation. So, it failed to encourage new businesses. Instead, Russia's economic reformers inadvertently paved the way for too sharp a rise in highly concentrated ownership and the emergence of oligarchies.

Many of the laws and enforcement institutions necessary for a new legal framework to be functional were not implemented apace. Weak

the issuance of 150 million vouchers with a face value of RUB 10,000 each that were purchased by employees and the general public for a nominal fee of 25 RUB per voucher. The sale process then followed three stages: first, employees and managers were offered a percentage of the privatized firm (to be paid for in the form of both cash and vouchers); next, a second tranche was sold via a voucher auction, with participation by voucher funds that had accepted the vouchers in return for shares in their fund; and, finally, a competitive tender process was conducted for the remainder of the shares not purchased during the first two stages. The outcome of the mass privatization was that control of newly privatized firms passed to existing corporate managers and insiders.

[3] In 1995 the federal government facing a severe fiscal situation initiated the 'loans-for-shares' scheme, in which the government lodged its shareholdings as security with domestic Russian banks in return for loans representing a fraction of the value of the shares. The net result was that substantial stakes in some of Russia's largest enterprises were transferred to bank ownership at a fraction of their value. Auctions were often administered by the banks, which could participate in them as both bidders and depositories for bids (Hare and Muravyev, 2002).

institutions, insider dominated privatization, and the nature of the Russian industrial structure—with highly capital intensive production, characterized both by a high degree of asset specificity and significant economies of scale—resulted in an unintended concentration in the private ownership of industrial assets.

The result of ownership concentration was the consolidation of power and wealth in the hands of a small number of powerful Russian entrepreneurs, the so-called 'oligarchs' who were well connected with powerful state officials. Most of the oligarchs headed private corporations that were former SOEs, such as oil companies, banks, and metallurgical plants. Typically, the oligarchs accumulated their initial capital stock through commodity trading of oil, gas, and metals, importing scarce consumer goods and selling them at artificially high prices in a sclerotic economy that was in the incipient stages of opening up, or financial brokerage. They used this seed capital stock to expand by acquiring more SOEs as they were privatized.

Through their large-scale acquisition of formerly public owned assets, the oligarchs created obstacles to the emergence and development of a competitive business climate and influenced policy-makers to adopt public policies conducive to their private interests. State institutions were so weak that the federal authorities simply lacked the administrative capacity to implement reforms. The State thus found itself faced with the need to govern an economy dominated by a small number of relatively large private companies—whose owners meddled extensively in electoral and policy-making processes[4] to advance their own interests.

Given a weak, nascent legal order, and inadequate administrative and regulatory capabilities, the Russian State immediately felt threatened by the rapidly growing power of oligarchic private owners. The inevitable reaction of the succeeding government was to resort to direct control over the cash flows of former SOEs that had been too hastily privatized. This was done through effective renationalization to counter what the State saw as an encroachment upon, and dilution of, its former powers over

[4] The industrial structure and the high concentration of ownership present two political problems, which can be particularly acute in situations of state weakness. Such companies tend to be very demanding vis-à-vis the State: their size means that they are likely to be politically powerful and their asset specificity is likely to make them relatively inflexible and will therefore lobby the government to adapt its policies in order to support or protect them.

resource mobilization and allocation. As a result, since 2004, Russia has seen a major reversal of previous trends with an increase in the share of the State sector in the economy (EBRD 2009).

The Russian State found it easier to exert direct control over the operations and finances of these large enterprises rather than to rely on the regulation of contracts with private firms and their subsequent taxation. This route was taken because the Russian State possessed substantial coercive capacities as the default option for achieving its 'regulatory' aims (Tompson, 2007).

Some observers have suggested that the reversal was part of a broader process of correcting past abuses and creating a more orderly and stable set of property relations in Russia. They have argued that chaotic, corrupt privatization processes of the 1990s necessitated the renationalization of 'strategic enterprises'. However, with the overt manipulation of political, legal, and regulatory processes in the country since the early 2000s, the renationalization of all too many SOEs are as suspicious and notorious as the privatizations of the 1990s in reasserting state power and control over the economy.

Since 2004, the reversal away from privatization back to state expansion has been remarkable. The reassertion of state domination has, of course, been most pronounced in the energy sector, along with banking and manufacturing. Yukos has been the most visible and controversial sign of the shift towards greater state control. Unsurprisingly, earlier privatization plans have since been scaled down. For example, the privatization plan adopted in 2010 predicated the privatization of 1,500 enterprises, including several of the largest companies in banking, energy, telecoms, and transport. But, while many stakes were sold, most large transactions were delayed. This was apparently because of an unfavourable market situation, according to official sources (OECD, 2013b).

In June 2013, the Russian government unveiled yet another Privatization Plan for 2014–2016. The plan rolled back significantly the scope of privatization and involved, to a large extent, the Russian government maintaining 'golden shares' in large SOEs. Since 2004, Russia has developed its own unique form of State capitalism, with its coercive state reasserting control over enterprises engaged in the exploitation of its natural resource endowments. The boundaries between the state and the private sector are no longer clear. Private businesses (many owned by high-level state officials) occupy a grey area in this unique system where they are not independent of the state nor fully part of it. They are expected to obey state mandates and directives in the same way as SOEs.

The nature of historical industrial production State ownership patterns in Russia, the mechanics of transition, a strong, historical interventionist tradition, and administrative structures that have not kept pace with economic liberalization are crucial in understanding Russia's dysfunctional State-owned sector today.

The legacies of the communist era continue. Many key reforms that concern the 'unfinished business of transition' are in abeyance. Despite its ostensible commitment to its earlier plans to privatize, the Russian State, with its reassertion of industrial enterprise control through ownership, has again become an extremely important player in the economy with continuing ownership of substantial productive assets and its coercive influence throughout the economy.

Regulation and State ownership of enterprises

With abundant natural resource endowments shaping its industrial structure, Russia would probably have had a fairly high ownership concentration of industrial assets—public or private—under any circumstances. This structurally influenced predominance of large enterprises in a natural resource dominated economy poses a severe challenge to market entry and competition and preserves protected pockets of inefficiency, irrespective of ownership.

The post-2004 Russian State has opted to reassert direct control and ownership of these assets, instead of regulating private owners, in an economy dominated by a small number of relatively large private companies exploiting hydrocarbon and mineral resources. Relying on direct State ownership and control (rather than on regulation, taxation, or contract) suits much better a State accustomed for more than a century to exercise substantial coercion in getting its way.

The Russian regulatory framework recognizes that private companies do not compete on equal terms with SOEs that enjoy state support. Policies have called for a decrease in the number of State entities, and have tasked the Federal Anti-Monopoly Service (FAS) to protect market competition by ensuring that (a) every economic sector contains no less than three firms, one of which should be privately owned; (b) the number of breaches of anti-monopoly legislation by the state is reduced; and (c) the share of SMEs in state procurement (both of government and SOE's) is increased (Di Bella et al., 2019).

However, the renewed post-2000 emphasis on the State's direct control over the economy has resulted in various parts of the government continuing to issue new regulations and decrees regardless of the State's capacity to implement and enforce them. Uneven implementation has created further complications, with various officials, branches of government, and jurisdictions interpreting and applying regulations inconsistently, with the decisions of one state entity often being overruled or contested by another.

In sectors where the State is deeply involved as regulator and owner, state authorities have been torn between their desire to make monopolies and oligopolies more efficient and their inclination to make provision for the heavy 'social obligations' that these State-owned monopolies have traditionally fulfilled. These obligations are often 'compensated for' through fiscal subsidies or regulatory privileges. Policy-making in these sectors is characterized by long delays and frequent reversals of course.

Attempts to challenge such behaviour have yielded little by way of results. Nowhere is this more evident than in the hydrocarbons sector. The Russian government has delayed reform of the subsoil legislation for years, while continuing to use the defects of the current licensing regime to pressure companies into behaving as the government would wish rather than as commercial profitability and efficiency considerations might dictate. With the government now intervening more directly in industrial sectors that it regards as 'strategic', SOEs with monopoly or near-monopoly positions have extended their reach into related sectors through vertical and horizontal integration.

Such behaviour by large SOEs may in part be conditioned by economic habits formed under central planning[5] when companies had limited options to procure raw materials and market their output. Even supposedly

[5] The industrial structure of the Soviet Union was characterized by very long chains of dependence, which lacked the resilience and flexibility built on redundancy in markets. The absence of alternative suppliers and customers left Soviet enterprises vulnerable and one response to that vulnerability was to take direct control of up- and down-stream activities.

private firms in major industrial sectors face a future of being monopolies or oligopolies, thus suppressing or preventing the emergence of competition in many markets. The absence of an effective competition policy, and delayed reform of firms in infrastructure, has added to the daunting challenge of creating a level playing field.

Other sectors, characterized by equally high levels of state or private oligarchic ownership concentration, witness collusive behaviour, and abuse of market power in preventing new entry or stunting the growth of competing firms. This has led to considerable doubts about the 'relative autonomy' of the State. State bodies are often penetrated, or 'captured' by private interests (OECD, 2006). This weakens rule enforcement. Although the State bureaucracy is large and pervasive, it has limited substantive administrative capabilities. It is often unresponsive to both public and political masters. In addition, informal governance systems are riddled with corruption. These weaknesses impinge directly on the State's ability to devise, adopt, and implement effective regulatory policies.

Broad-based regulatory reforms began in the early 1990s through the liberalization of prices and free trade. Russia replaced Soviet institutions with a two-track judicial system. Commercial courts were built on the remnants of the former administrative dispute resolution forum for Soviet enterprises. These commercial courts were tasked with economic disputes and administrative conflicts between firms and the state. The courts of general jurisdiction were set up to handle civil litigation and criminal matters (Gans-Morse, 2011).

By the mid-1990s, a new Arbitration Procedural Code, a Civil Code, a Law on Joint-Stock Companies, a Law on the Securities Market, and other legislation essential for the functioning of a market economy were promulgated.

However, the implementation of essential reforms needed to support successful and durable privatization was too slow. Such reforms included the creation of effective regulatory institutions; reform of public administration; creation of a judicial system on which economic agents could rely for timely adjudication and effective enforcement of contracts; protection of property rights; and new market-oriented forms of regulation. SOEs and large private firms have successfully circumvented formal legal institutions, which they perceive as slow, corrupt, or incapable of enforcing court rulings (Edwards, 2009).

Since 2004, the Russian government has expressed its intent to level the competitive playing field in sectors where SOEs play a dominant role. Paradoxically, however, the government is extending its holdings in some key sectors, rather than reducing them. The state is extensively involved in natural gas, electricity, rail transport, and banking sectors, not only as a regulator but also as the owner of the SOE monopolies that dominate in each. In these sectors, the State-controlled monopolies have, with total impunity, acted at times in ways that have distorted or suppressed competition.

In the banking sector, for example, State-owned banks have successfully blocked regulatory reforms that would level the playing field. Previous administrative linkages between the Soviet banks, regional administrations, and state enterprises have continued. However, regulatory privileges enjoyed by State-owned banks have been slowly reduced, and the adoption of deposit insurance legislation has deprived all but Sberbank of their explicit state guarantees, extensive State ownership has intensified conflicts of interests within the Central Bank (CBR). The CBR is at once the sector's regulator, its largest single creditor, and the owner of its biggest bank. It also has considerable control over most aspects of insolvency proceedings in the sector (Frye, 2005).

Regional governments continue to intervene, sometimes quite heavyhandedly, in local banking activity, suppressing competition and impeding entry into local markets by 'alien' non-local banks. They often use the banking business generated by their own local budget accounts as a form of patronage in supporting local banking (Tompson, 2004) by excluding non-local banks. Consequently, many regional banks have established near-monopoly positions in local markets with official backing.

Attempts to challenge SOEs' behaviour have generally been unsuccessful, owing to the weakness of the competition authority; the general weak framework of competition law and policy in Russia; the weak institutional capacity of State-controlled sector regulators; and the lack of enforcement. Sector regulators exist but they are subordinated to their respective ministries. These ministries often overturn the regulators' decisions.

There is an exceedingly high level of government intrusion in private business as well. In part, this reflects a carryover of the previously established SOE culture of 'command-and-control' in regulation, giving rise to seemingly arbitrary policy decisions. The government owns a large number of 'golden shares' in private companies that allow it to have seats on boards and veto any commercial decisions of the firm that it may not like. Such shares were created in private firms operating in sectors deemed to be of strategic importance. The Russian government owns golden shares in 181 companies in which it has no conventional equity stake (Sprenger, 2008).

If the privatizations of the 1990s occurred during a period of 'wild-west' lawlessness, when the state was too weak to protect businesses from criminals and unscrupulous competitors, the threat to effective market competition in recent years has emanated from within the state itself. There has been a drift towards more interventionist, less rules-based state behaviour in many sectors.

In the Putin era, Russia has focused not on reducing the State's role in ownership but on transforming it for the worse. In many cases, State ownership has created conflicts of interest for the authorities and distorted or suppressed competition. Extensive State ownership and interference have led to regulatory uncertainty and a business climate that is not conducive to fair competition.

With markets typically characterized by a small number of large firms, the temptation to increase profits by reducing effective competition is high. Both the legal/judicial framework and the State's administrative and regulatory capacities have remained weak. The State therefore has relied on direct intervention in the economy through its coercive power.

Crony capitalism vis-à-vis SOEs as it has evolved in the Putin Era

SOEs enjoy definite advantages in Russia but most importantly, SOEs function as a mechanism of political control and rent extraction in Russia's system of vertical power by enriching allies and neutralizing any political opposition (Aslund, 2019).

Such authoritarian State capitalism has resulted in a country where, although there is private business and supposed market competition, it is the State that always determines who wins. The misuse of state power through confiscation of assets and criminalizing competitors has generated internal instability. The State has maintained control by rewarding loyalists and punishing dissent. If Yukos was the most visible sign of the transition to greater state control, Yevroset the cell phone retail chain, which was forced to be sold by one oligarch (who fell out of favour) to another oligarch at an artificially low price, is a sign of the State's egregious involvement and interference in the private sector in rewarding its cronies.

Economic reform in the early 1990s created opportunities for the Soviet administrative elite to acquire state assets through corrupt, quasi-legal means, laying the foundation for crony capitalism. Crony capitalism has since been nurtured and matured through state monopolies. In a World Bank study on industrial concentration, as of 2001, the country's 23 largest firms were estimated to account for 30% of Russia's GDP. These firms were controlled by a mere 37 individuals. By international standards, this was an astonishing concentration of wealth and industrial power in such a large country, all the more surprising given that such a privileged economic elite did not even exist two decades ago (Rutland, 2008).

The first phase of 'wild privatization' in the early 1990s was followed by a period of gradual consolidation. Powerful competitors pushed out weaker rivals. Economic power was concentrated in the hands of a few individuals—in oil and gas, banking, and metallurgical sectors—who had direct access to political leadership at both national and regional levels (Rutland, 2008).

Leaders had a vested interest in preserving the status quo. There was no significant coalition of groups with a stake in further reform (i.e. introducing effective competition). Private companies used their leverage to block legislation on higher excise taxes or revisions to laws favourable to foreign investment. An attempt was made in 1997 to curb corruption and introduce more competition into the 'crony capitalist system' that had been forged between the newly emerged oligarchs and the weakened state. But the reform drive failed in the face of effective opposition from regional governors and oligarchs, who mobilized their supporters in the State Duma.

Virtually all the wealth the oligarchs have owned came from insider seizure of Russia's raw material assets which until 1992 had been owned and managed by the State. But, until 2000, almost none of the oligarchs restructured or improved the productivity of the assets they had acquired from the State. By 2000, the economy had been sufficiently liberalized to enable the oligarchs to enrich themselves, but not so much as to expose them to effective competition and efficiency.

The fact that Russian private business evolved into a narrow oligarchy that was 'unpopular and widely regarded by the public as illegitimate' made it relatively easy for the State to recapture the commanding heights of the economy under President Putin. The dense elite networks and 'crony capitalism' of the 1990s opened the door for political recentralization and hardening autocracy. The heart of the Putin project was to reassert state control over the economy, including renationalizing 'strategic' industries in the supposedly larger interests of internal order and social stability.

Although Russian leadership advocates privatization, the actual government strategy is focused on consolidating, maintaining, and expanding political and economic power for the ruling elite through the control of select industries and enterprises whether publicly or privately owned. The high commodity prices of the last decade helped the State in successfully pursuing that strategy. Since Western sanctions were imposed in 2014, the Russian State has been providing opportunities to its oligarchs in new industries to make Russia less dependent on foreign imports.

The expansion of state ownership and control since 2004 has occurred against the backdrop of the State using its expanding array of commercial and fiscal activities to reward its supporters (Remington, 2008). State capitalism has taken root again with the goal of weakening the oligarchs and turning them into a subordinate group, subservient to the State. Putin moved swiftly to distance the oligarchs from the centre of political power by putting to use the coercive authority of the State. The handling of Yukos confirmed that tax inspectors, courts, and security services could all be used as willing tools of the State. In the absence of clear property rights, that could be defended in independent court system, Russian business became very vulnerable to state pressure.

The relationship between big business and the government became more opaque. It reasserted the dominance of political power over mercantile power and made oligarchs the 'minor' partners of politicians. The general pattern of the state's relationship with private business has since changed dramatically. Officials at all levels (regional and local) now resort openly to issuing directives to businesses. Even so, the crony networks that politicians have with the oligarchs have been maintained for the purposes of exerting the state's micro-management and control.

Putin made a coordinated effort to regain control over privatized companies by having his trusted aides appointed to their boards. His administration is noted for the presence of former security service personnel at the helm of affairs at important SOEs. These personnel have in turn placed individuals from their own networks into key posts in the railway industry, banking, customs, energy, and so on. Crony capitalism in Russia has thus led to inefficient state control over public- and *privately* owned companies for purely political reasons, thus endangering the economy.

Even though Putin was successful in pushing back the political challenge he faced from rising private capitalists, the oligarchs as a class have not disappeared. On the contrary, under Putin they have increased in number. But they have become 'his' oligarchs. The political stability and economic growth that Russia has experienced during Putin's presidency has enabled them to multiply their wealth many times over. Russia's well-connected elite continues to enrich itself (and the public officials with whom it works hand-in-glove) unfairly with the active connivance of the State, not by seizing control of firms at a pittance any longer, but by benefitting directly from state spending programmes.

The oligarchs provide a considerable proportion of the financing for elections at all levels of the government and the political activities of the government elite. In return, the government allows the oligarchs to extract considerable rents—a part of which are funnelled back into financing the electoral success of supportive politicians. The most common way for politicians to carry out their part of the crony capitalism bargain is to grant domestic monopolies and government contracts to individual oligarchs (Kimbugwe et al., 2012). Holders of monopoly rights granted by politicians are able to raise prices and extract monopoly rents, often enforced by the State.

In many regional markets too, it is typical to have a few incumbent firms operating in cooperation with regional or local officials. As well as reflecting corruption and rent-seeking behaviour, these arrangements often arise as a result of limited fiscal autonomy at lower levels of government. Many of the regional governments and municipalities pursue their social objectives through shadow budgets that employ the quasi-fiscal services of large incumbent enterprises operating in their territory.

The system—which propagates crony capitalism and has been given formal shape during Putin's presidency—is characterized as '*Sistema*', coined by Ledeneva (2012). It stands for the workings of power networks and methods of informal governance applied by political elites, intertwined with the existing formal institutional structures. *Sistema* refers to the outcome of the existing clash between official policies and unofficial influences, between formal hierarchies and informal networks. It functions with some elements of the soviet 'administrative-command' system. Administrative-command methods used to mobilize cadres and to allocate resources have been adjusted to accommodate present-day objectives and priorities.

The private agenda of public officials

The Soviet administrative hierarchy, despite its complex and seemingly well-defined formal institutions, relied heavily on an informal set of personal networks within the party-state apparatus. Authority was often vested more in persons than in offices. In the post-Soviet era, such 'personalistic' administrative practices bred graft and corruption. Post-Soviet governments did not succeed in tackling this problem. Senior officials still seek to bolster their authority over the institutions they run by placing trusted personal associates in key posts.

The merging of the informal networks with official hierarchies has led to personalization of the bureaucracy. The highly personalized nature of the administrative system is one of the paradoxes of Russia: it is a weak state with strong officials. The top management at SOEs has had long tenures; CEOs of Gazprom, Rosneft, Aeroflot, Transneft, Sberbank, VTB have been in post on an average for 15 years. CEOs with long tenures risk falling into the traps of conservatism, lethargy, and routine. They have the trust and support of Putin and this makes any move to replace them dependent on them having lost that trust.

The patronage dispensed by individual officials—particularly those responsible for managing state property or large financial flows—can be enormous. The weakness of the administrative machinery makes it easy for officials to use that power to pursue narrow private or political ends. In addition, the unique feature of Russian capitalism, where private businesses are still under the direct influence of the state, opens significant possibilities to profit personally from public office. Insider–managers within all the major state monopolies have often been able to divert cash flows and siphon off assets, referred to as 'informal profit-seeking' at the state's expense. In the absence of hard budget constraints, effective competition and functioning capital markets, insider–managers have been able to entrench themselves and resist both restructuring and liquidation.

But the more significant challenge facing Russia is that of bureaucratic discretion. Russia with its weak regulatory institutions and lagging state capacity has provided considerable latitude for bureaucrats to interpret and implement laws as they wish. This has created uncertainty that deters long-term investors by undermining the predictability with which regulatory policies are interpreted and applied[6] (Beazer 2012). The combination of excessive regulation, frequent rule changes, and inconsistent application makes it difficult for private businesses to be sure they are on the right side of the law. This situation has left considerable discretionary power in the hands of Russian officials dealing directly with businesses and has created opportunities for large-scale corruption. Corruption is the reason for the bankruptcy or closure of one of every seven businesses in the country (Cohen et al., 2014).

Russian officials have abused regulatory codes to extort firms. They have adopted harsh techniques, including the threat of jail time, for extortion. Officials have proved resilient to reforms aimed at restraining their influence over business. They have maintained excessive regulations in order to profit from firms which are forced to pay bribes in order to cut through red tape, acquire necessary permits and licences, and avoid fines and sanctions. Private profiteering by public officials in Russia has been facilitated by an environment of political and economic uncertainty and the government's intrusive role in a pervasive system of licensing, inspections, and authorization requirements.

[6] Unpredictable policy application caused by bureaucratic leeway can lead longer-term investors to seek alternative locales where future costs and returns will be more predictable. Although firms can find strategies to mitigate potential enforcement-related surprises and make some level of investment possible, such actions divert precious capital away from investment activities that could have been possible under more predictable conditions.

For most firms, the most pressing concern is harassment from lower-level officials, whom the top leadership has struggled to control. Russia's legal system has remained in a state of flux. Keeping up with legislative changes, presidential decrees, and government resolutions is a challenging task for private companies as well as SOEs. Big companies have played their role in maintaining this status quo in the hope that tougher and ever-changing rules of the game will force smaller competitors to exit. In addition, they lobby for tax breaks, protective tariffs, and government contracts by directly approaching public officials.

The misallocation of resources in and by SOEs

The distinguishing feature of the attempted privatization of the Russian State-dominated economy has been *transition without economic transformation*—i.e. a transition to a market economy without the transformation of production through greater management efficiency. The introduction of the market economy in Russia took place overnight. In the rush, the more dysfunctional features of the old order were exacerbated not obliterated. Those features include a highly inefficient and self-serving banking system; overdependence on natural resources; the State's direct involvement in pricing and allocation decisions; one-industry or one-company dependent towns; and the procurement system.

The State's continuing dominance of the banking system and the involvement of the central bank in commercial banking activities have distorted competition and credit allocation and has encouraged expectations of bail-outs. Despite the advantages that State-owned banks enjoy with respect to private banks (implicit and explicit state guarantees and access to relatively cheap government deposits, among other), most State-owned banks (except the largest) have lower profitability than private banks (Di Bella et al., 2019).

SOBFIs have continued to pursue policies that reflect the non-commercial preferences of the State (property redistribution, especially with regard to assets pledged to banks by owners against loans received; provision of funds to socially or politically sensitive ventures, etc.).

Oil and gas are of critical importance to the Russian economy. They are, and will continue to be, the key source of national wealth. In 2012, oil and gas accounted for 52% of federal budget revenues and over 70% of export revenues. The involvement of state actors and interests is more apparent in the oil and gas sectors than in others. The State's involvement in these two sectors has seen significant growth in Russia's energy leverage over Europe, and is a source of power which it has used both to reward its friends and punish its enemies.

The critical issue for the State, however, is how the excess rents generated by these resources are used for the development of the domestic economy. There is a strong politically driven impulse to allocate rents in a manner that maintains and expands specific sectors of the economy that Russia inherited from the Soviet Union. These sectors have used hydrocarbon rents to expand production capacity; hire new workers; and build new plants and new cities. This has increased the need for generating more rents in the future and has made the withdrawal of rents exceptionally costly.

As the rents from oil and gas have grown, they have been diverted increasingly to inefficient sectors to maintain capacity utilization levels. Significant resource diversion has deepened and entrenched backwardness and inefficiency throughout the Russian economy. High oil prices in the 2000s resulted in an appreciation of the Russian rouble against other currencies, thus reducing the competitiveness of an already inefficient manufacturing sector.

Allocating rents extracted from oil and gas to much less efficient sectors has resulted in SOEs not maintaining adequate levels of investment in the hydrocarbon sector that is so critical to the Russian economy. Even the private sector, where the bulk of the profits are derived from the sale of oil, gas, and metals, makes almost no new investment in oil and gas technology or capacity, resulting in declining production, depleting reserves, and delayed exploitation of new reserves. This can be partly explained by the fact that the private sector still is faced with the risk of expropriations of successful businesses and other violations of property rights.

In 2012, the level of Russian investment per barrel of extracted oil was between US$9 and US$10 in comparison to the average investment per barrel by large international oil firms of US$15 to US$20 (Chrissikos,

2014). While their own production declines, the oil and gas SOEs compensate for their low investment by purchasing private companies[7] (by artificially minimizing the market value of their target enterprises and then forcing the management to sell them at those lowered prices).[8]

Workers, meanwhile, have had fewer incentives to migrate or invest in new occupational skills because unproductive jobs have remained available in obsolete factories, as the legacy of one-company towns, mono-towns[9] has continued. Rather than restructure or shut down enterprises, Russia's adjustment took the form of shrinking output while preserving capacity. Firms with concentrated employment have been able to lobby various levels of government due to the latter's sensitivity to high unemployment rates.

Showing excessive concern for maintaining social stability, the government has continued to channel resource rents to preserve employment in mono-towns. There have been instances of Putin publicly berating oligarchs in the wake of workers protesting the shutdown of factories and forcing them to keep obsolete factories going. Support to loci of concentrated employment, drawing on natural resource rents, may have achieved a degree of employment stability and abatement of social tension, but this has been done at a very high cost in the broader misallocation of resources (Commander et al., 2011).

SOEs in Russia provide higher total compensation to its employees than the private sector. The compensation differential has affected workers' job preferences and the relative ability of public and private sector firms to recruit skilled workers, and hence the efficiency of labour allocation in

[7] A case in point is State-owned Rosneft's purchase of the well-managed private corporation TNK-BP for $55 billion in 2012. In 2015, Rosneft's total market capitalization is less than that of TNK-BP alone. Rosneft is still benefiting from the windfall of the confiscated Yukos assets.

[8] The cheaply sold enterprises then end up under control of companies owned by family members and close confidants of Russia's high-ranking officials.

[9] Before 1989, single SOE owned mono-towns employed between 25 and 75% of the labour force in each region; concentrated in industries with four or fewer firms in that region (Brown, Ickes, and Ryterman, 1994). Even when a number of firms operated in a locality, these often belonged to the same sector, resulting in many local economies being dependent on one particular industry. This mono-industry-town economic geography arose as a combination of enterprise locations having been driven primarily by natural resources, reliance on economies of scale, and absence of market competition. One-company town enterprises tend to be characterized by significantly lower marginal products of labour and significantly higher marginal products of capital, suggesting substantial labour hoarding in one-company-town firms (Commander et al., 2011).

the economy. In the context of Russia's tight labour market, the relatively stronger pull of skilled labour towards the SOE sector has caused disproportionate skill shortages in the private sector. Existing studies find a statistically significant negative difference between the average productivity of Russian SOEs and equivalent private firms (World Bank, 2019). In Russian manufacturing firms, there is a strong and statistically significant negative relationship between state ownership and firm total factor productivity (Bogetic and Olusi, 2013).

In the domestic economy, the Russian government intrudes extensively in pricing and investment decisions of SOEs, through calibrated controls over the distribution of energy to end-users. It uses its control of key natural resource and infrastructure monopolies to funnel massive indirect subsidies to much of the economy via producer prices that are lower than what would prevail if determined by the market. The prices at which Gazprom is required to sell in the Russian market are, by some estimates, less than one-tenth of the market rates at which the company sells in export markets (Fleming). Large-scale energy and transportation subsidies to favoured companies also distort resource allocation in favour of large incumbent SOEs, reducing the pressure on loss-making enterprises to restructure, and erecting insurmountable barriers-to-entry for new firms.

From the supply side, the Russian State's size has contributed to concentration in several sectors including natural monopolies, defence production, energy, and finance. Economic concentration is high even in sectors in which the state's presence has been relatively low.

Although the government in Russia is not large by international standards, its relatively large SOE sector results in a disproportionately high volume of state procurement within the public sector and the economy at large. State purchases, including by SOEs, represented 28.5% of GDP (on average) in 2015–18. Legislation on government procurement has recognized that the state's demand of goods and services is large, and that it can have a significant impact on the economy. Misallocation of resources has been exacerbated by public procurement policies. Most SOE procurement occurs non-competitively and supplier concentration is high. The use of SME quotas by subsidiaries of larger firms, and unconstrained use of price advantages for domestic suppliers, has limited efficiency and value chain development (Di Bella et al., 2019).

Continuing state presence and influence in banking and energy, the misuse of resource rents, the widespread presence of mono-towns, and the high-volume of state procurement have locked in a pattern of sub-optimal resource allocation. It has impeded enterprise restructuring, modernization, and diversification of the economy. State capture by business in the 1990s, and a reversal in the (much more assertive, predatory) role of the State in the following decade, has now evolved into a strange stand-off situation. The Russian State with its strong coercive power is confronted by the countervailing power of highly concentrated private business. Thus, they hold each other mutually hostage. The Russian State still wields significant power over oligarchs who are obliged to agree to deals which afford an opportunity for personal payback to the state, but at the cost of pragmatic plans for investment in the growth of their enterprises.

Challenges confronting the internal management of SOEs

The Soviet system of planning gave the economy a monopolistic hue as targets were assigned to specific enterprises and duplication was regarded as wasteful. Enterprises sought to increase their bargaining power through expansion. In the absence of hard budget constraints, the need to expand led to further deepening of monopolistic tendencies and shortages. In the face of supply constraints, enterprises introduced vertical integration or circumvented the command economy by having informal relations with suppliers. The semi-legal system of bilateral barter was organized by regional party officials and by a class of intermediaries.

Being no longer subject to control either from the party or ministries, the monopolistic tendencies of large Russian enterprises continued unfettered. Local conglomerates transformed themselves into trading companies with a monopoly over specific resources and products. For much of the 1990s, the government did not try to exercise any systematic influence over the management of privatized companies in which it continued to hold shares (Burawoy, 2001).

After Yukos, Putin moved to tighten state control still further. The State reacquired and managed companies through somewhat unorthodox methods. The expansion of State ownership has not always been open, prices for the assets acquired varied widely from close to 100% of the estimated market value for Sibneft and Power Machines to well below market value for United Heavy Machinery and to almost zero for Yukos (Lazareva et al., 2008).

Government oversight of SOEs and large private companies is achieved through the placement of members of the executive branch on corporate boards, in some cases as the Chair. Many of these board members are drawn from Putin's own retinue. Russian business corporations are therefore not fully independent of the State. Decision making is opaque and hidden from public view brokered in face to face meetings between the leaders of state corporations and top government officials. They are expected to obey state mandates (Rutland, 2008).

In SOEs, the 'system of instructions', under which some state-appointed directors are required to vote at SOE board meetings according to the State's preferences on a set of issues, poses a significant challenge to the SOE functioning. Currently SOEs exist in a variety of corporate forms, including State Corporations and Unitary Enterprises that are not totally transparent. There are also diverse State ownership modalities, with prominent SOEs not subject to the oversight of the Federal Agency for State Property Management, Rosimuschestvo. This fractured pattern of ownership allows some SOEs to be included in ad hoc schemes that grant them exceptional status and limit the accountability of their senior management (OECD, 2013b).

Since 2000, the government has taken a slew of measures to streamline the activities of SOEs along with general improvement in the institutions of corporate governance. For example, the Joint-stock company law was passed in a new version; the Bankruptcy law was revised; a new Code of Corporate Behaviour was designed and introduced; and dissemination of best practices in corporate governance was promoted. In particular, formal monitoring of SOE performance was introduced, corporatization of Federal state enterprises was accelerated, competitive procedures for appointment of SOE managers were introduced, and contacts with them were formalized (HSE, 2003).

In recent years, Russia has adopted measures to strengthen the role of Rosimuschestvo. The focus has been on improving accountability and in improving the composition of SOE boards. Since 2011, independent professional directors have been brought into a number of enterprises (RZD, VTB, Rosneft, Gazprom) through the introduction of the special committee on the selection of directors. Board member remuneration has also been increasingly linked to achieving key performance indicators.

But the Russian government still wields significant influence over the functioning of the large SOEs, where CEOs require approval from the Kremlin for most decisions. Although Rosimuschestvo has increased its presence in the selection of board nominees for large SOEs, it is reportedly often overruled by sectoral ministries (Lehuede and Kossov, 2014).

More recently, listed SOEs have been required to upgrade their listing level at the Moscow Exchange and to adopt, comply, or explain the new Code of Corporate Governance.[10] Since 2014, the Russian government has required all SOEs to adopt key performance indicators in line with the strategy defined for each SOE and has declined to increase the size of the government subsidy supporting SOEs (Filatov et al.).

Yet, a comparison of return on assets (RoA) and return on equity (RoE) in the period 2012–16 between SOEs and privately owned firms suggests that latter outperform the former in most sectors, and across activities with both low and high value added. SOE performance seems similar to that of private companies in some sectors (for example, crude oil and gas extraction, oil and coke refining) but, in most other cases, the RoA of private sector firms is higher than that of SOEs. This is valid for agriculture, manufacturing (for example, the production of electrical equipment, machinery, and equipment), and public services (for example, electricity, gas, steam, sewage) (Di Bella et al., 2019). Figure 7.1 shows Russian SOE performance in comparison the private sector.

Likewise, analysis of RoE ratios shows that Russian SOEs are broadly underperforming private firms. None of the 10 largest SOEs listed on the Moscow Exchange has a P/E ratio of above 7x and price-to-book (P/B) ratios are particularly low in the cases of Gazprom, Rushydro, and Russian Grids. In 2013, shares traded in the Russian market at an average price of 5 to 6 times earnings compared to the average in Brazil at 13x; India at 15x; and China at 10x (EEMEA regional equities outlook, 2013).

[10] Currently, many SOEs are listed at the lowest B level, subject to minimal obligations towards corporate governance requirements, such as information disclosure and the number of independent directors.

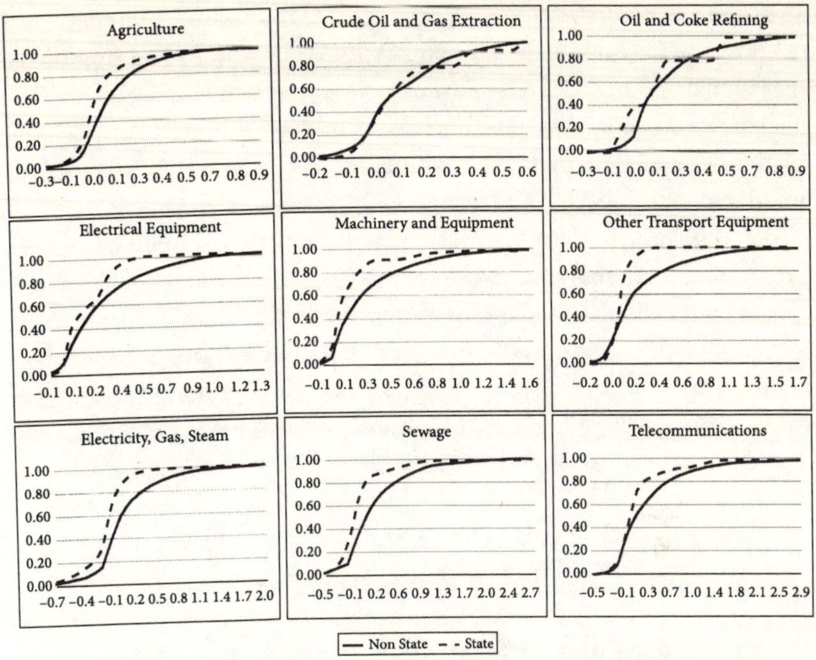

Figure 7.1 Performance of Russian SOEs compared to the private sector

Note: A curve to the left indicates lower cumulative returns.

Source: Di Bella et al., 2019.

Large SOEs, like Gazprom, have seen their market capitalization shrink. The Russian Railways' network has barely expanded in the last 10 years, while the average speed of freight trains has dropped 5% between 2004 and 2014, suggesting poor maintenance (Bershidsky, 2015).

The SOE sector's overall lagging performance is mostly attributable to the poor performance of small and medium State-owned companies. Small and medium SOEs have significantly lower labour productivity (revenue per worker) and efficiency (return on capital) than private firms of similar size, while the difference is not significant for larger SOEs (World Bank, 2019).

The privatization process has continued in parallel with state acquisitions offsetting most of the reduction in the size of the SOE sector. The Russian State will therefore remain a significant shareholder, with controlling or blocking stakes in several large and strategic enterprises.

Although the Russian authorities agree that SOEs should be streamlined and governance improved, the main problems for SOEs are at both the operational and board levels. At the operational level, the problem is inefficiency and rent extraction. Decision-making is based on personal relationships while structures, systems, or processes are ignored. At the board level, the focus is on achieving political objectives.

The SOEs under Kremlin-friendly management although inefficient have been the backbone of corporate Russia. The Russian version of capitalism under which the country's economy is run maintains the interests of the state and public officials. The current low energy prices may necessitate tighter cost controls and clampdown on corruption in SOEs. It will also require that the focus at SOEs moves from loyalty to competence.

Conflicts that arise in the State's primary role vs its ownership of enterprises

The demise of the administrative-command-control system of the Soviet era in 1989 resulted in the state abdicating all its responsibilities, which it no longer had the means to fulfil. Along with commercial and financial intermediaries, privatized companies appropriated profits by taking advantage of monopolized control over supplies and resources and tax avoidance. They maintained this control, through corruption and, where necessary, backed it up by threats and use of force.

Putin and his close circle's system of government—'*sistema*'—was effective in reducing the chaos of the rapid privatization of the 1990s, but now his system and the economy hold each other as mutual hostages. The paradox of this system is that the informal tactics deployed for getting things done have undermined the institutions that need to be modernized so that the state can play its legitimate role more effectively (Ledeneva, 2012).

The criminalization of Russian business through the 1990s and the lack of a firm legal basis for their rapidly acquired wealth made the new business elite vulnerable to attack by the state which targeted them with public support and approval on its side.

The state has intervened, albeit in a biased way, to correct past abuses of state resources and the flagrant misbehaviour of the oligarchs by radically resetting the business environment. The machinations of the state, under Putin, to regain control over the economy from the oligarchs, whom it considered undeserving, have been particularly aggressive and unscrupulous.

The return of the statists and their push for redress has set back efforts to make Russian business more transparent. The temptation for the state to directly control businesses has been heightened in this new uncertain business environment. So, instead of a great transformation, the Russian economy has seen an involution; instead of a self-expanding market-based society working together with a regulatory state, there is a retreat from the market, and an economy overwhelmed by networks of particularly malevolent form of 'crony capitalism'.

The 1990s was characterized by the fragmentation of the federal state, whose inability to exercise influence over the regulatory decisions of central and regional public authorities took place within an uncertain institutional context. Oligarchs became dependent on successfully lobbying (and buying) government officials for their survival. But, with their deeply divided interests, they have allowed the State to entrench its role as an arbiter between sectoral protection demands.

The Russian State has played a central role in implementing free market policies but, after more than three decades, it still finds it necessary to regulate the micro-level minutiae of market economy functioning by influencing the behaviour of individual firms.

The State, instead of laying foundation for the market to function, has continued to exert extraordinary powers, often administered in inexplicable ways. Instead of the rule of law, the state operates with slippery, unofficial rules that it does not observe consistently. It makes those rules up as it goes along depending on convenience.

Russia is clearly a market economy of an unusual sort, with significant lacunae. These include, for example, profound weaknesses in business and economic structures; an inability on the part of government to devise and implement coherent, consistent macroeconomic policies; a public administration that is unable to administer; regulatory frameworks that either do not exist or cannot be enforced; and the almost complete absence of the legal and institutional foundations required for smooth the functioning of a market economy. The absence of the legal foundations in Russia include, inter alia, well-defined property rights enshrined in legislation and protected by effective adjudication and law enforcement, a clear system of taxation, a bankruptcy law, arbitration and dispute resolution mechanisms for contract enforcement, etc.

Expanding its influence through state entrepreneurship, state monopolies and placement of members of the executive on corporate boards of private businesses have meant that the borders between the state and private sector have become blurred. The expansion of the State has made corruption even more entrenched and inevitable. It has driven business into 'grey areas'. It has hindered market growth from achieving its full potential and fostered an economy of high political risk in which relationships have mattered more than rules and policy risk in which rules have been designed to move into the broader space where the anticompetitive state acts.

Conclusions

There is no doubt about what ails the Russian economy—low productivity, lack of diversification, dependence on the volatile revenues from exhaustible natural resources, low investment and innovation, capital flight, ubiquitous corruption, and absence of the rule of law. Yet the present government's strategy to address these challenges is a reactive rather than a proactive one—it seems more a sequence of knee-jerk reactions to internal lobbying by powerful monopolies (both state and privately owned) and inappropriate adjustment to the severe economic shock caused by low energy prices.

The predominance of large enterprises in a natural resource dominated economy has posed a severe challenge to market entry and competition and has preserved protected pockets of inefficiency, irrespective of ownership. The post-2004 Russian State has opted to reassert direct control and ownership of these assets, instead of regulating private owners.

Extensive State ownership and interference have led to regulatory uncertainty and a business climate that is not conducive to fair competition nor effective market functioning. Both the legal/judicial framework and the State's administrative and regulatory capacities have remained weak. Resource abundance in the country has had a negative influence in poisoning policies, economy, and society, which has resulted in leakage of power from state to non-state actors. The Russian State with its strong coercive power is confronted by the countervailing power of highly concentrated private business. They hold each other mutually hostage.

Continuing state presence and influence in many sectors, the misuse of resource rents, and the widespread presence of one-company towns, and the high-volume state procurement have locked in a pattern of sub-optimal resource allocation. But this Russian version of capitalism has succeeded in maintaining both the interests of the state and public officials.

The Russian State has played a key role in implementing free market policies but, after more than three decades, it still finds it necessary to regulate the micro-level minutiae of market economy functioning by influencing the behaviour of individual firms.

8

Country case study 6: Saudi Arabia

SOEs in Saudi Arabia

The State in the Saudi economy has been historically dominant, reflecting the developmental role it has assumed to address large physical and institutional infrastructure needs since the early stages of state building. SOEs have represented an attempt to put oil surpluses to productive local use, while not simply redistributing all of them to the private sector. The Saudi regime has been conscious of keeping some degree of strategic control over the process of economic development and diversification. One advantage of SOEs has been that their activities have been easily embedded in national sector development strategies, and their activities have maximized synergies.

SOE-led development has allowed them to break new ground in sectors in which local business, with limited capacity, was reluctant to invest due to lack of experience and/or high perceived risk. SOEs have also been used to train the national manpower which the local private sector is not willing or capable of undertaking.

The Saudi government's asset portfolio, in the form of equity participation in SOEs and/or strategic investment projects, has increased since 2005. Stock exchange data on government shares in listed domestic companies held through the Public Investment Fund[1] (PIF) show that the value of these assets (based on market capitalization), and excluding shares held by the pension funds, are significant, amounting to close to $130 billion or 20% of GDP at end-2015. The PIF, which holds most of the government's equity stakes in Saudi companies, does not publish data on returns. Its holdings include very profitable companies, such as the Saudi Arabian Basic Industries Corporation (SABIC) and a number of banks

[1] The Saudi PIF was established in 1971 to invest state funds into strategic sectors or enterprises, in support of broader national economic development goals.

(IMF, 2016). Table 8.1 shows Saudi PIF listed shareholdings in majority- and minority-owned SOEs.

SOEs in Saudi Arabia are concentrated in a few key sectors which have been largely untouched by past privatization efforts. Even in sectors that were partially privatized, the government has retained a large stake. Figure 8.1 shows the sectoral distribution of SOEs in the PIF for the year 2015. Data on listed companies show that government ownership is still extensive in a variety of sectors, notably heavy industry, utilities, banking, communication, and petrochemicals.

These figures, however, do not include state ownership of several large, wholly government-owned corporations, on which information is not available. The government ownership stake in the non-oil sector is also high given that many large public enterprises and entities are not listed on the stock market including Saudi Airlines, the airports, Railroads Saudi, Gulf International Bank, and Saudi Agricultural and Livestock Investment Company (SALIC). The government dominates the provision of services in education and health, despite the opening up of these sectors to private investment (IMF, 2016).

Through numerous partial Initial Public Offerings (IPOs) of new SOEs, the State redistributed some of the oil wealth without creating direct budgetary entitlements among its population. IPOs of minority SOE holdings have been restricted to nationals and are often sold at below fair-value price. While underpricing is a well-documented phenomenon worldwide, empirical evidence suggests that it has been more evident in Saudi Arabia and other Gulf Cooperation Council (GCC) countries, reflecting perhaps the governments' desire for privatization to be a vehicle for oil wealth to be shared with citizens. This has led to windfall incomes for nationals in the short run. Gulf rulers have hoped that it might contribute to 'popular capitalism' in the long run, that would create a steady stream of dividends to the population—a less burdensome mode of rent recycling through widespread share ownership (Hertog, 2012a).

The public listing of the Saudi State energy company Aramco has been at the heart of economic reform plans to diversify the economy. The IPO raised $25.6 billion through its flotation on Riyadh's Tadawul stock exchange. Although, this time round the IPO was forced to rely on wealthy families and funds in the country and the Gulf region.

Table 8.1 Saudi PIF listed shareholdings

	Company name	State ownership %	Market value (USD Mn)
Electricity and Gas	Saudi Electricity Company	81.2	17,455
	National Gas and Industrialization	10.9	509
Finance	National Commercial Bank	54.3	27,243
	Samba Financial Group	38.0	12,443
	Company for Cooperative Insurance	23.8	2,113
	Riyadh Bank	21.8	9,936
	National Agricultural Development Bank	20.0	659
	Saudi Investment Bank	17.3	2,987
	Alinma Bank	10.7	5,908
	Saudi Industrial Development Bank	10.7	1,657
Manufacturing	Saudi Basic Industries Corporation (SABIC)	70.0	61,200
	National Petrochemical Company	16.3	2,138
	Saudi Pharma Industries and Medical Appliances	13.1	1,062
	Southern Province Cement Company	37.4	2,614
	Qassam Cement Company	23.4	1,681
	Eastern Province Cement	20.6	727
	Yanbu Cement Company	10.0	1,832
Other activities	Saudi Airlines Catering Company	35.7	2,691
	Dur Hospitality (Saudi Hotels)	16.6	714
Primary Sectors	Saudi Arabian Mining Company (MAADEN)	50.0	10,335
	Rabigh Refining and Petrochemical	37.5	2,869
Real Estate	Saudi Real Estate Company	64.6	735
Telecoms	Saudi Telecoms Company	70.0	36,496
Transportation	Saudi Ground Services Company	520.5	2,270
	National Shipping Company of Saudi Arabia	34.0	4,885
	Saudi Public Transport Company	15.7	559
Total	26 companies	7 SOEs, 19 minority-owned companies	2,13,718

Source: OECD, 2018c.

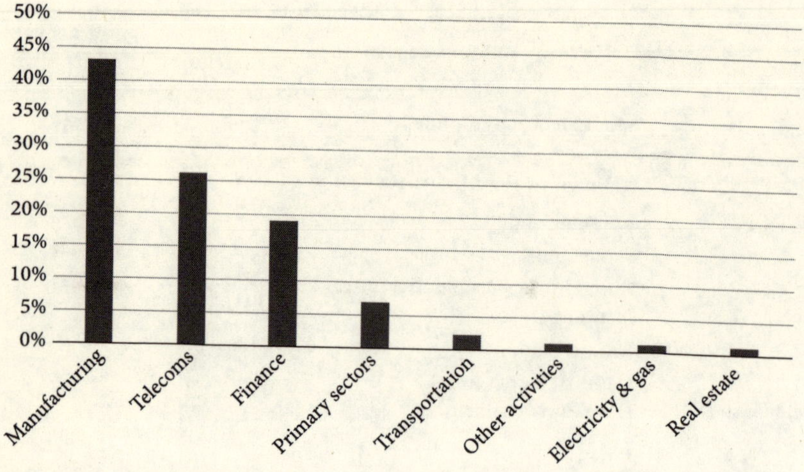

Figure 8.1 Sectoral distribution of SOEs in the Saudi PIF portfolio (2015, by value)
Source: OECD, 2018c.

The State has remained strong in Saudi Arabia, and despite its greatly enhanced capacities, the private sector still remains dependent on government. Most of Saudi business have operated with the State's direct and indirect fiscal stimuli. The State remains one of the largest employers, although generally in the GCC, over-employment tends to be more prevalent in the ministries than in SOEs. In Saudi Arabia, the salary and benefits bills for the entire public sector are more than double that of the private sector (Central Department of Statistics & Information, 2013).

The main role of the public sector in Saudi Arabia has been to strengthen the historical ties among members of the ruling family and their supporters. Prior to the discovery of oil, the ruling sheikhs played a central role in their societies. They were not simply political figures but were regarded as the 'figurative' fathers of their tribes who were compelled, by the principles of Islam, to look after their tribes' well-being (al-Kandari and al-Hadban, 2010). To fulfil their 'paternal' obligations, the sheikhs were expected to achieve justice and provide safety and protection against external threats in return for the financial tributes and political submission of their subjects (Biygautane et al., 2017).

Critical to the sheikhs' political survival was their relationship with the traditional merchant classes that constituted the pillar of the 'private sector' and the tribe's core economic resource. The modern state building process that began in Saudi Arabia with the direct flow of massive oil revenues to the 'personal purse of the sheikhs' reinforced their position in society from being a tribal alliance, to an 'autocratic' regime that 'constitutionally' positioned the sheikhs as members of the ruling family (al-Kuwari, 1978). Discovery of oil enabled the tribal sheikhdom to expand into a self-sufficient monarchy in which the al-Saud family members functioned as a 'ruling institution which operated its own patron-client networks' (Kostiner and Teitelbaum, 2000).

In the absence of any powerful political institutions, the government in Saudi Arabia has become a 'family corporation' (House, 2013) or 'family run government' (Dunford, 2013), where royal descents occupy key government and ministerial positions. As a consequence, Saudi Arabia's administrative system is highly personalized, and informal structures of authority determine the actual importance of institutions, and not necessarily the role they serve in society (Champion, 2003; Hertog, 2010a).

Although the Saudi State is fragmented, with different parts of it dominated by patronage networks of different senior princes, the presence of the family has been a unifying factor that guarantees the basic coherence of the system. The presence of hundreds of princes in the State apparatus, despite their internal squabbles, has worked towards a common survival interest.

The expansion of the Saudi oil state since 1970 has allowed for the parallel growth of a very diverse array of SOEs: the Americanized Saudi management in Aramco, the progressively ossified bureaucracy of Petromin, as well as the lean, but local management of SABIC. Several SOEs are now among the most successful and profitable enterprises that are recognized globally (for instance SABIC and MAADEN). Dividends from these enterprises accrue to the PIF (Hertog, 2008).

Different from a typical developing country SOEs of the 1960s and 1970s, some of the Saudi SOEs are outward oriented, exporting its goods and services regionally and, in many cases, globally. That Saudi Arabia has become the largest non-oil exporter in the Arab world is owed to a large extent to its State-owned heavy industry. The GCC's experience with SOEs calls into question the conventional wisdom about the inefficiency of public sectors and SOEs in the developing world. They have given a new lease of life to the 'developmental state' in the Gulf, which is able to maintain a leading role in the economy while avoiding its over-bureaucratization. The size of the state has therefore remained large in terms of its stake in public enterprises and its spending and investment.

In an Ernst & Young poll of citizens in 24 different countries, Saudis consistently gave the highest rank to management and services of their public companies and agreed more than any other nationality that strategic enterprises should be in state hands. This is partly due to the bureaucracy, tightly controlled by the central government in Riyadh, has managed to reach out to remote villages in Saudi Arabia and made Saudi nationals structurally dependent on, and oriented towards, the State. State employment has also served as a nation-wide patronage machine that has been used to bestow and withhold favours to villages, tribes, and individuals, resulting in most individuals and interest groups accommodating themselves to state-set norms (Hertog, 2015).

Large fiscal deficits brought about by the precipitous decline in oil prices in late 2014 and long-standing challenges with youth unemployment have been two of the dominant underlying themes driving economic policy in Saudi Arabia in recent years. As part of the Saudi Arabian government's plan to open up SOEs to more involvement with the private sector, in March 2018, Saudi Arabia's Council of Economic and Development Affairs approved the executive plan for the country's privatization programme (Quincy group). The programme was called Delivery Plan 2020, and its goal was to increase and strengthen the role of the private sector by opening State-owned assets for investment, making certain selected government services open to the private sector, consolidation of state assets under the PIF, and the pursuit of a more aggressive investment strategy and dynamic asset allocation.

At the same time, the State has continued to maintain a series of policies under the umbrella of 'Saudization', a term used to increase the share of Saudis in employment with reduced reliance on expatriates. Among other policies, this includes a growth in the scope and scale of SOEs, and other State-led initiatives, most prominently through the PIF. These two policies do not share a clear link—much in the same way the historical growth of the welfare state in the country constituted a type of rentier statecraft aimed at distributing patronage (Al-Sulayman, 2018).

Saudi Vision 2030, the current long-term development plan focuses its economic agenda on developing promising industries that are separated from state spending and independent of oil price fluctuations. In Vision 2030, the private sector's contribution to GDP is expected to increase from 40% to 65% (Oxford Business Group). However, this vision has not yet been accompanied by any strategy or policies regarding the redundancies among Saudis that will inevitably occur when State-owned assets (with attendant excess employment) are eventually privatized. Several key enterprises slated for privatization earlier, such as the airlines, airports, and utility companies, have been under or awaiting restructuring for many years. The water authority and electricity companies remain largely government owned and dependent on budget support despite their corporatization and some restructuring in preparation for privatization.

The State's attempt to encourage the growth of private sector employment while maintaining high levels of public sector pay, benefits, and bonuses, has continued to have a profound distorting effect on the labour market. This feature of public sector employment, along with the private sector's long-held reliance on cheap foreign labour, forms arguably the most significant challenges to the economic reform agenda (Al-Sulayman, 2018).

Ownership vs regulation

Developing new sectors through privileged public enterprises has been a useful strategy for Saudi Arabia by injecting surplus public capital into a growing and diversifying local economy. In terms of scale, planning capacity, time horizon, infrastructure investment, and bargaining power with international counterparts, the public sector has often had a strategic advantage over private players. Arguably no private Saudi group could have negotiated the world-scale petrochemical joint ventures that SABIC set up with international partners in the late 1970s and early 1980s (OECD, 2012b).

The concept of 'level playing field' for private players (whether domestic or foreign) therefore was irrelevant in areas that simply did not exist before the State started investing in them. Treating public enterprises and private investors the same in heavy industry in the early phase would arguably have stunted strategic development, leading to either misallocation or non-allocation of capital. There would quite likely be no chemical sector in

Saudi Arabia had SABIC not shown the viability of heavy industry in the Arabian desert. Most breakthroughs into new sectors were led by SOEs, be it in heavy industry, aviation, logistics, or telecoms.

SOEs, like SABIC, have benefitted from not only large initial capital injections but have also continued to receive concessionary loans from the government. The State has continued to provide dedicated infrastructure and—in the case of heavy industry—privileged access to cheap feedstock (OECD, 2012b). While this has become challenging in some cases, it was arguably a historical necessity to get new industries off the ground. SOEs have also been provided with other quasi-fiscal subsidies, including inputs at below market prices. Notable examples include the provision of cheap kerosene for national airlines (Saudi Airlines) and the supply of cheap gas and electricity for industrial companies (especially in heavy industry). SOEs often have access to separate infrastructure and public service providers.

The legacy of relatively successful State-led development and diversification has been a set of impressive, but often privileged SOEs whose relationship to a growing and maturing private sector has become tense. Yet this outcome appears preferable to one in which new sectors of economic activity might not have been developed at all without State intervention. After many years of pioneering development in key sectors, SABIC is in conflict with large local industrialists over access to feedstock and domestic sales of bulk petrochemicals. Although there probably would not have been any private players of note in this industry, had SABIC not played its crucial role as midwife in giving birth to the chemical/petrochemical sectors (OECD, 2012b).

In the Saudi heavy industry sector—the only one in which there is now significant investment by private local investors—SABIC still gets privileged access to feedstock. It resists pressure for further privatization or equal feedstock access to private investors by signing joint ventures with local investors. The increasing number of joint ventures SABIC has initiated with local investors has not resolved the issue. There is no independent sectoral regulator that can arbitrate such issues effectively. A competition commission exists but is relatively inactive. The nascent level of legal and institutional development has resulted in the regulatory framework—for assuring fair competition, among SOEs and private entities—very weak.

Sector regulators often function as specialized support agencies rather than enforcers of competition or transparency. For instance, in the mid-1970s, the Royal Commission for the Industrial Cities of Jubail and Yanbu in Saudi Arabia was given a dedicated mandate to bypass the rest of the Saudi bureaucracy in regulating SABIC's operations and creating enabling utility and other infrastructure (OECD, 2012b).

SOEs in Saudi have always been accountable almost exclusively to the top royal ruling elite, not to the broader public or to an independent regulator. Such centralization (and often personalization) meets its limits when regulatory tasks become more complex. But it has been an important substitute for formal regulation and accountability mechanisms when the State apparatus at large has not been sufficiently equipped for such tasks.

Some exceptional administrative and regulatory enclaves do exist in Saudi Arabia, like the Saudi Arabia Monetary Authority (SAMA) which regulates a small number of large, comparatively well-run banks, and the Royal Commission for Jubail and Yanbu which has successfully exercised oversight over a few large-scale public and private industries. But they are the exceptions, not the rule. The consumers services, retail, and light industry are less well-regulated in Saudi Arabia. Reform involving general regulation of Saudi business has remained stuck, as smaller SOEs have been harder to protect from bureaucratic and other predation.

Public sector wages and overall compensation packages (including a number of side benefits) have been another factor undermining the private sector. Compensation in ministries and SOEs remains comparatively high. While Saudi private enterprises must rely on low-cost, low-quality labour, they are unable to compete with the public and SOE sectors in attracting high-calibre Saudis in significant numbers. Some of the public sector's privileges have undermined a level playing field with the private sector, though they were necessary initial conditions for building insulated, efficient structures in an otherwise mediocre administrative environment (OECD, 2012b).

As a counterweight to their ability to operate in monopolistic or quasi-monopolistic industries or enjoy state protection or subsidies, SOEs have been required to perform functions that go significantly beyond their commercial mandates. In a number of cases, SOEs are expected to nurture or develop talent in their supply chain and also act as centres of excellence more broadly, which some of them carry out successfully (OECD, 2013c).

SOEs faced no competition in their respective sectors when they were first established when little domestic private sector capacity existed. But now, they have been joined by private investors inspired by the success of the public sector and encouraged by government to go into business and take risks. Trailblazer status made dedicated state support and subsidized access to essential infrastructure justifiable for SOEs, or even necessary, at the early stage of their establishment. Now such privileged treatment hampers the further diversification and expansion of the Saudi economy through greater private involvement (OECD, 2012b).

Diversification policies have achieved limited progress in meaningfully increasing the share of the non-hydrocarbons in GDP and the share of the private sector in economic activity, which has increased by only 10% since 2000. Research on the diversification experience in Saudi Arabia points to the presence of a large SOE sector and its wide-ranging mandates as a barrier to entry that limits competition and diversification (IMF, 2016).

Saudi Arabian style crony capitalism

Patron–client relationships, and patronage, have continued to characterize the Saudi regime. They form the building blocks of the royal family's political legitimacy, and administrative culture (Mansour, 2007). Economic patronage has been the means through which the Saudi ruling family has reinforced its political power. Vital economic decisions are taken by the King or other highly ranked officials, who have often prioritized the interests of the Saudi merchant classes (Malik and Niblock, 2005) over that of the public at large. Royal family members have been actively involved in private enterprise by collaborating and partnering with major businesses (Ali, 2009). The Saudi royals have thus created their own vested interest in steering economic policies to best serve the interests of the business elites from whose expanding fortunes they profit. The rest of the private sector has been left for smaller investors, who also 'rely heavily on the connections and support of members of the ruling family' (Ali, 2009).

The prevalence of favouritism, *Wasta*[2] (connections), and neo-patrimonialism have enabled influential members of merchant classes and government officials to continue their reliance on different forms of corruption to secure government contracts and benefits (Ali, 2010). Such favouritism, applied through informal connections, has created an entire segment of middle-men with strong ties to the Saudi bureaucracy (al-Hegelan and Palmer, 1985). Some middle-men have direct access to princes through informal Majlis meetings and have used such access to negotiate deals for ordinary citizens with no connections to merchants or royal members. They have sometimes even managed to bypass the formal channels of decision-making to secure loan approvals or land acquisitions for their clients (House, 2013).

To protect the economic interests of Saudi businesses against foreign competitors, government policies give local businesses precedence in acquiring state contracts and projects (Hess, 1995). Foreign companies have been forced to employ middlemen to manoeuvre through the complex Saudi bureaucratic machinery. Their role has included securing state contracts for their clients by matching them with Saudi partners to qualify for bidding for government contracts (Ali, 2010).

While the private sector has made significant progress since the first oil boom, most of its activities still amount to more sophisticated rent recycling rather than autonomous diversification (Hertog, 2013). Redistribution of state resources through the private sector has been the most unequal part of the Saudi state-building process—for there is little doubt that most of the original Saudi business fortunes were made with and through the State, via networked connections in the State apparatus. Divergence in private sector success might be explained through different levels of entrepreneurialism and pre-oil business traditions of different regions. But given the top-down nature of much of the rent distribution process, the helping hand received by the private sector from the regime and bureaucracy has played an important role. Non-ruling merchant and aristocratic elites have often done well materially out of the process of state expansion.

[2] It stems from the Arabic root for 'middle' and vividly depicts the idea of social intermediation. Having Wasta means knowing someone who can provide access to something otherwise inaccessible.

Business favouritism has been most directly visible in the field of agricultural support policies, which created a new class of agricultural entrepreneurs in the North, where there was no tradition of large-scale agriculture (Hertog, 2014). The private sector's demands on government have been rather similar in each region, focusing on protection against foreign competition and reduction of red tape.

The rapidly growing distributional state itself has become quite heterogeneous, comprising unreconstructed patrimonial fiefdoms in some of the still backward parts of the country, while efficient modern bureaucracies have emerged in other more progressive regions. Rapid state expansion has created new social and political hierarchies and a deeper social stratification, with ruling families in a very distinct position at the top not only in politics but also in other fields, such as business and State-licensed 'civil society' (Peterson, 2016).

The hub-and-spoke patronage system around the Al Saud royal family has undermined the autonomy of pre-oil economic networks in the kingdom's different regions. It has marginalized those economic elites who were not willing to be co-opted by the ruling family. It has also created strata of newcomers in business who were patronized by the Al Saud. This social mobility has further contributed to the creation of a new kind of nationally integrated business elite that is deeply tied up with the Al Saud system (Hertog, 2015).

The private agenda of public officials

The highly influential political and bureaucratic positions in Saudi have been commonly entrusted to members of the ruling family, or technocrats with strong allegiance to the rulers, as a strategy to entrench the latter's regime against political rivals (Davis, Pitts, and Cormier, 2000). Government entities have typically been led by princes and individuals with varying degrees of informal authority, influence, and interests. This has resulted in an administrative system which is 'fragmented' yet, in a strange way, competitive (intra-royal-family). Economic policies and their implementation are determined to foster the individual interests and personal agendas of members of the ruling family (Pierce, 2012).

With no national, democratic, political traditions and with most Saudis being disconnected from the administration, the society has not constrained the decisions that royals make in building the State or enriching themselves. It is largely intra-family patrimonial politics that determines who would receive which ministerial or SOE leadership post. Patrimonial intra-family politics also determine much of the institutional design of the rapidly growing state, tailoring institutions around personal needs and conflicts.

Similar predisposition was reproduced on a smaller scale by senior commoner administrators. Although skills often did matter when selecting commoner administrators, structures of clientelism and long-term loyalty played a prominent role. As a result, a unique pattern of bureaucracy was built in which yet-embryonic institutions became tokens of intra-elite bargaining among ambitious princes and a limited number of commoner clients. State institutions were used to build personal fortunes and to expand one's following. Most senior figures have used the institutions they controlled to personally distribute favours and conclude business deals (Hertog, 2007).

There was, of course, an underlying concern to build institutions that could administer the increasing flow of substantial oil income. But beyond this very general need, personal ambitions and bargains loomed large in determining specific outcomes. Most princes in bureaucratic positions quickly surrounded themselves with growing numbers of hangers-on, advisers, and business partners. Saudi Arabia, rooted as it was in a tribal nomad society, largely lacked an administrative tradition and societal checks on bureaucracy.

Combined with family politics, the unprecedented growth of bureaucracy since the 1950s has not been accompanied by any rationalization. Oil rents aided the uncontrolled expansion of the State based almost entirely on patronage. Informal authority has determined the actual importance of institutions. Institutions considered important were run by important princes or by commoners very close to the court.

Decision making on major national questions has remained largely informal, and although service provision improved in some sectors, governance has been marred by princely jealousies. In the 1950s when the formal State was small, unorganized, the combination of growing resources and institutional fluidity offered great opportunities for a small number of people who happened to be in the right place at the right time. The Saudi State expansion after the 1973 oil boom helped entrench those existing power centres (Hertog, 2007).

All of the major ministries confer enormous patronage power to their heads. It is exercised overtly and covertly through the sheer scale of employment, the provision of select services, and a never-ending flow of business contracts. The autonomous power of senior princes has meant that they can ignore budgetary rules governing public procurement, undermine coherent economic planning. State agencies with fiscal abundance have created and developed their own internal array of services. The parallel power bases of princes have made national decision making and, at a lower level, day-to-day policy coordination difficult.

Ever since the creation of modern bureaucracy in Saudi Arabia, the royal princes, and the connected commoners around them have been enmeshed in tightly knit patron–client relations. Royals have provided access to power, resources, and status, whereas the commoners provided technocratic ability, loyalty, and defended the interests of their patrons in society and in state machinery. These ties have kept elites with seemingly divergent interests—princes and technocrats—bound together for more than half a century. These ties have seldom been simple, but rather part of a complex network of patronage. Shifting individual interests and coalitions of the elite have been the main force determining how state institutions grew and change (Hertog, 2008).

Further state expansion in the 1970s and early 1980s has allowed for new islands of efficiency to emerge, staffed by the most promising technocrats and given relative autonomy from the rest of the civil service. These include the Saudi Ports Authority, SABIC, and the Riyadh Development Authority. These islands of efficiency, however, did not alter the core structures of the state and regime. In practice, the royals have been content to let islands of efficiency operate with considerable freedom. Their performance and managerial structures have, by and large, been stable over long periods. The elevated status of the senior management has depended on royal patronage. Since the 1960s, senior princes have personally identified and co-opted technocratic talent into these companies. The State has therefore created new bureaucratic elites—some descending from old social elites, others from more modest social backgrounds (Hertog, 2010c).

Saudi Arabia has large resources relative to its population, while productive technical capabilities in the economy are limited. An individual in a privileged position makes state resources—contracts, licenses, jobs, housing, benefits etc.—available to other individuals lacking the same access. Brokerage and informal intercession by higher-ups (*Wasta*), therefore have played an important role in State–society relations. Informal intercession has often happened to the benefit of individuals rather than larger groups. It has been channelled through new intermediaries around the State and the ruling family: courtiers, advisors, lower-level relatives of the rulers, well-placed bureaucrats, etc. (Hertog, 2016b).

This intentional, and formalized, creation of brokerage seems to differentiate the 'leakage' in rentier states from that in other developing countries (Reddy and Haragopal 1985). The regime has a clear motivation for this: in the face of limited local skills, creating formal privilege had been an effective way to include locals in the economy. By giving a special value to rentier state citizenship per se, Saudi government has created traditions of brokerage that have defined its business and State-society relations (Hertog, 2010c).

These rent and access peddlers have created vested interests in structures that will become inefficient in the long run, with an array of pointless intermediaries creaming off the returns generated by productive people. In Saudi Arabia not only have all the leading princes clung to their posts but also Saudi business has seen very few big newcomers since the 1980s. The turnover of technocrats in the cabinet has decreased markedly, with their average age strongly increasing (Hertog, 2007).

SOEs and the possible misallocation of resources

State institutions in Saudi, although all built with oil rents, are deeply heterogeneous. If oil has had any systematic effect in the domestic economy, it has been to provide the flexibility to the ruling royal family to embark on ambitious, institutional innovation and experimentation. Oil rents led to weak budgetary constraints and a simultaneous pursuit of both efficiency and redistribution objectives have led to diverse outcomes.

For the royal family to be able to experiment with SOEs or, more broadly, for state institutions to be moulded by elite preferences, the necessary condition was that the regime remained fairly insulated and autonomous from societal demands when decisions about the allocation of oil rents were made. This was the case in Saudi Arabia in the 1940s and 1950s, where patronage was largely localized and individualized and no large groups could stake systematic claims on the new riches. The ruling Saudi royal family has had, and continues to have, very different relationships with interest groups surrounding them. It has had to strike political deals, with local merchant groups in the pre-oil age in return for taxes or loans. The large-scale oil income rapidly made the incipient State fiscally autonomous from local society and endowed them with unprecedented power (Hertog, 2012b).

But over the years, the Saudi regime felt a political need to share the immense resource wealth with the wider population to create a wider, popular support base for the regime. The patrimonial and personalized rule of the Al-Saud family and the country's vast resources have together given the regime a unique degree of power over Saudi society. It has led to a high degree of material dependence of the average Saudi on the State's patronage exercised through the disbursement of oil revenue resources (Hertog, 2015).

The reach of the State has been reflected not only in its controlled consumer prices and expansive service provision to the Saudi population but also in its vast infrastructure. However, that infrastructure network has been built without due consideration to sound budgeting and oversight. A survey of 300 managers and supervisors in Saudi Arabia found that 97% of government mega-infrastructure projects were not completed on time, and more than 80% of them significantly exceeded their budgets (al-Turkey, 2011).

In addition to subsidized energy, Saudi Arabia has resorted to price controls on electricity, water, and other basic goods that are provided by SOEs. But, apart from this egregious waste of fiscal resources, the misallocation that occurs—through the three main tools of distribution, cheap energy, subsidized access to utility services, and public sector over-employment—has had lasting adverse effects on the economy. These forms of distribution might have been justifiable when there was excess hydrocarbon production and low domestic consumption, when the population was small, and the State apparatus was being built. But they have now become extremely costly.

Subsidized energy and unnecessary over-employment in the public sector are inefficient and regressive. They have serious deleterious consequences for diversification in non-oil sectors, fiscal sustainability, and, in the long run, the potential of local societies to find a growth-oriented compromise between domestic labour and business (Hertog, 2016). The opportunity costs of runaway energy consumption growth have been significant. Saudi Arabia now consumes more energy domestically than Germany, a country with three times its population and six times its GDP. Creating additional production capacity to satisfy these needs has proved to be increasingly costly (OECD, 2013c).

The opportunity cost of Saudi Arabia's provision of cheap gas, water, and transport fuel through various public enterprises has been estimated at 10% of the country's GDP (OECD, 2013c). Most economists concur that the current subsidization of petrochemical products in Saudi Arabia is economically sub-optimal. Better targeted subsidies are needed to reach the poor. Aramco representatives have publicly warned that if current trends of domestic energy consumption continued, the equivalent of 6 million barrel of oil per day would be consumed domestically by 2030, reducing the amount of energy available for export and hence affecting the fiscal balance as well as Aramco's own cash flow. Hydrocarbon rents per capita have been an effective predictor of declining productivity between 1990 and 2010. An additional US$1000 of rents implies a productivity loss of about 2.6%. For a country, like Saudi Arabia, with per capita rents of US$10,000, the predicted productivity loss will amount to 22%.

Dependence on resource-intensive technology has sapped incentives to move towards a more efficient production structure with the Saudi economy becoming more energy-intensive since the 1980s. Domestic energy suppliers moreover have hit hard constraints in recent years as gas—used for petrochemical production and electricity generation—has become scarce and expensive to produce. The growth of the private sector in Saudi Arabia has been highly factor intensive, relying on comparative advantages in factor prices resulting from state support. This growth model has resulted in weak incentives to increase productivity, invest in technology, and engage in research and development. Over-reliance on finite resources to expand production instead of augmenting productivity will be unsustainable in the long run (Hertog, 2013).

Saudi Arabia's rentier status has allowed for the creation of large-scale, formalized patronage structures. Probably, more than half of the economically active Saudi population is employed by the State. The public sector payroll has been expanding continuously even through the lean years of the 1980s and 1990s when the government ran large deficits. The share of bureaucrats has consistently increased in the total population. Moreover, jobs have usually been filled based on kinship and connections, rather than merit (Hertog, 2012b).

Saudi public sector employees are not incentivized to perform well, thus resulting in an over-staffed bureaucracy that is extremely inefficient, slow, and very expensive to maintain. Surplus employment has been extended to many non-royal ministries and agencies, in particular cabinet-level 'line ministries' which are not created by royal charters. Their efficiency is even lower.

The stickiness of bureaucratic employment has prevented institutional reengineering. The wage bill in Saudi rose to 27% of total government expenditure, while only 25% of government expenditure went towards capital spending in 2008 (Ramady, 2014). The wage bill has steadily increased as a share of public expenditure since the early 1980s. Since the 1970s, productivity as measured by output per employee has been declining significantly, another indicator of patronage employment to the detriment of institutional (and national) performance.

As more social groups have been tied to the state through employment and service provision, the government has become largely incapable or unwilling to impose cuts on the public payroll and subsidized public services. This 'stickiness' of mass distribution has been reflected in the broader budget figures: the government's capital spending declined precipitously in times of fiscal crisis—to the extent that Saudi infrastructure suffered significant damage.

The SOE growth model in Saudi Arabia is one of the privileged 'islands of efficiency'. These pockets of efficiency are comparatively free of surplus employment as they enjoy autonomy on employment decisions. But the rest of the Saudi State has provided a significant share of the rentier resource distribution to the Saudi populace at large (Hertog, 2012b). Islands of efficiency in the Saudi State have almost, by definition, been separated from the overall institutional environment through sharp boundaries, the policing, and defence of which they themselves have contributed to.

The under-performance of large parts of the Saudi system has created islands of efficiency; conversely, the presence of these islands has lowered the pressure to reform the overall system.

Performance of SOEs

Saudi SOEs comprise a few isolated 'islands of efficiency'—referred to earlier—in an ocean of mediocrity. They are a few key strategic SOEs that perform well, notably in the areas of hydrocarbons and petrochemicals, public service delivery, infrastructure provision, monetary and financial regulation, and public security. They have done relatively well since the 1970s. Their organizational identity has been strong; recruitment and promotion have been largely in-house; and other bureaucracies are kept at arm's length at all levels of hierarchy. But little information is publicly available on the performance and size of these SOEs which are believed to be well run and enjoy a high degree of operational independence (OECD, 2012).

The reasons behind their emergence, evolution, and growth were not predetermined. In the absence of powerful political forces outside of the regime core, it was instead contingent on the vagaries of a few princes and technocrats—their personalities, their patronage relations, administrative acumen, their intra-family petty conflicts, and jealousies (Hertog, 2008). The Saudi SOE sector has been characterized by remarkable heterogeneity, as the ruling family has used different parts of the State for different purposes: some primarily for providing public services and pushing economic diversification, others for keeping the balance of power and resources within the family, as well as broader patronage, co-optation of strategic sections of the population, and self-enrichment (Hertog, 2016).

Two of these exceptional SOEs are Aramco and SABIC. The national oil company, Aramco, has been State owned since its full nationalization in 1980. Its activities have been extended downstream—into refineries, petrochemical plants, and oil and gas services, including international operations—and beyond its core commercial mandate, such as building stadiums and universities. Saudi Aramco by most accounts is very well run and enjoys high operational autonomy. A product of a largely consensual process of nationalization conducted in the 1970s has retained the managerial structures and culture of its former US parent companies and has been governed in a hands-off manner by the country's Supreme Petroleum Council, which includes senior members of the Saudi royal family and ministers (OECD, 2013c).

Royal leadership has managed to prudently protect Aramco against royal and bureaucratic predation so far. Saudi Aramco has been able to operate the domestic oil sector without having to invite any foreign joint venture partners. It has enjoyed large operational autonomy and functions as yet another state within a state with its own infrastructure, clinics, schools, and residential compounds. It has a significant presence of independent and competent directors. Due to its high level of efficiency, Saudi Aramco has become a *de facto* national development agency that has been called upon to undertake activities outside its areas of core expertise.

For example, it has built a new high-profile international university (the King Abdullah University of Science and Technology), set up a world-class football stadium in Jeddah, provided SME support programmes, undertaken research in non-stream energy technology, and developed an industrial city in the south (built around an oil refinery for which the government did not find private investors). Many former Aramco managers have been invited to take up senior positions in other parts of the government as the company is regarded as a best training ground for good, all-round managers.

The other national industrial champion is SABIC, one of the world's largest and most profitable petrochemicals companies, which is 70% State owned. SABIC is an institutional 'fortress' that has defended itself successfully against bureaucratic encroachments or rent seeking by minor royals. This had to do both with direct senior royal interest in keeping SABIC functional with considerable protection afforded to the company by successive Ministers of Industry. The company's profit outlook was rated as dim by multinational petrochemical companies when it was created in 1976 with paid up capital of $2.7 billion. It has, however, produced creditable returns ever since its plants came onstream in the 1980s and remained profitable through market slumps when international chemical companies made significant losses. Its operating margins have been higher than those of both of its main rivals Dow and BASF.

These islands of efficiency have been protected from bureaucratic and other forms of predation through royal patronage. They are run by technocratic confidantes of senior princes and have been endowed both with ample resources and a clear mandate to hire competitively. They have built up lean, corporate efficient structures, and undertaken very efficiently a limited set of tasks in a delimited, high-priority policy area in which other bureaucratic entities are prevented from interfering. Their rapid emergence would have been unthinkable without the deployment of oil rents to buy foreign expertise, build infrastructure, and attract the brightest young nationals with competitive salaries. These islands of efficiency have been largely shielded from rent-seeking, which is more easily and profitably pursued in other institutions and SOEs (Hertog, 2012b).

The Saudi SOE model based on privileged 'pockets of excellence' demonstrates that the absence of conventional corporate governance mechanisms does not preclude good SOE performance or political accountability. Conversely, the formal presence of such mechanisms does not guarantee good performance. SOEs have an arm's length relationship to the administration at large. Companies, like SABIC, Saudi Aramco, are not under the regulatory purview of sectoral ministries, and they enjoy high *de facto* autonomy from these ministries (OECD, 2012).

These SOEs have been established by special decree. Their managers report directly to the ruler, the crown prince, or their close advisers. Their leadership has been judiciously picked by the ruling families with proven managerial capabilities as overriding selection criterion. Some rulers have sent out special recruiters to scour candidates with high potential in local business, bureaucracy, and universities. SOE managers have often enjoyed special access to the ruling family, allowing them to bypass the sluggish national bureaucracy on matters of regulation and infrastructure. Senior managers have developed long-term relationships of trust with rulers, resulting in less personnel turnover. Privileged SOEs have enjoyed managerial autonomy from the rest of the State. With such status and support, it has been easier for their managers to keep a consistent focus on generating profits. The chairs of boards have often been ruling family members, their principal executives are highly skilled 'commoner' technocrats (Hertog, 2010b).

Levels of corruption in these SOEs are much lower than in the rest of the State apparatus. Corruption has been harshly prosecuted by SOE leaders and incentives for it are weaker because of competitive hiring and excellent remuneration. SOEs have been autonomous in their recruitment and have had separate salary and staffing systems that enable them to attract top talent. These structures have often been deliberately set up in contrast to more rigid, less meritocratic public service employment. SOE budgets and capital resources have been protected through generous initial capital endowments and through financial autonomy (i.e. SOEs are taxed only on their net revenue and can expand through both retained profits) (OECD, 2012).

Some of these structures and practices have been informal and have proved to be difficult to re-create through formal legal instruments. These have evolved because of a leadership that has been autonomous and the absence of the populist economic ideology (OECD, 2012). These islands of efficiency have played a pivotal role in building up the Saudi private sector not only through infrastructure provision, contracting, and training initiatives but also through the transfer of skills (and networks) in the shape of public sector managers who move to the private sector.

SOE islands of efficiency are publicly recognized and appreciated in an economy characterized by rent seeking, and whose administrative and regulatory capacities are limited. They have defended themselves successfully against bureaucratic encroachment and predation by disenchanted minor royals. Their well-developed defensive reflexes have isolated them from other state institutions, making learning and adaptation harder and reducing their influence over their environment. The hierarchical hub and spoke system of state institutions around the royal family has made reform coalitions hard to construct. Each of these state institutions has owed its existence to royal support and patronage to operate outside of the regular bureaucracy, hire separately, and deliver results.

Successful Saudi SOEs have these features in common: they enjoy the direct protection of rulers; senior managers have long-term relationships of trust with rulers; and members of the ruling family are often company chairpersons. These SOEs have not been used for mass patronage employment and have been characterized by relative institutional autonomy. The relative autonomy is of course granted by the senior royal leadership (Hertog, 2006).

Apart from these exceptional pockets of excellence, the rest of the Saudi SOE sector is afflicted by many of the same problems that SOEs around the world suffer from. Factor-intensive and relatively low-tech growth, combined with corporate governance structures that have lagged behind international standards, has made it harder to attract international technology partners. Management structures often remain informal and business transactions relationship based, which has increased barriers of entry for newcomers.

In Saudi Arabia, entities with separate ownership functions have been passive shareholders. For example, PIF which controls most of the kingdom's large SOEs outside of aviation and the oil upstream sectors is *de facto* a unit of the Ministry of Finance with no strategic mandate. It has a limited number of lower-level representatives on the boards of the various entities it formally owns. Apart from Aramco whose operations are supervised by foreign board members, Saudi SOE boards have been by and large known to be fairly passive. SABIC is a representative example. The chairman is a member of the ruling family and is also the chairman of the Royal Commission for the Industrial Cities of Jubail and Yanbu, while the other members of the board include SABIC's CEO, one current and one former deputy minister, as well as three local private sector representatives. The board members, from the government side, are chosen on the basis of seniority (OECD, 2012b).

The board of Saudi Telecom (STC) is similar. It includes a number of local private sector representatives, several senior ministerial representatives, and the governor of SAMA, as its chairman. SAMA has been historically affiliated with the Ministry of Finance, which controls the PIF which formally holds a majority of STC's shares. The Ministry of Finance hence exerts indirect control through a chairman with no background in telecommunications and with extensive other obligations. As in SABIC, the PIF as a formal majority owner is not represented on the board (OECD, 2012b).

Rampant, indiscriminate over-employment of nationals since the 1970s has meant that performance standards have become hard to enforce. Some SOEs under long-term control of ruling family members have become impenetrable bastions of patronage and princely self-enrichment. Public sector employees strictly abide by the directions of their superiors and never question their authority or decisions (Hertog, 2016). As a consequence, risk-taking and innovation has been restricted while delaying decisions, complicating processes, and increasing red-tape.

At the macro-level, SOE performance in Saudi Arabia has been dependent on a conservative monarchical rule with a premium on political quiescence, working to keep the society state dependent. However, the basic coherence of the ruling family has been maintained through elaborate, intra-family deals, usually struck in the course of the negotiations over succession. They have allowed the perpetuation of a clear status hierarchy between the ruling family and the rest of the bureaucracy (Hertog, 2010a).

State ownership of enterprises and its other responsibilities

The MENA region's reliance on SOEs has been a consequence of a number of innovative, imaginative experiments with State capitalism in the Gulf countries, notably in Saudi Arabia and the UAE. As a result, for the foreseeable future, reliance on SOEs as pioneers of national infrastructure and as actors with diverse developmental mandates (e.g. construction of social housing, employment creation) is bound to continue regardless of fiscal pressures. Examples of the developmental and social activities of SOEs vary but have been visible across the region (Amico, 2017).

The Saudi economy remains deeply oil dependent and hence dependent on Saudi Aramco. It is too important an asset not to be used for future economic diversification aimed at greater self-sufficiency. It has consistently been given mandates related to developing firms in its value chain and a range of other tasks beyond its sectoral expertise (Amico, 2017). Saudi Aramco's prominent national role reflects its capabilities and gives it considerable political capital. It now functions as the surrogate government (Hertog, 2019).

In the Saudi context, the company has unrivalled managerial capacities. It has become a critical agent for the social, economic, and infrastructural development. This has presented both opportunities and risks for Aramco, which now operates beyond its traditional 'turf' of running the upstream oil and gas sector. Aramco is now been involved in activities that are more political and more closely scrutinized by the Saudi public (Hertog, 2019). Although its early role in national development has been a matter of some debate, it has played an important part in building Saudi infrastructure, especially in the strategic Eastern Province, in training an advanced industrial and managerial workforce and in providing health services (Hertog, 2013).

The company has become increasingly involved in training programmes that aim to shape the Kingdom's young managerial elites. It now has a significant stake in industrial diversification; domestic energy reform; national employment; entrepreneurship; and secondary, vocational, and higher education (Hertog, 2012b). In addition to non-oil domestic development tasks, the company has acquired growing international investments, and is set to indirectly raise significant debt for the Saudi government (Hertog, 2019).

As the Saudi State's policy challenges have grown, Aramco—because of its internal managerial capacity—has been pushed to the fore-front of social and economic development outside of the hydrocarbons sector. This has been partially an outcome of higher oil income and increased demands on the part of government and the royal leadership, but has also been driven by a more assertive vision of the company's role developed since 2009.

While the leveraging of Aramco's project implementation capacity might seem rational in the short run, there is a concern in some quarters that the company's objectives might become diluted and, in the worst case, could be dangerous first step towards Aramco's politicization.

The other issue is whether the breadth of all the combined tasks it is now undertaking might become overwhelming, thus diluting the managerial focus of the company with an ever-expanding list of follow-up tasks (Hertog, 2013).

While the kingdom's ambitious industrial diversification agenda has provided Aramco an opportunity to diversify, it has also pushed the company into a more complex political environment. At a minimum, the company will need a clear strategy to prioritize and put a shadow price on its development tasks. One of the company's core strengths has always been that of being perceived as separate from politics in Riyadh. This stance will be harder to maintain as Aramco takes on more industrial policy tasks (Hertog, 2019).

Conclusions

Reliance on SOEs as pioneers of national infrastructure projects and as actors with diverse developmental mandates has remained an important policy lever in the MENA region and will continue into the foreseeable future. The Saudi growth model is based on 'islands of efficiency'—SOEs that are drastically better than the rest of the Saudi State and significantly more efficient than the average emerging market SOEs. These islands of efficiency were strategic sectors notably in the areas of public service delivery, infrastructure provision, monetary and financial regulation, and public security. These islands of efficiency have been role models for the rest of the MENA region.

They have been protected from bureaucratic and other forms of predation through royal patronage. In practice, royals have been content to let islands of efficiency operate with considerable freedom, and their performance and managerial structures have by and large been stable over long periods.

While the rapidly growing distributional, but increasingly dysfunctional, Saudi State itself has become quite heterogeneous, consisting of patrimonial fiefdoms in some parts and efficient modern bureaucracies in others. Rapid state expansion has created new social and political hierarchies and a deeper social stratification but with the royal family remaining at its apex.

Apart from the exceptional, exemplar SOEs, the rest of the Saudi State provides a significant share of the rentier resource distribution to the Saudi populace. The under-performance of significant parts of the Saudi system has fed the need for islands of efficiency; conversely, the presence of these islands has lowered the pressure to reform the overall system.

The legacy of State-led industrialization, urbanization, and modernization has been created by these privileged SOEs. But their relationship to a maturing private sector has now become tense. Yet this outcome appears preferable to one in which new sectors might not have been developed at all.

9

Country case study 7: Singapore

The origins of State capitalism and SOEs in Singapore

The story of Singapore's success is the story of the government's extraordinarily successful interventions in the economy. The government played a pivotal role not only in mapping out the strategic direction for the Singaporean economy but also in driving the structural transformation that has taken (and continues to take) place over the past six decades.

No major strategic or structural change in Singapore since 1965 has occurred without a strong and well thought out push from the government. Unlike other developing countries, the State's ubiquitous, pervasive presence in the economy has remained significant over time; even as the economy has matured from developing to developed, with its markets and institutions now being considered as world class, equal to the best in the Antipodes, US, Europe, and Japan.

As part of its post-independence industrialization strategy, the Singapore government assumed a proactive entrepreneurial role by establishing SOEs in manufacturing, finance, trading, transportation, ship building, and services. The government was not reticent about investing in infrastructure and industries that it deemed critical to the development of the economy, especially 'sunrise' industries.

Compared with other dynamic Asian economies, government intervention in the Singaporean economy was more intrusive and extensive. Singapore is neither a socialist nor a communist country. It is decidedly a liberal market orientated economy. Yet, paradoxically, the government applied a *'State capitalism'* approach to the country's economic development when it separated from Malaysia in 1965, after gaining independence in 1963. That was long before that term came in vogue, following China's success in imitating (with important departures and variations) the Singaporean model.

At independence, the new People's Action Party (PAP) government inherited ownership of several public companies in telecommunications, aviation, and defence from the previous British administration. It continued with many earlier policies, for example, the establishment of industrial estates and providing tax incentives to attract new enterprises and encourage the expansion of existing ones.

At independence, industrialization was considered the means to economic growth that would create employment and help finance social reform and housing. To this end, the government acquired minority stakes in key-established companies and established start-ups in strategic sectors, like construction, shipbuilding, transportation, industry, engineering, and logistics to foster self-sufficiency and attract private investment (Cummine, 2015).

Unlike most other developing countries at the time, Singapore did not look, myopically, to protect its own small domestic market from foreign competition. Instead, it decided to look at the world as its market and took whatever measures it thought necessary to create or import 'best-in-class' firms, employing the best talent, technology, and the best standards to meet the needs of that global market. Not only did the Singapore government use traditional revenue and spending (fiscal) tools to mobilize and allocate resources but it also made extensive use of SOEs to undertake activities in a world-class way that influenced private sector behaviour significantly.

These SOEs—now called Government-Linked Companies (GLCs)-- all played critical roles in Singapore's economic development (Ministry of Finance, 2002) creating jobs on a large scale and contributing to nation building. In doing so, neither government nor SOEs sacrificed efficiency or productivity but emphasized them instead, as being critical to competitive success. Many of the SOEs have since been partially privatized and listed on the local stock exchange.

GLCs are classified into tiers: Tier 1 GLCs are directly owned by Temasek (or through special purpose investment vehicles owned by Temasek), whereas Tier 2 or Tier 3 includes GLCs that have another GLC as controlling shareholder (Table 9.1). There are 12 Tier 1 GLCs and 18 Tier 2 or 3 GLCs. GLCs account for 30 out of 742 issuers (4%) but about 30% of total market capitalization on the Singapore stock exchange. They account for an estimated 20% of Singapore's GNI (Teen, 2015).

Table 9.1 Singapore GLCs

GLCs	Definition	Examples
Tier 1	directly owned by Temasek (or through investment vehicle owned by Temasek)	Capitaland, DBS Group, Keppel Corp, NOL, Olam, SATS, Sembcorp Industries, SIA, Singtel, SMRT, ST Engineering, STATS ChipPAC.
Tier 2 and 3	Includes GLCs that have another GLC as controlling shareholder	Ascott Residence Trust, CapitaCommercial Trust, CapitaRetail China Trust, CitySpring Infrastructure Trust, K1 Ventures, Keppel Land, Keppel REIT, Keppel T&T, Mapletree Commercial Trust, Mapletree Greater China Commercial Trust, Mapletree Industrial Trust, Mapletree Logistics Trust, Sembcorp Marine, SIA Engineering, Singapore Post, Starhub, Telechoice, Tiger Airways.

Note: Company in which the government, through Temasek, another government agency, or another GLC, is the controlling shareholder with 15% or more of voting shares.

Source: Teen (2015).

GLCs have played a crucial role in Singapore's transformation within one generation. They continue to do so for the next. The important role given to SOEs was the idea of—the People's Action Party—closely associated with Lee Kwan Yew, Singapore's first Prime Minister, now acknowledged as modern Singapore's founding father. The party had a Fabian socialist background prior to independence in 1959, and therefore, it placed great initial emphasis on social equity, but in a highly pragmatic manner (OECD, 2014a).

Singapore's economy has performed impressively enough to be recognized as an 'economic miracle' (Huff, 1999). In a short span (1965–90) Singapore registered average annual GDP growth of 7.5% (Huff, 1999) with *per capita* income rising from S$500 in 1965 to S$10,000 in 1989 (Porter, Neo, and Ketels, 2013). By 2016, GDP per capita was S$52,960, among the highest in the world. Unlike city-States and emirates/kingdoms in the Middle East, Singapore is not just a rich (city-State) country. It is 'developed' in every sense. Although often criticized in the West as being 'guided' and therefore a restricted and highly imperfect democracy', its standards of governance, jurisprudence, human development, social, and institutional capital now rank as among the best in the world.

At independence, the Singaporean government did not concern itself with protecting the interests of local Chinese businesses, engaged as they were in petty entrepôt trade which did not create jobs. Rather, when Singapore separated from Malaya, the island's government decided that the key to growth was not import substitution but an exports-led strategy.

Such a strategy relied on significant foreign investment (for funds and technological as well as managerial know-how) of a kind that would create large-scale, domestic employment. The government, on its part, supported that objective by investing heavily and continually (unlike most other developing countries at the time) in healthcare, education, and social housing for its population to ensure that it would be productive with the required skill levels and continually adapting itself.

The government also believed that it could not, however, be dependent exclusively on foreign direct investors whom, when it came to a crunch, would show allegiance to their own countries. There needed to be a counterbalance to FDI in the form of domestic GLCs which would act as a substitute for absent domestic private entrepreneurs, who could make large investments and undertake risks (OECD, 2014a). That approach was diametrically opposite to the paradigm adopted by almost all other emerging economies in the 1960s--led by the examples of India and China. Almost all the colonies of former European empires, followed import substitution policies requiring a high degree of protection.

With some exceptions, the commercial profitability (as a proxy for efficiency and productivity) of GLCs was stressed uncompromisingly in the medium (if not short) term. GLCs were also directed to pursue simultaneously, the government's wider goals of generating large-scale domestic employment while achieving a measure of social equity.

Although the objectives set for GLCs have been clear for some time, and widely supported by their managements and boards, performance targets set for them have varied over the years. In the beginning, their emphasis was on creating employment, viewed as the best way for achieving social equity. By the mid-1980s, policy had changed to encourage increasing skill and income levels accompanied by regionalization, i.e. outsourcing low-skilled activities to less developed countries in the ASEAN region. Following the Asian financial crisis in 1997, policy objectives widened beyond regionalization to embrace globalization (OECD, 2014a).

GLCs were instrumental in initiating and leading the development of nascent, strategic sectors in the domestic economy—banking, telecommunications, industrial estates, logistics, the seaport, airport, air and sea transportation, shipbuilding and repair, defence technology, etc. These industries have remained significant to the Singaporean economy. State investment in GLCs was critical in enhancing the overall efficiency and total factor productivity in these strategic sectors/industries, as well as in the overall domestic business environment. This resulted in reducing setting-up and operating costs for MNCs from the US, Japan, and Europe which found Singapore to be the ideal, most hospitable, regional Asian base in which to establish themselves to serve markets in ASEAN, India, and China.

Singapore has always been clear about what was expected of GLCs, which have evolved and transformed over time in consonance with the changing demands of the city-State's rapid economic development and modernization. The State has also been clear; however, that although wider issues concerning the public good (for example, social equity) might not be the primary goal of GLCs, they still needed to support policies, such as land acquisition, social housing, and public health (OECD, 2014a).

The roles of EDB, DBS, Temasek, and GIC in Singapore's economic development

Government set up the Economic Development Board (EDB) in 1965 to replace Singapore's Industrial Promotion Board. The EDB's role was to attract new businesses to Singapore to enable the country to develop a deep, diversified, and strong manufacturing base. Industrialization—initially directed at import substitution, when Singapore joined the Federation of Malaya in 1963, before abandoning it in 1965—was to be export oriented with particular initial emphasis on significant employment generation.

However, the island's quantum of human capital needed for rapid industrialization was insufficient at the time. Local capital markets were relatively undeveloped with almost no domestic risk capital. The domestic private sector (mainly involved in petty trade) was risk averse and loath to undertake large industrial projects requiring unprecedented amounts of capital without sufficient knowledge of the complexities involved. In addition, the domestic market for consumption was too small to support a large and diversified industrial base.

Local business experience on the island was confined mainly to import/export trade and related financial services, like banking, and transport services, like regional shipping. The local private sector had little or no technical or managerial experience to establish or run large industrial enterprises. Relying on multinational corporations was one option for filling this crucial gap in industrial and management know-how. The other was to foster their localization through strong state involvement in certain key strategic sectors of the economy.

Singapore's government targeted the global economy as the consumption base for its domestic industry. They found control over key domestic markets and institutions the most effective way to respond to opportunities in the world economy to meet the objectives of absorbing surplus labour and promoting economic growth. To boost Singapore's ability to engage in international trade, a majority-state-owned company, Sembawang Shipyard, was established in 1968 to take over the UK military's Royal Naval Dockyard. To further promote the prospects of export manufacturing, in 1969 the government established a fully State-owned company, Neptune Orient Lines (OECD, 2014a).

The purpose of the latter was to limit Singapore's dependence on foreign shipping and facilitate the trade with centrally planned economies, like China and India. Other significant investments in 1968 and 1969 focused on the hydrocarbons sector to address the issue of Singapore's total energy dependence. Joint ventures with the US oil company Amoco and Japan-based Oceanic Petroleum led to the formation of the Singapore Petroleum Company, of which the government owned almost one-third (OECD, 2014a).

The Development Bank of Singapore (DBS) was established in 1968 to take over the development finance section from EDB. It was an important catalyst for Singapore's industrial development in the early years after independence. In the same year, the government established the International Trading Company (Intraco) to take over what had previously been EDB's export promotion division. Intraco was tasked with two objectives: the first was to develop overseas markets for Singaporean products, and the second, to source cheaper raw materials for local industries through pooled purchasing (OECD, 2014a).

GLCs became the means for the government to take the lead in establishing new industries, including in the services sector, where the presence of the private sector was weak. However, these public enterprises had to be run, and their performance judged, on a strictly commercial basis. They were not subject to political influence to achieve expedient social, distributional, and regional objectives at the expense of profitability, as was the case in many neighbouring Asian countries.

By 1973 the Ministry of Finance directly owned 26 companies and had partial ownership of an additional 33. The government was furthermore the beneficial owner through equity investments made by DBS (estimated at 50 companies) and Intraco (20 companies) (OECD, 2014a). Later, these equity holdings were streamlined when the government incorporated Temasek in 1974—as a fully owned company of the Ministry of Finance. Temasek is still a government holding company that is the apex shareholder in SOEs on behalf of the Singaporean government.

Temasek took over the ownership of a number of companies whose shares were previously held by a state body, such as statutory board or ministry. This allowed the government to have the GLCs owned and managed on a purely commercial basis, effectively separating the government's role as shareholder from its regulatory and policy-making functions (Israel, 2008). Temasek relieved the ministries of finance, trade, and industry from direct commercial management of GLCs, thus removing GLCs from the kind of political influence and interference that remains the bane of SOEs in most other countries.

The government's direct efforts in promoting industrial growth through GLCs created substantial employment. Singapore's industrialization strategy, aimed at export orientation for the global market, proved to be timely and spectacularly successful. The economy saw a large structural shift towards manufacturing whose share in total output grew from 16.6% in 1960 to 29.4% by 1979. In 1992, manufacturing contributed 27.6% of GDP, most of which was exported, and accounted for 27.5% of employment (Tan et al., 2015).

Singapore's economy is still heavily influenced by the State through Temasek and its portfolio of GLCs—many of which have global operations. Temasek is now one of two sovereign wealth funds (SWFs) in

Singapore, the other being the Government Investment Corporation Private Limited (GIC). Both are designated as 'government companies' in Singapore's Constitution.

The main difference between the two SWFs is that GIC 'does not own assets and only manages assets and foreign reserves on behalf of the Singapore Government', whereas Temasek has owned and managed its own investments and assets. In 2019 the net portfolio of Temasek was valued at SG$313 billion (US$229 billion) which has more than doubled in the last decade from SG$130 billion (FT, 2019).

The total contribution of Temasek and GIC to government in 2019 of SG$17.1 billion has surpassed corporate tax revenue of SG$16.7 billion and goods and services tax revenue of SG$11.6 billion. Together they comprise Singapore's largest income source. As social security spending rises with an ageing population, Temasek aims to invest in start-ups to support government income in the future (FT, 2019).

Temasek's initial portfolio comprised some 35 companies, but only twelve currently remain under its control. While the scope of Temasek's activities has changed considerably since its establishment, it continues to play a key role in fostering economic development and maintaining a strong Singaporean State influence in the economy (Cummine, 2015). In addition to GLCs held directly or indirectly by Temasek holdings, there are also a number of enterprises that are fully or majority owned by statutory boards. Such enterprises are also classified as GLCs, to the extent that their shares are owned ultimately by the State. Over the years, the government has refocused and fine-tuned state's role but has not dismantled it. Rationalization of the government's interventions in the economy (direct and indirect) through the ownership of SOEs, guidance over the way in which they operate, has not resulted in significant diminution of State capitalism.

Regulation vs public ownership of SOEs

Since 1965, the government has maintained its steady focus on GDP and per capita income growth, alongside the sustained accumulation of surpluses (of the government and private businesses) as the primary target of economic policy. It sees GDP/GNI growth as the main measure of economic success and the key to a 'better life' for its people. Over the years the primacy of economic growth has taken precedence over other development objectives.

Specifically, efficiency has been prized over equity. Although the PAP emphasized social equity in the early years of independence, discussions of 'equity' and 'income distribution' have since been sidestepped as being detrimental to the pursuit of efficiency and growth. This has resulted in the 'producer surplus' being given much greater priority over the 'consumer surplus'.

Policy incentives have favoured large corporates, i.e. MNCs and GLCs, because they generate greater producer surpluses through economies of scale. Small and medium enterprises (SMEs) have complained for many years that they have been neglected by the State and government policies have not been attuned to fostering them.

The Competition Act[1] was adopted in 2004 to help promote market competition and efficiency; but a large number of industries were excluded from its coverage thus giving firms in these industries a high degree of monopoly power. The objective of the law was clearly aimed at promoting market efficiency, and not necessarily at enhancing consumer surplus. However, the competition authority has doubled its efforts to promote competition in a small, open market economy characterized by concentrated ownership. The 119 enforcement actions in Singapore since 2007 have involved anti-competitive agreements (51 cases), prohibiting mergers and acquisitions (36 cases), and abuse of a dominant position (32 cases) (Wallar, 2014).

This highlights the government's pragmatism in continuously calibrating the balance between State intervention and the preservation of efficient competition and market discipline. While the government has been heavily involved in investment and production activities and has been competing directly with the private sector in many cases, it is conscious of the need to avoid the inefficiency, waste, and dissipation of

[1] The Singapore Competition Act is not applicable to the entire economy because various sectors, including the public sector, have been excluded from complying with the requirements of the Act. The sectors excluded include (i) government authorities, statutory bodies, or any other person acting on their behalf; (ii) activities that are excluded with ministerial permission due to exceptional and compelling reasons of public policy; and (iii) ten, that is, industries, like telecommunications, media, post, transportation, energy, and waste disposal that are partly regulated.

scarce resources associated with so many SOEs elsewhere. It is equally aware of the need to foster innovation and encourage genuine competition to bolster efficient market functioning to strengthen GLCs' position in global markets (Tan and Bhaskaran, 2015).

Efforts have been made to ensure sufficient competition (by allowing more than one player in an industry) while allowing GLCs to exist. The approach has been to intervene in the economy forcefully when needed but to leave the market to function so long as the balance leads to overall efficiency, high economic growth, and accumulation of surpluses (Tan and Bhaskaran, 2015).

GLCs have operated as 'for-profit' commercial entities, on the same basis as private sector companies. They are expected to provide commercial returns commensurate with risks taken and are subject to the same regulations and market forces as private enterprises. They do not receive any subsidies or preferential treatment from the government. For-profit commercial orientation was established early as a norm for all GLCs[2] (Ramirez and Tan, 2004).

To mitigate the risk that the GLCs might be politically and socially rather than commercially driven, the government has 'constructed a highly visible and well-tailored regulatory regime, which aims to prevent the government from abusing its position as the ultimate controlling shareholder'. This regulatory regime has multiple, complementary components:

- First, a variety of legal constraints are imposed on MOF's rights as a shareholder. For example, the Singapore Constitution provides that MOF's appointment, reappointment, or removal of Temasek directors must be approved by the President of Singapore.
- Second, restrictions are placed on Temasek's board to minimize the potential for politically motivated intervention.

[2] GLCs were expected to be run on a commercial basis, as expressed by then Deputy Prime Minister, Dr Goh Keng Swee: *'One of the tragic illusions that many countries of the Third World entertain is the notion that politicians and civil servants can successfully perform entrepreneurial functions. It is curious that, in the face of overwhelming evidence to the contrary, the belief persists' (Goh, 1972).*

- Third, GLCs and the holding companies do not belong to the civil service of Singapore and therefore have no legal privileges or immunities of government departments (Quah, 2017).
- Finally, although Temasek is legally exempt from public reporting requirements, it has chosen to publish detailed disclosures of its portfolio and performance, and subjects its financial statements to annual audits by international audit firms.

Notwithstanding these safeguards, it may be misleading to conclude that Temasek and the GLCs are entirely free from political influence. Members of the boards of both Temasek and its portfolio companies have historically been drawn from the Singaporean civil service (as indeed are most of its 'politicians' who run for election to parliament) and the military. Even today, the managers of Temasek's portfolio firms are chosen from the technocratic ruling elite.

Half of the directors in GLCs identified as independent have previously held positions in the Singapore government and/or government bodies. They have shared backgrounds, steeped in a powerful, civil service culture, and common world view. So, the objectives of the controlling shareholder, on one hand, and directors and managers of the GLCs, on the other, are met without direct intervention by the government. That has not been necessary to ensure that Temasek's GLC investment strategy fulfils the government's policy goals and strategic objectives (Milhaupt, 2017).

Yet at the same time, the primacy of the commercial *profitability* objective of the government in holding shares of the GLCs provides great clarity to managers operating within the system. This stands in contrast to the mixed commercial and social motives of SOEs in other countries which dilute their profitability significantly. The criticism frequently targeted at GLCs is that government support and favour gives them unfair competitive advantages in the local market, where they have 'crowded out private investment in new markets, products and technologies and usurped entrepreneurial activity'.

The main advantage of government ownership, however, has been the positive signal it sends to the national, regional (ASEAN), and global markets. Indeed, many GLCs have consistently posted a strong financial performance. But the rapid growth of GLCs both in size and in number—has led to concerns that they are encroaching into too many industries and hindering the development of a critical mass of local enterprises. Among small- and medium-sized private enterprises in particular, GLCs are still perceived to have unfair advantages in terms of access to funds, tenders, and opportunities.

Although, there has been no evidence that GLCs have had easier access to credit, they have been rewarded in financial markets with their publicly traded shares reflecting a premium of about 20% over their equivalent privately owned counterparts. The premium over non-GLCs has meant that GLCs' cost of capital has been lower. This is after accounting for GLCs being large, profitable, and less likely to go bankrupt. This GLC premium reflects the markets' perception of the benefits—whether real or illusory—of being linked to the government. This represents a capital market distortion (Ramirez and Tan, 2004).

Other criticisms are that the GLCs' diversified conglomerate structure and their management by former civil servants or military officials, who are conservative and risk-averse, results in economic under-performance. But available evidence and research suggests that most GLCs are 'both competently administered by professional managers and are profitable'.

The extensive economic and political reach of the Singapore State necessarily conditions the activities of the local private sector. Dependence on the State for contracts and awareness of the political nexus between the civil service and the PAP has promoted co-option. Singapore's GLC ecosystem can therefore be considered as being a perfectly legal and appropriate dispensation of state patronage of favoured individuals and electoral constituencies. The rents generated by GLCs are internalized through distribution to individuals within those monopolies, without involving the private sector which meets those rents through payments for corporatized public services.

These criticisms, however, do not detract from the remarkable overall success of the Singapore approach on most measures—financial performance, transparency, lack of corruption, and protection of minority shareholder interests. Its GLC strategy has allowed the government, acting through Temasek, to reap the benefits of a controlling shareholder in its portfolio companies; and at the same time, it has avoided the problems of minority shareholder exploitation that most controlling public shareholder regimes present.

Crony capitalism

Singapore has a long-established reputation as one of the least corrupt countries in the world. At the same time, the State owns and controls much of the economy, intervenes heavily in the public and private enterprise sector and is formally democratic. These are all conditions that in other countries have been positively correlated with high levels of corruption. Singapore's anti-corruption strategy has relied heavily on conducive values, meritocracy, and enforcement that goes along with stiff, draconian penalties for default, and high institutional efficiency (Lim 1998).

In addition, the generous financial rewards available to public servants vitiate any need for enrichment through corruption (Wei, 2000). For example, cabinet ministers' salaries are pegged to those of the CEOs in the largest multinational firms in the world. To quote Lee Kwan Yew: 'It's a simple choice, pay political leaders the top salaries that they deserve and get honest clean government or underpay them and risk the Third World disease of corruption'. He also often said that 'I am the best paid Prime Minister in Asia but probably the poorest'.

The lack of corruption in Singapore has been attributable to the relative economic weakness of the local private sector in the post-colonial era. It remained weak due in part to the PAP government's lack of interest in supporting the local Chinese business elite and its own social democratic ideology of the time, which did not allocate a major role to domestic capital in national economic development. The result was that that the PAP did not rely heavily on political support from business, did not develop an ideology that gave pride of place to indigenous firms, and therefore did not look to the local private sector as a central object of either policy or patronage (Haggard and Low, 2002).

Yet GLCs, and the wider (economic) interventionist role of the State, embody not just economic might but also power relations critical to the PAP. State control of capital and resources underscores the political paternalism that Lee Kuan Yew personified and remains central to the quintessential character of Singapore's governing regime. The dispensing of rewards is the most obvious dimension of this.

State capital has created a new establishment of political and economic elites (Worthington 2002). Senior government leaders, former senior government officials, former senior military commanders, current senior government officials, and current and former ruling party politicians have joined a select group of politically trusted senior civil servants as either directors or executives of GLCs (Tan 2002).

Their (often) multiple, sequential sources of employment, income, and ownership are involved directly in, or closely connected with the government's business activities through SOEs. However, this list does not necessarily indicate nepotism since the individuals are all highly qualified in terms of education and past employment.

This has been a coincidental outcome of a 'free market meritocracy' and the pervasiveness of GLCs and their collective monopolistic position as employers of senior local talent. The scarcity of talent in a small population has led to their multiple jobs and responsibilities. For example, senior government officials also hold paid appointments in GLCs while still in government (Lim, 2018).

The GLCs have provided opportunities to members of the political elite to advance their careers and create networks of power through the control of a variety of assets. There has been little evidence that political insiders have abused office for personal gain. The public perceives GLCs less in terms of providing political and career incentives to elites and more in terms of a fusion of the public good and private interests (Haggard and Low, 2002).

The importance of relative autonomy in government economic decision-making underscores that policy remains guided primarily by considerations of economic efficiency. However, social conflict theory underlines that the political autonomy does not, by any means, amount to the removal of vested interests or politics from the policy-making and implementation processes.

The reality is that the Singaporean *administrative* bureaucracy has little independence from the *political* PAP and its business nexus of power. The political elite, the administrative elite, and those who govern and direct the State's business interests comprise the same relatively small tightly interlinked group of people. For these privileged 'star performers' salaries represent only a fraction of the entire financial remuneration (augmented by large bonuses, board member fees and other perks) they can expect to receive legally during a working life spent in the civil service, military, or employment in statutory boards and GLCs (Lim, 2018). PAP has further co-opted prominent, accomplished members of the private business community by inviting some of them to sit on boards of economic agencies. Clearly, Singaporean economic policies are enmeshed in the PAP's political strategy and the interest of the Singaporean business community.

With firm control over both the political system and the economy, the Lee family has directed both Temasek and the GIC towards a mixed strategy of ensuring PAP dominance over the Singaporean economy. It has reinforced its obsession with generating long-term profits to accumulate unassailable surpluses and reserves for the benefit of future generations. The Lee family's political dominance has also enabled Singapore to undermine the positions of major economic and bureaucratic interests to increase the profits of Temasek and GIC (Shih, 2009).

Singapore has scored poorly on the crony capitalism index, as calculated by The Economist (May 6, 2016), because of its role as a financial entrepot for its ASEAN neighbours, and its dominant property and banking clans. The Economist has also remarked that Singapore is the 5th easiest place in the world to do business for politically well-connected businessmen.

There is no denying that, despite decades of industrial policy and State intervention, Singapore has grown rapidly, apparently without corruption. State-created (and state-controlled) rents have been efficiently allocated, without illegal payments having to be made by either MNCs or private investors. They have enjoyed tax breaks, highly efficient infrastructure services, and other subsidies on the input cost side to enhance their ability to compete globally. Any rent seeking has been checked by the need to compete in international markets.

In the domestic market, rents allocated to State agencies and GLCs which have enjoyed domestic market monopolies have been held to the high-performance standards necessary to attract foreign private investment in other sectors of the economy. Monopoly rents earned by GLCs, along with persistently large fiscal and current account surpluses, have been invested to increase efficiency and growth. They have been distributed legally and transparently to senior management, civil servants, and political leaders through generous remuneration packages (Lim, 2018).

The private agenda of public officials

The basic approach to state economic intervention in Singapore has been to run the economy almost like a corporation in the relentless pursuit of GDP growth and surplus accumulation. Political office holders and senior civil servants are remunerated, in part, according to the GDP growth that they deliver, much like corporates which reward their senior management with bonuses linked to profits made (Lim, 2015). Once the objectives of high economic growth and surplus accumulation are clearly defined, they are implemented efficiently by a task-oriented government bureaucracy. The decision to peg the remuneration of political office holders and senior civil servants to very top private sector pay, despite disagreement from many quarters, is an example of the government's ability to implement what it considers pragmatic policy measures undeterred by considerations of political costs and public opprobrium.

Given the critical, pervasive role that government plays in the economy, it has argued that the public sector must be staffed with high calibre people who are equal to the best in the private sector. Matching remuneration to that in the private sector is necessary to attract and retain such talent without the risk of infesting the system with corruption (Tan and Bhaskaran, 2015).

The social contract with the people that has kept the PAP government in power since independence is widely accepted to be the promise of employment and a fair distribution of economic benefits, a significant part of which is represented by the provision of good public housing where a large majority of Singaporeans reside in.

The performance of the GLCs has also been centre stage in the evolution of the social contract between government and citizens. Any serious decline in the performance of GLCs would have major implications for the political regime. Thus, fortuitously, from the outset, conditions to encourage the responsible management of GLCs have been put in place and reinforced. Civil servants who manage GLCs (and whose careers intertwine with positions in government ministries as well) find themselves acting at the behest of political masters who were formerly their seniors. They were also tasked in earlier years with managing GLCs, which they did by combining the goal of commercial profitability with that of economic development in mind (Tan and Bhaskaran, 2015).

In keeping with the goal of fostering good governance, the government has also adopted a zero-tolerance approach to corruption. This has undoubtedly contributed to GLCs being relatively well managed and not becoming victims of rent-seeking that often occur in SOEs elsewhere. Under Singapore law, a public servant who receives any gratification is presumed to have received such gratification corruptly, as an inducement or reward unless the contrary is proved by the public servant. Therefore, corruption has not been common in Singapore.

The PAP government, since self-government rule, has been determined to wipe out corruption in the civil service. Over the decades, the government has established several safeguards against corruption among civil servants. Among them are transparency in rules and regulations, severe punishment, including jail terms, confiscation of wealth accumulated illegally, and strict enforcement of rules and laws. However, the most effective deterrent against corruption has been the unparalleled remuneration and respect accorded to those with jobs in the civil service.

All these measures have ensured that civil servants do not collude with private businessmen who may want to buy privileges. In addition, all business transactions have to be formalized in order to provide redress to aggrieved parties as well as to prevent corruption and tax evasion (Kwok Bun Chan 2005).

Prior to independence human resources in Singapore were quite modest. As a result, the PAP government introduced a wide-ranging scholarship arrangement open to every stratum of society. Students were bonded after their study to the government for a period, resulting in a public sector elite that felt at ease in the business world. They were also products of the 'clean traditions' established early in Singapore. Unlike experience in other countries, civil servants who managed GLCs appear to have been rather effective, showing few signs of risk aversion noted in other countries (OECD, 2014a).

When civil servants ceased to manage GLCs, the best among them are appointed to their boards. In the past, the board of Temasek and its portfolio companies has had a high proportion of civil servants, and senior ex-military officers as directors. But this has slowly evolved towards independent, private sector boards and professional managements. The question that remains is why civil servants and the military have been so successful in managing and directing GLCs in Singapore, whereas their track record in other countries has been the opposite. The difference may be due partly to the 'clean society' concept that characterizes Singapore, with little corruption and with appointments always being based on merit, transparent, and competitive.

The allocation and use of capital resources through Temasek and GIC

Temasek has evolved from a holding company with an initial portfolio of 35 GLCs to a long-term, return-seeking institutional investor with both wealth management and development mandates. It has pursued its developmental mandate by buying direct stakes mainly in Singaporean and Asian companies. It has reinvested its proceeds from asset sales and dividend income into foreign assets, acting more as a private equity fund than a SWF.

As a result, Temasek has become primarily a government-owned (sovereign) institutional investor whose portfolio is concentrated in Asian equities. In 2014, 70% of its portfolio was held in liquid, tradable listed assets with 72% allocated to assets in Singapore and Asia, making it one of the least diversified SWFs globally. A further 10% was allocated to Australia and New Zealand, underscoring its geographic Asia-Pacific bias. The heavy regional orientation of Temasek's portfolio is a legacy of its original mission to assist in the State-led development of Singapore and its immediate regional neighbourhood (Cummine, 2015).

Temasek remained a domestically focused holding company until the late 1970s, when it adopted a more outward-looking approach. Since 2002, Temasek has been recast to move away from its historical domestic investment agenda aimed at diversifying and developing Singapore's economy to a new role as a commercial investment company to create and deliver long-term returns. The revised 2009 charter further emphasized Temasek's role as a commercial rather than strategic investor that must

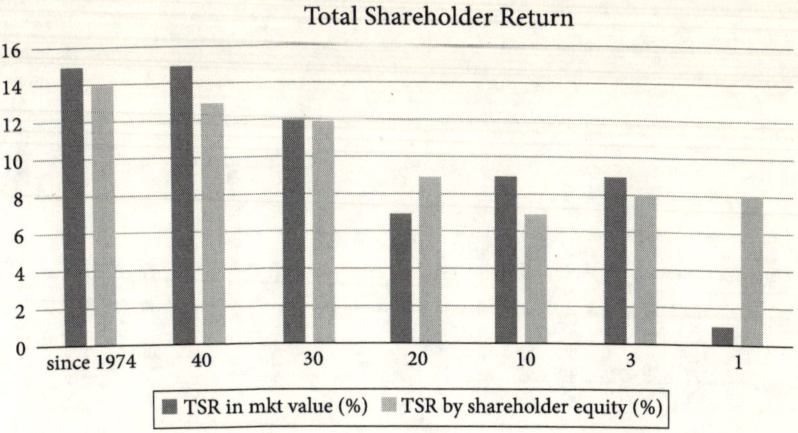

Figure 9.1 TSR of Temasek
Source: Temasek.com.sg.

prioritize long-term wealth creation over the pursuit of the government's national economic objectives.

The realization of this mission—at arms length from the government—has been made possible through Temasek's independent financing arrangements through five primary sources of funding—company dividends, divestment proceeds, distribution of fund investment earnings, and since 2005, long- and short-term debt issuance. A more fundamental implication of this funding strategy is the ability to help develop domestic capital markets (Cummine, 2015).

Singapore's SWF GIC and state investor Temasek Holdings have achieved an annualized real return of 3.7% for the 20 years that ended on March 31, 2017. Meanwhile, Temasek's investments delivered annual total shareholder return[3] of 7% over the same period (see Figure 9.1). Its net portfolio value was S$313 billion in 2018–19, compared to S$164 billion in 2006–07 (see Figure 9.2 below).

Temasek and GIC's investments have benefitted Singaporeans through the Net Investment Return Contribution (NIRC) to the annual Budget.

3 TSR by market value takes into account changes in the market value of the portfolio, dividends paid, and minus any new capital received. TSR by market value takes into account changes in the market value of the portfolio, dividends paid, and minus any new capital received.

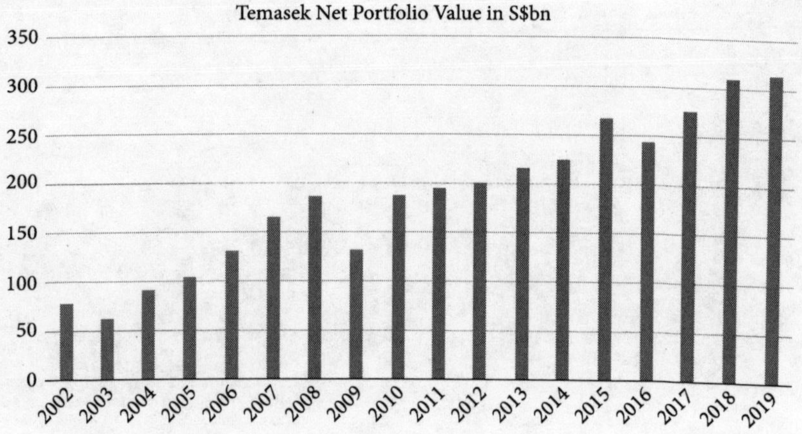

Figure 9.2 Temasek's net portfolio value in S$bn
Source: Temasek.com.sg.

The NIRC framework allows the government to spend up to 50% of the long-term expected returns from the reserves. The NIRC has become an increasingly important source of fiscal receipts. It accounted for about 18% of overall revenues in 2017–18, making it the single largest source of government revenues.

A study (by Balding, 2014) has questioned the veracity of Temasek's reported performance. The study claims that there appears to be a rather significant discrepancy between the returns claimed by Temasek and the returns produced by domestic equity markets. Singapore has produced an average annualized stock market return strikingly similar to other countries. The returns Temasek claims to have generated since its 1974 creation cannot be replicated relative to returns from Singaporean or international equity markets. While investment funds may outperform equity markets for periods of time, it seems unlikely given the known returns of Singaporean and global equity markets that Temasek produced the returns it has claimed.

However, Temasek's returns do not merely follow the overall performance of local and foreign stock market indices. It is necessary to look at the returns from the best 10% of the stocks in a market and the worst 10% to understand the performance of Temasek.

Long-term investors make changes in their asset allocation strategy over time to take advantage of investment opportunities based on their superiority at stock and company selection. In addition, unlike stock market indices which comprise listed equities, Temasek's portfolio includes unlisted investments whose real value is often more difficult to gauge in the absence of a market price.

The same study has suggested that if the government had invested its surpluses with Temasek, it would be currently holding between S$1.6 and 2.0 trillion. Since 1990, the Singaporean government has run a total accumulated surplus of S$271 billion (till 2012) averaging 8.64% of GDP. Government surpluses have been invested by GIC, with its distinct objectives and role of investing at the conservative end of the risk spectrum as part of the government's larger strategy for global investment diversification.

But a deeper look at their objectives and distinct investment missions, begs the following questions: (a) has the historical division of labour between GIC and Temasek now become artificial and unnecessary? (b) should the separate large, attendant administrative, and board overhead costs for Temasek and GIC be retained? and (c) might greater economies of scale and better overall returns not be achieved by merging the two?

A further critique of Singapore's State capitalist model has included the increase in its overall indebtedness. Singapore is the only country in the world to have sustained a fiscal surplus over a long period of time and yet, paradoxically, its sovereign indebtedness has increased to nearly 100% of GDP even though the country's portfolio of assets far exceeds this amount. So, in net terms it is not indebted at all when seen in conventional, comparative terms against the indebtedness of other countries. The increase in indebtedness provides an additional source of cash flow. But there is much debate over how this cash flow has been used. Approximately 80% of publicly held debt in Singapore is attributable to GLCs, while only 18% is attributable to the government.

GLC debt, the Temasek portfolio, and Singaporean nominal local currency GDP have grown at annualized rates of 9.5%, 8.9%, and 7.6%, respectively. In other words, GLC debt has grown faster than Temasek portfolio and nominal GDP (Balding, 2014). However, its large debt position has helped develop domestic capital markets. By undertaking its own debt raising activities, Temasek has expanded its access to short- and long-term debt and helped cultivate the local debt market. Access to short-term and long-term debt has allowed Temasek to use its debt instruments more creatively. Through debt Temasek has been able to systemically reduce its holding in an investee company at a premium over the current market price while enjoying nominally interest-free financing for a period of three years (Schena and Chaturvedi, 2011).

The limits of State-directed competitive advantages and the associated resource allocation have been highlighted by Singapore's experience with its SMEs and its regionalization strategy. Singapore's industrial ecosystem in export manufacturing has consisted primarily of MNCs with local enterprises being involved in supply chains providing essential supporting infrastructure. The government has set up various committees over the years to promote the growth of SMEs in Singapore, with limited success. One reason that has been highlighted is that the actual and effective assistance provided to SMEs is marginal as compared to the support extended to MNCs and GLCs because of the latter's perceived ability to expand GDP on a larger scale.

This reflects Singapore's inability to go beyond mobilizing resources and directing them to the narrow objective of economic growth. For future growth phases, when more complex and multi-faceted development is needed through globally competitive innovation and leadership in new technologies, the Singapore State's competence in mobilizing all the necessary human, financial, and knowledge-based resources has not appeared sufficient to the task (Tan and Bhaskaran, 2015).

Singapore's regionalization strategy focused around ASEAN has comprised mainly State-led and State-financed infrastructure projects, along with a range of incentives and regulatory innovations, designed to assist private companies and individuals move overseas. The government took a three-fold approach in its overseas park developments. It began with senior politicians negotiating with the host governments to establish a favourable institutional framework through concessions and endorsement for facilitating the parks. The second step involved GLCs investing heavily in the infrastructure and real-estate development of overseas parks. The final step was to promote the advantages of the parks to Singapore-based companies and MNCs looking to invest in the region. The Economic Development Board (EDB) encouraged MNCs to locate their regional support centres and headquarters in Singapore while setting up low value and resource intensive activities in the industrial parks (Yeoh, Neo, and Lee, 2003).

The parks have been sites of investment privilege, because of the quality of infrastructure. However, the privileges obtained have been vulnerable to changes in political allegiances, and infrastructure efficiency has been at risk from the uncontrollable broader environment in which the parks are located. There is no doubt about Singapore's expertise in industrial township development, and its reputation for transparency and efficiency. Although Singapore's search for alternative strategies and programmes to re-position the regionalization efforts has continued, this reengineering of economic space beyond Singapore did not fully account for the economic, or socio-political, realities in the host environments (Yeoh, How, and Sim, 2006). There is now quite rightly a greater emphasis on globalization and not just on regionalization. The challenge here is that many countries perceive SOEs as agents of foreign governments.

Performance of GLCs

By most accounts, the strategy of State capitalism followed in Singapore has been immensely successful. GLCs have evolved into important national institutions. The major GLCs have become well-recognized corporate names regionally and globally. GLCs bear a close resemblance to the best private enterprises, except they are even better. The government clearly subscribes to what has been termed the managerial view in the ongoing debate on public vs private ownership, which argues that competition rather than ownership per se is the key to efficiency (Tan and Ramirez, 2004).

GLCs are run on a commercial basis, with a focus on bottom line performance. They have not been used for social, distributional, or employment generation purposes. They compete with private firms and MNCs and, in some cases, with each other. Although their board members are civil servants, government control over GLCs is through loose oversight rather than micromanagement and political interference. The government makes no attempt to appoint managers or other personnel to manage the companies and normally does not interfere in the management of GLCs. The boards of GLCs are policy boards rather than functional (managerial) ones (Chen, 2017).

In the case of Temasek, it turned humble millions from Singapore's treasury into assets worth over S$313 billion 55 years later. In the five years leading up to the financial crisis, Temasek earned an average annual return of 10%, thus giving the Ministry of Finance nearly one billion dollars in dividend income every year. Likewise, GIC which manages well over US$100 billion in assets has produced a real annual return of 4.5% since 2000 through investing in a mix of public equities, fixed income, and alternative investment. Thus, both entities succeeded beyond expectations in their mission to 'preserve and enhance the purchasing power' of Singapore (Shih, 2009).

Research studies show that capital markets value GLCs more than non-GLCs. Studies have concluded that on average GLCs provided superior returns on both assets and equity. They have also found that GLCs in general managed their expenses better than non-GLCs. The lower expense-to-sales ratio among GLCs indicated that GLCs were more profitable because they ran leaner operations. These findings demonstrate that GLCs in Singapore have been different from the generally inefficient SOEs run by most other governments (Tan, Puchniak, and Varottil, 2015).

In addition, more recent studies have suggested that GLCs have implemented better corporate governance practices than non-GLCs. In view of its investment orientation and approach to its portfolio firms, Temasek is akin to an engaged, active-investor, pension fund—promoting good corporate governance and actively voting its shares, but not becoming directly involved in management.

There are no detailed objectives and Key Performance Indicators (KPIs) that are set for each GLC but there is a risk-adjusted rate of return which serves as a benchmark. Temasek monitors the companies and for their main investments it meets the board every three years. The emphasis is on the role of the boards in portfolio companies and the efficacy of their nomination committees. As a result, boards have tended to become more formally independent, and management more professional in line with the evolution of corporate governance standards in Singapore. Temasek has had the flexibility to take concentrated risks whether in owning up to 100% of a company or in deploying their investments into a particular country or sector (OECD, 2014a).

On accountability, the Singapore Companies Act confers on unlisted GLCs the room for opaque accounting. The Act provides for the 'exempt private company' (EPC), a type of company that need not file its balance sheet and profit and loss statements. It may lend money to its own directors and companies, even those in which its own directors have an interest. As an exempt private company, Temasek is exempted from financial information public disclosure. However, since 2004, Temasek has chosen to publish its Group Financial Summary and portfolio performance in its annual report, the Temasek Review. Overall, Temasek has improved its transparency by disclosing its governance structure, operations, and returns. In 2013, it achieved a rating of 10/10 in the Linaburg-Maduell Transparency Index, ranking Temasek among the most transparent of all SWFs (Sim, Thomson, and Yeong, 2014).

However, regionalization and globalization which made sense in the context of a small economy have not easily been achieved by GLCs as they have not always been welcome by recipient countries. State-owned or -controlled companies have always been open to charges that they operated as agents of foreign governments. It has been unclear to recipient countries whether Temasek was an investor or a GLC.

They have therefore faced problems with investments in India, Thailand, Indonesia, and Australia. Temasek was the controversial purchaser of the Thai conglomerate Shin Corp in 2006 (not the corresponding GLC, Singtel) that caused political problems with Thailand. This raised ethical questions since Temasek used nominee companies to evade Thailand's local equity rule. The corresponding GLC, Singtel, has also invested in many countries (for example, Optus in Australia) and has been in the process of integrating them into the company. These developments have led to changes at Temasek, including improved disclosure and transparency (Goldstein and Panamond, 2008). The banking group DBS (Development Bank of Singapore) has also been integrating several foreign purchases and has also now broadened the board to include foreigners (OECD, 2014a).

Common to all business, there have been failures at both GIC and Temasek. For example, Singapore Airlines (SIA) attempted to circumvent Australian foreign ownership limits in airlines by investing in Air New Zealand, which at that time controlled an Australian airline. The latter went into bankruptcy forcing SIA to write off the investment (OECD, 2014a).

Singapore has successfully followed the distinct strategy of using GLCs to grow the economy while using the government's share of the profits from these companies to pursue public policy objectives. Temasek has run its portfolio GLCs with a completely commercial, profit-maximizing orientation. The GLCs will not be completely privatized because of the PAP's strategy of using State ownership to reap political private benefits of control in the form of regime legitimacy and stability—an approach that has been highly successful. The long-term financial performance of Temasek's portfolio has been very favourable, and private investors in GLCs have shared *pro rata* with the State, in this success.

Ownership vs other state responsibilities

In 1960, a year after Singapore attained full internal self-governance, it had a GDP per capita of US$428 that was close to the developing world average and faced significant challenges. As a newly independent country in 1965 with no natural resources, Singapore faced much uncertainty. From its days as a small and underdeveloped nation, Singapore has emerged from various challenges over the years to transform into one of the most affluent countries in the world today (ranked ninth wealthiest nation in the world in per capita terms) (Tan, Puchniak, and Varottil, 2015).

With virtually no natural resources, good, effective governance has been the key to Singapore's success. The government has played a pivotal role not only in setting the strategic direction for the economy but also in driving much of its structural transformation. It used economic growth to raise the living standards of Singaporeans through education, healthcare, and a radical public housing policy. To a large extent, the story of Singapore's economic development success is the story of the government's successful interventions in the economy (Tan and Bhaskaran, 2015).

The founder of independent Singapore, Lee Kwan Yew, understood that to put Singapore on a sustainable growth trajectory required more than just sound economic policy. Lee built a country whose institutional set-up has been unparalleled, including the rule of law, efficient government structures, the continuous fight against corruption, and overall stability. Free education helped encourage social mobility, supporting the doctrine of self-reliance and meritocracy which were the cornerstone philosophy of Lee Kwan Yew (Huang and Yeung, 2018).

Lee Kwan Yew built a Singaporean model of economic development which depended externally on services as much as manufactured exports with extensive government intervention and planning. However, his approach was to intervene in the economy forcefully when needed but to leave the rest to the market so long as the balance led to high economic growth and accumulation of surpluses. The government's pragmatism has helped it to continually calibrate the balance between state intervention and preservation of market discipline for the last 55 years. The need to be pragmatic and the ability to experiment with new policies also helped in fostering an unusual degree of innovativeness and risk-taking in the policy-making process.

The government sought to achieve, early in the days of independence, a 'social contract' between the government and the governed in which some civil rights were traded off against the State's powers and the political control that it felt were needed to pursue high economic growth. High GDP growth then enabled the government to deliver various public services and public goods and legitimize its rule. The government has counted on a strong civil service and a system of statutory boards, together with other state institutions, to implement its policies. In general, these institutions, based on meritocratic management and low corruption, have been effective in delivering the desired outcomes (Lim, 2015).

The government attracted talent from all over the world. Lacking other natural resources, human resources have been the city State's most precious asset, and they have been carefully nurtured and developed. Singapore's education system created multiple pathways for students to produce the skilled labour force needed to achieve the ever more ambitious economic goals. Other than human capital, the need to develop hard infrastructure was not overlooked. To jump start the country's development, the government offered tax incentives and drew in foreign investments to build industrial and business parks, world-class ports, and airport (OECD, 2010c).

The government has always introduced various new initiatives to maintain a competitive and business friendly environment in Singapore. The government has adopted a pro-business policy, the key aspect of which is a functional set of corporate and financial laws. Singapore has built up its corporate governance standards to promote investor confidence in companies listed on the Singapore Exchange and put Singapore on the global map as a trusted international financial hub. It has a robust intellectual property regime to ensure that city remains a preferred location for innovation in every industry. It has been committed to introducing and updating its laws regularly, so that the legal regime can keep up with the ever-evolving business environment. Singapore's public enforcement sends a strong signal of their commitment to hold the city's reputation as a trusted trade, financial, and logistics hub.

Lee Kwan Yew's greatest achievement was to promote the concept of good governance in southeast Asia, a region long plagued by corrupt, inefficient governments. His perfectionism, far-sightedness, elitism, authoritarianism, and intolerance for corruption, along with his obsession for security, cleanliness and order, are reflected in nearly every aspect of modern Singaporean life (Straits Times, 2015).

The success of Singapore challenges the claim that private enterprise rather than the State is necessarily more efficient at allocating capital to its most productive use. The Singaporean State has been equally effective in dedicating itself to its core activities of public security, providing justice, law, and order, defence of the country from foreign aggression, and running a stable, sustainable, and efficient macroeconomy. Singapore is all about the strong correlation and balance between political and economical realities. The unusual effectiveness of the Singapore government has won worldwide acclaim over the years and has rarely been matched elsewhere.

The Singaporean economic model, which began as a mixture of socialist nationalism and paternalistic authoritarianism, moved towards shareholder capitalism in the 1990s. Prosperous and technologically advanced, the city-State has appeared to have shielded itself against the decline that seem to characterize other developed economies. Its political and economic conditions in the early days are reminiscent of those in many emerging countries today, and its development story is relevant to many of those emerging countries. But can key aspects of the Singapore model be copied or replicated to any meaningful extent in other countries?

The answer to this question can be discerned from Singapore's experience in creating regional business parks. The objective behind these large infrastructure projects was the government's intent to draw on its state enterprise network and extend this network to facilitate business ventures in the region. Singapore's positive reputation for infrastructure efficiency and corrupt-free administration was transplanted to locations where these attributes were less prevalent (Shaw and Yeoh, 2000).

The progress of Singapore's overseas parks over a comparatively short period of time indicates the ability of GLCs network to mobilize economic and political resources to create economic space for the city-State. The projects have obtained government endorsements which further underlined the significance of the projects. Nonetheless, the complexities of the individual environments, as well as the rude intrusion of the economics of competition, have hindered the progress and hobbled the commercial effectiveness of the parks (Yeoh, How, and Leong, 2005).

Conclusions

The State has played a pivotal role not only in mapping out the strategic direction for the Singaporean economy but also in driving much of its structural transformation. The State's ubiquitous, pervasive presence in the economy has remained significant over time, even as the economy has matured.

Singapore has been very clear about what was expected of GLCs, and these have evolved over time in line with ever more sophisticated demands for economic growth. The State has also been clear, however, that wider issues, such as social equity, were not the primary goal of GLCs.

Over the years the primacy of economic growth has taken precedence over other development objectives. Specifically, efficiency has been prized over equity. Social equity was emphasized in the early years of independence, discussions of 'equity', and 'income distribution' have since been shunned as being detrimental to the pursuit of efficiency and growth.

By most accounts, the strategy of State capitalism followed in Singapore has been extremely successful. GLCs bear quite a close resemblance to the best run private enterprises in the world though most GLCs are better. GLCs are run on a commercial basis, with a focus on bottom line performance. The long-term financial performance of GLCs has been very favourable, and private investors in GLCs have shared *pro rata* with the State in this success.

In the domestic market, rents allocated to State agencies and GLCs have been held to the high-performance standards necessary to attract foreign private investment in other sectors of the economy. Rents earned in monopoly GLCs have been distributed legally and transparently to senior management, civil servants, and political leaders through generous remuneration packages.

However, GLCs are targeted because of government backing and favour that gives them unfair competitive advantages in the local market and because they have 'crowded out private investment in new markets, products and technologies and usurped entrepreneurial activity'.

10

Country case study 8: South Africa

The historical context of State involvement in the South African economy

South Africa has an unusual, if not unique, political history that has shaped public policy and influenced the nature of the State's ownership and deployment of commercial enterprises—differently in each phase. South Africa has relied on the State to own and direct major commercial enterprises—over successive political eras and governments. SOE strategy was shaped by early colonial history, characterized by a prolonged internal conflict through the 19th century between the English and Afrikaaners to resolve which side would govern the State.

This was followed by the *apartheid* era of racial segregation and separate development from 1920 to 1994. During that period, major SOEs were created to play a significant role in the economy. Full elections were held in 1994, won by the African National Congress (ANC) with Nelson Mandela becoming President.

Each of these phases reflect different motivations, orientations, directions, and priorities of the State in creating and running SOEs. From the end of the Boer War to the end of the first world war, the South African State, run mainly by Afrikaaners, aimed to be as autarchic as possible. The Boers remained anxious to retain their cultural heritage and be independent of their remote British colonial parent, especially for essential national infrastructure. This impulse also triggered early attempts at rapid indigenous industrialization and infrastructure creation, to support commercial farming, and burgeoning gold and diamond mining. These activities, along with financial and other services, remain mainstays of the South African economy today.

After the first world war, *apartheid* was pursued aggressively by the South African State. It was met with growing domestic resistance with opprobrium heaped on it from rest of the post-independence, developing world. *Apartheid* made the South African government realize the need for a different kind of import-substituting self-reliance. It was made necessary by the political choices the State pursued, achieved mainly via the SOEs.

With the inevitable collapse of *apartheid* regime, and the onset of plural democracy, South Africa's economically significant SOEs became instruments for achieving social and political change through expanded black employment and empowerment objectives. Financial and commercial viability of SOEs, that were stressed heavily during the *apartheid* regime, receded in importance. Massive corruption (especially during the Zuma presidency) in government spilled over into the operations of SOEs, gaining a firm foothold. This has compromised the viability of SOEs since the mid-2000s and has damaged them, perhaps irreparably.

Understanding that historical context is essential in divining where South Africa's SOEs now stand. There are over 300 public sector organizations consisting of 9 constitutional institutions, 21 major public entities, 153 national public entities, 26 national government business enterprises, 72 provincial public entities, and 18 provincial government business enterprises. Constitutional institutions are Schedule 1 organizations, major public entities are Schedule 2 organizations, and the remainder are Schedule 3 organizations (Fourie, 2014).

Together the aggregate assets of all SOEs was valued over R1 trillion, or about 27% of GDP in 2016 (Kikeri, 2018). There are eight major public companies which provide infrastructure services and undertake development programmes. These have been separated from their associated policy-making ministries. They come under the Department of Public Enterprises (DPE) as the apex SOE shareholding ministry with the Minister of Public Enterprises representing the interests of government as shareholder, while the relevant line ministry focuses on dealing with policy-related issues.

One (Telkom)—listed on the Johannesburg Stock Exchange (JSE)—is overseen by the Department of Communications. There are several SOEs, commercial and non-commercial, active in a broad range of activities, at the sub-national level. The economic importance of SOEs is concentrated in the top 30 companies of which just four account for 91% of the assets, 86% of gross turnover, and 77% of SOE employment (Government of

South Africa, 2011). The total revenues of SOEs amount to 8.7% of GDP and are among the main sources of urban employment.

Sector-wise, transport (28.8%), energy (27.3%), communications (16.2%), financial services (8.03%), and water (3.61%) account for most of the revenue generated by SOEs (OECD, 2015e). DPE oversees some Schedule 2 SOEs, such as Transnet Ltd, SAA, Eskom, Pebble Bed Modular Reactor, Denel, Alexkor Ltd, and South African Forestry Company Ltd. Other SOEs fall under their lead ministries. For example, the Airports Company South Africa (ACSA) falls under the Ministry of Transport, the Central Energy Fund falls under the Department of Energy, and the Armaments Corporation of South Africa falls under the Ministry of Defence.

SOEs in South Africa have played a vital role in terms of the direct services they provide. The population's access to water, electricity, sanitation, and transportation is almost entirely dependent on the State (OECD, 2015f). SOEs in South Africa have also played a key role in certain vital industries that serve as inputs to other industries (DPE, 2002). The electricity, transport, and fixed-line telecommunications sectors are dominated by SOEs (Steyn, 2012). These sectors account for a significant proportion of input costs for potential high-growth industries, like mining, manufacturing, tourism, information and communication technology, and export industries (Goldstuck, 2012).

The discovery of diamonds (1867) and gold (1886) accelerated the introduction of electricity on a commercial scale, with gold mining as the major driver of electricity consumption (Development Bank of Southern Africa [DBSA], 2012). Since 1994, the government has been implementing plans to overcome South Africa's persistent infrastructure deficiencies, including addressing the pressing need to upgrade the country's power generation capacity.

SOEs have become indispensable in fulfilling the State's developmental mission in South Africa. This is, to some extent, an outcome of disappointment with privatization experience in some sectors, especially over concerns about employment equity, preferential procurement, and unemployment. The State was consequently forced to depend on SOEs after the turn of the 21st century and, in doing so, to abandon the privatization of state assets that occurred in the late 1990s at the urging of multilateral institutions. But reliance on State capitalism is also the result of a development strategy that aspires to diversify the economy, using SOEs to support private sector development by providing essential services and infrastructure. Since the global financial crisis of 2008–10, the government's strategy to bring the economy out of recession has been to continue with the historical pattern of investing heavily in infrastructure.

The significance of SOEs to the RSA economy can be discerned from the 2016 *Budget Review* which showed that R867 billion was budgeted to be spent by all branches of government—between fiscal years 2016/17 and 2018/19—on infrastructure. The share of this accounted for by SOEs was R422 billion or 49% and the rest of the balance being accounted for by national, provincial, and local government departments.

The evolution of State capitalism and South African SOEs since 1920

The government's role in shaping the South African economy has been particularly evident since the 1920s when the foundations of *apartheid* and many of the present SOEs were established. These enterprises were initially given a mandate to strengthen import-substitution industries and operated as exclusive franchises. Some of the larger companies included the Electricity Supply Commission, which later changed its name to Eskom. Its task was to develop, produce, and maintain electrical power distribution.

Then the Iron and Steel Corporation (later Iscor) was established for domestic production of a core input. It was followed by the Industrial Development Corporation (later IDC) to assist in the establishment of new industries, such as the Phosphate Development Corporation to mine and process phosphate minerals to advance agricultural and peripheral practices. The South African Coal, Oil and Gas Corporation was set up by IDC to produce synthetic fuels and derivatives from coal, and the Southern Oil Exploration Corporation to locate and exploit crude oil resources to combat the oil and petroleum embargoes imposed on South Africa (Fourie, 2014).

Other examples are as follows: the South African Broadcasting Corporation (SABC), a news broadcast service in Afrikaans, English, and other indigenous languages; the Armaments Development and

Production Corporation and later Armaments Corporation of South Africa (Armscor), responsible for all research and development pertaining to munitions and the production of military equipment; and South African Airways (SAA) (Rangata, 2003). Many State corporations also established subsidiary companies in partnership with private firms, and several held controlling shares of stock in private firms (Jerome and Rangata 2003). Although the initial goal for the establishment of SOEs was import substitution, by the 1980s, the then National Party-led government—which was increasingly isolated in the world—opted to focus on economic development through export-oriented policies. Armscor was one of the more successful companies, so armaments and military equipment formed the mainstay of exports. During this period, South African SOEs contributed the highest proportion to the GDP of any country outside the former Marxist Socialist Bloc.

By the late 1980s, the South African government, through its SOEs, owned and managed about 40% of all economic output, including iron and steel, weapons manufacturing, and energy. SOEs were also vital to the services sector. The government's main concern, since the discovery of gold in 1886, has been to balance the growth of the mining industry against the need to diversify the South African economy in a way that sustained development and enhanced self-sufficiency. Overall, the SOE strategy was characterized by fiscal support for business enterprises through limited taxation, infrastructure support, and guaranteed input costs. The bulk of the country's most profitable products have always been exported, whether wool, diamonds, or gold, making the government in turn reliant on those industries and thus willing to continue beneficial support to ensure their continued profitability (Clark, 2014).

Successive governments have tried to encourage and to support local industries that could reduce imports, provide jobs, and create a multiplier effect by encouraging further industrial growth. Premier Paul Kruger, who had led the Transvaal in the late 19th century, had granted monopoly concessions to industrialists; the 1920s governments of Jan C. Smuts and J.B.M. Hertzog had initiated SOEs, and the post-1948 National Party government had tried industrial decentralization. Yet, even after decades of policies designed to spur diversification, South Africa's exports in the 1980s were still primarily gold and diamonds (Byrnes, 1996).

The government continued to protect its import-substitution industries. Its core economic strategy advocated a shift to more market-oriented policies, but left room for government intervention in response to rapidly changing social and political demands. The strategy emphasized local industrialization in order to cut imports, create jobs, and strengthen export industries, especially to increase value added through local processing of raw materials for export (Jerome and Rangata 2003).

Attempts at privatization and their subsequent reversal

By the late 1980s, however, the government decided that a number of SOEs needed to be privatized because they were (a) financially unsustainable; (b) funded from limited state resources which could not be stretched further; (c) not financially attractive to acquire immediate capital for additional projects; or (d) so inefficient that they elicited criticism of the government in wasting public resources (Klopper 2010).

Private individuals were then allowed to purchase shares in many SOEs. When privatization was first attempted, anticipated private sector participation in SOEs did not materialize. For example, Iscor suffered the embarrassment of an unsuccessful public offering in 1929. At the time, most SOEs were viewed as inherently unprofitable, requiring to be funded by the government because of a lack of private interest, or private incapacity to run such large, complex businesses. Fifty years later, in 1979, however, after oil sales from Iran had been cut off, the synthetic fuel corporation, SASOL, offered shares to the public. Investors eagerly bought all the shares that were available and fully supported two more such offerings (Byrnes, 1996).

In 1988, President P. W. Botha announced plans to privatize several SOEs, including Eskom, Foskor, and Iscor, as well as State-operated transport, postal, and telecommunications services (Transnet). This was done in response to public criticism of the government's role in these enterprises as they were no longer profitable and a drain on the exchequer. SOEs had been the recipients of large foreign loans that were called in and cut-off in 1985, as UN-approved sanctions against *apartheid* took hold, leaving them with serious capital shortages (Byrnes, 1996).

Sale of the SOEs' assets could both ease the debt burden and provide the government with new revenue for urgent social programmes. Iscor was the first major SOE to be sold, in November 1989. Its sale raised R3 billion for the Treasury. The government then scaled down its plans. In the early 1990s the future of privatization was unclear. Officials estimated that the R250 billion needed to finance purchase of the largest SOEs probably could not be found within the country. The argument for privatization was weakened by the worsening investment climate as political negotiations for plural democracy stalled and violence increased. Government opponents, especially the ANC, vigorously opposed privatization—viewing it as a ploy to maintain white control before majority rule materialized (Phaahlamohlaka, 2006).

In 1994 the newly formed Government of National Unity continued the economic policies of its predecessors. Although SOEs were viewed as part of the apartheid legacy, their critical importance could not be denied or overlooked. The shift towards greater market orientation of the SOEs was re-emphasized by the ANC government under Mandela, though it allowed for government intervention when necessary. Import-substituting industries continued to be supported while trying again to spur industrial development towards greater export orientation.

In 1995 the government came up with a new privatization programme, seeking equity partners in major SOEs, like Telkom and South African Airways, while trying to sell several smaller SOEs outright. This provoked strong protests from labour unions over the threat of job losses and the exclusion of labour unions representing workers from the policy decision-making process. The resulting compromises in privatization and restructuring policies and their associated processes resulted in a range of suboptimal developmental impacts (Byrnes, 1996).

In the early 2000s, the government's agenda shifted from privatization to improving SOE profitability through corporate restructuring aimed at achieving greater efficiency. The government formally decided to retain ownership of key SOEs and gave them strategic economic mandates to guide their strategies and business plans. SOEs were instructed to undertake aggressive investment programmes. These were later expanded to support the needs of the growing economy, rather than focus on what their balance sheets could accommodate. It also reoriented SOEs more towards achieving social and other wider development goals.

Subsequently the government devised yet another programme to restructure SOEs through its '*Policy Framework: An Accelerated Agenda towards the Restructuring of SOEs*'. In parallel, it went through with an initial public offering of Telkom on the JSE. The 2003 listing of Telkom was reportedly not a popular move. Trade unions opposed it because of the job losses incurred following listing (APRM, 2007). Bowing to public pressure, the government again refocused its efforts on reinforcing the sustainability of SOEs and delivering on specific strategic mandates.

In 2010, a Presidential State-owned Entities Review Committee was appointed to review the role of SOEs and how they might support the 'developmental state' aspirations of government (Chabane, 2010). The recommendations emerging from the Committee were made public in 2013. The Review concluded that the State should (1) clearly define and communicate a consistent strategy for SOEs; (2) ensure that effective contact between regulators, government, and SOEs is maintained; (3) redefine the purpose of SOEs; (4) monitor and evaluate all SOEs regularly based on criteria modelled on global best practices; and (5) enable high operational performance of SOEs so that they can meet economic and developmental objectives in a cost-effective and financially viable manner.

Despite their turbulent and confused history, and the many attempts made since 1994 to transform them, SOEs will remain important in South Africa because of its unique set of cultural circumstances, shaped by *apartheid*. That underscores government's felt need for SOEs to remain involved in promoting pro-poor expansion of positive externalities, more employment, rapid social transformation, a more sustainable approach to developing and supporting the growth of domestic and international supply chains of indigenous small- and medium-scale businesses, and a broad-based economic growth.

The ANC, which is ideologically committed to radical economic transformation, believes that this can be achieved in part by using government procurement to favour black businesses. However, the politicization of public procurement as a means to achieve economic transformation has resulted in the subversion of service delivery mandates. It has opened SOEs to massive corruption, competition, and rivalry.

Regulation vs public ownership of SOEs

In South Africa, dominant public and private conglomerates have shaped the evolution of its industries. Although their power has been diluted somewhat over the years, the economy has not diversified away from energy and resource-intensive industries dominated by these conglomerates.

For over a century, the South African economy has been characterized by limited competition, extensive government intervention, and explicit exclusion of the majority of the population from participation except, of course, as consumers. The *apartheid* regime pursued policies that resulted in a sharply dual economy, with a prosperous, developed part for 20% of the population co-existing with a grossly underdeveloped part for the other 80%. These trends have persisted into the post-1994 era.

Extensive, prolonged government intervention has prevailed in telecommunications, mining, agriculture, and energy. Strong linkages developed between these sectors and other related industries (for example, finance) under *apartheid*. In South Africa, not only the political connections of the incumbents in these sectors but also their strategic behaviour, (through vertical integration and leveraging market power into related markets) have allowed entrenched dominant positions to be maintained and strengthened (Makhaya and Roberts, 2014). This has led to the emergence of dominant corporate conglomerates across key sectors.

Established incumbency has allowed them to extract rents and shape the regulatory regime in their self-interest. In 1994, the ANC faced an enormous challenge in transforming public administration and the management/orientation of SOEs inherited from the apartheid era, into vehicles for service delivery and development. The South African economy has been opened to the global market in the last two decades, but the benefits from liberalization have been muted and poorly distributed. The structure of the economy has not changed significantly (Makhaya and Roberts, 2014). Consequently, there is now widespread dissatisfaction across society, and within the ANC itself, with the performance of SOEs.

OECD's product market regulation indicator on South Africa highlights that businesses are faced with a high overall administrative burden. Burdensome regulation is the result of high government involvement in the economy, high tariff, and non-tariff barriers as well as barriers-to-entry in many sectors. The government's inclination to protect existing businesses from competition (particularly in the network industries) has only exacerbated the situation. The degree of regulatory protection for incumbents is particularly high in the utilities (for example, gas and electricity, transport, and telecommunications) which are mainly State owned. The concentrated structure of the South African economy makes it difficult for small firms to enter some markets and compete, although the country uses preferential access to public procurement to empower and encourage disadvantaged groups, which include black-owned small businesses.

Many infrastructure SOEs are in a dominant if not complete monopoly position in the value chain that they operate in. Regulators have often been ineffectual in protecting other players from monopoly abuse by the SOE incumbent. Examples include Independent Communications Authority of South Africa (ICASA's) failure to introduce effective competition against Telkom, and the difficulties faced by private sector generators (including co-generators and independent power producers (IPPs)). Telecommunications regulation in practice has not paid sufficient attention to competition because of the presence of the State-owned Telkom and its repeated abuse of its dominance in excluding competitors (Das Nair and Roberts, 2015). This has resulted in poor outcomes in terms of rollout, speed, and price of broadband internet access.

The actions of the State as owner of Telkom have contradicted its objectives as a reformer and economic policy-maker. Government's shareholding in Telkom is held by the Department of Communications (DoC) which is also responsible for policy framework for the sector. This has compounded conflicts of interest (and of objectives) and has reduced the incentive to encourage ICASA to develop into a strong, effective, impartial regulator.

Telkom's long battle to keep competitors from offering voice services has been facilitated by the DoC's delays in clarifying the extent to which value-added services providers could also provide voice services (Banda et al., 2015). Similarly, the idea of encouraging new IPPs to invest in power generation has been compromised by covert political pressure, Eskom's market power, and the influence of large electricity users (Das Nair and Roberts, 2015).

The Centre for Competition, Regulation and Economic Development (CCRED) at the University of Johannesburg finds that anti-competitive behaviour has failed consumers by maintaining unjustifiably high costs for goods and services and has disadvantaged rival entrants. The support for the national airline SAA, its subsidiaries, and associated companies have undermined many of its rivals. Such conduct has included repeated violations of competition laws—from price fixing to predatory and cartel behaviour.

Abuse of dominant cases involving price discrimination, excessive pricing, and exclusionary arrangements, including vertical arrangements, and loyalty rebates, have been referred to the Competition Tribunal[1] since 1999. Most cases have involved SOEs, like Sasol, Telkom, SAA, Safcol, and Foskor. Under the 'abuse of dominance' provisions some SOEs have incurred penalties, while others have made divestitures. While the competition authorities have obliged SOEs to divest or pay penalties, overall, the Competition Law has not proved to be effective in dealing with the market dominance of entrenched SOEs bent on resisting regulatory discipline (Makhaya and Roberts, 2014).

The legislative framework which empowers regulators to provide an independent review of the economics of new projects has failed to provide the important check-and-balance on decisions related to large SOE projects. For many new projects, by the time the SOE approaches the regulator with the licence application, the decision has often been a fait accompli; or regulators are simply not adequately resourced or interested in taking on the large-vested interests behind such projects (Steyn, 2011).

Since the mid-2000s, the overall economic environment in South Africa has been shaped largely by five key drivers that include as follows: (1) the Radical Economic Transformation (RET) policy; (2) infrastructure-led growth; (3) the Broad-Based Black Economic Empowerment (B-BBEE) policy; (4) the economic dominance of key SOEs; and (5) State-investment institutions, like the Public Investment Corporation. Together, they

[1] The Competition Commission makes recommendations on large mergers and refers findings of anti-competitive conduct to the Competition Tribunal for decision-making. The Tribunal members typically have a legal or economics background, and a panel of three members is formed to hear and decide on each matter apart from intermediate mergers, decided by the Commission.

have created conditions conducive to a small group to repurpose state institutions and have resulted in unintended adverse consequences.

A report entitled The State of Capture (2016) by a former government ombudsman has detailed how the planned vision of a 'professional public service and a capable state' has been subverted by a symbiotic relationship that has emerged between a *constitutional state* with clear rules and laws and a *shadow state* comprising well-organized patronage networks that facilitate corruption for the enrichment of a small group (Bhorat et al., 2017).

The shadow state has rendered formal institutions incapable of executing their responsibilities. The same report has highlighted the perversion of corporate governance norms in SOEs with access to rent-seeking opportunities being secured by diluting regulations. Government ministers acting in concert with private interests have used regulatory instruments or policy decisions in an arbitrary manner to extort from incumbent SOEs and favour private business interests. The extent to which state capture has spread can be seen from selective prosecutions following publication of the report.

Given Eskom's near monopoly status, consumers have relied on the National Energy Regulator of South Africa (NERSA) to protect them from exorbitant tariff increases. Even though Eskom is currently permitted to increase energy tariffs by 13% a year, NERSA in the past has granted only part of the price increases sought by Eskom—which at one stage threatened power blackouts if its requests were denied (Kane-Berman, 2016). Yet electricity tariffs in South Africa are among one of the highest in the region (Figure 10.1). SOE incumbents in pursuit of maintaining their status quo have often resisted and deliberately delayed changes asked for by regulators. They have been able to shape the new regulatory frameworks in their favour to protect their rents. This has been done through, *inter alia*, extensive and prolonged litigation in competition proceedings (Makhaya and Roberts, 2014).

If large SOEs have resisted change, politicians have also played their role in reducing the powers of regulatory bodies. Regulators have been expected to resolve policy contradictions. But resolving such problems has been beyond the mandate of regulators. So, they end up fudging the issue. They have been forced to depart from their official regulatory methodology and determine tariff increases on the basis of an ad

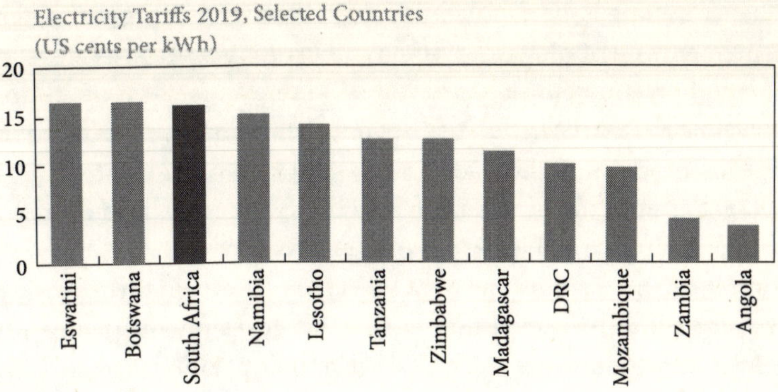

Figure 10.1 Electricity tariffs in selected countries (2019)
Source: IMF, 2020.

hoc subjective judgements that try to achieve a balance between political pressures and economic forces. When politicians feel that regulators have 'impinged on the political terrain' they call for regulatory powers to be reduced. In this way, policy failures have undermined regulators by setting them up for future failures. Often, what appear to be regulatory failures are, in fact, symptoms of underlying policy failures caused, invariably, by political pressure (Steyn, 2011).

The functioning of SOEs has been affected by delays in clarifying policy and regulatory frameworks. Late or incomplete clarification of sector policy has led to rushed and inadequate project planning, design, and project execution by SOEs. These have been exacerbated by ineffective regulatory processes. Together, they have led to cost overruns and economic waste and resultant higher costs to consumers.

Crony capitalism

Through the 20th century, the South African economy was centred around mineral extraction, energy, and finance. Most of the linkages across these economic activities were realized through coordination by the State. If there was a contest among conglomerates in these sectors, particularly between the interests of Afrikaaner and English capital, it was mediated through the State. For example, the State supported the development of

Afrikaner mining houses, notably Gencor, through interventions in coal procurement and mining rights (Fine and Rustomjee, 1996).

Corruption and political patronage were central features of the *apartheid* regime in South Africa. They became increasingly pronounced from the 1970s onwards as the *apartheid* system began to disintegrate. The Afrikaner establishment was unable to discipline its followers and prevent the ensuing 'scramble for personal enrichment'.

Patron–client relationships were also endemic within the African-run homeland authorities such that 'homeland government became a byword for corruption and incompetence' (Hyslop, 2005). The growth of neo-patrimonial politics after 1994 is not just a continuation of the old practices during *apartheid*. The roots of recent corruption and patrimony have been at the core of the history of the ANC itself (Lodge, 1998). What is clear, however, is that it was not until 1994, when the ANC took over the State that patron–client relations began to assume the scale and character that are being witnessed now. Suddenly, gaining access to a vast array of resources, ANC activists utilized positions of party authority to leverage themselves into positions of state authority, whether as parliamentarians, cabinet ministers, mayors, councillors, civil servants, or employees in the rapidly expanding state machinery.

Such processes have been facilitated by the ANC itself. The party has promoted the deployment of its cadres' control over the State, as part of a broader effort to encourage the political and socio-economic transformation of South Africa and to help the growth of a black capitalist class (Gumede, 2005). The role of the SOEs and, in particular, the expenditure on procurement by the SOEs has been the centre of focus in ANC's policy documents to engender RET. Eskom and Transnet have been the two key special centrepieces of this strategic focus on SOEs as the drivers of RET.

Over the last 20 years the value of goods and services that government has purchased, largely from the private sector has grown by R400–R500 billion a year. This figure is testament to the near complete outsourcing of government's core functions. Essentially the government has become a massive tender-generating machine. It constitutes the core of a system for allocating beneficial rents to drive development (Polity, 2017).

In reality, it has provided many opportunities for entrenching clientelism and patronage networks that become dependent on people who make the decisions at the top of the pyramid. Decisions have been made by the ruling party 'acting as both player and referee' in the process of awarding tenders, rather than being a neutral, impersonal actor in the public interest. Individuals and consortia with a history of making donations to the ANC have benefited directly from share deals, using the profits from these shareholdings to finance party activity (Beresford, 2015).

The ANC's funding model has simply been 'business fronts benefiting from state contracts that pass profits back to the ANC treasury' (Holden, 2012). Access to the networks of public authority has become a vital facilitator of private capital accumulation. In 1994 the promise of ANC-led pluralism was to build a state that would serve the much wider public good encompassing all races. But evidence suggests that the state institutions have been repurposed to serve narrower private interests.

The consequent deepening of corrosive culture of corruption within the State and grafting a shadow state onto the existing constitutional state has brought RET to a halt. Just as large sections of the old Afrikaaner capitalist class were dependent on state support under the *apartheid* regime, so too is the emerging black elite on its connections to the new state authorities (Beresford, 2015).

The unique characteristic of the South African public rent-seeking system is its hybrid nature because of a well-structured constitutional order. Even after the relentless repurposing of the State institutions in the last 10 years, President Zuma found himself strangled by the constitutional requirements that he could not dispense with, for example, reporting to Parliament and being subordinate to the Constitutional Court; and the competitive dynamics within the shadow state.

The private agenda of public officials

In numerous organizational reports and strategy documents, the ANC has claimed that it is a movement, rather than a political party, precisely because of its special duty to 'lead society'. This explains the dramatic politicization of the public service in South Africa after 1998, principally through the expansion of the Senior Management Service Programme. It was intended to have a maximum of 3,000 members, but it comprised 10,000 people by 2017. By expanding the size of the programme, the ANC has tried to establish its total control of the State (Bhorat et al., 2017).

Turbulence and dysfunctionality in government administration is often related to competition between the ANC, government, and constitutional bodies competing for the right to appoint officials to key state positions (Bhorat et al., 2017). The use of cadre deployment to capture SOEs has long been part of the policy of the ANC, committed, as it is, to bringing about a RET in South Africa.

The blurring of the distinction between party and State has increasingly characterized the ANC's leadership behaviour, coloured by neo-patrimonial predispositions. While formal distinctions between private and public concerns were widely recognized, officials have, nevertheless, used public powers for private purposes (Lodge, 2005). Since the late 1980s, the ANC has believed that it needed massive funding to win elections and it began to rely on resources generated by party-controlled enterprises or by politically motivated contracting.

As the ANC Youth League displaced the trade unions as the core of its organized base, the party became increasingly amenable to a politics in which authority is manifest in the exercise of personal power and individual generosity (Beresford, 2015). These insights explain corruption as a direct consequence of the ANC's history, of structural constraints on its finances, and of its organizational culture. Since 2011 state institutions have been repurposed at an increasing pace towards a rhetorical commitment to RET.

The deepening of the corrosive culture of corruption within the State has refocused the energies of ANC leaders, senior party officials, and their cronies, on private wealth accumulation. What officials have been unable to achieve via the constitutional state, they have attempted to achieve via the shadow state. Some senior officials and politicians have participated unwittingly in this project because they have been insufficiently aware of how their specific actions would contribute to the wider process of systemic betrayal (Bhorat et al, 2017).

Even when SOEs have not been pressed into undertaking unviable capital projects for political reasons, SOE managers have faced inappropriate incentives. They are biased towards supporting larger, and technologically more complex projects, and far more expensive projects, rather than incremental or mundane additions that might be more economical, efficient, viable, and more appropriate in the public interest (Steyn, 2006).

In certain cases, unviable projects were selected by top managers acting as aspirant pseudo-capitalists with grandiose ambitions, who have interpreted their mandate too widely, while other projects were selected on the basis of the preferences of political leaders. The Petroleum, Oil and Gas Corporation of South Africa (Petro SA), which belongs to the State-owned Central Energy Fund, failed to buy Engen, a fuel refining and retailing company whose majority shareholder is Petronas of Malaysia, due to a lack of resources. But this constraint did not stop Petro SA from putting in a bid in 2016 to buy a refinery, a lubricants plant, and 845 Caltex fuel stations in South Africa from the American oil giant Chevron (Kane-Berman, 2016).

This was a case of SOEs run by aspirant, swashbuckling SOE managers pursuing ambitions in the expectation that any losses can be passed on to the taxpayer and/or the consumer. Eskom's determination to increase its nuclear generating capacity has been partly rooted in personal preferences of political leaders and those of some favoured business associates.

Allocation of resources

Most SOE investment projects are not selected as part of their commercial mandate. They are effectively imposed on them by politicians or senior government officials for political, 'strategic' or social reasons. Such projects are typically not financially viable. A range of non-commercial transactions have been imposed on SOEs by the government for which SOEs have not been compensated, leading to undesired outcomes and unintended consequences.

For non-financial institutions, non-commercial transactions often take the form of underpricing through the extension of favourable pricing contracts, while for financial institutions, the most common forms are directed lending and concessionary loans. In all these instances, there exists some form of cross-subsidization. Lending by one SOE to another is another form of non-commercial transaction. There is an absence of official reporting on non-commercial transactions which makes quantification of the costs from such activities difficult and therefore difficult to measure how resources have been allocated. Rather than approaching the Treasury for funding to make up the viability gap, politicians and senior officials often find it convenient to press SOEs to undertake these projects without providing a solution for the viability problem (Steyn, 2011). The costs of such projects, sometimes referred to as 'unfunded mandates' have resulted in an additional increase in tariffs to existing consumers, who are forced to pay for the subsidy the project requires.

SOEs have typically financed their projects through borrowing, which, at least implicitly, is guaranteed by the government and thus constitutes a fiscal risk for the Treasury. Once SOEs have committed to projects, the next risk they encounter is the possibility of substantial cost overruns. Most large SOE projects end-up costing much more than the budgeted amount on which the decision to proceed with the project was premised. Examples in South Africa include the King Shaka International Airport, and Medupi and Kusile power stations (Steyn, 2011).

When such costs are disallowed to be recovered by tariffs, they are inevitably passed on to the taxpayer, in the form of loss of dividend payments to the fiscus or the need for SOE bailouts. Regulators' ability to deal with this problem has been mixed so far. Political interference and misallocation of resources can be gauged from the following examples: ACSA, a majority State-owned company, owns and operates almost all major commercial airports in South Africa. Airport tariffs, which are subject to regulation, have risen substantially in recent years.

The main reason for the tariff increase has been due to profligate expenditure made by ACSA in its facilities. These were, arguably, not sound business decisions. King Shaka International Airport in Durban was built without an identified need for expanded airport facilities. ACSA had determined there would be no need for a new airport until 2017–20 and that the project would not be economically viable until then (Steyn, 2011). This led to a disagreement over tariff increases between ACSA and the regulator. Delay in resolving it led to a huge tariff increase of 68.6% in order to allow ACSA to 'claw-back' the required annual tariff (Banda et al., 2015).

Transnet operates rail freight, ports, and constructs pipelines. It has used ports as a cash cow by levying high port tariffs in order to subsidize its other loss-making operations. Historically, port tariffs in South Africa were high to support the country's import substitution strategy. The tariffs for container vessels in Durban, South Africa's second-largest port in terms of tonnage handled, are twice as high as the average tariffs for 12 international ports (ITF-OECD, 2014). South African port charges were 173% higher than the global average, undermining the country's competitiveness (IMF, 2016).

Prior to its commercialization in 2002, Eskom provided electricity to rural areas at a lower price than to urban areas. In 2012 Eskom disclosed in its annual report that its supply of electricity to certain large energy-intensive mining companies through Special Purchasing Agreements (SPAs) was below cost. These SPAs were brokered as part of South Africa's industrial policy strategy to attract FDI through cheap energy. This was at a time when Eskom possessed excess capacity in its national grid. Low electricity prices were seen at the time as a quick route to guarantee South Africa a competitive advantage to attract foreign capital, create jobs, and improve the country's trade balance. The beneficiaries included major multinational corporations, such as BHP Billiton and Anglo American. The implication of this is that other electricity users were effectively subsidizing these large MNCs. This made the SPAs a special form of subsidy Eskom paid to large mining companies for which it was not compensated by government (Dawood, 2014).

One of the main planks in the government's strategy to enhance the inclusiveness of economic growth is the black economic empowerment (BEE) programme. BEE has used public procurement policy, via a points system, to induce SOEs to include larger numbers of historically disadvantaged population groups in their production and supply chains as workers, managers, and owners (OECD, 2015f). The protagonists of BEE have insisted that 30% of government contracts, especially in SOEs, be set aside for black-owned companies, irrespective of their experience, capacity, or the price at which they offered to provide services or goods. This has led to an expansion of a competitive kleptocratic culture across all levels of government. There were 166 cases of fraud and corruption between 2010 and 2016 that have been related directly to procurement by state institutions and SOEs. These cases involved amounts ranging from R70, 000 to R2.1 billion and the total amount at stake in all these cases has been R17 billion (Bhorat et al., 2017).

The South African Constitution requires any withdrawal from the National Revenue Fund to be approved by Parliament. Hence, a state subsidy requires parliamentary approval. This, in effect, is what the B-BBEE caucus had demanded, a subsidy given to black companies for doing business. The bar, however, for guarantees was lower. It only needed a letter from the Minister of Finance. With a guarantee, SOEs can borrow from private lenders/banks to finance their investment plans and pay the growing number of black-owned sub-contractors. This indeed was how SOEs in South Africa have tended to finance their investments. If SOEs defaulted on interest payments, banks have a 'first call' on the South African fiscus.

Similar to other SOEs, Eskom is also mandated to assist the government in fulfilling its economic empowerment initiatives through affirmative procurement. The costs of affirmative procurement include longer tendering periods to secure procurement from designated groups, training on emerging businesses, and administrative costs to do with policy enforcement. One of the causes of the countrywide blackouts that started in 2008 was that Eskom redirected some of its contracts for coal to small black-owned companies unable to meet the demand. The country still needs more generating capacity. Eskom will need an estimated R300 billion in the next few years to complete Kusile and Medupi, two huge new coal-fired power stations, whose costs have escalated, and which have been several years behind schedule, again leading to either higher tariffs for consumers or recapitalization by the government (Kane-Berman, 2016).

Performance of South Africa's SOEs

Taken as a whole, commercial SOEs in South Africa have had mixed performance results. The Presidential Reform Commission on SOEs (PRC) Review for 2006–10 showed that the overall performance of commercial SOEs in terms of revenue and profits was positive but return on assets (RoA) was low (Figure 10.2). During this period, total aggregate revenue grew by a compound annual growth rate of 6.9%, while the average net profit margin was 13.8%. RoA was low, with an average of 0.7%. Among the profitable SOEs were Transnet, Central Energy Fund (CEF), DBSA, and South Africa Post Office (SAPO). However, South African Forestries Company (SAFCOL) and South Africa Broadcasting Corporation (SABC) made significant losses for two of the five years, SAA had two years of losses, and Denel and Alexkor incurred losses all five years (Kikeri, 2018). Figure 10.3 shows South African SOEs' RoE.

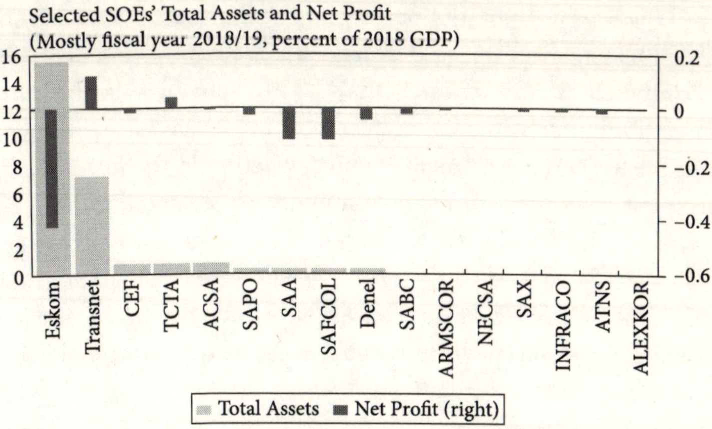

Figure 10.2 Total assets of South African SOEs and their net profits (2018–19)

Source: IMF, 2020.

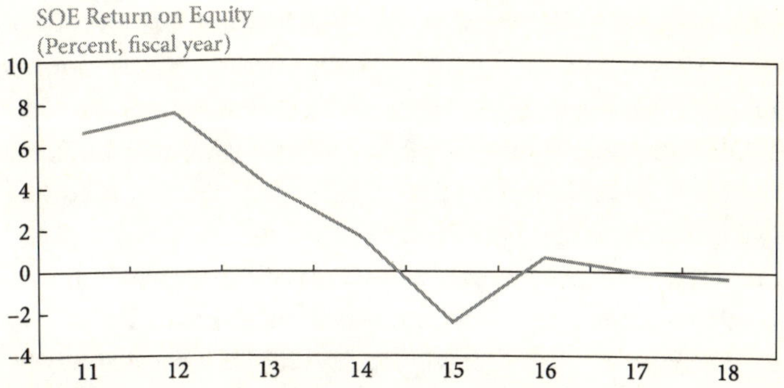

Figure 10.3 South African SOEs' RoE

Source: IMF, 2020.

According to Treasury data, SOEs had a net asset value of R305 billion in 2014–15. However, their RoE had dropped from +7.5% in 2011–13 to −2.9% in 2014–15. Figure 4.6 shows selected SOEs' total assets and net profits for the fiscal year 2018–19. Most of the decline was due to large losses at CEF and SAA. Moreover, government guarantees to SOEs (R467 billion) had reached the upper limit of what could be considered prudent given the total government debt. These guarantees amounted to 11.5% of GDP and were a 'source of pressure on the sovereign rating'. Although many SOEs were solvent and performing well, others posed significant risks to public finances (Kane-Berman, 2016).

On the whole, South African SOEs have been characterized by chronic under-performance with poor returns on public investment and continuous reliance on government support, whether in the form of explicit government guarantees or subsidies. There are essentially three financial problems with SOEs: (a) their overall return on equity is negative; (b) their aggregated cumulative losses pose a severe risk to public finance; and (c) SOEs with fragile balance sheets have difficulty raising the money to invest in the economic infrastructure and structural transformation that the country needs.

Chronic financial problems at SOEs are partly a function of operational inefficiencies, poor governance structures, and of much weaker executive management at senior and middle levels post-1994. They have manifested themselves through poor service delivery and serious liquidity shortfalls that in some cases required government bailouts, jeopardizing fiscal consolidation plans and weighing heavily on debt accumulation. After years of poor performance by Eskom, the government agreed to support it with exceptional financing, committing so far to transfers equivalent to 4.75% of GDP over 10 years. Transfers to other SOEs, including SAA, have been also persistent. But these transfers to finance SOE current spending have not been growth enhancing (IMF, 2020).

Most SOEs have faced elevated costs arising from bloated wage bills and costly procurement. Cost increases have outstripped tariff increases and cuts in capital expenditure, and debt service burden has risen, keeping SOEs' net cash flows negative (Figure 10.4). Eskom is by far the largest SOE and its position is particularly critical, with an operational balance insufficient to service its high debt—around 10% of GDP (Taylor, 2020). Figure 10.5 shows the debt of South African SOEs. Amid declining sales, elevated procurement costs, and a rising wage bill, Eskom faced a liquidity crisis in March 2019 that prompted a bridge bank loan and urgent budget support. SAA was placed in an insolvency protection mechanism in December 2019 after an additional bailout, and the passenger railway company, Passenger Rail Agency of South Africa (PRASA), has been put under administration after continued poor operational and financial performance. To partially compensate for the support to Eskom and other SOEs, the government has

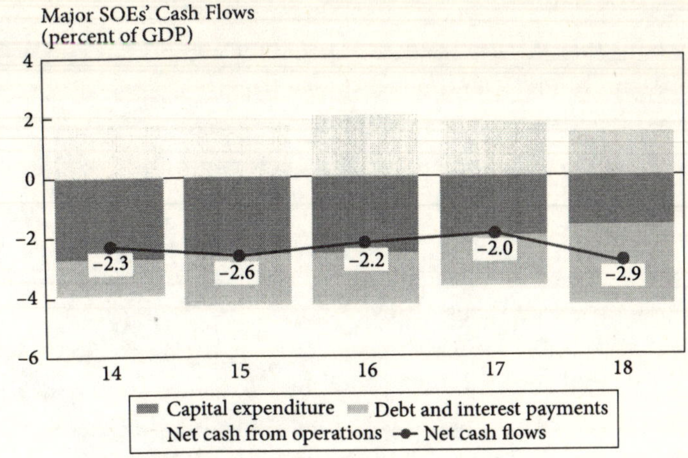

Figure 10.4 South African SOEs' cash flows
Source: IMF, 2020.

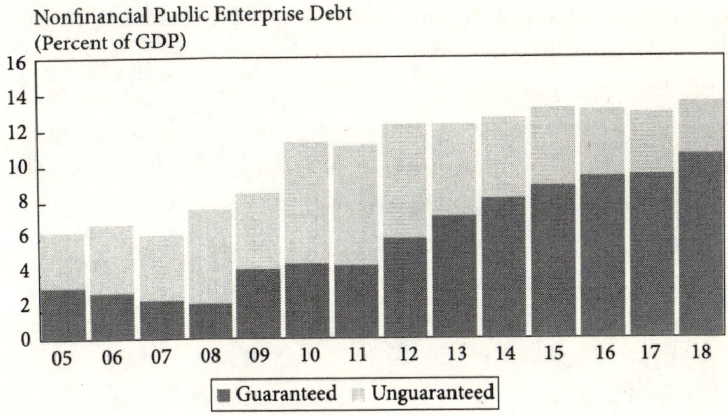

Figure 10.5 South African SOEs' debt
Source: IMF, 2020.

planned cuts in transfers to local governments and spending on goods and services (IMF, 2020).

DPE is the apex agency responsible for overseeing and managing the government's interest in some major SOEs as a shareholder. While the ownership of the remaining SOEs is dispersed across ministries for tele-communications, agriculture, transport, water affairs, defence, trade and industry, minerals, energy, and finance. The multiple, fragmented jurisdictions that govern South African SOEs complicate sector policy development, hinder coordinated implementation, and fail to achieve of desired outcomes. They also impede resource sharing and prevent synergies from developing across SOEs. There is currently no clear methodology to determine whether a particular SOE should be placed under its line ministry, DPE, or another statutory body. A case in point is ACSA, which comes under the Department of Transport, while SAA falls under the DPE (Kanyane and Sausi, 2015).

DPE is responsible for incentivizing SOEs to maximize financial performance, as well as coordinating with them to achieve non-commercial objectives that they have been assigned. It is involved in other aspects of SOE governance: informing the public procurement policies of SOEs, overseeing skills development; overseeing board appointment processes; board induction; and board remuneration. The recommendations of the Presidential Review Commission have alluded to new institutional arrangements, consolidating the oversight of SOEs falling outside the current portfolio of the DPE (OECD, 2014b).

The Companies Act of 2003 and the Public Finance Management Act (PFMA) of 1999,[2] regulate SOEs in conjunction with other laws, rules, and regulations. The South African legislative and policy framework under which SOEs operate is fragmented, often contradictory, and therefore does not facilitate the execution of fiduciary duties satisfactorily. For that reason, it constrains SOEs from achieving their developmental, strategic, and socio-economic objectives. Studies carried out by the DPE point out many incongruences between the PFMA and the Companies Act. The Companies Act and PFMA were not originally meant to grapple with the specific issues confronting SOEs on a day-to-day basis. They served as stopgap measures (SOEs Policy Dialogue Report, 2012). SOEs find it difficult to compete with private companies, as they have to operate within the stringent standard operating protocols of the PFMA (Kanyane and Sausi, 2015).

[2] PFMA intends to secure accountability and sound management of the revenue, expenditure, assets, and liabilities of public sector institutions. It applies to government departments, public entities (including SOEs) listed in schedules 1, 2, and 3 and provincial SOEs.

The proliferation of government departments at the national and provincial levels from 2009 onwards, to extend political patronage networks, followed decentralization of financial accountability to departmental heads. Together with contracting-out, such decentralization was seen as an essential reform for improving the efficiency of the public sector. Since then a systematic process has ensured control over SOEs by chronically weakening their governance, operations, finances, and management/organizational structures. Loopholes in the PFMA have been exploited to make it possible to use the procurement procedures of SOEs to benefit selected politically connected contractors (Bhorat et al., 2017).

SOEs are not required to table their budgets and expenditure plans in Parliament, unlike government departments. The details of SOE expenditure can, therefore, evade public scrutiny (Bhorat et al., 2017). Having independent boards and professional managements in SOEs has been eschewed because it did not fit the key aspects of ANC policy, including affirmative action and the deployment of party loyalists to positions of power in SOEs. Independent directors drawn from the private sector who have served on some of the boards of SOEs have complained about constant political interference from ANC. As a result, SOEs have been turned into playground of patrimonial political leadership and crony capitalism, with their organizational integrity compromised and their balance sheets hollowed out (Kane-Bernal, 2016).

Ownership vs other functions of the State

South Africa suffers among the highest levels of inequality in the world. The top 20% of the population earns over 68% of income, while the poorest 40% possess only 7% of income (IMF, 2020). The historic wealth of South Africa, making it the second largest economy on the continent, was based on enormous mineral wealth combined with a racially discriminatory legal system that resulted in an abundant, disenfranchised, and poorly paid workforce. Not surprisingly, democratic South Africa started the 1990s with extreme inequality because *apartheid* excluded the bulk of the population from economic opportunities. However, South Africa's Gini coefficient has increased further in the early 2000s and has remained high ever since.

The South African government has used different tools to tackle the stubborn levels of inequality, including progressive fiscal redistribution. Efforts to reduce inequality have focused on higher social spending, targeted government transfers, and affirmative action to diversify wealth, property ownership, and promote entrepreneurship among the previously marginalized (IMF, 2020). Policies, including the Radical Economic Transformation (RET) policy; the B-BBEE policy; the economic dominance of key SOEs; and by State-investment institutions like the Public Investment Corporation, have been implemented to create more space for historically disadvantaged South Africans in business and government.

As fiscal mismanagement and rising public debt have reduced the scope for continuing to use fiscal policy for redistribution, SOEs were expected to provide capital for attaining BEE objectives. The New Growth Path (NGP) launched in 2009 was aimed at redirecting state support to black-owned small businesses, new entrepreneurs, and stem the tide of deindustrialization. Although SOEs are aware of their role in supporting social, economic, and political objectives, financial and resource constraints,[3] the breakdown of their structures, and all-pervasive corruption have been impediments to achieving results on the ground. The PRC Review has indicated that BEE programmes have not worked optimally. SOEs have failed to achieve both their main objectives (i.e. to provide key utilities to support industry, build infrastructure) and their secondary, non-commercial objectives, as a direct consequence of state capture.

Redistribution programmes implemented through SOEs created conditions conducive to a small group in the ANC hierarchy to repurpose state institutions. The lack of transparency at SOEs in generating redistribution through non-monetary transfers allowed that small group to enrich themselves at the expense of the survival of the SOEs. In addition to strategic economic mandates, SOEs were burdened with a social agenda to rectify inequalities created in the *apartheid* period.

[3] SOEs are required to function sustainably on the strength of their balance sheets but they continue to depend on Government for financial support. Many SOEs doubt their ability to meet future funding requirements without Government support, but South Africa's self-imposed limit on a debt/equity ratio of no more than 40% constrains the extent to which the Government can support SOEs (Kikeri, 2018).

Ambitious developmental goals were imposed on SOEs without any consideration as to what their balance sheets could comfortably accommodate. Over time, given often contradictory policy objectives, these new tasks stretched the SOEs' operational capacities and balance sheets to breaking point.

The primary obstacles to the development of key manufacturing industries have been identified as high electricity prices and the 'monopolistic pricing' of inputs that are key to manufacturing. This is clearly because of large SOEs that pass-on high costs to businesses, thus sustaining elevated price levels and reducing the economy's competitiveness (IMF, 2020).

Also, given existing limits on SOE capability, approximately 40% of their build programmes depend on imports. This has created both a security-of-supply problem for the SOEs and a balance-of-payments constraint at the macroeconomic level. In trying to align SOEs' operations with the developmental goals of the government, SOEs have become financially unstable with far reaching consequences for the economy. Viewed through an historical lens, SOEs were used as sources of employment for politically important groups, as low-cost suppliers of inputs for industry, and as financiers for new technologies. Overall, they were used to promote capital accumulation in the private sector, and especially in the mining and energy industries. SOEs in fact have facilitated the generation of great profits for the private sector, but at their expense.

Now, however, the accumulated annual costs and debt burden of South Africa's dysfunctional SOEs, in terms of jobs losses, deterring investments, and reducing economic growth, are so high that they threaten the country's fiscal position and economic sustainability. Gross SOE debt in 2018–19 was 55% of South Africa's GDP of which Eskom's debt is equivalent to 10% of GDP. On current policies, public debt would exceed 70% of GDP in the near term and would not stabilize (IMF, 2020).

Nearly 30 years after the demise of *apartheid*, the SOEs that were established by that regime to provide electricity for the mining industry, to circumvent international embargoes, are hindering the development of post-*apartheid* South Africa, when South Africans still suffer from poverty, inequality, and unemployment on a scale not unlike their condition under *apartheid*.

Conclusions

SOEs in South Africa form a significant part of certain vital industries that serve as inputs to other industries. They are indispensable in fulfilling the State's developmental mission. This is, to some extent, an outcome of disappointment with post-democratic privatization experience in some sectors in the late nineties.

Since the mid-2000s, the overall economic environment in South Africa has been shaped largely by the RET policy; infrastructure-led growth; the B-BBEE policy; the economic dominance of key SOEs; and by State-investment institutions, like the Public Investment Corporation.

But the combination of these policies and strategies has led to many unintended adverse consequences. It helped in the emergence of a symbiotic relationship between a *constitutional state* with clear rules and laws and a *shadow state* comprising well-organized patronage networks that facilitated corruption for the enrichment of a small group. Repurposing the SOEs to become the primary mechanisms for rent seeking at the interface between the constitutional and shadow state became the strategic focus of that small group.

As a result, most SOE investment projects were not selected as part of their commercial mandate. Instead, they were effectively imposed on them by politicians or senior government officials for political, 'strategic', social, or self-serving reasons. SOEs have been turned into playground of patrimonial political leadership and crony capitalism, with their organizational integrity compromised and their balance sheets hollowed out. The accumulated annual costs and debt burden of South Africa's dysfunctional SOEs, in terms of jobs losses, deterred investments, and reduced economic growth, have become so high that they now threaten the country's fiscal position and economic sustainability.

Deepening of a pervasive, corrosive culture of corruption within the State has brought the RET transformation programme to a halt. South Africans therefore continue to suffer from poverty, inequality, and unemployment on a scale not unlike their condition under *apartheid*.

11

Conclusions from a review of SOEs in the country case studies

State capitalism re-emerged, with a new lease of life, after the GFC of 2008–10. Interest surged in the large emerging economies that had survived the crisis relatively unscathed. The resilience of Brazil, China, India, Indonesia, and others was attributed (perhaps somewhat hastily and superficially) to widespread state involvement in their economies, especially through State-owned enterprises (SOEs) and state-owned banks and financial institutions (SOBFIs).

Despite the many economic shocks and traumas of the 1970s through to the 1990s, SOEs have remained popular for many reasons: national defence and economic security/independence; fending off excessive foreign influence in the economy; promoting employment and regional development of backward areas; supporting various kinds of affirmative action, and empowerment, programmes for hitherto dispossessed, or otherwise disadvantaged minorities; developing a wider national base of industrial skills and new technologies; and providing essential services in situations of a natural monopoly and national crises.

They have also been useful to governments as sources of non-tax funding; providing for the general welfare of citizens; achieving scale economies; and for enabling the exercise of patronage and political influence. Governments have, therefore, protected and promoted SOE monopolies in utilities, public transport, and communications.

But the presence of SOEs creates conflicts of interest—like—those between the roles of government as owner and regulator, as well as between the commercial and non-commercial objectives of SOEs. These are difficult to resolve and often put the State in a contradictory position. Having SOEs in any economy compromises and weakens the functioning of *neutral factor markets* which should be available to all players on an equal basis. It also impairs the efficient functioning of *markets for goods and services* by creating various producer biases that disfavour competitors, consumers, and taxpayers.

State capitalism, therefore, now incorporates: fostering greater market competition; providing advanced forms of hard (technology) and soft (organization and management) infrastructure; creating new industries; encouraging innovation, if necessary through disruption; mediating in ensuring sound, productive, unconfrontational industrial relations; and compensating or repurposing those workers and communities left behind by globalization of supply chains and other essential transformational changes. Streamlining and reorienting SOEs to become more efficient, profitable, and entrepreneurial has now become hallmarks in fusing (successfully) state intervention with market liberalism to achieve (and sustain) unprecedented outcomes.

The State's preferred instruments of intervention have altered accordingly (Chatterjee, 2020). Many former monopolies and large SOEs are now subject to the discipline of market competition, public listing, and minority shareholder activism (Mussacchio and Lazzarini, 2014). Development banks and other State-owned financial institutions have taken on a renewed role, but with lending reoriented towards a broader pool of recipient firms beyond favoured SOEs (Thurbon, 2016). In parallel, government-SOE-private business interactions have become part of a coherent, integrated development policy process, with different forms of public–private partnership becoming increasingly common across a number of countries.

While the GFC renewed interest in State capitalism, experience with the outcomes of privatization in many emerging economies over the last two decades proved that privatization was no panacea. In many countries, privatization replaced state monopolies with private ones, with worse economic consequences, rewarding crony oligarchic owners with windfall gains. Crony capitalism became a bigger problem than SOE inefficiency, with income distribution at stake.

This book sought to examine the role of the State in actively shaping and co-creating markets and fixing them when they went wrong. If State capitalism can manage markets effectively and foster competition for specific policy ends, nurture innovation, and help build future leading sectors as well as, or better than, market capitalism, should it not be encouraged to do so? Must conflicts of interest, and other internal contradictions, always constrain the State from playing a meaningful role as a long-term and strategic investor in commercial enterprises?

The studies of eight countries from different regions undertaken for this book, sought to provide answers to these key policy questions related to state capitalism. Generalizing from the results of multi-country studies to arrive at universally applicable predictions, prescriptions, and policy recommendations, is inherently difficult. Individual countries are quite different in their socio-economic, historical, political, and institutional circumstances. So are their experiences, as the eight country studies highlight, even as the book attempts to extrude, from available research, the principal common characteristics of, and practices followed by, successful SOEs independently of country context.

In the post-COVID-19 world, a new form of 'state-private symbiosis'—of a kind unimagined in any detail yet—will—have to emerge. After the twin experiences of acute global exigencies in 2010 and 2020, in both of which the State was obliged to play a role it had not earlier envisioned, such a concept may need to combine structurally: (a) those aspects of the State's intervention role that are indispensable *in extremis*; while preserving (b) the efficiency of resource allocation and mobilization functions of markets in normal times; and (c) the role that the State and the private sector play in fostering innovation.

The GFC of 2010 and the COVID-19 pandemic in 2020 have twice underscored, within one decade that, in existential crises, markets cannot function nor survive without emergency support from the State *in extremis*. Both these crises have highlighted the critical and indispensable role of the State in saving lives and protecting livelihoods. In many countries, SOEs have been a crucial part in delivering on that effort as agents of the State. Likewise, during financial crises, SOBs grow in stature in a 'flight to safety' away from private banks. For SOEs to be able to play that role for the State during crises, it is imperative that they are well governed and are financially healthy. Only well-governed and financially healthy SOEs can help combat economic and financial crises, foster innovation, and promote development goals. Research suggests that SOEs underperform when they have to respond quickly to pressures from their external environment, as the problems of 'liabilities of stateness' (a phrase coined by Lazzarini and Musacchio) constrain and inhibit their reorganization. But as the two crises have demonstrated, for the State to play that crucial role, governments need to work towards reducing these 'liabilities of stateness' to prepare SOEs to respond to crises.

Contrary to widespread public perception, active and involved state participation in the ownership of commercial enterprises has proven, in many instances (though not across-the-board) to be beneficial for government budgets. Financially sound, wealthy SOEs constitute valuable assets for the State. Loss making, or overly indebted, SOEs represent liabilities that may require frequent capital injections or other forms of financial support which can become a perennial drain on the fiscus.

Governments, therefore, need to ensure that SOE financial structures are strong and they are always properly funded, to achieve their economic and social mandates. This is also critical in responding not only to crises—so that public banks and utilities have enough resources to provide subsidized loans, water, and electricity during crises—but also to help build leading sectors of the future and promote development goals.

Therefore, the relationship of SOEs to their shareholders, and the way in which they are governed, is of prime importance as governments seek to nurse damaged economies and stabilize domestic financial markets—rendered excessively volatile and made dysfunctional by global crises. Consequently, a radical reappraisal of corporate governance principles and values within SOEs should be an overriding priority. In addition, SOEs will need autonomy and tacit support from the State to make hard choices related to labour and redundant technology. In other words, how an enterprise is managed (and given the right to do so by itself) is as important as who owns the enterprise (IMF-EBRD, 2019).

In addition, a regulatory policy framework with an overarching guiding principle to state regulation is equally important. An uneven regulatory policy framework leads to distortions in the market. Private interests with deep pockets in concert with politicians take advantage of these distortions to extort from incumbent SOEs. Regulatory capture by private (near) monopolies has led to rising market concentration with existing competitors faced with extreme financial distress and overwhelmed to provide any meaningful competition.

Many policymakers, their interlocutors, and the wider public in emerging economies believe that the debate between private versus state ownership should not be focused exclusively on creating profitable State-owned entities. It should also (necessarily) include issues of institutional transparency, accountability, responsibility, equal opportunity, and the rule of law.

When SOEs operate inefficiently and are poorly governed and regulated, they not only create a strain on public resources, but come to be used inappropriately as tools for political patronage, or for self-enrichment by corporate insiders, at the expense of society at large. This, in turn, erodes the trust of citizens, companies, and investors in public institutions and markets. The reputational damage that results from poorly-governed or mismanaged SOEs ultimately turns away private capital—both domestic and foreign—which is crucial for financing development.

SOEs and the issue of conflicts of interest arising with regulation

The standard paradigm for economic regulation is premised on two key assumptions, i.e. (a) independent regulation is a valuable but fragile arrangement that contributes to better implementation of policy by reducing conflicts of interest and (b) regulated companies, and their managers, are primarily motivated by maximizing profits and enhancing shareholder value. Thus, regulators are focused mainly on ensuring that the behaviour of the *producers* of goods and services in the industries being regulated, are legal, reasonable, and kept within appropriate bounds to ensure fair competition and a level playing field.

These assumptions have become the basis on which regulators in emerging economies create incentives for companies to improve efficiencies and service quality. That regulation should also strive to protect the interests of direct players in viable industries, while protecting the related, pertinent interests of other stakeholders—i.e. consumers, sub-contractors, suppliers, creditors, and service—is taken account of much less than it should be.

In many emerging economies, regulation is not just about efficiency but also about the appropriate distribution of rents and surpluses, between producers and consumers, or among different types of producers and consumers. For this reason, regulation intrinsically involves political choices. Attempts make regulation purely a servant or function of 'economic science' in setting prices or tariffs and pretend that regulation must be devoid of political preferences in society, might be misplaced, and may have unintended consequences.

Regulatory preference for, and regulatory protection of, SOEs continues to be high in most emerging market countries. Regulators have limited authority and freedom to enforce regulations against SOEs to the same degree as against their private counterparts. Regulatory preference, therefore, follows a hierarchy in which SOEs, and crony capitalist firms are protected the most, followed by domestic private firms, foreign firms, and SMEs.

Protections, like exemptions from sound principles of enterprise management and competition law, have continued to be provided to SOE monopolies. Utilities in general have exemplified SOEs undermining regulatory independence, the dilution of rule-based decision-making, and disregard for contractual arrangements for political gains. They do not appear to have much reason to abide by regulatory directives that are in direct conflict with populist measures and political, policy decisions taken by the executive.

Large SOEs, to maintain their status quo, have resisted and deliberately delayed essential changes in their operations, management, technology, and finances which regulators may have demanded or suggested. They have been able to shape the regulatory frameworks in their favour to protect their rents. Large SOEs have colluded to form the core of a public enterprise sphere of influence and have been successfully proactive in determining the terms of the government's support to SOEs. Government backing and favour have given SOEs unfair competitive advantage in their domestic market, where they have crowded out private investment in new markets, products, and technologies and usurped entrepreneurial activity.

The setting of tariffs is one of the State's significant regulatory responsibilities, and it has had to balance the influence of many competing constituencies. Current regulatory model in some countries selects bidders on the basis of those able to offer low tariffs rather than on the basis of their capacity to deliver quality services, again favouring incumbent large SOEs. Correspondingly, the pace of private sector-driven upgrading of the relevant facilities has lagged. Regulators have been forced to depart from their official regulatory methodology and determine tariff increases on the basis of an ad hoc subjective judgements that try to achieve a balance between political pressures and economic forces.

Inadequate institutional distance between regulators and SOEs has meant that regulators have been ineffectual in protecting other players from monopoly abuse by SOE incumbents and in promoting efficiency-enhancing competition and have, indirectly helped SOEs in maintaining their dominance. Many large SOEs have provided services at below cost to preferred political constituencies for electoral gains and have consequently failed other consumers by maintaining unjustifiably high costs for goods and services. If large SOEs have resisted change, politicians have also played their role in reducing the powers of regulatory bodies.

In economies where the legacy of State-led diversification has led to privileged SOEs, their relationship to a maturing private sector has become tense. This is partly due to the nascent level of legal and institutional development in enforcing fair competition, i.e. the framework within which SOEs contend with private sector entities.

Effective regulatory systems of governance need specific capacities and institutional endowments. They presume the efficient operation of administrative practices and procedures. Regulators manifest their weak autonomy when many of the capacities they need are insufficient and only partially (or superficially) present. Building capable, effective, and responsive regulatory institutions for oversight of SOEs has been challenging in environments that still reek of powerful vested interests and the vestiges of a patrimonial state.

The operational functioning of regulatory bodies has been a constraint in creating a level playing field in terms of ensuring a competitive and fair business environment. Increasing direct, public control over the economy in some countries has resulted in different parts of the government issuing a plethora of new regulations and decrees without any attempt at coordination and without taking into account the State's capacity to implement and enforce them.

Uneven implementation has created further complications, with various officials, branches of government, and jurisdictions interpreting and applying regulations inconsistently, with the decisions of one state entity often being overruled or contested by another. Multiple institutional actors, agencies, and a plethora of bureaucracies compete within the SOE ecosystem, blurring lines of authority, and responsibility, thus contributing to rule confusion.

Politicians, acting in concert with private interests, take advantage of these weak regulatory capacities to extort from incumbent SOEs and favour particular interests. Regulatory bodies are not only 'captured' by private interests but also are often subordinated to the ministry of the sector they regulate. Ministerial departments have had overriding powers over regulatory bodies' decisions. As a result, over time, the regulatory bodies have been reduced to advisory bodies which lay down rules that do not conflict with ministerial departments. Regulatory bodies, therefore, have limited ultimate authority.

Regulatory bodies have often operated with varying and sometimes ambiguous and controversial—degrees of independence from the political executive. This has led to a different set of norms being applied to SOEs or being partially applied by the regulator due to pressures on its functioning. The absence of strong and independent regulatory bodies in creating the necessary checks and balances against discretionary governmental action has sometimes threatened the performance of SOEs.

In addition, the legislative framework which empowers regulators to provide an independent review of the economics of new projects has failed to provide the important check and balance on decisions related to large SOE projects. For many new projects, by the time, the SOE approaches the regulator with the license application, the decision has often been a fait accompli. These large SOE projects then become a source of their underperformance.

The best assurance of competitive neutrality in the treatment of SOEs is to keep regulatory enforcement independent of the missions of industrial policy and promotion. But many regulators are responsible for the promotion and development of certain industries as well. Regulators have often functioned as specialized support agencies. Consequently, they have not promoted enough competition and have become involved in turf battles with competition authorities. It is not uncommon, therefore, to witness SOEs in strategic sectors being involved in a peculiar seesaw/cycle of deregulation–liberalization–reregulation.

In addition to playing a role in industrial policy, there are situations, where regulators are expected to resolve policy contradictions. But as this is beyond their mandate, they end up fudging the issue. In this way, policy non-performance is blamed on regulators and set them up for future failures.

While playing multiple roles in the economy including ownership of enterprises, regulation, and financing, the State often exacerbates the conflict-of-interest problem and achieves the opposite of what it intended in terms of its enunciated policy goals. In the utilities sector, for example, when governments do not allow essential tariff adjustments, it not only creates a regulatory risk for service providers in terms of the future path of tariff adjustments and the transparency of their setting and enforcement but also risks creating liquidity problems for the service providers. The financial precariousness then negatively affects lenders (in most cases State owned).

The State's multiple roles also mean that it is uniquely positioned to shape the applicable legal regime with its interests as the shareholder in mind, at the expense of other minority shareholders.

Ensuring a level playing field for firms is, therefore, paramount and would create positive effects by fostering greater productivity and avoiding protectionism. Experience from successful SOEs has demonstrated clearly that it is competition and regulation rather than ownership per se which are key to efficiency.

SOEs and crony capitalism

Oligarchic control in business is often prevalent in countries in which bureaucracies are less efficient, in which government directs economic activities, in which political rent-seeking opportunities are lucrative, in which financial markets are dysfunctional and where uneven regulatory policy framework is responsible for distortions in the market. The State's role in granting property rights to land and influencing the value of property; granting licenses for the exploitation of natural resources; influencing the development of infrastructure and its pricing; granting tax benefits; public procurement; spectrum allocations for telecommunications; etc., have created opportunities to extend favours of large economic value to private interests.

Not surprisingly, in many countries, most business fortunes were made with/through the State and through connections with networks in the state apparatus. Crony capitalism has undoubtedly brought huge benefits to entrepreneurs who could not have existed otherwise. Crony businesses have survived not on the genius of their business acumen, but on their ability to buy and manipulate politicians and civil servants. Political connections have served as a substitute for missing or weak property rights.

Political connections have also helped businesses in manipulating the public banking system. Businesses borrow from multiple lenders and invest less equity than expected and function through asymmetric risk sharing between Public Sector Banks (PSBs) and themselves in large projects.

The evolution of rent management systems within neo-patrimonial regimes around the world has taken many forms. They can be characterized within a spectrum that ranges from centralized-coordinated to chaotic. To secure favourable policy and regulatory decisions, especially, protection against foreign competition, large crony businesses have often exploited their close personal links with politicians.

Politicians rely on donations from these businesses to finance party activity and to fund increasingly expensive and fiercely competitive election campaigns. In some countries, crony capitalists cut out the middlemen and become politicians themselves.

The most common way in which politicians carry out their part of the crony capital bargain is to grant domestic monopolies and government contracts to supportive businesses resulting in different outcomes in different countries:

- With the mutual back scratching that occurs in many developing 'democracies', crony businesses benefitting from state contracts, pass the excess profits they make back to finance the electoral success of supportive politicians.
- In China, the domination of the communist party and the state's economic control have bred a virulent form of crony capitalism, as ruling elites have converted political power into economic wealth and privilege, at the expense of equity and efficiency.
- In authoritarian democracies, SOEs function as a mechanism of political control and rent extraction, by enriching allies and neutralizing any political opposition.

- Crony capitalism is nurtured and matured through SOE monopolies. The crony networks that politicians have with businesses are maintained for the purposes of exerting the state's micro-management and control.

The pervasive corruption surrounding the relationship between an SOE and its contractors has significantly raised regulatory risk in many countries. It has threatened future investment. Entrenched clientelism/patronage networks have deepened and broadened the corrosive culture of corruption within the state, by grafting a *shadow state* onto the extant constitutional state. However, there have been cases where countries with extensive corruption managed to grow rapidly in the 1980s and 1990s. In those countries, if rent-creating corruption led to significant efficiency losses then, by sharing the profits from corruption with SOE managements, there was a paradoxical incentive created to enhance efficiency so as to generate more such profits.

Exercising the private agenda of public officials

If big private businesses and SOEs have resisted essential reforms related to their operations, management, technology and finances, politicians, and bureaucrats have equally resisted administrative reforms that separate policy making from implementation. Separating policy making from policy implementation reduces the ability of SOE insiders and the state to shower favours on cronies. Bureaucrats have been the vanguard of resistance to attempts to any reform that affects their personal interests or makes more demands on them in the way they discharge their duties.

Given the significant protection provided to public officials, both by stature and exceptions in laws related to fiscal responsibility, public officials have been allowed to pursue their private agenda with impunity. In the absence of effective factor markets, the government naturally plays an influential role in allocating scarce resources through: the sale of state assets, bank loans, tax benefits, awarding of infrastructure projects, regulatory fees, sale of land, appraisal of state assets, and arbitration/resolution of business disputes. State officials understand the key role that they play in determining who gets what and have created opportunities for themselves to create and extract rent. In the process, treasuries have been deprived of large sums of revenue.

Excessive regulation, frequent rule changes, and inconsistent application of regulations, combined with weak administrative machinery, make it difficult for private businesses to be sure they are on the right side of the law. This deliberate creation of 'destructive ambiguity' has left considerable discretionary power in the hands of public officials dealing directly with businesses, and has created opportunities for large-scale corruption.

The most common form of corruption in many emerging markets has involved interest groups engaging in bribing and lobbying government officials to influence SOEs' resource allocation—including the sale of control rights or physical assets or licenses under illicit agreements that confer undue gains on both public officials and their buyers. Corruption has been exacerbated by competitive multiparty politics, when political parties and related entities compete to establish their own patronage networks. State control over monopoly SOEs has provided ruling parties with access to a large resource base.

If politicians and bureaucrats have resisted administrative reforms, at the firm level, SOE managers face inappropriate incentives. They are often biased towards larger, technologically more complex projects that cost more. They eschew more incremental or mundane solutions that might be more appropriate in the public interest. In some cases, unviable projects are selected by top managers acting as aspirant pseudo-capitalists with grandiose ambitions, who interpret their mandate to suit their own pecuniary interests. Top SOE managers in all major state monopolies divert cash flows and siphon off assets, referred to as 'informal profit-seeking' at the state's expense. In the absence of hard budget constraints, effective competition, and functioning capital markets, SOE managers are able to entrench themselves and resist both restructuring and liquidation (Steyn, 2006).

Countries have experimented by pegging the remuneration of public officials to the very top bracket of private sector pay and reward senior SOE managers with bonuses linked to profits. Governments have implemented these remuneration policies as pragmatic measures to deter corruption but have had mixed results. Full transparency in the activities of the SOEs is paramount to improve accountability and to reduce corruption. Including SOEs in budget and debt targets is another way to create better incentives for fiscal discipline (Gaspar et al., 2020).

SOEs and the misallocation of resources

Governments in all countries face many and diverse political and policy pressures. In their attempts to address this complexity, it is often tempting to expect SOEs, which typically control vast resources, to assist with achieving multiple objectives. SOEs are expected not only to deliver on their core functions but also assist with a myriad of economic and social policy objectives.

For non-financial SOEs, non-commercial transactions often take the form of underpricing through the extension of favourable pricing contracts, while for state-owned financial institutions and banks, the most common forms are directed lending and concessionary loans. The wider the set of objectives for an SOE to achieve, the more its resources are stretched, and the more they make trade-offs to attain their objectives. How SOEs allocate their resources is, therefore, dependent on what kind of policy trade-offs are made by SOE managements.

Governments have often used SOEs to provide public goods and services. Frequent political interference in the pricing of such goods and services and inadequate funding of SOEs have resulted in their inefficient delivery. Profitable business units within SOEs end up cross-subsidizing unprofitable public service delivery.

Non-commercial investment projects imposed on SOEs for political, 'strategic' or social reasons are typically not financially viable. The majority end-up costing far more than the budgeted amount on which the decision to proceed with the project was premised. These 'unfunded mandates' lead to undesirable outcomes such as an additional increase in consumer tariffs to pay for the cost of unviable projects. There is an absence of transparent reporting on non-commercial projects which makes quantification of the costs of such activities difficult and, therefore, difficult to measure how resources have been allocated.

In terms of the allocation of state resources, the other important challenge has been the functioning of SOBFIs and the state's inability or reluctance to discipline well-connected large firms. Misallocation results from their focus on extending credit to firms that are not necessarily financially constrained. Although there are growing credit lines to small firms, large corporations still represent a large portion of state-owned banks' borrowers.

Many large private firms, as well as SOEs, have benefited from the state's generous incentives to make heavily leveraged investments. These have often resulted in structural imbalances, e.g. overcapacity in certain sectors. The state's presence in the banking system has not only distorted competition and credit allocation but has also encouraged expectations of bailouts, when businesses fail. It leaves state-owned banks and financial institutions over exposed to non-performing assets, thus, necessitating a resource-sapping flow of public resources from treasuries to public banks.

Misallocation of resources has also been exacerbated by procurement policies. Most SOE procurement occurs through non-transparent, non-competitive methods and supplier concentration is high. The unconstrained use of price advantages for domestic suppliers, have impaired efficiency and impeded the development of value chains.

In many resource-abundant countries, SOEs often provide higher total compensation to employees than the private sector and tend to over-employ. The compensation differential affects workers' job preferences and the relative ability of public and private sector firms to recruit skilled workers, and hence the efficiency of labour allocation in the economies.

In these resources endowed countries, SOEs that exploit key natural resources and are tasked with developing infrastructure are invariably used to funnel massive indirect subsidies to much of the economy. They do so via reduced or controlled (often uneconomic) producer prices and direct subsidies to consumers that are lower than would prevail if determined by the market. As rents from natural resources grow, they are often diverted to inefficient sectors to maintain capacity utilization levels, or for ostensible diversification through new investments, without sound budgeting and strong oversight. Significant resource diversion without proper budgeting and oversight has led to project delays and cost over runs, deepening and entrenching inefficiency throughout the economy. Resource diversion has also resulted in SOEs and government not being able to maintain adequate levels of investment in the resource sectors that generate surplus rents.

The state control of factor markets, therefore, creates some pernicious side effects which include rent seeking by both governments and enterprises, thus, distorting resource allocation. Moreover, the existing prices of capital, land, and energy do not reflect the environmental cost of production, making for a widespread misallocation of resources.

SOEs and State's other responsibilities

There are a few notable exceptions (like Singapore) where the state has intervened extensively in the economy successfully (without adversely affecting the business environment) while also owning and managing enterprises. Elsewhere, reliance on SOEs to build national infrastructure projects and as actors with diverse developmental mandates (e.g. construction of social housing, employment creation, healthcare provision, etc.) continues regardless of fiscal pressures. Profitable SOEs are considered too important as assets not to be used for economic diversification. They are given mandates related to developing firms in their value chain and assigned a range of other tasks in new policy sectors beyond their sectoral expertise. Profitable and successful SOEs end up playing a prominent national role that uses their proven managerial and execution capabilities in areas beyond those that their initial mandates allowed for.

Most successful SOEs which are required to play a bigger role are aware of their responsibility in supporting social, economic, and political objectives. But financial and other resource constraints (mainly in administrative capacity and know-how); the unsuitability or incongruity of their corporate structures for doing off-line tasks; and pervasive, systemic corruption impede achieving results on the ground. So, in several countries, SOEs have not only failed in fulfilling their main objectives (i.e. to provide key utilities to support industry, build infrastructure) but also their developmental objectives.

Large and successful SOEs are often induced to undertake development projects by their governments through; capital increases, limiting dividend payments, increasing access to concessional finance, project guarantees, and asset securitization. Expanding investment in non-core activities, funded by higher leverage, has exposed SOEs mandated with development projects to cash-flow difficulties, especially when they suffer from institutional and coordination weaknesses. Thus, inducing SOEs that are successful in their core businesses, to undertake off-line development projects, risks immediate financial viability and dilutes their core capabilities, while increasing long-run fiscal risk.

Successful state interventions have included: effective governance; a pivotal role in mapping out strategic directions for the economy; driving structural transformation; and raising overall living standards especially through education and public housing policy.

But when an intrusive state is unwilling to withdraw itself from certain activities, it can lead to negative synergies between the state and the private sector, resulting in sub-optimal outcomes. Therefore, two key successful features of developmental states include understanding the futility of doing more but doing it less well, and providing space for dynamic and competitive private enterprises to emerge, survive, and grow. This needs governments to review regularly if SOEs are still necessary in the economy and whether they deliver value for taxpayers' money. The case for having SOEs in competitive sectors, such as manufacturing, is weaker because private firms usually provide goods and services more efficiently (Gaspar et al., 2020).

When the state overstretches its economic intrusion and influence, it hinders market growth from achieving full potential and fosters an economy of high political risk in which relationships matter more than rules. The quasi-fiscal activities of SOEs, especially of national oil companies, have included curbing inflation through energy price caps, have resulted in a growing gap between the prices of domestic oil and gas byproducts and the prices charged by international oil companies in international markets. These subsidies are 'implicit price support for fossil fuel' that has discouraged use of alternatives, like ethanol, and has reduced incentives to achieve energy efficiency.

Due to these quasi-fiscal activities, national oil companies do not face any discernible pressure from governments to set up other public services and infrastructure in the communities affected by their activities. Governments have also failed to take responsibility for environmental and social damage or loss caused by national oil companies in the course of oil/gas exploration activities. This has created several dilemmas for oil SOEs that must deal with environmental issues and, at the same time, are expected to serve the interests of politicians.

Evaluating the performance of SOEs in all the countries studied

Despite the different constraints faced by most SOEs, some SOEs as a group of privileged entities enjoy considerable autonomy in operational terms and with loose oversight by government are able to generate profits for their shareholders. These SOEs bear a close resemblance to private enterprises with a focus on bottom line performance.

Autonomy has not only allowed many SOEs to increase profitability and expand output relative to other SOEs but also allowed them to perform effectively relative to the private sector. Dividends and retained earnings have increased too. Consequently, as majority (or only) shareholders, governments have received substantial non-tax revenues from profitable SOEs. But without significant autonomy, internal allocations are driven by reasons other than SOE efficiency alone.

These privileged 'pockets of efficiency' in several countries show that the absence of conventional corporate governance mechanisms does not preclude good SOE performance or political accountability. Conversely, the formal presence of such mechanisms does not guarantee good performance.

The corporate governance of SOEs offers a puzzling irony. The state is expected to lead by example since it imposes governance rules on private enterprises whether by laws or voluntary codes. However, majority of SOEs do not implement corporate governance principles.

Among many inefficiencies present in the state-majority model, it is disadvantageous for minority shareholders. When governments hold a majority stake in SOEs that are important to a country's stability—e.g. energy, banking and telecommunications—it 'opens the door to minority investors taking a hit, when a SOE holds down price adjustments in order to benefit voters'.

In contrast, the state minority model allows for partial mitigation of the negative effects present in majority-owned SOEs. It allows financially constrained firms to undertake long-term strategic projects by benefitting from government resources and political assistance (Inoue, Lazzarini, and Musacchio, 2013). The state's minority stake positively affects SOE performance providing that they are able to promote sound long-term investments and are shielded from governmental interference.

But the state minority model runs the risk of exacerbating cronyism as these businesses 'jockey to curry favor with government for preferential investments or loans based on political connections'.

The top management of most SOEs are torn between their desire to make their entities more efficient and profitable and to provide for their 'social obligations' that involve trade-offs against maximization of profits. The financial problems with most SOEs that are not natural resource driven, are not large, and are not a protected monopoly position in the industry are manifested as follows: (a) their overall return on equity is negative; (b) their aggregated cumulative losses pose a severe risk to public finance; and (c) their fragile balance sheets make it difficult to raise capital to invest further.

In addition, higher leverage, especially external indebtedness in the face of inadequate hedge against their foreign exchange exposure, is another significant challenge faced by SOEs. SOE profitability has steadily declined since the GFC. SOEs have handled the post-2008 slowdown poorly, hampered by less pressure to reform and more pressure to spend to support growth. The low returns on SOE investments mean that they may not be able to pay back these debts.

Chronic financial problems at SOEs are partly a function of poor governance structures (lack of accountability and ineffective oversight) and partly symptomatic of rampant political interference in their core and non-core activities, and weak (if not incompetent) executive management at senior and middle levels. SOEs' inefficiencies, therefore, stem from the dysfunctional conditions in which they operate and weak governance structures that affect their operating procedures.

Drawing from a sample of about 1 million firms in 109 countries, an IMF study found that SOEs are less productive than private firms by one-third, on average. Productivity of SOEs in countries with perceived lower corruption is more than three times higher than those in countries where corruption is severe (Gaspar et al., 2020).

Countering that unfortunate impression, the stellar performance of SOEs in Singapore over a long period of time, of a few key SOEs in Saudi Arabia and India (the islands of excellence in a sea of mediocrity), and the dominant role that SOEs have played in propelling China to the top of the world league of nations cannot be set aside and completely overlooked dismissively. Most countries do not have the public ethos and absence of corruption that Singapore enjoys. Its conditions cannot be easily replicated elsewhere, not even in China, which has tried to emulate the Singaporean approach but with significant variations to reflect Chinese ground realities.

Still, the many examples of successful, profitable SOEs in several (but not all) of the eight countries studied, provide significant hope of SOEs' continued relevance and use. The financial and public health crises have highlighted the need for more state productive capacity, government procurement capabilities, and symbiotic public–private collaborations. Governments argue that fulfilling nonfinancial and public service objectives should outweigh the fact that SOEs are less profitable, efficient, or productive than private firms. But further investment in state's productive capacity in order for SOEs to play an effective role during economic crises will be dissipated, if it falls on weak and poorly managed structures in SOEs; if regulation follows a pecking order in which SOEs, and crony capitalist firms are protected the most, followed by domestic private firms, foreign firms, and SMEs; if politicians continue to undermine the functioning and independence of regulators; if there is pervasive corruption surrounding the relationship between an SOE and its contractors; if political connections serve as a substitute for missing or weak property rights; if state control of factor markets leads to rent seeking by both governments and enterprises; if political interference disallows price adjustments of goods and services provided by SOEs.

Competition and regulation rather than ownership per se are key to efficiency. Ensuring a level playing field for firms is imperative to foster greater productivity and avoiding protectionism. Equally important is for governments to regularly review where SOEs play an indispensable role and to understand the futility of doing more and instead facilitate dynamic and competitive private enterprises to emerge, survive, and grow.

Bibliography

Abrahams, L. (2011). South Africa's e-development still a futuristic task. Journal of Knowledge Economics 2, pp. 145–171.

Ahluwalia, I. J. (1995). New economic policies, enterprises, and privatization in India. In: Cassen, R. and Joshi, V. (Eds.), India: The future of economic reform. Delhi: Oxford University Press.

Ahuja, G. and Majumdar, S. K. (1998). An assessment of the performance of Indian state-owned enterprises. Journal of Productivity Analysis 9(2), pp. 113–132.

Aivazian, V. A., Ge, Y., and Qiu, J. (2005). Can corporatization improve the performance of state-owned enterprises even without privatization? Journal of Corporate Finance 11.

de Alcântara, J. N., Calegario, C. L. L., de Andrade, L. P., and de Alcântara, J. N. (2017). A propriedade estatal. a condição dos paraîsos fiscais e o desempenho finaneiro: uma análise dasmultinacionais brasileiras no perîodo de 2000 a 2015. In: Encontro Nacional de Programas de Pós-graduação em Administração. Anais. São Paulo: Anpad. October/2017. Estratégia em Organizações.

Ali, S. (2010). Dubai—Gilded Cage. New Haven: Yale University Press.

Amann, E. and Baer, W. (2005). From the developmental to the regulatory state: the transformation of the government's impact on the Brazilian economy.

Amann, E., Baer, W., Trebat, T., and Villa, J. M. (2014). Infrastructure and its role in Brazil's Development Process. International Research Initiative on Brazil and Africa, IRIBA Working Paper 10.

Amann, Edmund, Baer, W., Trebat, T., and Villa, J. M. (2016). Infrastructure and its role in Brazil's development process. The Quarterly Review of Economics and Finance 62.

Amico, A. (2017). Arab States as Shareholders: Origins and Consequences. International Development Policy. Graduate Institute of International and Development Studies, Geneva.

Amsden, A. H. (2001). The rise of the rest: challenges to the west from late-industrializing economies. New York: Oxford University Press.

Apriliyanti, I. and Kristiansen, S. O. (2019). The logics of political business in state-owned enterprises: The case of Indonesia. International Journal of Emerging Markets 14(5).

APRM. (2007). South Africa: Country Review Report no. 5. APR Secretariat, Midrand.

Aslund, A. (2019). Russia's crony capitalism. Yale University Press.

Aspinall, E. and Sukmajati, M. (2016). Patronage and clientelism in Indonesian electoral politics. In: Aspinall, E. and Sukmajati, M. (Eds.), Electoral dynamics in Indonesia: Money politics, patronage and clientelism at the grassroots. Singapore: NUS Press, pp. 1–38.

Aspinall, E. (2013). Popular agency and interests in Indonesia's democratic transition and consolidation. Indonesia 96, pp. 101–121.

Astami, E. W., Tower, G., Rusmin, R., and Neilson, J. (2010). The effect of privatisation on performance of state-owned-enterprises in Indonesia. Asian Review of Accounting 18(1), pp. 5–19.

Bacchiocchi, E., Ferraris, M., Florio, M., and Vandone, D. (2019). State-owned banks in the market for corporate control. Journal of Economic Policy Reform 22(2), pp. 120–147.

Bai, C.-E., Hsieh, C.-T., and Song Z. (M.) (2014). Crony Capitalism with Chinese Characteristics.

Bajaj, V. and Yardley, J. (2012). Scandal poses a riddle: Will India ever be able to tackle corruption? The New York Times, September 16, p. 6.

Baker, J. (2012). The rise of Polri: Democratisation and the political economy of security in Indonesia. Ph.D. Thesis, Department of Government, London School of Economics and Political Science.

Balding, C. (2014). A brief research note on Temasek holdings and Singapore: Mr. Madoff Goes to Singapore.

Banda, F., Robb, G., and Roberts, S. (2015). The Links between Competition Policy, Regulatory Policy and Trade and Industrial Policies. Centre for Competition, Regulation & Economic Development Working Paper No. 5/2015.

Bardhan, P. State and capital in Chinese and Indian economic development. University of California at Berkeley.

Bardhan, P. (1998 [1984]). The political economy of development in India (Expanded Edition). New Delhi: Oxford University Press.

van Basten, C. (2007). Economic Regulation of SA's public utilities. Pretoria: TIPS.

Batson, A. (2017). The state of the state sector. Gavekal Dragenomics.

Beazer, Q. H. (2012). Bureaucratic discretion, business investment, and uncertainty. Journal of Politics 74(3), pp. 637–652.

Beresford, A. R. (2015). Power, patronage, and gatekeeper politics in South Africa. African Affairs 114(455), pp. 226–248.

Bershidsky, L. (2015). Vladimir Putin may be tiring of corrupt cronies running down Russian SOEs. Financial Review, August 19.

Bertrand, M., Mehta, P., and Mullainathan, S. (2002). Ferreting out tunneling: An application to Indian business groups. Quarterly Journal of Economics 117, pp. 121–148.

Bhargava, J. (2013). Descent of Air India. New Delhi: Bloomsbury Publishing.

Bhaya, H. (1990). Management efficiency in the private and public sectors in India. Public enterprise at the crossroads, pp. 228–240.

Bhorat et al. (2017). Betrayal of the promise: How South Africa is being stolen.

Biygautane, M., Gerber, P., and Hodge, G. (2017). The evolution of administrative systems in Kuwait, Saudi Arabia, and Qatar: the challenge of implementing market based reforms. Digest of Middle East Studies 26(1).

Bogetić, Ž. and Olusi, O. (2003). Drivers of firm-level productivity in Russia's manufacturing sector. World Bank Policy Research Working Paper 6572.

Box, R. (2005). Critical social theory in public administration. Armonk, NY: M E Sharpe.

Breuer, L., Guajardo, J., and Kinda, T. (2018). Developing infrastructure. Realizing Indonesia's economic potential. Washington, DC: IMF.

Buchanan, J. M., Tollison, R. D., and Tullock, G. (1980). Toward a theory of the rent-seeking society. College Station: Texas A&M University Press.

Buge, M., Egeland, M., Kowalski, P., and Sztajerowska, M. (2013). State-owned Enterprises in the global economy: Reason for concern? VOX: CEPR's Policy Portal.

Burawoy, M. (2001). Transition without transformation: Russia's involuntary road to capitalism. East European Politics and Societies 15(2), pp. 269–290.

Byrd, W. (ed.) (1992). Chinese industrial firms under reform. Oxford: Oxford University press.

Byrnes, R. M. (ed.) (1996). South Africa: A Country study. Washington, DC: GPO for the Library of Congress.

Cai, H., Fang, H., and Xu, L. C. (2011). Eat, drink, firms, Government: An investigation of corruption from the entertainment and travel costs of Chinese firms. The Journal of Law and Economics 54(1), pp. 55–78.

Carney, R. W. and Hamilton-Hart, N. (2015). What do changes in corporate ownership in Indonesia tell us? Bulletin of Indonesian Economic Studies 51(1), pp. 123–145.

Carney, R. W. and Travers Barclay, C. (2013). Changes to the ownership and control of east Asian corporations between 1996 and 2008: the primacy of politics. Journal of Financial Economics 107(2), pp. 494–513.

Carrera, Jr. and Marcos, J. (2018a). State ownership and Brazilian multinational enterprises: degree of internationalization and financial performance. FUNDAÇAO GETULIO VARGAS ESCOLA DE ADMINISTRAÇAO DE EMPRESAS DE SAO PAULO.

Carvalho, D. (2014). The real effects of government-owned banks: evidence from an emerging market. The Journal of Finance 69(2), pp. 577–609.

Cary, E. (2013). Reforming China's state-owned enterprises. The Diplomat.

Central Department of Statistics & Information (2013). www.cdsi.gov.sa

CFA Society Brazil (2016). Corporate governance of state-owned enterprises in Brazil.

Champion, D. (2003). The paradoxical kingdom—Saudi Arabia and the momentum of reform. London: Hurst.

Chan, K. B. (2005). Migration, ethnic relations and Chinese business. Routledge.

Chandra, R. and Chatterjee, E. (2019). State capitalism in India. Oxford Handbook of State Capitalism and the Firm. Oxford: Oxford University Press.

Chang, H.-J. (2007). State owned enterprise reform. United Nations, Department for Economic and Social Affairs.

Chang-Tai, H. and Klenow, P. J. (2009). Misallocation and manufacturing TFP in China and India. The Quarterly Journal of Economics 124(4), pp. 1403–1448.

Chatterjee, E. (2017). Reinventing state capitalism in India: a view from the energy sector. Contemporary South Asia 25(1), pp. 85–100.

Chatterjee, E. (2020). New developmentalism and its discontents: State activism in Modi's Gujarat and India. Development and Change.

Chawla, P. (2012). The crusade against corruption is missing the big, bad, dirty picture. Indian Express, November 4.

Chen, D. (2013). China's state-owned enterprises: How much do we know? From CNOOC to its siblings. The School of Public Policy Research Papers. University of Calgary 6(19).

Chen, Weitseng (ed.) (2017). The Beijing consensus?: How China has changed Western ideas of law and economic development. Cambridge, UK: Cambridge University Press.

Chi, H.-Y., Weng, T.-C., Chen, G.-Z., and Chen, S.-P. (2019). Do political connections affect the conservative financial reporting of family firms? Sustainability 11, p. 5563.

Chibber, A. and Gupta, S. (2017). Public sector undertakings: Bharat's other Ratnas. NIPFP Working Paper No. 186.

China Economic Review (2012). Decoding China Inc. August 6.

China Economic Review (2012). Awash in cash—State companies are outspending the private sector—to China's detriment.

Chu, S. N. and Song, L. (2014). State control, entrepreneurship and resource allocation. In Song, L., Garnaut, R., and Fang, C. (Eds.), Deepening reform for China's long-term growth and development. Canberra: Australian National University Press.

Clark, N. (2014). Structured Inequality: Historical Realities of the Post-Apartheid Economy. Ufahamu: A Journal of African Studies 38(1), pp. 93–118.

Coats, D., and E. Passmore (2008). Public value: The next steps in public service reform. London, UK: The Work Foundation.

Correa, P. (2007). What it takes to lower regulatory risk in infrastructure industries: An assessment and benchmarking of Brazilian regulators. Gridlines No. 29. Washington, DC: PPIAF, World Bank.

Cull, R., Li, W., Sun, B., and Xu, L. C. (2015). Government connections and financial constraints: Evidence from a large representative sample of Chinese firms. Journal of Corporate Finance 32, pp. 271–294.

Cummine, A. (2015). How Temasek has driven Singapore's development. East Asia Forum.

Daroesman, R. (1981). Survey of recent developments. Bulletin of Indonesian Economic Studies 27(2), pp. 1–41.

Das Nair, R. and Roberts, S. (2015). The interface of competition and regulation in energy, telecommunications and transport in South Africa. The Centre for Competition, Regulation and Economic Development.

Das, S. K. (2001). Public office, private interest: bureaucracy and corruption in India. New Delhi: Oxford University Press.

Davis, J. A., Pitts, E. L., and Cormier, K. (2000). Challenges facing family companies in the Gulf Region.

Dawood, G. (2014). State-owned enterprises and quasi-fiscal activities in South Africa. International Budget Partnership.

DBSA (2012). The state of South Africa's economic infrastructure: Opportunities and challenges.

De Paula, G. and Avellar, A. (2008). Reforms and regulation in Brazil: The experience of ANTT and ANTAQ. Quarterly Review of Economics and Finance 48, 237–251.

Deng, Y., Morck, R., Yu, J., and Yeung, B. (2011). Monetary and fiscal stimuli, ownership structure, and China's housing market. NBER Working Paper No. 16871. National Bureau of Economic Research.

Denizer, C., Dethier, J.-J., and Gelb, A. (2011). Development Economics and the International Development Association. The World Bank Policy Research Working Paper 5541.

Dholakia, B. H. (1978). Relative performance of public and private manufacturing enterprises in India: total factor productivity approach. Economic and Political Weekly 13(8), pp. M4–M11.

Di Bella, G., Dynnikova, O., and Slavov, S. (2019). The Russian State's size and its footprint: Have they increased? IMF Working Paper WP 19/53. Washington, DC: IMF.

Dickie, M. (2005). China's merchant adventurers set off in search of global conquests. Financial Times, 16 March 2005.

Dollar, D. and Wei, S. (2007). Das (wasted) Kapital: Firm ownership and investment efficiency in China. IMF Working Paper WP/07/9. Washington, DC: IMF.

Dowding, K. (1995). The civil service. London: Routledge.

Dreze, J. and Sen, A. (2013). An uncertain glory: India and its contradictions. Princeton, NJ: Princeton University Press.

Duckett, J. (2002). Political interests and the implementation of China's urban health insurance reform. Social Policy and Administration 35(3), pp. 290–306.

Dun and Bradstreet (2019). India's Top PSUs 2019.

The Economist (2012). Corruption in India: Digging deeper into the pit. August 22.

The Economist (2017). Most of India's State-owned firms are ripe for sale or closure. June 2017.

Elliott, R. and Zhou, Y. (2013). State-owned enterprises, exporting and productivity in China: A stochastic dominance approach. The World Economy.

Fan, G. and Hope, N. (2014). The role of state-owned enterprises in the Chinese economy.

Ferrari, A., Mare, Davide S., and Skamnelos, I. (2018). A glimpse into state financial institution ownership in Europe and Central Asia. World Bank Blogs, 22 January.

Filatov, A., Tutkevich, V., and Cherkaev, D. Board of directors at state-owned enterprises (SOEs) in Russia. Russian Corporate Governance Roundtable. Paris: OECD.

Filho, J. and Alves, C. (2018). Control mechanisms in the corporate governance of state-owned enterprises (SOEs): A comparison between Brazil and Portugal. Cad. EBAPE.BR 16(1).

Fine, B. and Rustomjee, Z. (1996). The political economy of South Africa—from minerals—energy complex to industrialisation. London: Hurst.

Finn, D. (2006). Fumbling in the dark: The case for a paradigm shift in analyzing China's capital market regulation.

Fitriningrum, A. (2006). Indonesia experience in managing the state companies. OECD-Asian Roundtable on Corporate Governance Network on corporate governance of SOEs, May 2006, Singapore.

Fitriningrum, A. (2015). Are State-owned enterprises successful vehicles for attaining their government stated objectives? Ph.D. thesis in Commerce. Research school for accounting. Australian National University.

Fourie, D. (2014). The role of public sector enterprises in the South African economy.

Florencio, P. (2016). Technology and innovation in the Brazilian oil sector: Ticket to the future or passage to the past? The Journal of World Energy Law & Business 9(4), pp. 237–253.

Florio, M. (2013). Network industries and social welfare. The experiment that Reshuffled European utilities. Oxford: Oxford University Press.

Freedom House (2017). Freedom in the world 2017: Indonesia profile. Available at: https://freedomhouse.org/report/freedom-world/2017/indonesia (accessed 1 December 2017).

Fukuoka, Y. and Djani, L. (2016). Revisiting the rise of Jokowi: The triumph of reformasi or an oligarchic adaptation of post-clientelist initiatives? South East Asia Research 24(2), pp. 204–221.

Gao, S. (1996). China's economic reform. Macmillan, Basingstoke.

Gans-Morse, J. (2011). Threats to property rights in Russia: from private coercion to State aggression. Post-Soviet Affairs.

Garnaut, R., Song, L., and Yao, Y. (2006). Impact and significance of state-owned enterprise restructuring. The China Journal 55, pp. 35–65.

Garshman, M., Roud, V., and Thurner, T. (2018). Open innovation in Russian state-owned enterprises. Industry and Innovation.

Gaspar, V., Medas, P., and Ralyea, J. (2020). State-owned enterprises in the time of COVID-19. IMF Blog Insights and analysis on Economics and Finance.

Gaspari, E. (2003). A ditadura derrotada. Sao Paulo: Companhia das Letras.

Gibson, D. and Crutcher, L. L. P. (2012). Indonesian oil and gas regulator held to be unconstitutional.

Goldstein, A. and Pananond, P. (2008). Singapore Inc goes shopping abroad: Profits and pitfalls. Journal of contemporary Asia 38(3), pp. 417–438.

Goldstuck, A. (2012). Internet matters: The quiet engine of the South African economy.

Gonzalez-Garcia, J. and Grigoli, F. (2013). State-owned banks and fiscal discipline. IMF Working Paper No. 13/206.

Gonzalo, J. A., Pina, V., and Torres, L. (2003). Objectives, techniques and valuation of state-owned companies inprivatization processes. Public Management Review 5(2), pp. 177–196.

Green, S. and Liu G. S. (2005). Exit the Dragon? Privatisation and state control in China. London: Chatham House and Blackwell Publishing.

Grossman, A., Okhmatovskuy, I., and Wright, M. (2015). State control and corporate governance in transition economies: 25 years on from 1989. Corporate Governance 24(3), pp. 200–221.

Guha Thakurta, P. (2014). Gas wars: Crony capitalism and the Ambanis. FEEl Book.

Guj, P. (2012). Mineral royalties and other mining-specific taxes. International Mining for Development Centre—Mining for Development: Guide to Australian Practice.

Gumede, W. M. (2005). Thabo Mbeki and the battle for the soul of the ANC. London: Zebra Press.

Guo, K. and Yao, Y. (2004). Causes of privatization in China: Testing several hypotheses. China Center for Economic Research. Working paper No. E 2004-004.

Gupta, M. (1982). Productivity performance of the public and the private sec-tors in India: A case study of the fertilizer industry. Indian Economic Review 17(2/4), pp. 165–186.

Gupta, N. (2005). Partial privatization and firm performance. The Journal of Finance 60(2), pp. 987–1015.

Gupta, S., Jain, P. K. and Yadav, S. S. (2011). Impact of MoU on financial performance of public sector enterprises in India. Journal of Advances in Management Research 8(2), pp. 263–284.

Gupta, A. (2017). Changing Forms of Corruption in India. Modern Asian Studies 51(6), pp. 1862–1890.

Gylfason, T., Herbertsson, T. T., and Zoega, G. (2001). Ownership and Growth. The World Bank Economic Review 15(3), pp. 431–449.

Hadiz, V. (2004). Decentralization and democracy in Indonesia: A Critique of neo-institutionalist respective. Development and Change 35(4), pp. 697–718.

Hadiz, V. (2010). Localising power in post-authoritarian Indonesia: A southeast Asia perspective. Redwood City, CA: Stanford University Press.

Hadiz, V. and Robison, R. (2005). Neo-liberal reforms and illiberal consolidations: the Indonesian paradox. The Journal of Development Studies 41(2), pp. 220–241.

Haggard, S. and Low, L. (2002). State, politics and business in Singapore. In: Edmund Gomez (Ed.), Political business in East Asia. London: Routledge.

Hall, R. H. (1963). The concept of bureaucracy: An empirical assessment. American Journal of Sociology 69(1), pp. 32–40.

Hallward-Driemeier, M., Kochanova, A., and Rijkers, B. (2020). Does democratization promote competition? Indonesian manufacturing pre and post Suharto. World Bank Policy Research Working Paper 9112. Washington, DC: World Bank.

Hancock, T. and Xueqiao, W. (2019). State-owned investors dominate China's new tech exchange. FT August 11.

Hare, P. and Muravyev, A. (2002). Privatisation in Russia. Russian-European center for economic policy research paper series. Moscow.

Al-Hegelan, A. and Palmer, M. (1985). Bureaucracy and development in Saudi Arabia. Middle East Journal 39(1), pp. 48–68.

Hellman, J. and Kaufmann, D. (2001). Confronting the challenge of state capture in transition economies. Finance and Development 38(3), p. 31.

Hertog, S. (2006). The new corporatism in Saudi Arabia: limits of formal politics.

Hertog, S. (2007). Shaping the Saudi State: Human Agency's Shifting Role in Rentier-State Formation. International Journal of Middle East Studies 39(4), pp. 539–563.

Hertog, S. (2008). Petromin: The slow death of statist oil development in Saudi Arabia. Business history 50(5), pp. 645–667.

Hertog, S. (2010a). Princes, brokers, and bureaucrats: Oil and the state in Saudi Arabia. Ithaca and London: Cornell University Press.

Hertog, S. (2010b). Defying the resource case: Explaining successful state-owned enterprises in rentier states. World Politics 62(2), pp. 261–301.

Hertog, S. (2010c). The Sociology of the Gulf rentier systems: Societies of intermediaries. Comparative Studies in Society and History 52(2), pp. 282–318.

Hertog, S. (2012a). The role of MENA business in policy-making and political transitions. In: Hertog, S., Luciani, G., and Valeri, M. C (Eds.), Business politics in the Middle East. London: Hurst & Co Publishers Ltd.

Hertog, S. (2012b). Good, bad or both?: The impact of oil on the Saudi political economy.

Hertog, S. (2013). The private sector and reform in the Gulf Cooperation Council.

Hertog, S. (2014). Arab Gulf States: An assessment of nationalisation policies. Technical Report, GLMM, Research Paper, 2014/1, Migration Policy Centre.

Hertog, S. (2015). The political economy of regional development in post-World War II Saudi Arabia. In: Bernard, H., Thomas, H., and Stéphane, L. (Eds.), Saudi Arabia in transition: Insights on social, political, economic and religious change. New York: Cambridge University Press.

Hertog, S. (2016a). Rent distribution, labour markets and development in rent countries. LSE Kuwait Programme Paper Series 40.

Hertog, S. (2016b) The oil-driven nation-building of the Gulf States after World War II. In: Peterson, J. E. (Ed.), The emergence of the Gulf States: Studies in modern history. London: Bloomsbury Academic.

Hertog, S. (2019). In the spotlight: Demands on Saudi Aramco are increasing.

Hertog, S., Luciani, G., and Valeri, M. (2013). Business politics in the Middle East. London/New York: Hurst/Oxford University Press.

Hertzmark, D. (2007). Pertamina Indonesia's State-owned oil company. The James A. Baker Institute for Public Policy. Houston: Rice University.

Hess, D. (1995). Science and technology in a multicultural world. New York: Columbia University Press.

Hill, H. (1987). Survey of recent developments. Bulletin of Indonesian Economic Studies 23(3), August, pp. 1–33.

Hill, H. (2007). The Indonesian economy: growth, crisis and recovery. The Singapore Economic Review 52(2), pp. 137–166.

Hill, H. (2015). The Indonesian economy during the Yudhoyono decade. In: Aspinall, E., Mietzner, M., and Tomsa, D. (Eds.), The Yudhoyono presidency: Indonesia's decade of stability and stagnation (pp. 281–302). Singapore: Institute of Southeast Asian Studies Publishing.

Hirschman, A. (1958). The strategy of economic development. New Haven, CT: Yale University Press.

Holden, P. (2012). Ensuring reproduction: The ANC and its models of party funding. In: Plaut, M. and Holden, P. (Eds.), Who rules South Africa? Pulling the strings of power. Johannesburg and Capetown: Jonathan Ball Publishers.

House, K. E. (2013). On Saudi Arabia: Its people, past, religion, faultlines and future. New York, NY: Vintage Books.

Hsueh, R. (2011). China's regulatory state: A new strategy for globalisation. Ithaca, NY: Cornell University Press.

Huff, W. G. (1999). Turning the corner in Singapore's developmental state? Asian Survey 39(2), pp. 214–42.

Huang, F. and Yeung, H. (2018). Institutions and economic growth in Asia: The case of Mainland China, Hong Kong, Singapore and Malaysia. Routledge.

Hyslop, J. (2005). Political corruption before and after apartheid. Journal of Southern African Studies 31, 4.

International Business Publications (2007). Indonesia—Privatisation programs and regulations handbook.

IMF (2012). Brazil: Financial System Stability Assessment. IMF Country Report No. 12/206.

IMF (2015). Indonesia—Selected Issues. IMF Country Report 15/75.

IMF (2016). Saudi Arabia—Selected Issues. IMF Country Report No. 16/327.

IMF (2017). Brazil: Fiscal Transparency Evaluation. IMF Country Report No. 17/104.

IMF (2018a). Indonesia—Staff report for the 2017 Article IV consultation.

IMF (2018b). Indonesia—Selected Issues. IMF Country Report 18/33.

IMF (2020). South Africa: Bridging the income divide. February 7.

IMF-EBRD (2019). Reassessing the role of State-owned enterprises in central, eastern, and southeastern Europe.

Inoue, C. F. K. V., Lazzarini, S. G., and Musacchio, A. (2013). Leviathan as a minority shareholder: Firm-level performance implications of equity purchases by the government. Academy of Management Journal 56(6), pp. 1775–1801.

Israel, S. C. (2008). Temasek Holdings: A dependable investor in the United States—Temasek's testimony to the US House Financial Services Committee. Foreign Government Investment in the United States Economy and Financial Sector, Washington, DC.

ITF-OECD (2014). The competitiveness of ports in emerging markets: The case of Durban, South Africa. Paris: OECD.

Jain, R. (2017). Public sector enterprise disinvestment in India: Efficiency gains in a political context. Journal of Asian Economics 53, pp. 18–36.

Janeway, W. H. (2018). Doing capitalism in the innovation economy. New York: Cambridge University Press.

Jarvis, D. (2012). The regulatory state in developing countries: Can it exist and do we want it? The case of the Indonesian power sector. Journal of Contemporary Asia 42(3).

Jenkins, R. (1999). Democratic politics and economic reform in India. Cambridge: Cambridge University Press.

Jerome, A. and Rangata, M. (2003). The tortuous road to privatisation and restructuring of state assets in South Africa: Lessons from African privatisation experience. Cape Town: Development Policy Research Institute.

Jia, R., Kudamatsu, M., and Seim, D. (2014). Political selection in China: The complementary roles of connections and performance. IFN Working Paper 1003.

Jingrong Lin, K., Lu, X., Zhang, J., and Zheng, Y. (2020). State-owned enterprises in China: A review of 40 years of research and practice. China Journal of Accounting Research 13(1), pp. 31–55.

Johansson, A. (2014). Political change and the business elite in Indonesia. Stockholm School of Economics Asia Working Paper No. 34, pp. 143–172.

Joseph, K. L. (2010). The politics of power: Electricity reform in India. Energy Policy 38(1), pp. 503–511.

Al-Kandari, Y. and al-Hadban, I. (2010). Tribalism, sectarianism, and democracy in Kuwaiti culture. Digest of Middle East Studies 19(10), pp. 268–285.

Kala, N. (2019). The impacts of managerial autonomy on firm outcomes. NBER Working Paper No. 26304.

Kane-Berman, J. (2016). What to do about our SOEs?—IRR.

Kanyane and Sausi (2015). Reviewing state-owned entities' governance landscape in South Africa. African Journal of Business Ethics 9(1), pp. 28–41.

Kaplan, S. B. (2016). Banking unconditionally: The political economy of Chinese finance in Latin America. Review of International Political Economy 23(4), pp. 643–676.

Kapoor, D. and Khosla, M. (eds.) (2019). Regulation in India: Design, capacity, performance. Bloomsbury.

Kaur, K. and Kumar, S. (2010). Corporate ownership and the technical and scale efficiency of pharmaceutical firms in India-empirical evidence. South East European Journal of Economics and Business 5(2), pp. 95–106.

Kaur, S. (2004). Privatisation and public enterprise reform: A suggestive action plan. Australia South Asia Research Centre Working Paper. Canberra: The Australian National University.

Khanna, S. (2012). State-owned enterprises in India: Restructuring and growth. Copenhagen Journal of Asian Studies 30(2), pp. 5–28.

Khanna, S. (2015). The transformation of India's public sector political economy of growth and change.

Kikeri, S. (2018). Corporate governance in South African State-owned enterprises. World Bank Republic of South Africa systematic country diagnostic.

Kim, K. (2018). Matchmaking: Establishment of state-owned holding companies in Indonesia. Asia and the Pacific Policy Studies 5(2), pp. 313–330.

Klopper, H. (2010). Research report on State Owned Enterprises.

Kompas (2015). 16 politisi dan Relawan Jokowi jadi komisaris bahaya menanti BUMN. Available at: http://nasional.kompas.com/read/2015/04/12/11412621/16.Politisi.dan.Relawan.Jokowi.Jadi.Komisaris.Bahaya.Menanti.BUMN

Kostiner, J. and Teitelbaum, J. (2000). State formation and the Saudi monarchy. In: Kostiner, J. (Ed.), Middle East monarchies: The challenge of modernity. London: Lynne Rienner, pp. 131–149.

Kovaleva, E., Volkov, A., Malyh, S., and Gerasimova, E. (2019). Public sector in the Russian economy. Analytical Center for the Government of the Russian Federation. Bulletin on Competition Development.

Krueger, A. O. (2002). Why crony capitalism is bad for economic growth? In: Haber, S. (Ed.), Crony capitalism and economic growth in Latin America: Theory and evidence. Stanford: Hoover Institute.

Kung, J. K.-S. and Ma, C. (2016). Friends with benefits: How political connections help sustain private enterprise growth in China.

Al Kuwari, A. K. (1978). Oil revenues of the Gulf Emirates. London: Bowker for Durham University Middle East Center.

Kwiatkowski, G. and Augustynowicz, P. (2015). State-owned enterprises in the global economy—analysis based on fortune global 500 list. Managing intellectual capital and innovation for sustainable and inclusive society. Management, Knowledge and Learning Joint International Conference May 2015, Italy.

Lardy, N. (2016). The changing role of the private sector in China. Reserve Bank of Australia Conference Papers.

Lazareva, O., Kachinsky, A., and Stepanov, S. (2008). Corporate governance, ownership structures and investment in transition economies: The case of Russia, Ukraine and Kyrgyzstan. SSRN Electronic Journal.

Lazzarini, S. G. (2011). Capitalismo de laços: os donos do Brasil e suas conexões. Rio de Janeiro: Campus/Elsevier.

Leahy, J. and Schipani, A. (2017). Culture of corruption engulfs Brazilian elite. FT May 25.

Ledeneva, A. (2012). Cronies, economic crime and capitalism in Putin's *sistema*. Oxford: Oxford University Press.

Leff, N. H. (1968). Economic policy-making and development in Brazil, 1947–1964. New York: John Wiley & Sons.

Lehuede, H. J. and Kossov, A. (2014). Corporate governance of Russia's State-owned enterprises.

Li, H., Zhang, J., and Meng, L. (2006). Why do entrepreneurs enter politics? Evidence from China. Economic Inquiry 44(3), pp. 559–578.

Li, W., Roland, G., and Xie, Y. (2019). Crony capitalism, the party-state, and political boundaries of corruption. Working paper, University of California, Riverside.

Li, X., Liu, X., and Wang, Y. (2012). A model of China's State capitalism. SSRN Electronic Journal.

Lieberthal, K. G. (1992). Introduction: The 'fragmented authoritarianism' model and its limitations. In: Lieberthal, K. G. and Lampton, D. M. (Eds.), Bureaucracy, politics and decision making in post-Mao China. Berkeley: University of California Press.

Lim, L. (2018). Business, government and labor: Essays on economic development in Singapore and Southeast Asia. World Scientific.

Lim, L. (2015). Singapore's economic development: Retrospection and reflections. World Scientific.

Lim, V. (1998). An overview of Singapore's anti-corruption strategy and the role of the CPIB in fighting corruption.

Lin, L. W. (2010). Corporate social responsibility in China: Window dressing or structural change? Berkeley Journal of International Law 28(1), pp. 64–100.

Lin, L.-W. and Milhaupt, C. (2013). We are the (National) Champions: Understanding the mechanisms of state capitalism in China. Stanford Law Review 65(4), pp. 697–759.

Lodge, T. (1998). Political corruption in South Africa. African Affairs 97, p. 387.

Lu, D., Thangavelu, S., and Hu, Q. (2005). Biased lending and non-performing loans in China's banking sector. Journal of Development Studies 41(6), pp. 1071–1091.

Majone, G. (1994). The Rise of the regulatory state in Europe. West European Politics 17(3), p. 77.

Majone, G. (1999). The regulatory State and its legitimacy problems. West European Politics 22(1), pp. 1–24.

Makhaya, T. and Roberts, S. (2014). The changing strategies of large corporations in South Africa under democracy and the role of competition law. University of Johannesburg Working Paper 2/2014.

Mansbridge, J. (2014). The role of the state in governing the commons. Environmental Science and Policy 36, pp. 8–10.

Mansour, A. M. R. (2007). Public policy and privatization: The case of the Qatari experience. Public Administration and Development 27(4), pp. 283–292.

Mauro, P. (1995). Corruption and growth. Quarterly Journal of Economics 110, pp. 681–713.

Mazzucato, M. (2013). The entrepreneurial state. London: Anthem Press.

Mazzucato, M. (2018). Who really creates value in an economy? Project Syndicate, September 11.

McLeod, R. (2000). Soeharto's Indonesia: A better class of corruption. Agenda: A Journal of Policy Analysis and Reform 7(2), pp. 99–112.

McNally, C. A. (2013). The challenge of refurbished state capitalism: Implications for the global political economic order. DMS—Der Moderne Staat 6(1), pp. 33–48.

Megginson, W. L. (2017). Privatization, state capitalism, and state ownership of business in the 21st century. Foundations and Trends in Finance 11, pp. 1–153.

Mertha, A. (2009). Fragmented authoritarianism 2.0: political pluralization in the Chinese policy process. China Quarterly 200, pp. 995–1012.

Musacchio, A., and Lazzarini, S. G. (2014). Reinventing State Capitalism. Cambridge: Harvard University Press.

Musacchio, A., Lazzarini, S. G., and Aguilera, R. V. (2015). New varieties of state capitalism: Strategic and governance implications. Academy of Management Perspectives 29(1), pp. 115–131.

Micco, A., Panizza, U., and Yañez, M. (2007). Bank ownership and performance. Does politics matter? Journal of Banking and Finance 31, pp. 219–241.

Mietzner, M. (2015). Dysfunction by design: Political finance and corruption in Indonesia. Critical Asian Studies 47(4), pp. 587–610.

Milhaupt, C., and Pargendler, M. (2017). Governance challenges of listed State-owned enterprises around the world: National experiences and a framework for reform. Cornell International Law Journal 50(3), pp. 473–542.

Minogue, M. (2006). Apples and oranges: Comparing international experiences in regulatory reform. In: In Minogue, M. and Carino, L. (Eds.), Regulatory governance in developing countries, CRC Series on competition, regulation and development, Chapter 4. Edward Elgar Publishing.

Minogue, M. and Carino, L. (2006). Introduction: Regulatory governance in developing countries. In: Minogue, M. and Carino, L. (Eds.), Regulatory governance in developing countries, CRC series on competition, regulation and development, Chapter 1. Edward Elgar Publishing.

Mohan, T. T. and Ray, S. C. (2003). Technical efficiency in public and private sectors in India: Evidence from the post-reform years.

Molnar, M. and Lu, J. (2019). State-owned firms behind China's corporate debt. OECD Economics Department Working Papers No. 1536. Paris: OECD.

Moran, M. (2003). The British regulatory state: High modernism and hyper-innovation. Oxford: Oxford University Press.

Mourougane, A. and Piso, M. (2011). Promoting infrastructure development in Brazil. OECD Economics Department Working Papers No. 898, pp. 1–33.

Murphy, K. M., Shleifer, A., and Vishny, R. W. (1989). Industrialization and the big push. Journal of Political Economy 97(5), pp. 1003–1026.

Musacchio, A. and Pineda, E. I. (2019). Fixing State-owned enterprises in Latin America: Old problems, new solutions. Washington, DC: Inter-American Development Bank.

Mushkat, M. and Mushkat, R. (2012). The political economy of China's regulatory state: A reappraisal. Brigham Young University Journal of Public Law 27(1).

Nagaraj, R. (2006). Public sector performance since 1950. Economic & Political Weekly 41(25), 2551–2557.

Najberg, S. (1989). Privatização de recursos públicos: Os empréstimos do sistema BNDES ao sector privado nacional com correção monetária parcial. Rio de Janeiro: PUC-RIO.

Nasution, A. (1995). Market mechanism and government: The case of Indonesia following the economic reforms since the 1980s. Paper presented at the Conference on the 'World Economy in Transition', organized by the Institute of Economic Research, Hitotsubashi University, Tokyo.

Nathan Economic Consulting India Private Limited (2013). National competition policy and economic growth in India—Electricity sector study.

Nem Singh, J. and Chen, G. C. (2018). State-owned enterprises and the political economy of state–state relations in the developing world. Third World Quarterly 39(6), pp. 1077–1097.

Niblock, T. and Malik, M. (2007). The political economy of Saudi Arabia. London and New York: Routledge.

Nolan, P. and Xiaoqing, W. (1999). Beyond privatization: Institutional innovation and growth in China's large state-owned enterprises. World Development 27(1), pp. 169–200.

Nolan, P. (2004). Transforming China—Globalisation, transition and development. London: Anthem Press.

OECD (2000). Reforming China's enterprises. Paris: OECD Publishing.

OECD (2005). OECD economic surveys—China. Paris: OECD Publishing.

OECD (2009). OECD reviews of regulatory reform—China. Paris: OECD Publishing.

OECD (2010a). OECD economic surveys—China. Paris: OECD Publishing.

OECD (2010b). OECD investment policy reviews: Indonesia. Paris: OECD Publishing.

OECD (2010c). Singapore: Rapid improvement followed by strong performance. Paris: OECD Publishing.

OECD (2011a). State-owned enterprise governance reform: An inventory of recent change. Paris: OECD Publishing.

OECD (2011b). Corporate governance of listed companies in China—Self assessment by the China Securities Regulatory Commission. Paris: OECD Publishing.

OECD (2012a). Public-private partnership governance: Policy, process, and structure. In OECD Reviews of Regulatory Reform Indonesia. Paris: OECD Publishing.

OECD (2012b). Towards new arrangements for state ownership in the Middle East and North Africa. Paris: OECD Publishing.

OECD (2013a). OECD economic surveys: Brazil. Paris: OECD Publishing.

OECD (2013b). Russia—Modernising the economy. OECD better policies series. Paris: OECD Publishing.

OECD (2013c). State-owned enterprises in the Middle East and North Africa: Engines of development and competitiveness? Paris: OECD Publishing.

OECD (2014a). Managing state assets to achieve developmental goals: The case of Singapore and other countries in the region by Grant Kirkpatrick. Workshop on state-owned enterprises in the development process. Paris: OECD Publishing.

OECD (2014b). State-owned enterprises in Southern Africa: A stocktaking of reforms and challenges. OECD corporate governance working papers No. 13. Paris: OECD Publishing.

OECD (2015a) State-owned enterprises in the development process. Paris: OECD Publishing.

OECD (2015b). OECD economic surveys: Brazil. Paris: OECD Publishing.

OECD (2015c). OECD economic surveys—China. Paris: OECD Publishing.

OECD (2015d). China in a changing global environment. Paris: OECD Publishing.

OECD (2015e). Corporate governance—State-owned enterprise reform. OECD South Africa policy brief. Paris: OECD Publishing.

OECD (2015f). OECD economic surveys: South Africa, Paris: OECD Publishing.

OECD (2016). Combating corruption and promoting business integrity in State-owned enterprises: Issues and trends in national practices. Mexico City: OECD; Paris: OECD Publishing.

OECD (2017). The size and sectoral distribution of State-owned enterprises. Paris: OECD Publishing.

OECD (2018a). State-owned enterprises and corruption: What are the risks and what can be done? Paris: OECD Publishing.

OECD (2018b). OECD economic country surveys Indonesia. Paris: OECD Publishing.

OECD (2018c). State ownership in the Middle East and North Africa. MENA-OECD Working Group on Corporate Governance. Policy options to achieve sound corporate governance for competitiveness. Paris: OECD Publishing.

OECD (2019). Brazil—OECD Peer reviews of Competition Law and Policy. Paris: OECD Publishing.

Oxford Business Group. More private sector participation to stimulate growth in Saudi Arabia industry. https://oxfordbusinessgroup.com/overview/roadmap-progress-vision-2030-initiatives-increase-private-sector-participation-are-stimulating

Pandey, M. and Dong, X.-Y. (2009). Manufacturing productivity in China and India: The Role of institutional changes. China Economic Review 20(4), pp. 754–766.

Pangestu, M. and Habir, A. D. (1989). Trends and prospects in privatization and deregulation in Indonesia, ASEAN Economic Bulletin 5(3), pp. 224–241.

Pargendler, M., Musacchio, A., and Lazzarini, S. G. (2013). In strange company: The puzzle of private investment in state-controlled firms. Cornell International Law Journal 46(3), Article 3.

Pargendler, M. (2014). Corporate governance in emerging markets. In: Gordon, J. N. and Ringe, W.-G. (Eds.), Oxford Handbook of Corporate Law and Governance.

Pargendler, M. (2016). Governing state capitalism—the case of Brazil. In: Liebman, B. L. and Milhaupt, C. J. (Eds.), Regulating the Visible Hand?: The Institutional Implications of Chinese State Capitalism. OUP.

Pei, M. (2006). The dark side of China's rise. Foreign Policy. Carnegie Endowment for International Peace.

Pereira, T. and Simões, A. (2010). O papel do BNDES na alocação do custo fiscal do empréstimo de R$100 bilhões concedido pela união em2009. Revista do BNDES 33, Rio de Janeiro.

Peterson, J. E. (ed.) (2016). The emergence of the Gulf States: Studies in modern history. London: Bloomsbury Academic.

Phaahlamohlaka, L. A. (2008). The impact of privatization on the electricity industry with specific reference to Guateng. Masters Thesis. Faculty of management and Economics. University of Johannesburg.

Pierce, J. (2012). Oil and the house of Saud: Analysis of Saudi Arabian oil policy. Domes: Digest of Middle East studies 21(1), pp. 89–107.

Polity (2017). SAFTU: SAFTU demands Zuma's resignation over corruption evidence. 30 May.

Porter, M. E., Neo, B. S., and Ketels, C. (2013). Remaking Singapore. Harvard Business School Case 710-483.

Prag, A., Röttgers, D., and Scherrer, I. (2018). State-owned enterprises and the low-carbon transition. Environment Working Paper No. 129. OECD.

Pratap, K. V. (2011). Sustaining privatization. Unpublished PhD thesis, University of Maryland.

Preqin (2018). Sovereign wealth fund review. 10th ed. New York: Preqin.

PricewaterhouseCoopers (2015). State-owned enterprises: Catalysts for public value creation?

Prochnik, M. and Machado, V. (2008). Fontes de Recursos do BNDES 1995–2007. Revista do BNDES 14(29), pp. 3–34.

Qian, Y. (1996). Enterprise reform in China: Agency problems and political control, Economics of Transition 4(2), pp. 422–447.

Quah, J. S. T. (2017). Learning from Singapore's effective anti-corruption strategy: Policy recommendations for South Korea. Asian Education and Development Studies 6(1), pp. 17–29.

The Quincy group. The importance of State-owned enterprises in Saudi Arabia.

Raffiudin, R. (2015). Withering of patrimonial state-business relations in Indonesia following the 1997-8 economic crisis? Case Studies of the Electronics and Palm Oil Industries. Ph.D. Thesis, University of Victoria, Australia.

Rai, S. and Shah, A. (2014). Rethinking the policy framework in coal. https://ajayshahblog.blogspot.fr

Rama, M. (1999). Public sector downsizing: An introduction. The World Bank Economic Review.

Ramady, M. (2014). Political, economic and financial country risk: Analysis of the Gulf cooperation council. Springer.

Ramaswamy, K. (2001). Organizational ownership, competitive intensity, and firm performance: An empirical study of the Indian manufacturing sector. Strategic Management Journal 22(10), pp. 989–998.

Ramirez, C. and Hui Tan, L. (2004). Singapore Inc versus the private sector: Are government linked companies different. IMF Staff Papers 51(3). Washington, DC: IMF.

Ray, D. and Ing, L. Y. (2016). Addressing Indonesia's infrastructure deficit. Bulletin of Indonesian Economic Studies 52(1), pp. 1–25.

Reddy, G. R. and Haragopal, G. (1985). The pyraveekar: 'The Fixer' in rural India. Asian Survey 25, p. 11.

Robison, R. and Hadiz, V. R. (2004). Reorganising power in Indonesia: The politics of oligarchy in an age of markets. London: Routledge Curzon.

Rodrik, D. (2007). Normalizing industrial policy. Working paper. John F. Kennedy School of Government.

Rose-Ackerman, S. (1999). Corruption and government. Causes, consequences and reform. Cambridge: Cambridge University Press.

Rutland, P. (2008). Putin's economic record: Is the oil boom sustainable? Europe-Asia Studies 60(6), pp. 1051–1072.

Sadli, M. (1988). The private sector. In: Ichimura (Ed.), 199, pp. 354–69.

Salna, K. and Dahrul, F. (2020). Indonesia's new worry is its debt-saddled State-owned businesses. Bloomberg, April 8.

Sari, S. A. and Tjoe, T. F. (2017). Board remuneration and good corporate governance in Indonesian state-owned enterprises. Global Business Review 18(4), pp. 861–875.

Saxena, N. (2010). The IAS officer—predator or victim? Commonwealth and Comparative Politics 48(4), pp. 445–456.

Schena, P. J. and Chaturvedi, R. S. (2011). Sovereign wealth funds, debt issuances, and the development of capital markets. The sovereign wealth fund initiative. Center for Emerging Market Enterprises, The Fletcher School, Tufts University.

Schneider, B. R. (1999). The desarrollista state in Brazil and Mexico. In: woo-Cumings, M. (Eds.), The developmental state. Ithaca: Cornell University Press.

Schneider, B. R. (2015). The developmental state in Brazil: comparative and historical perspectives. Revista de Economia Poliٰtica 35(1).

Sim, I., Thomson, S., and Yeong, G. (2014). The State as shareholder: The case of Singapore. Centre for Governance, Institutions and Organisations. NUS Business School.

Simandjuntak, D. (2014). Riding the hype: The role of State-owned enterprise elite actors in the promotion of Jatropha in Indonesia. Sustainability 6, pp. 3780–3801.

Singh, R. P. (2009). Grids of change: Managing power games and power lines. Delhi: Penguin Enterprise.

Song Z., Storesletten K., and Zilibotti F. (2011). Growing like China. American Economic Review 101, pp. 202–41.

Shaw, M. and Yeoh, C. (2000). Singapore's overseas industrial parks. Regional Studies 34(2), pp. 199–206.

Sheng, H., & Carrera Jr., J. M. (2018b). The top 20 Brazilian multinationals: A long way out of the crises. Emerging Markets Global Players (EMGP) Report—Report of the Fundacao Getulio Vargas and the CCSI—Columbia Center on Sustainable Development.

Shih, V. (2009). Tools of survival: Sovereign wealth funds in Singapore and China.

Shirley, M. (1999). Bureaucrats in business: The roles of privatization versus corporatization in state-owned enterprise reform. World Development 27(1), pp. 115–136.

Shleifer, A., and Vishny, R. (1998). The grabbing hand. Cambridge: Harvard University Press.

Shleifer, A. and Vishny, R. W. (1993). Corruption. Quarterly Journal of Economics 108, pp. 599–618.

Shourie, A. (2009). Navigating reforms: lessons from India. Economic Affairs, September, pp. 68–73.

Sprenger, C. (2008). The role of state-owned enterprises in the Russian economy. Paper written for the OECD Roundtable on Corporate Governance of SOEs.

Statement by Minister Colins Chabane (2010). On the terms of reference and review framework and methodology of the Presidential State-owned enterprises review committee.

Steyn, G. (2006). Investment and uncertainty: Historical experience with power sector investment in South Africa and its implications for current challenges. Management Programme in Infrastructure Reform and Regulation. Cape Town: UCT Graduate School of Business.

Steyn, G. (2011). The impact of economic regulation on the management and performance of State-owned Enterprises. Presidential State-owned Enterprises Review Committee, Meridian Economics.

Straits Times (2015). Mr Lee Kuan Yew was embodiment of new Asian dynamism. March 24.

Strange, Susan (1996). The retreat of the State: Diffusion of power in the world economy. Cambridge: Cambridge University Press.

Al-Sulayman, F. (2018). State business relations and the new economic agenda in Saudi Arabia. Rice University's Baker Institute for Public Policy Issue Brief.

Sungkar, Y. (2008). Indonesia's State enterprises: From State Leadership to International Consensus. Journal of Indonesian Social Sciences and Humanities 1, pp. 95–120.

Suryadinata, L. (2001). Ethnic Chinese in Southeast Asia and their economic role. In: Armstrong, et al. (Eds.), Chinese Populations in contemporary Southeast Asian Societies: Identities, pp. 55–73. New York: Routledge.

Sutherland, D. (2003). China's large enterprises and the challenge of late industrialization. Routledge Curzon, London and New York: Taylor & Francis Group.

Szamosszegi, A. and Kyle, C. (2011). An analysis of state-owned enterprises and state capitalism in China. U.S.-China Economic and Security Review Commission.

Tan Boon Seng (2002). Why it might be difficult for the government to withdraw from business. 10 February, http://www.singapore-window.org

Tan, C. H., Puchniak, D., and Varottil, U. (2015). State-owned enterprises in Singapore: Historical insights into a potential model for reform. SSRN Electronic Journal.

Tan, K. S. and Manu, B. (2015). The role of the state in Singapore: Pragmatism in pursuit of growth. Singapore Economic Review 60(3), pp. 1–30.

Taplin, N. (2019). China's corruption paradox. Wall Street Journal. November 1.

Tautz, C. S. F., Fabricia de Andrade Ramos, João Roberto Lopes Pinto, Pedro Amaral Serra, and Rodrigo Valente Serra (2014). The state-of-the-Art of State-owned Enterprises in Brazil. International Budget Partnership Case Study.

Taylor, T. (2020). South Africa: Mired in Stagnation. February 10.

Teen, M. Y. (2015). Governance of government-linked companies in Singapore. Nus Business School, EU Asia Corporate Governance Dialogue 2015.

Tett, G. (2013). Insane financial system lives post-Lehman. Financial Times, September 12.

Thatcher, M. (2005). The third force? Independent regulatory agencies and elected politicians in Europe. Governance 18(3), pp. 347–373.

Thatcher, M. and Vlandas, T. (2016). Overseas state outsiders as new sources of patient capital: Government policies to welcome sovereign Wealth Fund investment in France and Germany. Socio-Economic Review 14(4), pp. 647–668.

Thee, K. W. (2006). Policies for private sector development in Indonesia. ADB Institute Discussion Paper No. 46.

Thelen, K. (2012). Varieties of capitalism: Trajectories of liberalization and the new politics of social solidarity. Annual Review of Political Science 15(1), pp. 137–159.

Thurbon, E. (2016). Developmental mindset: The revival of financial activism in South Korea. Cornell University Press.

Tompson, W. (2004). Banking reform in Russia: Problems and prospects. OECD Economics Department Working Papers 410. OECD Publishing.

Trebat, T. J. (1983). Brazil's State-owned enterprises: A case study of the state as entrepreneur. Cambridge University Press.

Al Turkey (2011). The reality of projects in terms of organization and structure, and the reasons for success and failure in Saudi Arabia. Al-watan Newspaper.

Ulfa, A. (2017). Mengurai Benang-Benang Kusut BUMN. Yogyakarta: Deepublish.

University of Alberta, China Institute (2016). State-owned enterprises in the Chinese economy today: Role, Reform, and Evolution.

Van der Eng, P. (2004). Productivity and comparative advantage in rice agriculture in South-East Asia since 1870. Asian Economic Journal 18(4), pp. 345–370.

Vial, V., and Hanoteau, J. (2010). Corruption, manufacturing plant growth and the Asian paradox: Indonesian evidence. World Development 38(5), pp. 693–705.

Wallar, J. (2014). Competition policy for a prosperous ASEAN Economic Community.

Wang, Jiangyu (2014). The political logic of Corporate Governance in China's State-owned Enterprises. Cornell International Law Journal 47(3), pp. 632–669.

Warburton, E. (2016). Jokowi and the new developmentalism. Bulletin of Indonesian Economic Studies 52(3), pp. 297–320.

Waterbury, J. (1993). Exposed to innumerable delusions: Public enterprise and state power in Egypt, India, Mexico and Turkey. Cambridge: Cambridge University Press.

Weber, M. (1978). Economy and Society: An Outline of Interpretive Sociology. Berkeley, CA: University of California Press.

Wicaksono, A. (2009). Corporate governance of State-owned enterprises: Investment holding structure of government-linked companies (dissertation). St Gallen, Switzerland: University of St Gallen.

Wildau, G. (2014). China announces plan for reform of State-owned enterprises. FT.

Winters, J. (2011). Oligarchy. New York: Cambridge University Press.

World Bank (2010). ROSC Corporate governance Country Assessment—Indonesia.

World Bank (2014a). Corporate governance of State-owned enterprises: A toolkit. Washington, DC: World Bank.

World Bank (2014b). Corporate governance of State-owned enterprises in Latin America—Current trends and country cases. Latin America and Caribbean region: World Bank, Global Governance Practice.

World Bank (2017). Indonesia economic quarterly: Closing the gap. Jakarta: World Bank.

World Bank (2018a). Approach Paper World Bank Group Support for the Reform of State-Owned Enterprises, 2007–2018: An IEG Evaluation. Washington, DC: World Bank.

World Bank (2018b). Indonesia Snapshots—private participation in infrastructure (PPI). Washington, DC: World Bank.

World Bank (2019). State-Owned Enterprises in the Russian Federation: Employment Practices, Labor Markets, and Firm Performance. Washington, DC: World Bank.

Worthington, R. (2002). Governance in Singapore: Myth and reality. London: Curzon.

Xu, X. and Yan, Y. (2014). Does government investment crowd out private investment in China? Journal of Economic Policy Reform 17(1), pp. 1–12.

Xu, Y.-C. (ed.) (2012). The political economy of state-owned enterprises in China and India. New York: Palgrave Macmillan.

Yarrow, G. (1986). Privatisation in theory and practice. Economic Policy 2, pp. 323–378.

Yeoh, C., Neo, A. K., and Lee, C. (2003). Regionalization and Transborder Industrialization: Singapore's Industrial Parks in China and Vietnam Examined. Narrowing the Competitive Gap of Emerging Markets in the Global Economy: 1st

International Conference of the Asian Academy of Applied Business. 197–205. Research Collection Lee Kong Chian School of Business.

Yeoh, C., How, W., and Yeong, A. L. (2005). Enclaves for ENTERPRISE: An empirical study of Singapore's industrial parks in Indonesia, Vietnam and China. Lee Kong Chian School of Business. Singapore Management University.

Yeoh, C., How, W., and Sim, V. (2006). Re-engineering economic space: The case of Singapore's transborder industrialization 'Gambits' in Asia.

Yeyati, E. L., Micco, A., and Panizza, U. 2004. Should the government be in the banking business? The role of state-owned and development banks. RES Working Papers 4379, Inter-American Development Bank, Research Department.

Yu, H. (2013). The Ascendency of State-owned Enterprises in China: Development, controversy and problems. Journal of Contemporary China 23(85), pp. 161–182.

Zhang, Z. (2019). China's SOE reforms: What the latest round of reforms mean for the market? China Briefing, May 29.

Zhang, R., Rezaee, Z., and Zhu, J. (2010). Corporate philanthropic disaster response and ownership type: Evidence from Chinese firms' response to the Sichuan earthquake. Journal of Business Ethics 91(1), pp. 51–63.

Zhou, X., Cai, H., and Li, Q. (2014). Property rights regimes and firm behavior—Theory versus evidence. In: Tsui, A. S. and Bian, Y. (Eds.), China's domestic private firms: Multidisciplinary perspectives on management and performance. New York: Armonk, pp. 97–119.

Index

For the benefit of digital users, indexed terms that span two pages (e.g., 52–53) may, on occasion, appear on only one of those pages.

Tables and figures are indicated by *t* and *f* following the page number